THE SURPRISE RIVAL

About the author

Alan Gregory was born in Melbourne, educated at the University of Melbourne (BCom, DipEd, MEd) and Simon Fraser University Canada (PhD). He was a teacher in Victorian high schools, then on the staff of the Faculty of Education at Monash University for 25 years, including periods as a visiting scholar to several overseas universities. He was made a Member of the Order of Australia in 1989 for services to education and the community, was Master of Ormond College, and served on several government boards including the Migration Review Tribunal and Refugee Review Tribunal. He has published widely in the field of economics education and history, and his books include: *It's Only the Game that Counts: A history of Lord Somers Camp and Power House 1929–1989*; *The Ever Open Door: A History of the Royal Melbourne Hospital 1848–1998*; the centenary history of Melbourne High School *Strong Like its Pillars*; and books on two principals of the school, Brigadier George Langley and William (Bill) M Woodfull. He undertook this book in a voluntary capacity.

THE SURPRISE RIVAL

A History of the Education Faculty, Monash University, 1964–2014

ALAN GREGORY

© Copyright 2014 Alan Gregory
All rights reserved. Apart from any uses permitted by Australia's Copyright Act 1968, no part of this book may be reproduced by any process without prior written permission from the copyright owners. Inquiries should be directed to the publisher.

Monash University Publishing
Building 4, Monash University
Clayton, Victoria 3800, Australia
www.publishing.monash.edu

Monash University Publishing brings to the world publications which advance the best traditions of humane and enlightened thought.

Monash University Publishing titles pass through a rigorous process of independent peer review.

http://www.publishing.monash.edu/books/sr-9781922235473.html

Series: Education

Cover Design: Kristian Lofhelm

National Library of Australia Cataloguing-in-Publication entry:

Author:	Gregory, Alan, 1938– author.
Title:	The surprise rival : a history of the Education Faculty, Monash University, 1964–2014 / Alan Gregory.
ISBN:	9781922235473 (paperback)
Notes:	Includes index.
Series:	Education, Higher
Subjects:	Monash University. Faculty of Education--History.
	Education--Study and teaching (Higher)--Victoria--Melbourne--History.
	Universities and colleges--Victoria--History.
Dewey Number:	378.9451

Printed in Australia by Griffin Press an Accredited ISO AS/NZS 14001:2004 Environmental Management System printer.

The paper this book is printed on is certified against the Forest Stewardship Council ® Standards. Griffin Press holds FSC chain of custody certification SGS-COC-005088. FSC promotes environmentally responsible, socially beneficial and economically viable management of the world's forests.

Contents

About the author. ii

Preface vii

Author's introduction xi

Abbreviations xvi

Deans of the Faculty of Education. xviii

1. Foundation and first year 1
   Founding Monash University

2. Early years and issues 16
   1965–1971

3. Consolidation 73
   1972–1980

4. Special education. 124

5. Good times 139
   1981–1988

6. Silver jubilee and amalgamations 188
   1989–1999

7. Entrepreneurial times 259
   2000–2010

8. Humanising the corporate Monash 316
   2011–2014

9. Students and recollections 370

10. 100,000 up – concluding thoughts. 426

Index. 443

Preface

It is a privilege to be the Dean of the Faculty of Education at Monash University, especially so at a time such as this when, through this book, we have the opportunity to celebrate our history. As a staff member in the faculty for the past 25 years I have witnessed many changes at both faculty and university level. However, one defining feature of the faculty that has been constant through the changing times has been our high standing in the international education community. The strength of our scholarship continues to define the faculty.

When the idea of writing a history of the faculty was first suggested, Alan Gregory very kindly volunteered to take on the task. His long-standing connection with the faculty and ability to trace back to the beginning has been important as he has spoken with, interviewed, researched and hunted down issues, ideas and stories in the archives. The time, energy and effort associated with writing this book should not be underestimated and Alan has worked tirelessly to complete the task in a timely manner.

The title Alan has chosen for the book highlights the early and quick steps the faculty took as it moved out onto the world stage, and now, 50 years into our existence, that position has become well and truly entrenched with our consistent ranking in the top six of the QS World Rankings. However, rankings are not the only measure of success. Today the faculty is larger than it has ever been with close to 6,000 enrolments across undergraduate, postgraduate and higher degree by research programs. Beyond the faculty as a home base, we teach across Australia through online and flexible delivery as well as internationally with program offerings in countries such as Singapore, Hong Kong, South Africa, Malaysia, Italy (Prato), Saudi Arabia and the Cook Islands as well as research and ongoing collaboration with leading universities in Chile, USA, Canada, UK, Europe and Asia. All of this is only possible because the faculty comprises people who individually and (even more importantly) collectively continue to build on the legacy of our past. Through a commitment to education more generally and a concern to 'make a difference' more specifically, our staff generously share their knowledge, skills and ability in myriad ways that continue to be well recognised and respected at home and abroad.

In this our 50th year, it is interesting to reflect on how the faculty has changed. We now have 24-hour access to our facilities, a far cry from the

9-to-5 routines of the early years. Our ever growing international student involvement brings a diversity and vibrancy to bear in ways that positively support and extend our community. The web has changed not only the way we teach and research, but has also dramatically changed the immediacy of communication – all of which carry new demands on our time and a greater sense of urgency. Student assessment and assignments are online and in diverse forms and long gone are the days of posting multiple hard copies of a journal article off for review and then waiting months for a reply – actually, the wait for a response hasn't changed and might even have become longer.

Despite such demands, the sense of collegiality and teamwork remains strong and is never taken for granted. In fact our open and inviting working environment is well recognised across the university as a defining feature of the faculty, not least because of our exceptional professional staff who consistently perform at a very high level in an environment that increasingly stresses accountability and compliance.

There are a number of 'great themes' that stand out in our history. Clearly, the faculty's research profile and international standing – something which has continually been a magnet for overseas scholars who, across the generations, have always sought to spend some time at Monash – is a matter of great pride. However, there are many other themes that stand out. There is our history of pre-service teacher education programs that are innovative, responsive to the needs of the profession, thoughtfully researched and skilfully delivered; these have always been to the fore. In-service teacher professional learning and the development of qualifications (e.g. Master of Educational Studies) designed to help teachers advance their knowledge have been a hallmark of the ways in which the faculty has enhanced the education system. Throughout the 1980s and early 1990s it could well be argued that the faculty supplied many of the academic leaders for other Australian Faculties of Education (and some internationally) as careers were established following completion of a Monash Education PhD. Importantly, at a time when career progression and senior positions for women were much more limited than today, a number of outstanding female scholars emerged from the faculty to make their mark in academia in very impressive ways, not only creating new research agendas and leading debate based on their work, but also accepting leadership positions across the university system.

The history of the faculty also illustrates how some fields of study for which we have been well known and internationally regarded have changed over time, whilst others have remained constant. Clearly, the work of the Krongold Centre and the impact of those colleagues involved in special and inclusive education was based on a solid foundation. Similarly, the Centre for Science, Maths and Technology Education has been exceptionally well regarded since its inception and most certainly continues that way. The esteemed work of the professors and staff in history of education, philosophy of education and sociology of education have seen the ebbs and flows of demand while in recent times, early childhood education, sport, physical and outdoor education have grown and begun to make their mark.

In our first 25 years, we were a postgraduate faculty of education located at the Clayton campus. The 'Dawkins era' saw amalgamations and expansion that included the Gippsland and Peninsula campuses in concert with a move into undergraduate programs through double degrees which led to changes in the faculty's organisation, structure and offerings. As the faculty grew, there were challenges. Nonetheless, the opportunities created were grasped by all and as our geographic and academic reach expanded, so too our influence in the field was extended.

Throughout 2013 as the Gippsland campus prepared itself to combine with Ballarat University to create a new regional institution, the faculty's expansion to the Berwick campus illustrated yet again the importance of the faculty to the university. In 2014 the Faculty of Education has become the major discipline at Berwick, pushing toward 1,000 students as a consequence of the introduction of new and innovative undergraduate programs as well as the new Master of Teaching.

As the next 50 years begins, I am sure there will be more change in the faculty because Monash University does not sit still for long. But whatever those changes bring, I feel confident that the faculty will continue to build on its strong and proud heritage. I trust that those who follow will feel the same sense of gratitude and honour for that which went before that those of us working here now continually experience. The contribution of today creates the legacy for the future. This faculty is most grateful for the precious gift of the heritage we enjoy as a result of the effort of those who came before.

Professor John Loughran

Author's introduction

> We have no direct access to historical truth, and what we feel or assert to be true depends as much on our imagination as our senses.
>
> Oliver Sacks, *New York Review of Books* 21 February 2013, p. 21

The *Times Higher Education Supplement* in its issue of 23 January 1987, undertook an evaluation of education departments/faculties in the United Kingdom. As well as publishing these rankings, which were based on peer opinion on the basis of teaching and research, they also ascertained opinions on departments outside of Britain, and reported that 'Monash University in Australia was the surprise rival to Stanford and Harvard'. This immediately catapulted the Faculty of Education at Monash to international and national attention. So the term 'the surprise rival' seemed an apt title for this book. Especially as in 2013 it also gained a high ranking as a faculty – number six in the world!

The first five chapters had been completed before the history of Monash University came out in May 2012. This was *University Unlimited: The Monash Story* by Graeme Davison and Kate Murphy, Allen and Unwin, Sydney, 2012. It was not my intention to go over the issues covered in this work, and so I have given a chronological narrative of the story of the Faculty of Education. It has been impossible to include every event, or every name – in some ways each chapter brings a sample of events and people of each period covered. To those who have seemingly been overlooked I apologise. Dr Paul Gardner in looking at the manuscript rightly advised that a thematic approach would be far more readable. He was right. However, to produce a thematic book would require first much chronological research before the story could be told as initial teacher training, graduate coursework, research, staff, amalgamations and so forth. There is a bias too, as I was a member of the faculty from 1965 to 1990. This book is inevitably Clayton centred. The faculty had its origins at Clayton, which in many ways still remains its 'home base'. It was the only location from 1964 until 1992. It also raised the issue of how far to cover the other locations at which the faculty was housed. For example, one could write a fine history of Frankston Teachers' College as an outstanding institution in its own right. I also had an association with the Churchill campus well before it became part of Monash.

Thanks

I have many people to thank – firstly the Dean, Professor John Loughran for entrusting me with this task.

My faculty mentor and liaison person has been Dr Rosalie Triolo – I could not have had a better encourager. Rosalie has been unceasing in her help.

I owe much to Jan Getson and Lyn Maloney from Monash University Archives. They have been very patient and helpful with my many visits to the archives. In addition Lyn has helped considerably with the preparation of Monash University photographs. I am grateful to Monpix for permission to use these images. Each image includes the Monpix number or the source of the photo, and, where known, the photographer.

Within the faculty I would also like to thank Darlene McGown, PA to the Dean, Candice Schultz, Lydia Loriente, Executive Officer of the faculty, and Naren Chellappah, formerly of the faculty administration, and then organiser of the jubilee celebrations, for invaluable help.

Deaths

During the preparation of this book I note with regret the passing of the following people who had associations with the faculty: Zainu'ddin, Professor Peter W Musgrave, Professor Marie Neale, Warren Mann, John Fyfield, Max Oldmeadow, Roy Wigg, Lindsay Shaw, Dr Brian Bullivant, Dr Mary Nixon and Dr Ann Shorten.

Interviews

I have had interviews with the following members of staff (or former members of staff): Professor Richard Gunstone, Professor Sue Willis (Pro-Vice Chancellor and former Dean 2000–1010), Dr Michael Dyson, Dr Jill Robbins, Anita Forsyth, Associate Professor Tony Taylor, Professor Simone White, Professor Richard White AM (former Dean), Dr Warren Mellor, Professor Fazal Rizvi, Dr Paul Gardner AM, Professor David Aspin (former Dean), Professor Ron Taft, Professor R J W Selleck, Dr Richard Trembath, Dr Jill Robbins, Associate Professor Shane Phillipson, Associate Professor Jane Southcott, Rosamund Winter, Professor John Loughran, Associate Professor Alan Reid and Peter Lawford (Faculty Business Manager).

Submissions

My thanks to former staff members who either by written or verbal submission have provided input into this book:

John Fyfield, Dr John H Theobald, Dr Gerald Burke, Professor Dick White, Dr F J (John) Hunt, Meigs Ghent, Hec Gallagher, Professor Maurie Balson, Professor R J W Selleck, Professor Ron Taft, Dr Brian Bullivant, Alan Trethewey, Lindsay Shaw, Professor R P (Dick) Tisher, Dr Richard Trembath, Dr Warren Mellor, Professor John Biggs, Dr John Lawry, Dr Terry Hore, Professor Fazal Rizvi, Dr Ian Mitchell, Dr Margaret Gill, MacKenzie (Ken) Clements, Professor Simone White, Bev Story (Pocknee), Associate Professor Ann Knowles, and Helen Hill.

Claude Sironi, who served the faculty so well for 36 years, has given freely of his photographic expertise, and loaned many photographs.

Heather Phillips has proven an invaluable help both in providing material, calling on her excellent memory of her 34 years in the faculty, and also providing photographs.

Rosamund Winter with her experience of the faculty has been invaluable in her help.

Thanks too, to Kristian Lofhelm, Audio Visual and Educational Technology Officer, for his help with scanning and photography. The front cover has been designed by Kristian with the main photograph being of faculty staff on a Faculty Day. Thanks too, to Debing Wang for his work in scanning; nothing was too much trouble. Thanks to Bronwyn Dethick for help with photographs and unravelling problems.

Some former students have also provided help: Dr Philip Dutton, principal of Burgmann College, ANU; Rupert MacLean, senior UNESCO post; Andrew Mackenzie, principal of Hume Anglican Grammar School; Professor John Miller AO, Judith Jesser and Suzanne Pinchen.

External

Eleanor Elizabeth Peeler of the University of Melbourne; Dr Lawrie Shears, former Director-General of Education, both in his capacity as a person who taught in the faculty, served on Faculty Board and in his official capacity.

Professor Kwong Lee Dow AO, former Dean of the Faculty of Education at Melbourne University and later Vice-Chancellor of Melbourne and Ms Sarah (Sally) Musgrave.

Editorial

Rosalie Triolo, Professor Diana Davis, Dr Paul Gardner, Professor Dick White, Professor Dick Gunstone, Professor Gerald Burke, Professor Dick Selleck, Professor David Aspin, Professor Peter Fensham, Garry Bell and Dr Margaret Gill have all helped with editorial advice. My thanks too, to the editor for the publisher, McKinley Valentine, and for layout, Kathryn Coulehan.

My thanks too, to those who have kindly contributed their reminiscences, which form Chapter 9: Peter Anderson, Professor John Biggs, Howard and Jenny Brown, Professor Gerald Burke, Professor Peter Fensham, Dr Paul Gardner, Dr Margaret Gill, Professor Gilah Leder, Suzanne Pinchen, Professor Dick Selleck, Dr John Theobald, Dr Rosalie Triolo, Rosamund Winter, and Dr Ailsa Zainu'ddin.

Staff

The following staff members or former staff members have provided input and material, for which I am grateful.

Professor David Aspin, Professor Maurie Balson, Garry Bell, Dr Gil Best, Professor John Biggs, Dr Dudley Blane, Howard Brown, Jenny Brown, Dr Brian M Bullivant, Professor Gerald Burke, Professor Judith Chapman, Dr MacKenzie (Ken) Clements, Professor Diana Davis, Margrette Fairbanks (Waldron), Professor Helen Forgasz, Anita Forsyth, John A Fyfield, Hec Gallagher, Meigs Ghent, Dr Margaret Gill, Professor Richard Gunstone, Helen Hill, Dr Terry Hore, Dr F J (John) Hunt, Dr Ann Knowles, Peter Lawford, Dr John Lawry, Professor Gilah Leder, Dr Warren Mellor, Dr Ian Mitchell AM, John Mooney PSM, Bev Pocknee (Story), Associate Professor Paul Richardson, Professor Fazal Rizvi, Professor R J W (Dick) Selleck, Lindsay Shaw, Associate Professor Jane Southcott, Dr Ann Shorten, Dr Brian Spicer, Dr Martin Sullivan, Professor Ron Taft, Dr John H Theobald, Professor R P (Dick) Tisher, Dr Richard Trembath, Alan Trethewey, Dr Max Waugh, Jim Wheeler, Professor Simone White, Professor R P White and Dr Ailsa Zainu'ddin.

While my approach has also been to include as much of faculty events and people as possible, it has not been possible to cover every event or activity or mention every person who made a contribution.

I have tried to include brief CVs of all the academic staff as appendices to the chapters. It has not been possible to be wholly successful in this venture, as Monash records are not complete nor do they cover much about a staff member's academic work. Not wishing to invade people's privacy I have not examined records of recent and current members of staff. I have relied on public sources or releases, and then have asked staff to submit a CV. I have often added to these, so do not see positive comments as self-promotion. It has not been possible to do the same for the all-important professional staff, formerly called administrative staff. The abolition of Faculty Handbooks made the whole venture even more difficult. So apologies to those not listed, I have tried to include as many as possible.

The historian E H Carr has stated that history 'is by and large, a record of what people did, not what they failed to do; to this extent it is inevitably a success-story.' As well as this 'success' bias, there is the further problem of even finding out what people did. Paper records of the faculty are incomplete; for some periods documents are missing. Of course documents do not reveal all, indeed many events are not recorded on paper. The story of this faculty is an important one to be told and it has been an honour trying to tell it.

Alan Gregory, May 2014

Abbreviations

ACER	Australian Council for Educational Research
ad eundem statum	with equivalent status
AQF	Australian Qualifications Framework
AUC	Australian Universities Commission
AUQA	Australian Universities Quality Agency
AM	Member of the Order of Australia
AM	Master of Arts (USA)
AO	Officer of the Order of Australia
APS	Australian Psychology Society
AC	Companion of the Order of Australia
Ass Prof	Associate Professor
ARC	Australian Research Council
ATAR	Australian Tertiary Admission Ranks
AVCC	Australian Vice-Chancellors Committee
OAM	Medal of the Order of Australia
BEc	Bachelor of Economics
BCom	Bachelor of Commerce
BEd	Bachelor of Education
BSpecEd	Bachelor of Special Education
BA	Bachelor of Arts
CEET	Centre for the Economics of Education and Training
CTEC	Commonwealth Tertiary Education Commission
DEET	Department of Employment, Education and Training
DEECD	Department of Education and Early Childhood Development
DEEWR	Department of Education Employment and Workplace Relations
DEETYA	Department of Employment, Education, Training and Youth Affairs
DipEd	Diploma in Education
DipEd Psych	Diploma in Educational Psychology
EAS	Effective Full-Time Staff
ECOPS	Faculty of Economics and Politics
EdD	Doctor of Education
ENTER	Equivalent National Tertiary Entrance Rank
EFTS	Effective Full-Time Students
EFTSL	Equivalent Full-Time Student load
EFTSU	Effective Full-Time Student Units
ERA	Excellence in Research for Australia
ERDC	Education Research and Development Committee
ESOS	Education Services for Overseas Students
FAUSA	Federation of Australian Universities Staff Associations

FACE	Fellow Australian College of Education
GIAE	Gippsland Institute of Advanced Education
Go8	Group of Eight (universities)
HEARU	Higher Education Advisory & Research Unit
HERU	Higher Education Research Unit
Honoris causa	honorary
MA	Master of Arts
MACE	Member Australian College of Education
MEd	Master of Education
MEd Stud	Master of Educational Studies
MICAS	Monash Institute for Child and Adolescent Studies
MUA	Monash University Archives
NUAUS	National Union of Australian University Students
PhD	Doctor of Philosophy
Ed Dept	Education Department (Victoria)
P & D	Planning and Development Committee
OBE	Order of the British Empire
SCV	State College of Victoria
SES	Socio-economic status
SGS	School of Graduate Studies
SPECE	School of Primary and Early Childhood Education
TEC	Tertiary Education Commission
TITC	Trained Infant Teachers Certificate
TPTC	Trained Primary Teachers Certificate
TEQSA	Tertiary Education Quality and Standards Agency
TSTC	Trained Secondary Teachers Certificate
TSpTC	Trained Special Teachers Certificate
UC	Universities Council
VIC	Victoria Institute of College
VTAC	Victorian Tertiary Admissions Centre
VUAC	Victorian Universities Admission Committee
VUSEB	Victorian Schools and Examinations Board

Monash grades

HD	High Distinction
D	Distinction
C	Credit
P	Pass
N	Fail
S	Supplementary
NN	Bad Fail

Deans of the Faculty of Education

Richard Selby Smith	1964–1971
Syd S Dunn	1971–1975
Peter W Musgrave	1977–1981
Peter J Fensham	1982–1988
David N Aspin	1989–1993
Richard T White	1993–2000
Sue Willis	2000–2010
John Loughran	2010–

Chapter 1

Foundation and first year

Founding Monash University

A second university for Melbourne was a long time coming. The 1950s experienced a rapid expansion of population, through both migration and natural increase, and the beginnings of an increased retention rate at schools. Both factors began to exert pressure on the resources of the University of Melbourne. Governments were slow to respond to an obvious need. There was not only a reluctance to confront the expense involved, but the process of establishing another university was a venture into the unknown.

A need for more science and technology education was also felt. The launch of the satellite Sputnik in October 1957 by the USSR was to have an enormous impact. As in the USA, there was in Australia a feeling that the education system was lacking, a feeling reinforced by a number of critical accounts of education in the USA by some eminent scholars. There were many ramifications. For example, the US Government funded a number of major curriculum projects, initially in physics, involving the top physicists in the land who brought their expertise to bear on the creation of a better and more imaginative physics curriculum, and better resource materials for schools. The development of one of these, the innovative Physical Science Study Committee physics course, had a direct effect on Australia. In 1964 the Monash physics department hosted a major teacher development workshop where Victoria's physics teachers were introduced to these new materials, and they were adapted for introduction in 1965. Some of the early appointments to the new Faculty of Education were staff with experience in this area.

Students in Victoria contemplating university tended to think only of the University of Melbourne; it was unusual to go interstate or overseas for a first degree. The long-established University of Melbourne was very much part of the culture of Victorians. It was consequently to cast a long shadow over any newcomer. Monash University would inevitably be judged by the community in comparison to the University of Melbourne, the only university most knew.

Various groups and enquiries all reiterated not just the demand for more places but especially for places in science and technology. Victoria's second university was originally conceived as a science and technology university, partly reflecting the need for more skilled technical people in the workforce.

The emergence of Monash University came on the initiative of the state government. Education in that period was very much a state matter. The Honourable John Bloomfield was the education minister in the Bolte Government which established Monash University.

Two committees of enquiry were important in the beginnings of Monash University: the Ramsay Committee (headed by the Director of Education, Sir Alan Ramsay) which recommended a university of technology, recognising the need for graduates in this field, and the Murray Committee (headed by Sir Keith Murray from the UK), which was set up by the Commonwealth Government. The Murray Committee reported in 1957 and recommended major financial assistance be given by the Commonwealth Government to the universities. What emerged from this was an Australian Universities Commission (AUC) which would make recommendations for funding of grants from the Commonwealth to the universities. The Murray Committee was in agreement with the Victorian Government's idea of having a second university with an emphasis on science, engineering and technology. It also envisaged other areas being added: law, economics and medicine.

The Victorian Government passed an Act of Parliament in 1958 to establish a university – Monash University – the first since Melbourne was set up 106 years before. An Interim Council was established with Robert Blackwood as chairman, with a brief for a technology-based university. The first meeting of the Interim Council was held in June 1958.

Having decided on a new university, the choice of a name became an issue. The choice of Monash was inspired. Sir John Monash, regarded as the most able general of the First World War, a brilliant engineer who pioneered reinforced concrete in Victoria, and who also headed the innovative brown coal development as head of the State Electricity Commission (SEC), was also a scholar and Vice-Chancellor (honorary) of the University of Melbourne. A truly great Australian, he had in many ways been overlooked. There had been neither a biography of him at that stage, nor much recognition. The selection of Monash's name for the new university was acclaimed, especially by the Jewish community.

There was speculation that one of the first choices for a site was Caulfield racecourse, a suggestion vetoed by the horse-racing devotee Premier Henry Bolte. Instead, the site for an institution for epileptics was eventually chosen. The existing buildings on the 115-acre Clayton site were to be important in the early days for the new university.

The Interim Council of Monash University had to make major decisions about the new university, and seek appropriate funding. It decided on a university which would reach a size of 12,000 students and engaged a firm to design a master plan for the campus. The council was shocked when the Australian Universities Commission discovered a major demand for places in arts and economics – more than for science and technology – and asked the council to change direction. The AUC also indicated it would not have the funds required by Monash for a 1961 opening. A compromise was reached with the council agreeing to a much reduced student intake in 1961, and to commencing with five faculties, with arts and economics added to science, engineering and medicine. So the Interim Council began the process of making the key appointments of Vice-Chancellor, Registrar, librarian, and professors of chemistry, physics, biology and engineering. From early 1960 appointees to these new posts began to arrive, none more important than the new Vice-Chancellor Professor Louis Matheson, originally from Manchester. Previously professor of electrical engineering at the University of Melbourne, he made an ideal appointment for what was envisaged as a science and technology university.[1]

Matheson and his team faced innumerable decisions, many of which had to be made quickly. Statutes and a system of university governance had to be agreed upon and further appointments made. While the University of Melbourne remained a dominant model for the new university, there were significant changes. Faculty boards, much smaller than the official governing bodies of Melbourne University faculties, were established. Also significant was the decision to have full-time deans, and not to follow the Melbourne model of the deanship rotating among professors. Moreover, the chair of the Academic Board was to be held by the Vice-Chancellor.

Matheson and the Council decided that no temporary buildings would be built at Monash University. This was clearly a reaction to the Melbourne experience where temporary buildings had become a blot upon the landscape, an excuse to defer new buildings, becoming effectively permanent. So, existing buildings on the site were used, and what buildings were erected had to serve many purposes in the early days.

---

[1] Professor Sir Louis Matheson KBE CMG 1912–2002.

The university was officially opened on 11 March 1961 and the first students started on 13 March 1961. This first intake had 371 students.

Education

Teaching in education was established for functional vocational reasons – many of the graduates were to seek careers as secondary school teachers, and so the traditional path was to follow a first degree with a year of teacher training, traditionally a Diploma in Education (DipEd). In a sense, having an education offering at Monash was a late thought, probably pushed by the Victorian Government for teaching studentship holders, who had undertaken to complete a degree and then teacher training before joining the state Department of Education. The shift of emphasis with Monash taking students in arts and economics, as well as science, meant that many of these students would seek teacher training at the end of their degree. Here was also a practical solution to a rapidly growing population which required more schools and so more teachers.

Education faculties had tended to suffer a 'Cinderella' status among Australian universities, and this was certainly so at the University of Melbourne, where it was given little attention. For many years the faculty had only one professor of education and it was only much later, with the senior posts held by Professor Kwong Lee Dow, that professors from education became important forces within the university and were given leadership roles.[2]

The indifference by many faculties or disciplines to the teaching of education is not readily explained. Was it ignorance, scepticism, or cynicism? Some regarded education as 'soft', lacking in rigour. Despite a vice-chancellor who believed that each faculty should have equal status, this attitude towards education was identifiable at Monash University too. Matheson, however, upheld two important principles: education was to be taught by a faculty, and that faculty should enjoy the same status and rights as any other faculty. This included a key principle that Monash should have one professor for every 100 students.

The main role of the education faculty at Melbourne was to provide the professional development year for students with a first degree, to enable them to qualify as secondary school teachers. The Diploma in Education was considered the first year of a Bachelor of Education, although only a minority continued on to complete the full degree. Most students took the

---

[2] Kwong Lee Dow served as deputy Vice-Chancellor for many years and then Vice-Chancellor.

short route of completing the diploma as a means of entering secondary teaching. The bachelor degree was there – but tended to be undertaken by teachers on a part-time basis as a postgraduate qualification, and in much smaller numbers than those doing the DipEd. Three subjects were required to complete the BEd – and they were challenging subjects then.

The DipEd at Melbourne comprised four core subjects called General Method, History and Philosophy of Education, Education Psychology, and Comparative Education. In addition, students undertook three 'method' subjects, related to the subjects they taught. Instruction in the 'methods of teaching' was given by part-time staff, usually competent practitioners, seconded from the state school system or in some cases from private schools. The full-time academic staff lectured in the four core subjects.

When teaching in education commenced at Monash, the faculty was housed in the west wing of the multi-purpose Sir Robert Menzies Building (the Ming Wing as it became known). The multi-storied building was built in stages, with the west wing being completed first. The small staff of Education was housed on the 11th floor. Later they shifted to the completed east wing and occupied the 10th and 11th floors. Teaching occurred in various locations.

The appointment of a dean was an especially important and urgent decision. Students who wished to undertake teacher training had commenced in 1961, so education had to be offered from 1964. The Interim Council set up a sub-committee to deal with this appointment in August 1962. The assumption was clearly the Melbourne University pattern of a one-year Diploma of Education, following a first degree (BA, BSc, MusBac, etc). A first meeting of a committee set up to advise on courses in education met in October 1963, with the Vice-Chancellor in the chair. Richard Selby Smith (not yet formally appointed as a professor) was present, and secretary to the committee was Lindsay Shaw.[3] This committee estimated that up to 50 students would want to enrol in the DipEd in 1964 and set about accommodating a head of department, secretary, three full-time staff and 3–4 part-time staff.[4] A second meeting of what had become a steering committee on education reporting to the Professorial Board was held on 5 May 1964 and among those present at this meeting were the Director of Education,

---

[3] Lindsay N Shaw, a respected administrator, was later faculty secretary for education from 1974 to 1985. He died in 2013, aged 91 years.

[4] Monash University Archives MON Faculty of Education Minutes 1963–1970, meeting 3 October 1963.

1.1 Menzies Building second stage under construction 1964, Education was initially housed in stage 1, top floor.
MUA IN-3973

Alec McDonell, and the Director of ACER, Dr W C Radford, as well as Professor Selby Smith.[5]

Not clear is how Richard Selby Smith, then headmaster of Scotch College, was appointed the foundation Dean of Education. Matheson implies that he sought him out as someone suited to this special task.[6] Selby Smith took over early in 1964 and with a small staff which he had appointed the previous year, teaching commenced in education at Monash University. In keeping with university policy set out by Matheson, a Faculty of Education was established in 1965 with Professor Richard Selby Smith as permanent dean.

In the first year the diploma course was offered there were 38 students, most of whom had completed a first degree at Monash. In addition to the four core subjects taken, the students took 'one other subject to broaden their

---

[5] Ibid., Meeting 5 May 1964.
[6] Louis Matheson *Still Learning*, South Melbourne, Macmillan Australia, 1980, p. 18. This is also confirmed by Selby Smith's remarks at the opening of the Education Faculty building which imply he was invited to take the chair. His son Peter Selby Smith indicates that after the initial selection committee found no candidate they considered suitable, they decided to offer the position to Richard Selby Smith.

academic background as a foundation for a career as a teacher.'[7] There was also a full program of teaching practice using both education department and independent schools.

Early in the life of the faculty, a curriculum laboratory was established. This was intended to contain a variety of school textbooks, curriculum materials, audio visual aids, equipment, and to act as a resource centre for the students in their lesson preparation. Blackwood saw it also having a wider role 'when more fully developed, for teachers generally'. The curriculum laboratory was to form part of the faculty for many years, although its role changed under different supervisors.

1.2 Professor Richard Selby Smith.
MUA IN-7402

---

[7] Robert Blackwood *Monash University: The First Ten Years*, Melbourne, Hampden Hall, 1968, p. 164.

The foundation Dean and staff

So who was this new Dean and who were his foundation staff? Richard Selby Smith – known as 'Dick' by his equals but 'Selby' by his senior staff, was an Englishman who had come to Australia as principal of Scotch College (1953–64) where he was successful and well regarded. Selby Smith completed a BA Oxford (1937) which became Master of Arts, and a Master of Arts (Teaching) at Harvard. He taught classics at schools in the UK. He then served in the Royal Navy, enlisting as an ordinary seaman. He became a Lieutenant-Commander. During the war he served on the light aircraft-carrier *HMS Attacker* which, in fact, was a converted Liberty Ship and after the war was refitted as the Sitmar liner *Fairsky*, well remembered by the 'Ten Pound Poms', as it was one of the chief ships used to transport British emigrants to Australia after the Second World War. After the war he became an education officer with the Kent Education office (1946–50), then deputy chief education officer for Warwickshire (1950–53). Appointed as the foundation professor of education at Monash in 1964, he became Dean of the Faculty of Education in 1965 and held this position until he left in 1971 for posts in Tasmania. Tall and lean with a sharp angular face characterised by large dark eyebrows, he was a warm man with an expressive personality.[8] He taught Comparative Education in the DipEd.

Four foundation staff taught the course in 1964: Henry Schoenheimer as a senior lecturer, and John Theobald, Dr Maurice Balson and Alan Trethewey as lecturers. In fact, John Theobald[9] started late 1963 and was able to secure schools for teaching practice and put in place basic administrative arrangements. Selby Smith commenced after Easter 1964, and Alan Trethewey later in the year. Theobald, Balson and Trethewey began their teacher-training careers sharing an office at the then Secondary Teachers' College in Melbourne. In 1962 the national conference of the newly founded (1959) Australian College of Education was held at the University of Melbourne on the theme of the teaching profession. Involved in the organising committee were Richard Selby Smith, then principal of Scotch College, and two lecturers of the Secondary Teachers' College, John Theobald and Maurie Balson. Through the nitty-gritty of conference organising, those on the committee came to know each other well, often under trying circumstances.

---

[8] He married Rachel nee Pease (1911–1999) and they had two sons Christopher (1942–2007) and Peter (1948–) Emeritus Professor Richard Selby Smith received the OBE and an Honorary Doctorate of Laws from Monash University. He died in 2005 in Tasmania.

[9] John Theobald's recollections of his time at Monash.

1.3 *Schoenheimer on education* edited by Leon Allwood for the Australian Council of State School Organisations, Drummond Publishing, Richmond, 1980.

Henry Schoenheimer had a philosophy background and also taught English. Originally from Queensland, he had trained as a teacher and completed a BA.[10] He then came to Victoria where he taught and also completed his DipEd (1955), BEd (1956) and MEd (1961) at the University of Melbourne. He lectured at Swinburne Technical College before coming to Monash. He was a tall bearded figure with a strong yet engaging personality. He had published a popular book on spelling for primary schools and was a prolific writer. In addition to his spelling books, two key books were *Good Schools* (1970) and *Good Australian Schools and their Communities* (1973). Keen on educational reform, he was a leader in the alternative schools movement and was active in his work in linking schools and their communities. He was also education correspondent for the *Australian* newspaper, writing under the name of Homer Sweet. He was entrepreneurial and as well as his press articles he would present radio programs. He was involved in many curricular projects. Colleagues could expect phone calls from Henry any time of the day or night on a range of educational topics. An excellent lecturer, he was popular with students, regarded as an idealist and a caring character they would always remember. He was to teach in the philosophy area as well as take English method in the DipEd. After Monash, he taught at La Trobe University (from 1971) then held posts with ACER. Depressed by the state of the world, he took his own life in 1976. One student from 1965 recalls the first lecture given by Schoenheimer in the philosophy of education course. Schoenheimer said 'You all have questions in your mind don't you? The main question is "Is it possible to fail this course?" The answer is "Yes" but it is very difficult.' The student said this immediately relaxed the whole class.[11]

John Theobald, after starting medicine, decided to become a teacher and changed to science. He completed the DipEd, then BEd. He taught science and biology at the University High School. He became a lecturer at the Secondary Teachers' College and his expertise was in teaching educational measurement and science education. He also became a Schools Board examiner in biology.[12] Sensing the need, he wrote a key book on educational measurement, *Classroom Testing*, aimed at teachers and education students. In its time this book was widely used and ran to many editions. He later

---

[10] For details of his life see Margaret H White's entry *Australian Dictionary of Biography*, Vol. 16 Melbourne University Press, 2002, pp. 191–192.

[11] Related by Gordon Lowing, a student in 1965 and later a legendary teacher at Melbourne High School.

[12] The body setting matriculation courses and examinations.

1.4 Dr John Theobald.
Education Faculty

completed his PhD which examined teacher–student interactions in the teaching of biology.

Maurie Balson, a gifted sportsman as well as scholar, had undertaken a BCom then DipEd and BEd, teaching commercial and economics subjects. He took himself off to California (UCLA) where he did a doctorate in education, in the area of educational psychology. He returned to teach educational psychology first at Toorak Teachers' College and then at the Secondary Teachers' College before his Monash appointment. He soon became known as an outstanding teacher and later in his career he became sought after as a speaker and facilitator to many school and parent groups. His publications *Becoming Better Parents* and *Understanding Classroom Behaviour* were widely read. The former became ACER's only book to be listed in the *Age* newspaper's 'Top Ten'.

1.5 Associate Professor Maurie Balson.
John Clark, MUA IN-649

Alan Trethewey was trained as a primary teacher and, following a BA and DipEd, taught in secondary schools. A history graduate, he later did a BEd and then MEd in the history of education. He taught at the Secondary Teachers' College and developed a particular interest in comparative education. This became his main field at Monash University. He wrote a key book, *Introducing Comparative Education* (Pergamon Press, Australia, 1976), which was used internationally. He left Monash after 10 years to take a post as head of the school of professional studies at the State College of Victoria, Toorak. Later he became Dean of the Faculty of Teacher Education at Victoria College, now incorporated within Deakin University. A popular member of staff, he was known as an excellent lecturer.

Why did many academics regard education as a 'Cinderella'?

First, there was a perception that the DipEd was dominated by 'methods' subjects and that such subjects were lacking in rigour. Furthermore, feedback to the faculty members was often unfavourable. Philosophy students, for example, found the History of Educational Thought subject of the DipEd rather elementary; psychology students thought the same of Educational Psychology. (Later there was an alternative Ed psych subject for students who had a psychology major.) Arts students well versed in sociology and history found Education in Society too prosaic.

While method subjects did and should include certain bread-and-butter basics for the classroom that might not be viewed as academic, much of the method work was solidly founded. For example, in science education, Monash Education had a team of scholars at the forefront of new ideas and thinking and had a first class international reputation. Many academics from undergraduate faculties would have been ignorant of the significant scholarship in many of the methods of teaching fields, science education, mathematics education, social education, economics education, English language teaching and TESL work, not to mention scholarship in foreign language teaching.

The Monash education faculty treated method subjects as of equal standing to other subjects and the method work at Monash also featured at the postgraduate level and saw many important developments in subject areas from these staff.

DipEd students were required to take seven subjects and also complete teaching practice. The subjects were Comparative Education, Educational Psychology, Philosophy and History of Education, Principles of Teaching and two methods of teaching subjects, plus a special course in some other university discipline. Subject results were to be graded as other Monash University subjects: High Distinction (HD), Distinction (D), Credit (C), Pass (P), or Fail (N or even NN).

Selby Smith's vision

Initially, the direction of the faculty was shaped by Richard Selby Smith, who made staff appointments in line with his vision of what a Faculty of Education should be and do. His philosophy is summed up in his introduction to the first *Faculty Handbook* for 1965,[13] and also in a paper he issued in October 1966 entitled 'Notes on the Possible Development of the Faculty of Education at Monash University'. [14]

---

[13] This was prepared in 1964. Initially though it was not a faculty, and so the first handbook simply referred to 'Courses in Education'. It became a faculty in 1965, but for ease we will refer to it as a faculty from the outset.

[14] Monash University Archives MON 496 (17) 1965–67 'RSS 28 October 1966', paper presented to a special staff meeting held on 31 November 1966.

In the *Handbook* he gave the stated aim as to 'help those graduates who intend to make their careers in teaching to begin to acquire the basic skills and knowledge which will enable them to take their places happily and effectively as members of school staffs.' He then spelled out in more detail how he saw the basic aim being achieved:

> ...they must learn to understand something of how children develop and of the ways in which knowledge, skills and attitudes to life are acquired. They must study methods appropriate to classroom work and have practice teaching under the guidance of those experienced in this work so that they will be able to introduce students to the subjects they have been studying in their own first university degree course.

Selby Smith went on to talk about students studying the best educational theory and practice and to 'develop a critical overview of the process of education and its aims and values in a democratic society'.

Matheson, in a book written after he had retired as Vice-Chancellor, said 'Monash decided that the Faculty of Education, although established with the prime purpose of providing courses leading to the Diploma of Education for intending teachers, would not be restricted to this task.'[15] As the faculty grew, staff did not accept the view that they were only there to provide initial teacher training. Concern with research and higher degree students became very important and later there was a significant shift in emphasis. This is reflected in Selby Smith's paper of October 1966. In the early years the prime purpose was pursued vigorously and it also provided the funds to employ staff and to develop the faculty.

Staff

Selby Smith was engaged in a massive task of employment of staff in those early years. He followed the adage of Vice-Chancellor Louis Matheson that 'a good vacancy is better than a bad appointment'[16] and this was especially apposite in those early days when nearly all appointments were tenured.

First year: 1964

In that first year with their 38 students, the small staff took all the subjects between them. Henry Schoenheimer took Philosophy of Education and

---

[15] Louis Matheson *Still Learning*, p. 30.
[16] Louis Matheson 'Monash Retrospect and Prospect' Oscar Mendelsohn Jubilee Lecture 22 May 1986, in *Addresses Given During the Silver Jubilee Celebrations 1968*, Monash University 1986.

English Method. Comparative Education was at first taken by Selby Smith then by Alan Trethewey. Maurie Balson taught Educational Psychology and Economics Method. John Theobald, who had taught at University High School and was an examiner in biology, took Principles of Teaching and Biology and Science Methods. Some part-time lecturers were brought in to cover other methods, such as David Scott, a teacher at Scotch College, who was brought in to handle mathematics, and Walter Butler from Glamorgan to take Modern Languages Method. A key member of the team was Hilda Mayberry, nominally secretary to Selby Smith, who did the secretarial work for all the staff as well as handle general administration, which was later taken over by a faculty secretary. All this, housed in one floor at the top of the only wing then built (now called the east wing) of the Menzies Building. A tremendous spirit of camaraderie and great sense of excitement developed between this small but cohesive group as they went about founding a Faculty of Education.

During this first year the foundation group of four (Alan Trethewey came later in the year) held staff meetings weekly and as well as conducting the DipEd program, planned the course of the future for what was to be a large education faculty.[17] There were basic questions of organisation to work out – what should constitute the DipEd, when should the BEd start, how should it be constituted? They had to settle on rules and regulations for students in terms of satisfactory progress and basic requirements, matching what other faculties had, and prepare regulations to determine the faculty's governance and procedures. There were practical matters to resolve – books and journals, clerical assistance, furniture for rooms, schools for teaching practice, provision of basic equipment. While a building had been promised, it would be a few years before it would be realised, so lecture and seminar rooms had to be found, as well as offices for a rapidly expanding staff. Fortunately all four of the founding staff were excellent administrators, as was Hilda Mayberry, and so all these issues were conscientiously pursued. John Theobald was especially skilled at organisation and he played a key role.[18]

---

[17] The first recorded staff meeting appears to be on 6 March 1964, John Theobald has handwritten minutes of these early meetings. The first typed minutes were of a meeting held on 17 June 1964. Monash University Archives MON 531, Box 44 papers of Dr J H Theobald.

[18] This is clear from the number of tasks he was given and how quickly he resolved them, as shown by the Minutes of Staff Meetings for 1964.

Chapter 2

Early years and issues

1965–1971

The faculty's first year, 1964, had been a make-shift year, with a handful of staff covering all the subjects for the Diploma in Education (DipEd) while simultaneously preparing to set up the full Faculty of Education. Until the Faculty Board was established, the Steering Committee for Courses in Education (which reported to the Professorial Board) handled all matters relating to Education.

At first there was no Faculty of Education, only 'Courses in Education' which had a two-page entry in the *Faculty of Arts Handbook* for 1963. When the first dedicated education handbook came out it was simply called 'Courses in Education 1965' and it was not until the second handbook was issued for the 1966 year that the book was called the *Faculty of Education Handbook*. Entries in the 1965 *Handbook* (made in 1964) were often inaccurate because of the long lead time – there were staff members listed who did not turn up, while staff who were there, but were appointed late in the year, did not make the list.

The DipEd at Monash expanded rapidly. The 38 students in 1964 increased to 147 in 1965, of whom 85 were Monash graduates and 88 were teaching studentship holders (31 students were part-time). In 1966 there were 215 students, 112 being Monash graduates and 144 studentship holders (47 part-time).[1]

The first Bachelor of Education (BEd) subjects were offered in 1965 with 19 students enrolled. Three subjects were required for the degree. The subjects offered in the first year were Educational Psychology, History of Education, and Child Development and Measurement in Education.

When all the statutes and regulations were in place, a first Faculty Board meeting was held on 30 October 1965. It was a special moment for the

---

[1] J H Theobald 'The Monash Faculty of Education' in *Monash University Gazette* Vol. III, no. 1, September 1966, p. 12

faculty. The Dean, Professor R Selby Smith, reported on student numbers: 116 full-time and 31 part-time for the DipEd and 18 for the BEd. He also announced that a second chair was being advertised and that a separate building for Faculty of Education had been foreshadowed and was proposed for the 1967–69 triennium. Greeted less enthusiastically was the news that the faculty colour for graduation dress was to be 'banana', with the yellow-coloured silk to be added to the blue Monash academic hoods.[2]

The method of teaching subjects offered in the DipEd in 1965 were English, History, Mathematics, Science, Geography, Economics, Modern Languages and Primary Teaching. Several more were to be added in 1966: Biology, Physics, Chemistry, Social Studies and Commercial Studies.

As well as basic faculty issues, other matters seriously canvassed in these early years were a concurrent degree, a course in librarianship, a course for teachers of physical education (especially seeing as the Diploma in Physical Education at the University of Melbourne was being phased out), offering of external studies, Aboriginal education and specific post-graduate diplomas.

Late in 1965 it was announced that Sydney S Dunn, assistant director of the Australian Council for Educational Research (ACER) had been appointed to the second chair of education. A graduate of the University of Adelaide and the University of Melbourne, Dunn has been in charge of all test development work carried out at the Australian Council for Educational Research since 1957. He was a part-time lecturer in Measurement in Education, a subject in the Bachelor of Education course at the University of Melbourne. He also gave courses on aspects of applied psychology at the Royal Melbourne Institute of Technology and the Australian Institute of Management. In 1956 he was awarded a Carnegie Grant to visit the United Kingdom and the United States of America. He visited these countries again in 1963.

Syd Dunn had been particularly interested in examining procedures and their effects on teaching methods and on the study habits and thought processes of students. He was also involved in research in the development of abilities, in concept formation and in the way in which these are affected by different disciplines and teaching methods. Dunn was the author of some 30 papers in educational books and journals and since 1961 has been consulting editor of the Australian Journal of Psychology. In 1962 he was president of the Australian Branch of the British Psychological Society and from 1963 he had been chairman of its Standing Committee on the Profession of Psychology.

---

2 MON 61 Faculty Board Minutes, Meeting 20 October 1965.

A decision was made to name the chairs, and this one was first called the 'Cunningham Chair of Educational Measurement'. Syd Dunn was not only from ACER and an expert in Educational Measurement, but Dr Ken Cunningham had been the foundation Director of ACER.[3] Nothing seemed to create more controversy than the actual names chosen for each of this and successive chairs. How the name was styled was tossed back and forward from Faculty Board to Professorial Board several times before any agreement. The chair eventually became the K S Cunningham Chair of Education.

Studentships

The studentship scheme run by the Victorian Department of Education commenced in the 1950s and aimed to secure teachers for the state's secondary schools. If a student gained a studentship it would pay most of their university fees and provide a living allowance. The living allowance was more generous than that given to Commonwealth Scholarship holders and, unlike the Commonwealth scheme, was not means tested. The recipient had to sign a 'bond', promising to teach in the service of the Education Department for three years, or else repay the funds received.

There was a higher living allowance for country students and in addition the education department ran a series of hostels which provided low-cost board and lodging for such students. Most of the studentship holders on completion of their degree and DipEd would be sent to country schools. This was a scheme which worked well – it meant the state secondary schools were staffed and usually with able and enthusiastic young teachers. Of the 38 students who undertook the DipEd in 1964, all but two were studentship holders. In 1968 there were 144 studentship holders out of 215 students.

The Department of Education generally dealt kindly with students who for reasons of marriage or circumstances such as an allergy to chalk wished to leave teaching short of the three years. It also gave many young people from middle class families the opportunity of tertiary education.

As the scheme continued, there was in the 1960s a problem of students who, while gaining admission to the university, failed some subjects in their first degree. Many of these were able students who had for various reasons suffered a short setback. As university places became harder to get, failure often meant exclusion. The education department had a Secondary Teachers'

---

[3] Kenneth Stewart Cunningham (1890–1976). Foundation chief executive of ACER and director from 1939 to 1954. An outstanding researcher and writer, he was much revered.

2.1 Professor Syd Dunn, Dean of Education.
MUA IN-7408

College at Melbourne University which gave extra tutorial help for students in some subjects, although it mainly functioned as an administrative unit to pay studentship holders.[4]

The education department started a scheme to give students who had failed a further opportunity by providing a college course, initially called a TSTC (Trained Secondary Teachers Certificate). In many cases TSTC students were able to cover lost ground, repeat their failed subjects and end up with a degree. The TSTC course was a concurrent course – the DipEd

---

[4] Studentship holders were also required to spend some of their long vacation time in schools in an observer capacity, although many also took lessons. Commerce students were obliged to do rudimentary training in shorthand (Dacomb system) and typing so they could teach these subjects in secondary schools.

component was covered as well as foundation subjects in the appropriate field: science, English, history, geography, commerce or languages. The education department opened Monash Teachers' College nearby on Blackburn Road for these purposes but it later widened its remit and taught in areas not covered by the university: physical education, domestic science and theatre arts. This later became Rusden State College, part of the State College of Victoria system.

Teaching practice

An important component of the DipEd was a period of teaching practice in schools. Monash retained the traditional pattern of three periods of teaching practice during the year, each of three weeks. Students were expected to teach a number of lessons in their two method subjects as well as observe. They were placed under the care of supervising teachers. Up until then, the University of Melbourne was the only institution to offer secondary teacher training, and so they had a monopoly on schools to use for teaching practice, both government and private. Monash had to make an agreement, firstly with the University of Melbourne and later with other educational institutions, about teaching practice places in the various schools. The schools also had to be amenable to the new institution they would receive students from. There was an initial allocation of government schools between Melbourne and Monash, and many non-government schools were approached and brought in. Supervising teachers did receive an honorarium for taking students, although in some schools this was pooled to be used for staff resources rather than apportioned individually.

During the late 1960s and 1970s, as the number of trainee teachers exploded, finding places in schools for teaching practice became a major problem. Other institutions arose, for example the state colleges and the Catholic teacher training institutions, which were also seeking placements. Students were usually visited by a member of the method staff from the education faculty during each teaching round. The faculty engaged extra people for these visits, but also required most of the non-method academic staff to make supervisory visits as well. Selby Smith enthused over new appointments who could also take some teaching practice supervision. The staff themselves were often not quite so enthusiastic.

Methods

Knowing the number of students who would complete their degrees in 1963 – and how many of these students were on Department of Education studentships and so obliged to complete a course in teacher training – helped with planning the DipEd course for 1964. It was especially useful in selecting the method of teaching subjects for the first year. The majority of students were involved in history and English, but provision needed to be made for a small number of students who required method work in economics, mathematics and science and modern languages. While some of these methods were covered in the first year by permanent staff (for example, Schoenheimer for English, Theobald for science and Balson for economics), use was made of teachers from government and private schools, with the backing of the Department of Education. The government was very supportive of teacher training, with the goal of increasing the number of secondary school teachers. The Department of Education not only provided studentships, but also seconded teachers from departmental schools to the Faculty of Education at both Monash and Melbourne to be part-time lecturers in the method of teaching subjects. The department was also generous in increasing the secondment time for a teacher as demand required. For example, one method lecturer commenced at Monash on half a day per week secondment, which eventually became two and a half days per week as the student numbers for that method subject increased. In addition to the lectures and tutorials, the method lecturer had to undertake the bulk of visits to schools to see students doing teaching practice on their teaching rounds, three times a year.

Selby Smith also wanted to include primary teachers in the life of the faculty and indeed his idea for a concurrent or first degree BEd was to make provision for primary teachers.[5] To secure an appropriate lecturer for primary method Selby Smith approached the principal of Burwood Teachers' College, Dr Lawrie Shears, and to his delight Shears indicated that he would take the course himself.[6] Shears did this successfully until he was appointed director of education. Shears became director-general of education but retained an active interest in the faculty at Monash.

---

[5] Monash University Archives MON Faculty of Education Minutes, 1963–70 Minutes of Meeting of Steering Committee for Education 13 October 1964. It was noted in these minutes that a specialist first degree would especially cater for those wanting to be primary teachers.

[6] Monash University Archives MON 531 Box 44 Dr J H Theobald's papers, Minutes of Staff Meeting 5 August 1964.

Concurrent course

One of Selby Smith's aims was to have a concurrent course. This was in contrast to the prevailing course where a student would complete a first degree, a Bachelor of Arts, Science, Economics, Music or Jurisprudence, and follow this with an additional year of professional training as a teacher (the DipEd). The concurrent course envisaged by Selby Smith would be one where students would take education subjects alongside normal first degree subjects from the start of the course. Some advantages to this 'concurrent course' arrangement included a closer linking of education with the student's major discipline and an appreciation of issues related to teaching from the outset. Selby Smith did not envisage the concurrent course as the only option for students, only that they should have a choice. His case was strengthened when the Melbourne State College and the University of Melbourne started discussion about a similar course for science students, which eventuated as a Bachelor of Science Education – a concurrent four year course.

Plans for such a degree at Monash University engaged many staff in hours of discussion and negotiation over a long period and even then the resulting plan did not enjoy unanimous staff support. The key group in this long process was a committee chaired by Ken McAdam. The McAdam report on 'ways and means' of achieving a first degree in education (concurrent degree), was approved by the Faculty Board at its meeting on 14 May 1969. This news was greeted with great relief as the issue had absorbed much time of many staff members for a long period. Negotiations with other faculties, mainly the Faculty of Arts, proved even more difficult. It eventually became clear that the arts faculty had no intention of participating in a concurrent course, no matter how it was arranged. This was reported by the Dean at the July Faculty Board meeting. It was a sad end to a long and at times torrid campaign. The whole notion of a first degree in education lapsed. Vice-Chancellor Louis Matheson saw Selby Smith's subsequent departure from Monash as at least in part influenced by his disappointment on this issue.[7]

Links with other faculties

Selby Smith was very keen on closer relations between education and other faculties of the university. One idea was to have students in the DipEd undertake an extra subject from another faculty, which he said would

---

[7] Louis Matheson, *Still Learning*, Melbourne, MacMillan, 1980, p. 19.

'bring Education close to the Faculties'.[8] He also encouraged teaching within education of people from other faculties, which did happen with some – notably Don Hutton from physics and John Stillwell from the mathematics department – but not to the extent Selby Smith had hoped. Hutton took over teaching Environmental Education which was jointly a masters subject for education and for the Master of Environmental Science. He also taught part of a physical science subject for MEnvSc in the 1990s. Stillwell was involved from 1970 to 1984, during which he worked for 20 per cent of his time in the education faculty, in science and mathematics methods, as well as the advanced methods offerings in these fields for the BEd and MEd courses.

Selby Smith had in mind the making of joint appointments between education and other faculties. He envisioned the Faculty of Education advising the rest of the university on curriculum, teaching methods and assessment (which had its fruition in the Higher Education Research Unit). Inter-faculty cooperation was also crucial for his hope for a concurrent degree or first degree in education.

Child Study Centre

From early on there had been faculty discussion about the possibility of a Child Study Centre. An advisory committee was set up in early 1966. This centre was primarily the creation of Elwyn A Morey.[9] Morey, an expert in child and adolescent psychology, was a warm caring person who had a vision of a significant centre where students could learn about child development and also undertake research. A functioning kindergarten was to be part of this centre.

Morey was an early appointment to the education faculty – it was announced in 1964 before her arrival in 1965. She had a BA (Hons) and then an MA majoring in English from the University of Melbourne. She later added majors in pure mathematics and French. She completed a DipEd and BEd and taught before going to the University of California. There she completed a PhD on 'The vocational interests and personality characteristics of

---

[8] Monash University Archives, MON Faculty of Education Minutes 1964–70, meeting 5 May 1964. Some believed this idea came from the other faculties; this was not so. Selby Smith partly derived the idea from Conant at Harvard and his views on the Harvard degree in teaching, which insisted that continuing study should always be part of a teacher's life. Monash University Archives MON 480 Box 39, Letter from Professor R Selby Smith to Alex McDonell Director of Education, Victoria, 11 February 1964.

[9] MON 61 Faculty Board Minutes, Meeting 20 April 1966.

women teachers' which earned her a National Research Award for the best PhD research by a woman in the USA. A qualified psychologist, she returned to Australia and worked as a research assistant with ACER, and from 1948–57 was lecturer, then senior lecturer, in the Department of Psychology at the University of Western Australia. In 1957 she held a similar post at the University of Melbourne, but in 1961 transferred as a senior lecturer to Monash's Faculty of Education. She joined the new faculty as an associate professor. Her main fields of interest were cognitive development in infants and young children and also the adjustment of children and families to disability.

Morey was greatly respected for her work on the Child Study Centre, securing a serviceable red brick house, one of the cottages left on the original Talbot Colony site, for its use. It was known as Birch Cottage and served as a 'play group', an informal kindergarten or child minding group. Morey was also very hospitable and Birch Cottage held weekend barbecues in the early days of the faculty for staff and partners to meet together socially.

Research and higher degrees

The faculty emphasised the value it placed on research by the setting up in November 1965 of a Research and Higher Degrees Committee, which was to consider research proposals from candidates for higher degrees, consider proposals from staff for research grants and make recommendations on higher degree and research needs.[10] Associate Professor Elwyn Morey (chair), Dr John Hunt and John Theobald comprised the first committee.

Library

While a staff library had been contemplated early on, the idea was discontinued in 1966.[11] University policy held that there would not be faculty libraries – despite the fact that there was the Hargreaves Library (for the Science, Medical and Engineering Faculties), and the Law Library in addition to the Main Library (now called the Sir Louis Matheson Library). However, there was the matter of the Curriculum Laboratory and the extent to which it exercised a library function. The education faculty had representatives both on the Main Library Users Committee and the General Library Committee. The Curriculum Laboratory staff handled

---

[10] Monash University Archives MON 496 (17) 1965–67 Minutes of Staff Meeting 16 November 1965.

[11] Minutes of Staff Meeting, 12 September 1966. The staff voted to discontinue a staff library.

2.2 Associate Professor Elwyn Morey.
MUA IN-66

staff orders for books and periodicals for the Main Library. Early in 1965 the Main Library experienced a problem with cataloguing, and built up a backlog of 28,000 books. They were acquiring new books at the rate of 2,000 volumes a month. The library grant to the Faculty of Education increased from $2,800 to $5,200 in 1966. While financial matters were to loom large as a constraint, in these early days the Faculty of Education had problems spending its allocation. There was a breakthrough in 1970 when the library agreed to spend funds on materials other than books and journals.[12]

---

[12] Minutes of Staff Meeting 5 August 1970. This enabled curriculum materials to be purchased as well as audio-visuals.

Monash High School

Almost in emulation of the relationship that the University of Melbourne Faculty of Education had with University High School, it was proposed that the Monash Faculty of Education have access to a school nearby, with which they would have a special relationship and serve as a demonstration school.[13] In 1964 Selby Smith was advised that the Department of Education had land in Blackburn Road that could be used, but the school was likely to start elsewhere.[14] It was referred to as 'Westerfield High School' and it started in temporary buildings in 1965.[15] The land in Blackburn Road was used for what was to become Monash Teachers' College, the equivalent of the Melbourne Secondary Teachers' College at the University of Melbourne. Monash Teachers' College extended its courses in physical education, drama and later home economics when it absorbed Larnook Teachers' College. Over the years, the education faculty, together with Monash Teachers' College, persisted in trying to establish links with what became Monash High School. While there was some use of the school by the science method staff, in terms of micro-teaching,[16] and with some other special projects, the hoped for close relationship never eventuated. The principal at the time did not prove cooperative to any proposed initiatives.

New staff appointments

Several additions were made to the Faculty of Education during 1965. Dr F J Hunt (known as John) was the first leader of the 'social foundations' area and an effective administrator. He brought a critical view to many issues within the faculty and functioned as a useful devil's advocate. He fought for the cause of the social sciences, often feeling they had been overlooked or overpowered by the sciences/maths group in the faculty. An active and respected staff member, he assumed many administrative positions during his career and shouldered a heavy supervision load.

---

[13] Monash University Archives MON Faculty of Education Minutes 1963–70, meeting 5 May 1964.

[14] Director of Education Mr Alec McDonell was present at the 5 May 1964 meeting and expressed these opinions. He also pointed out that the proposed high school would be a district school and not a selective school but that it could be a teacher-training school.

[15] Monash University Archives Faulty of Education Minutes 1963–1970 MON Meeting of Steering Committee for Education 13 October 1964.

[16] Microteaching is a method to improve teaching practice by having the student undertake a segment of a potential lesson and get feedback on this either by a video or audio tape or by an observer such as a lecturer or experienced teacher.

2.3 Dr John Hunt (right) with his PhD student John Nunn.
Education Faculty

Before his appointment as senior lecturer in education he had graduated BA and MEd from the University of Western Australia and had recently completed the requirements for a PhD at Stanford University. His doctoral thesis was entitled 'The Role of the Faculty in Junior College Organization Change'. He had extensive teaching experience in secondary schools and at the Western Australian Teachers' College. In 1962 he was a visiting lecturer in the social foundations of education at the University of Western Australia. His research interests were in the social foundations of education and the sociology of education. Hunt pioneered the course titled Education in Society which was a marked departure from the traditional offering of Comparative Education. Hunt felt Comparative Education was inappropriate with the 'emphasis shifted to an examination of education in its societal context and an appraisal of social science approach to the study of educational problems'.[17]

---

[17] Minutes Meeting of Faculty Board 19 April 1967.

His appointments reflected his interests, with political scientists, economics and sociologists joining the group. He brought sociology firmly within all sections of the education faculty. He was also influential within Australia in bringing more attention to social science teaching and research in the social sciences. He was a key participant in the UNESCO conference on the teaching of the social sciences in 1967 organised by Professor Perc Partridge.[18] He published widely. Among his publications were: *The Social Dynamics of Schooling* (1971), *Social Science and the School Curriculum* (1971), *Resources and Achievements in Melbourne Secondary Schools* (1975), *Socialisation in Australia* (1978), and *The Incorporation of Education: An International Study in the Transformation of Educational Principles* (1985). After he retired he wrote about his time at Monash in *Education at Monash: A Personal Experience*.

Ailsa Zainu'ddin (also known as Tommy; before marriage she was Ailsa Thomson) had a BA and MA from the University of Melbourne, majoring in history. She also completed a DipEd and a BEd. She taught history in the law faculty at Melbourne, and had been research assistant to Manning Clark. Manning Clark dedicated one his books to her and her husband. Zainu'ddin had also been one of the early volunteer graduates, or *pegawi*, in the Volunteer Graduate Scheme to Indonesia pioneered by Herb Feith.[19] In this scheme young Australian graduates went to work in Indonesia, not as foreign experts but as local employees would work and on their rates of pay. As well as maintaining her strong academic credentials in history, she became well known for her work in South-East Asian and Indonesian affairs and in promoting the cause of women's education. She brought together a group called HEGG (History of Education of Girls Group), which met regularly for seminars and presentation of papers.[20] Her *A Short History of Indonesia* (1968) was acclaimed, as was her centenary history of Methodist Ladies College: *They Dreamt of a School* (1982). She also wrote *Kartini Centenary: Indonesian Women Then and Now* (1980). Zainu'ddin published many articles in learned journals on the three areas of expertise and in which she also taught and undertook research. She retired in 1992.

---

[18] Director of the Research School of the Social Sciences, Australian National University, Canberra. There had been a strong Monash presence at the conference and one upshot was the book edited by D G Dufty, *Teaching About Society*, Adelaide, Rigby, 1970.

[19] Professor of politics at Monash University, Feith was a famous Indonesian scholar of unique qualities who took on many worthy causes.

[20] For Ailsa Zainu'ddin's personal recollections of HEGG see Chapter 9.

Other 1965 appointments included new method lecturers Max Oldmeadow OAM[21] (History), Hec Gallagher[22] (Geography) and Alan Gregory[23] (Economics). Hilary Webster was appointed to look after the Curriculum Laboratory and there were new secretarial and technical staff. Concerned about the speech of students undertaking the DipEd, the Dean obtained the services of noted elocution and speech teacher Keith Hudson who in his time had been a leading radio actor. Hudson commenced sessionally, but was eventually appointed a senior tutor. He gave one-on-one help to students and sometimes staff and would also visit students during teaching rounds. Always immaculately dressed and beautifully spoken, Keith Hudson had the air and manners of an English gentleman. He retired in 1986 due to ill-health, and sadly passed away four years later.

Morning tea

With the rapid expansion of student numbers and staff there was a great air of excitement in this newly created faculty. Morale was high. The staff room became an important element of faculty life. Morning tea, always at 10.30am, was a special event. All would be there, unless they had teaching commitments. Information was passed around, announcements were made, banter and debate was had, football victories and defeats were analysed and much fun was had. No one needed to make appointments to see the Dean or a colleague – a chat was always possible at the morning tea. It also meant a profitable mix of all staff, academic and general (later called the 'professional' staff). Lesley Hardcastle, recollecting those years has stated 'The stimulating discussions in the common room. Unlike any other place I have worked in there was high calibre intellectual exchange. We learnt from each other. I can still remember learning about the second law of relativity from Dick Gunstone, and a 'bear' like economy from an economist, and from other stimulating minds like Dick Selleck, Peter Fensham and Ron Taft'.[24] The downturn came with expansion; hygiene at the kitchen bench became of concern with the large numbers of people using and storing tea,

---

[21] A well-known teacher in the Dandenong area, with history being his specialty. He was later a member of the Commonwealth Parliament as Member for Holt 1972–75.

[22] A secondary school teacher, he was attached to Monash Teachers' College teaching Geography Method. He later became an inspector of schools and assistant director of secondary education.

[23] A teacher at Brighton High School.

[24] E-mail to the author.

coffee, milk and all the other substances regarded as essential to sustain one throughout a working day.

While the concept of morning tea was supported by all, the means of achieving it were subject to much disagreement. Over the years various solutions were tried and there were even committees of enquiry set up to ascertain the most efficient way to run a Tea Club and maintain kitchen hygiene.[25] A constant of faculty life over its whole existence had been disappearing teaspoons and cups. Subscriptions were debated – what deduction for those who do not take milk? At one stage a tea lady was employed both to serve the tea and clean up afterwards.[26] Many times the Dean had to bail out the Tea Club from his contingency funds to avert a financial crisis.

Various strategies were employed over the years to improve the situation. Technology helped as the urn was replaced by a constant hot water unit. There was also a happy phase when Howard Brown became 'tea lady.'[27] Ultimately peace only came to the Monash tea room when the Dean absorbed all the supply of materials and costs. Over the years this issue, together with the location of the staff mail boxes, have been the most contested. The mail boxes have oscillated between the staff room and the ground floor reception area. At Clayton campus they are currently in the staff room.

Rapid growth

There was concern about the rapid increase in demand for DipEd places. In 1966 there were 930 studentships awarded and the survival rate of students throughout their degree was 54 per cent. It was estimated that in 1970 there would be 1,000 studentships awarded with a survival rate of 60 per cent. New method staff in 1966 were Miss B S Shalley, A R Dickinson and D I Allen, and in 1967 Evelyn Ashcroft came to look after Geography Method. In 1966 the method numbers were as follows: History 120, English 100, Geography 30, Economics 15, Mathematics 15, Science 15, Modern Languages 12, Commercial Studies 10 and Primary Teaching 30.[28]

---

[25] Monash University Archives MON 496 Minutes of Staff Meeting 15 June 1966, 'Hygiene in Staff Room' and also Staff Meeting 15 February 1967.
[26] This was Mrs Mountain. Staff paid $2 a month to cover costs. Minutes of Staff Meeting 4 February 1970.
[27] Howard Brown acknowledges considerable help from Bev Pocknee.
[28] Monash University Archives, MON 531 Box 44, J H Theobald, Faculty of Education, Minutes of Staff Meeting 26 October 1965.

In 1966 there was also a large intake of staff, all of whom were to make significant contributions to the faculty: Ken McAdam (psychology), John Radvanksy (philosophy), Brian Sureties (English), Ray McCulloch (administration), Hugh Batten (science and media), John Cleverley (history), Lindsay Mackay (science and measurement), and Barbara Lewis as director of the kindergarten. The appointments reflected the fields Selby Smith saw as appropriate for the faculty to develop. In 1966 the faculty was regarded as sufficiently important for the Minister for Education, the Hon. John Bloomfield, to come and visit.[29]

In 1967 there were 290 full-time DipEd students, 80 part-time, and 100 students enrolled for BEd. The higher degree area was making a modest start with 14 students enrolled for the research MEd and two for the PhD. The DipEd was still the major business of the faculty. However, the various committees in charge of the various degrees were established and reported to the Faculty Board. The committees had been expanded to allow representation from the various areas of interest in the faculty. As a result there was a blossoming of the subjects offered for the BEd in 1967, especially with the new staff appointments and their interests. Among the new staff in 1967 were those who made an impact but did not stay that long, such as Gerald Johnston (political science), John Lawry (history), Merrill Jackson (psychology), Denis Phillips (philosophy). Other 1967 additions made a similar impact but ended up staying with Monash far longer: John Fyfield (administration, mathematics and measurement), Mary Nixon (psychology), Paul Gardner (science), Norm Dobson (history method) and Phyllis Scott (early childhood). Experienced educator Dr John Leese from Yorkshire Teachers' College was also appointed for a short term. With two chairs, in place the filling of the third chair was an important move.

A key event in 1967 was the appointment of Peter Fensham as a professor.[30] Dr Peter Fensham was reader in chemistry at the University of Melbourne. As well as his PhD in chemistry from Bristol and an international reputation in this field, he had a second doctorate from Cambridge in social psychology. He was involved in physical chemistry, in particular magnetochemical studies of oxides. A Melbourne graduate in science (BSc 1948, MSc 1950), he did his Bristol doctorate 1950–52, was at Princeton 1952–53, and completed his second doctorate in social psychology at Cambridge in 1953–56. He had

---

[29] Bloomfield was the Minister for Education who set up Monash University. A talented amateur painter in retirement, by then Sir John, he did a watercolour of the Monash grounds for the faculty which hung in the Dean's conference room for years until it disappeared.

[30] For Peter Fensham's recollections of his time at Monash, see Chapter 9.

published widely and held a post at the University of Melbourne since 1957. He was also well known for his broad range of interests as an active Christian, being involved with World University Service, Christian Frontier and the World Student Christian Federation. He was also part of the immigration reform movement, and was involved in Pugwash's campaign for nuclear disarmament. Some of his science friends were appalled at his decision to accept a chair of education when a chair of chemistry was within his reach but they did not take into account Fensham's broader interests. A remarkable career was to follow, a career that put the Monash Faculty of Education on the international map. His chair was named in honour of Sir Ian Clunies Ross, a notable Australian scientist and chairman of CSIRO. As with other chairs the name was revised several times.

In 1968 the faculty held an important series of seminars on the Universal Declaration on Human Rights, which was highly regarded and resulted in a book edited by Peter Fensham, who had been behind the project called *Rights and Inequalities in Australia*. Later in 1973 another successful seminar was held on the new Schools Commission.

Soon after came the appointment of a professor who was not thought of as an education person at all: Ron Taft. The Monash chair appealed to Taft because the structure devised by Selby Smith did not see professors assuming the traditional administrative load of a department. Selby Smith was after scholars for this multi-chair faculty and Taft, like Fensham, came without any direct school teacher or education background. It was not that Taft lacked administrative competence – indeed in the period he acted as Dean (after Syd Dunn's resignation) he showed himself to be highly effective in that regard. He also took his share of service on faculty and university committees.

The main thrust of his teaching was in social psychology and personality but he also covered general and educational psychology. As well as playing a key administrative role in the faculty, serving as head of psychology area, and Acting Dean, he established a distinguished and diverse research and publication record in fields such as personality assessment and dynamics, ethnicity and immigration, and social and cultural psychology.[31]

Melbourne born, he graduated in arts from the University of Melbourne in 1939 and obtained his MA in psychology at Columbia University, New York. During the Second World War he worked as an industrial psychologist in war industries, and then taught at the University of Melbourne. Taft was a foundation member of the Australian branch of the British Psychology

---

[31] Diana Davis and Frank Coulter were among the first of Ron Taft's PhD candidates.

2.4 Professor Peter Fensham.
Tony Miller, MUA IN-256

Society in 1946 and later became chairman. He also played a leading role in the affairs of the Australian Psychology Society, holding the status of honorary fellow. In 1951 he was appointed senior lecturer in psychology at the University of Western Australia and was reader from 1957 to 1965. In 1966 he became reader in psychology at the University of Melbourne, and then in 1968 he took a chair in the education faculty at Monash University which he held until his retirement in 1981.

He earned an international reputation for his three decades of pioneering research and publications in the field of ethnicity and the psychology of immigration. His work in the 1950s on personality assessment was also heavily cited in the international literature. In 1976 Taft was awarded the Silver Medal by the Royal Society of Victoria for his contributions to scientific research. He played an important part in promoting psychology as a discipline and as a profession. Taft was also active as the Australian representative in international psychology organisations. He was president of the International Association of Cross-Cultural Psychology and was

2.5 Professor Ron Taft.
Education Faculty

on the executive committees of the International Association of Applied Psychology and the Union of Psychological Science. He is also fellow of the American Association of Psychological Science.

Ron Taft had opted for his chair to be named the H L Fowler Chair of Social Psychology.[32] University Council rejected this suggestion and finally settled on the name of an eminent Queensland psychologist, Professor Schonnell. Taft had a diverse team of psychologists in the faculty – those with strong teacher backgrounds like Maurie Balson and Ken McAdam, mainstream psychologists like Mary Nixon (who became an honorary fellow of the APS), Phillip Greenway, Norm Nettleton and Wyn Owen, and those

---

[32] Hugh Fowler was a teacher in Western Australia and pioneer educational psychologist with the Department of Education in WA. He founded the psychology department at the University of Western Australia, only the second such department in Australia (H T Lovell set up the first at the University of Sydney in the 1930s) and became departmental head as associate professor.

more involved in special education: Fred Perry, Lawrie Bartak, Gil Best and Merrill Jackson. Initially, Professor Marie Neale was also to join this group, before special education assumed a separate identity. Taft also inherited the Child Study Centre created by Elwyn Morey; some of the psychologists with interests in child development served on a committee that administered the centre.

At that time Ross Day was professor of psychology. He had little interest in social psychology and happily left its teaching to the education faculty. The faculty offered courses in both educational psychology and social psychology, serving a special need in offering advanced courses to those who wished to qualify for membership of the Australian Psychological Society as registered psychologists. The Diploma in Education Psychology which the area developed especially served this purpose as well as cater to the interests of educational psychologists.

Taft recollects that Monash during his time was the first education faculty in Australia to offer PhDs, and also that a high number of professors emerged from the faculty. He felt the faculty gave important opportunities by offering late developers a second chance, which they took to good effect.

In 1968 there were 300 full-time and 70 part-time students doing the DipEd. For BEd there were 95 part-time students and 3 full-time. There were 13 students enrolled for the MEd and 3 PhD candidates. A significant appointment in 1968 was the appointment of Dr Gerald Burke as a lecturer. Gerald had come from Economics and Politics and he was to have a long and significant role in the Faculty. His initial academic field was the economics of education.

New building

Accommodation for the growing faculty was very tight. It quickly outgrew the space provided in the Menzies Building, and there was pressure on the limited number of seminar rooms that were available. The problem became so acute in 1968 and 1969 that there were 38 people from the education faculty housed in the law building, many of them higher degree students but also Professor Peter Fensham, Gerald Burke, Andrew Spaull, Alan Gregory and the HERU team. There had been the promise of a building of its own which for an education faculty was quite special. It would be the first separate building designed in Australia for the exclusive use of a Faculty of Education.³³ The firm selected to be architect for the new education building was John F D Scarborough and Partners, with the architect who did the work being Ken Atkins. Selby Smith had experience with Atkins in a building project at Scotch College. It was Monash policy to engage one firm to do the overall master plan for the university, but engage different architects for the various buildings.

The brief specified that the building was to 'provide a congenial and appropriate setting for the professional education of those intending teachers who are selected for university courses.'³⁴ The brief, set out in October 1966, defined the location as east of the Alexander Theatre and south of Birch Cottage, and it was to take maximum advantage of existing trees. There was an awareness of its being near the main entrance to the University. The building was to consist of a gross area of 48,900 square feet with construction costs estimated to be $115 per square foot. There would be a net usable area of 29,300 square feet. There was also to be a Child Study Centre. The funds allocated by the Australian Universities Commission (AUC) were $924,000. A project sub-committee was set up within the faculty with the Dean, Professor R Selby Smith, as chairman.³⁵ The New Building Project Sub-Committee had its first meeting on 13 July 1966.³⁶

The areas of rooms now had to conform to national standards set down by the AUC. A professor was entitled to an office of 240 square feet, an associate professor or reader 200 square feet, a senior lecturer 150 square feet, a lecturer 150 square feet, a tutor or demonstrator 120 square feet and a professor's secretary 100 square feet. Lecture rooms were to be 520 square feet, seminar rooms either 320 or 240 square feet, and a common room 450 square feet. The staff room on the second floor achieved its more spacious size by being placed adjacent to a seminar room with a temporary partition separating them. The temporary partition was soon removed, making the staff room large enough to accommodate the number of staff in the building. There were also limits to where carpet could be placed and these were limited to the Dean and his secretary and professors and their secretaries. Seminar rooms were allowed carpets – but not for any staff below the level

---

[33] Brief for the Architect for Education Building, 31 October 1966, Monash University Archives MON 531 Files of Dr J H Theobald.

[34] Ibid.

[35] Other members of the committee were Associate Professor Elwyn Morey, Dr F J Hunt, John Theobald, by invitation Dr A E Wilmot and representatives of the building officer of the university.

[36] Minutes of Faculty Board 29 July 1966.

2.6 Education Building, 1972.
MUA IN-3632

of professor. The brief also specified a foyer, a programmed instruction room, an educational media room, a theatre, a science laboratory and preparation room and a room for the Curriculum Laboratory.

The new building was occupied by late November 1969 and was officially opened on 20 February 1970 by Sir Henry Basten, the chairman of the AUC. He said in his address that 'education as a professional subject in universities has been a Cinderella everywhere – I do think, thank heaven, that these pockets of prejudice are fading'.

Selby Smith was greatly moved by the opening of the building; it was not only the first dedicated Faculty of Education building in Australia, it was also, to him, 'the end of the first phase in the development of our Faculty.'[37] It was also the first multi-professorial education faculty.

---

[37] Monash University Archives, MON 480 Box 39, Address of welcome by Professor R Selby Smith at opening of the education faculty building 20 February 1970. Gerald Burke recounts how many staff at the time lamented the frugal nature of the building which was designed and built with economy in mind.

He outlined what he felt were the two main tasks for the faculty: 'the education of our students, passing on to them the best that is known today and also the attempt to extend the boundaries of knowledge.' He also put in a plea for creativity, seeking to stimulate a continuing zest for learning as well as to ensure that less fortunate groups in the community were given opportunities. Both Basten and Selby Smith foreshadowed a growth and commitment to research.[38]

The new building, given the faculty's enormous growth, soon proved inadequate and within two years an extension was already being mooted, with the a project sub-committee chaired by Professor Peter Fensham.[39] The plan was to add 10 bays to the existing building (which was 24 bays), and also add a floor to the Child Study Centre. The building was to be five storeys, one more than the original. This extra floor had to be omitted due to budget cuts, and the number of bays of the proposed extension was reduced from 10 to 8. Budget cuts also meant that no provision could be made for an elevator.

Higher Education Research Unit

The beginnings of the Higher Education Research Unit were in 1966 when psychologist Dr John Biggs[40] was appointed education research officer to Monash University. Much of Biggs' work was concerned with providing data to the university administration to discover educational trends and predict student numbers. He was responsible to the Steering Committee for Education, and ultimately to the Professorial Board. In 1968 the Professorial Board accepted a proposal that incorporated the work of the education research officer into a unit with the wider purpose of assisting staff to solve educational problems relating to their curriculum, teaching methods, or forms of assessment. The unit, called the Higher Education Research Unit (HERU – later HEARU, with the A standing for Advisory), would undertake research on faculties or the university as a whole. A study was specifically requested for student work-loads, another request was to look at the 'drift from science'. The unit was also engaged in the study of higher education and the example of tertiary education choice was cited.[41]

---

[38] Monash University Archives, MON 480, report of the opening of the faculty building 20 February 1970.
[39] Other members of the committee were Professor Syd Dunn, John Theobald, Fred Perry, Alan Gregory and John Lawry.
[40] For John Biggs' recollection of his time at Monash and the foundation of HERU, Chapter 9.
[41] *Monash University Gazette* Vol.7:1 November 1970, 'Higher Education Research Unit', p. 9.

HERU was to be housed within the Faculty of Education, as was its budget. Professor S S Dunn was part-time director of the unit. Initially the academic staff within it consisted of John Clift (a New Zealander) and Dr Noel Ryan (a Jesuit priest). Both Clift and Ryan were not only well qualified but personable. Clift had used videotapes of seminars to help improve teaching in one subject. The unit started functioning in 1969. In 1971 a Diploma of Education (Tertiary) was introduced, a long hoped-for development for the faculty.[42]

Death of Elwyn Morey

Associate Professor Elwyn Morey's death early 1968 came as a great shock to the faculty. She was in a car crash on her return from a conference in Sydney. Morey was a much loved member of staff – a warm and compassionate person. Her work with children had been path-finding as well as outstanding. Professor Ross Day in an obituary remarked how much her death 'profoundly affected a large and varied circle of friends, associates, colleagues and students' and extolled her deep interest in the handicapped and her practical approach as a gifted intuitive practitioner.[43] The centre for the study of children and their development, which she was creating, had attracted much interest and showed enormous potential. It was a loss that was never filled. At the staff meeting following this tragic event in February 1968, all stood in silence as a mark of respect.[44] A trust fund was established in her memory and the planned Child Study Centre was named the Elwyn Morey Child Study Centre. Her death changed the direction of research in this area. With the appointment of Professor Neale the emphasis shifted away from child and adolescent development to studies in the area of special education.

General office

As the faculty expanded in every direction – courses, teaching, research, writing – there was a corresponding upsurge in typing and duplicating. It was the era of the stencil and duplicator, with photocopying, slow and expensive, being still in its infancy. There was an average of 20,000 pages of paper produced by the duplicator per week, sometimes this rising to 31,000

---

[42] Minutes of Faculty Board Meeting 15 July 1970.
[43] Professor Ross Day, Obituary of Assoc. Professor Elwyn Morey, Monash University Gazette, 1968, pp. 34–5.
[44] Monash University Archives MON 496 (18) 1968 Minutes of Staff Meeting 1/68, 7 Feb 1968.

sheets. Before personal computers the general office served as a typing pool for the staff (other than the professors, who had their own secretary). Some staff were heavy users of the office, especially those involved in two or three fields; others were infrequent users. There were often complaints as everyone expected their work not only on time but often at short notice. Some felt research typing was given a lower priority. Mrs Greenway had been succeeded by Bev Schneider as head of the general office and she had an excellent team with the likes of Heather Phillips and Elaine Scott. The office team were not only capable but well-liked by the academic staff.

A committee was set up to look into the complaints, and this committee recommended that there be two duplicating staff, that a typist should be allocated research typing for half of the week, that professors share one sixth of their secretary's time with other staff and that an additional collation machine be purchased. They also recommend the faculty have a building attendant to reduce some of the pressures on the general office. The attendant's duties would include receiving essays and assignments, collecting mail, issuing notes to students, being a shuttle to the general office, and even picking up the milk. It was recommended that the attendant have a reception desk in the foyer of the building.[45]

Much of this report was implemented. Professors shared their secretary with other staff in their area and two duplicating officers were engaged: Frances Boyle and her sister Hazel Evans, who were both superbly efficient. A building attendant was employed in the form of the laconic Dave Murphy of uncertain age[46] who became a much loved character and source of faculty gossip. His wife Mollie headed the faculty cleaning staff. Elaine Scott was designated as research typist, a post she held with great skill until serious ill-health forced her retirement.[47] A manual spirit duplicator was also purchased, as was a collation machine and a machine to address envelopes for large mailings, such as to schools.

The years of protest

Louis Matheson, Vice-Chancellor at the time, in typical understatement, speaks of 1967 to 1971 as the years of 'student difficulties'. The Vietnam War engendered strong protests against it, and in Australia conscription to

---

[45] MON 1164, 31, Faculty of Education, Staff Meeting Minutes, 5 February 1969. Denis Phillips and Alan Gregory comprised this committee.
[46] When Dave Murphy retired at age 65 he revealed he was actually 10 years older than that.
[47] Elaine Scott commenced 1969 and retired in July 1990.

fight in that war roused considerable anger. Monash soon became part of what was an international phenomenon of rebellion and unrest. While this general movement affected nearly all universities, unrest had been especially strident and violent in Berkeley in the USA and at the Sorbonne in France. Student leaders like Danny the Red became household names, and the occupation of university offices and destruction of university property became commonplace in a number of centres. Universities were vulnerable places to well organised revolt. There were areas too where injustices and what Matheson called 'discourtesies' were present – and the changing times demanded more democratic and equitable processes. Mistakes and injustices made by a department quickly became sparks for protest and rebellion. Monash University became known as the university in Australia with the most active and violent student unrest.

Generally the Faculty of Education was spared direct trouble from these events, however the atmosphere created affected everyone on campus. Brian Bullivant recalls that in a tutorial, as everyone introduced themselves, one student, with his rather dirty feet on the table, proclaimed 'I have no interest in teaching but want to get access to schools in order to smash the Victorian education system.'[48]

The most direct effect on education was when it became known that Albert Langer, the most well-known leader of the student revolt at Monash, intended to follow his first degree in mathematics by doing the DipEd. This attracted much publicity and the press implied he would be denied admission to the course because of his political views and actions, noting especially his conviction for offences that entailed a gaol term. The meeting of the Monash selection committee for the DipEd was watched with great interest. There was speculation about the Machiavellian plans the faculty had to exclude him. The truth was rather different. The committee simply looked at each candidate's eligibility in terms of their first degree, and whether they had the necessary prerequisites to undertake two method of teaching subjects. As Langer had the qualifications he was admitted without debate – his name was not even raised at the meeting.[49] Ironically at the same time as a form of Marxism had been embraced to underpin the student protests, there was a turning against Marxism in Prague and Warsaw.[50]

---

[48] Reflections of Brian Bullivant (1927–2013), former reader in education, July 2011 to the author.
[49] Author Alan Gregory was present at this meeting.
[50] Langer was exemplary in his first two teaching rounds under Dr Theo MacDonald, and did his third successfully in Pentridge prison with Theo's help.

At a staff meeting in October 1970 the Dean tabled a document from Vice-Chancellor Louis Matheson entitled 'Limits of Protest', which tried to outline what was acceptable protest and what was not, stressing that no one wished to stem dissenting voices. The document was supported by the staff.[51]

As a response to the early student protests a Commission on University Affairs was established to look into some of the issues raised. The main thrust of the report of the commission was to give more participation by students and non-professorial staff in university governance. The commission met 42 times and while various other matters were raised, it really only agreed on opening governance to more participation by students and non-professorial staff.[52] Matters relating to improved education techniques by the lecturing staff, better methods for conducting tutorials, having education officers in faculties, encouraging experiments in teaching methods and examining methods of evaluation were given lip service only. Aside from reinforcing the role of HERU, nothing much happened in these areas.

There was an irony to this, as the Faculty of Education was already leading the way in giving a bigger role to non-professorial staff – only to have its knuckles rapped for doing so a few years later. In the meantime the faculty quickly accepted the recommendations and acted to implement them. Students were placed on all committees of the faculty, and non-professorial staff in the few cases where they did not have representation already.

The student unrest issues at Monash gave it a reputation for radicalism. This also had an impact on staff. While some like Matheson and those associated with the Commission on University Affairs realised there was a need to reform various aspects of university administration, it was felt by others, such as some of the senior professors and members of the University Council, that they needed to throw off this radical image, and consequently they became more conservative in their approach.

New staff 1969–70

Two chair appointments were made in late 1969. Dr Marie D Neale was only the third woman to take a chair at Monash University. A senior lecturer in education at the University of Sydney, she was also an honorary clinical psychologist at the Royal Alexandra Hospital for Children. On the heels of receiving her MA from Auckland University, she went to the University

---

[51] Minutes of Staff Meeting 1 October 1970.
[52] Recommendation of the Commission on University Affairs, Monash University, October 1969.

of Birmingham in 1946 on a graduate scholarship. There she completed a Diploma of Psychology and then her PhD in a study of children's reading ability. She became a lecturer at the University of Birmingham and had other posts there as a clinical psychologist. She took up her Sydney appointment in 1961.

Professor Neale's major research interests were in exceptional development, children's learning, guidance, communication disorders, and patterns of talent and disability and reading tests. She had published numerous papers.[53]

Dr Peter Musgrave was appointed to a chair in the sociology of education. Musgrave had a BA from Cambridge, MA 1954, and did the Postgraduate Certificate of Education (PGCE) in 1956. After five years teaching he became lecturer, then senior lecturer, at Homerton College Cambridge. He had served in the armed forces, first for the Royal West Kents and then in India as a captain in the 2nd Punjab regiment. Musgrave also had experience working in the wool industry, which had previously brought him to Australia. In 1964 he was awarded a PhD from the University of London. In 1965 he was head of the Education Department at Bede College, University of Durham and from 1966 was senior lecturer at the University of Aberdeen.

His main research area was the sociology of education, and Musgrave had published many papers along with six books including *The Sociology of Education*, a significant book in this field, which was widely used and already in a fourth impression.[54] He was described by his UK referees as 'one of the foremost educationalists in this country' and 'an indefatigable worker' with 'considerable energy'.

An interesting group of people all joined the faculty in 1969 as senior teaching fellows: Diana Davis (English and psychology), Dermot Little (English method), Barbara O'Connor (sociology), Andrew Spaull (social foundations) and Brian Bullivant (anthropology). All of these people were to have important careers within the faculty.

While from early on the faculty had received many visitors, the first formal visiting professor came in 1969, in the form of US psychologist Professor Bruce Biddle. At this point it became faculty policy to keep a lecturing or staff post vacant to allow funds to offer visiting appointments to overseas scholars. This was to become an important aspect of faculty life and it enabled some outstanding scholars to spend time at Monash, to the benefit of staff and students.

---

[53] *Monash University Gazette* Vol. 6:1, November 1969, p. 39.
[54] *Monash University Gazette* Vol. 6:1, November 1969, pp. 39–40.

2.7 Professor Peter Musgrave, Dean of Education.
MUA IN-7404

In addition to the two professors Marie Neale and Peter Musgrave, the new staff welcomed in 1970 were Val Hawkes (political science), Geulah Solomon HET (who had been a research student), Brian Spicer (geography), Fred Perry (Psychology), and in HERU Dr Noel Ryan replaced John Biggs. At the end of 1970 it was announced that Dr Theo MacDonald had been appointed to handle Mathematics Method and that a PhD student in the faculty, well known to staff, Richard T White, had been appointed a lecturer from 1971.

Restructuring the faculty

Administratively, Selby Smith was keen to have the faculty as one 'unified without departments', like law. However, he did not want it to be like other education faculties in Australia, which at that stage had only one professor.

Selby Smith recognised that as happily as the faculty had been administered as one department up until 1967, some change was required. In many ways the staff meeting had already played a key role in faculty administration. Selby Smith warned that it:

> was important not to allow our Faculty to divide into relatively watertight departments, each capable of going their own way and of destroying the unity of purpose which a Faculty needs to be fully effective.[55]

Selby Smith saw the answer in a degree of delegation, and posited re-examining the committee structure and having coordinators for the various areas of study.

With the faculty becoming more and more complex the existing committee structure was proving cumbersome and so an ad hoc committee was set up to look at the constitution of committees in the faculty. A key recommendation was that a Planning and Development Committee be set up. This was to advise the Dean on medium and long-term planning issues, and should consist of the Dean and six other members, these being the six persons designated by the Dean as coordinators of the 'areas of study'. The 'areas of study' were specified as educational psychology, sociology of education and comparative education, history and philosophy of education, measurement and experimental education, methods and practice of teaching, and educational administration. Selby Smith wanted a carefully planned administrative structure that would encourage the academic staff to concentrate on teaching and research and not be bound up in administration.[56] He envisaged that the full-time faculty secretary along with the Dean would handle the bulk of the administration. A professor or associate professor should be the leader of the 'areas of study', coordinating the work 'without being run into the ground by administration as often happens to chairmen of departments'. In his paper Selby Smith stressed that he did not want an over-compartmentalised structure, which he said could only lead to empire building.[57]

Among the other recommendations of the Faculty Board meeting of October 1969 was first, the need for a horizontal sampling of interests. The recommendation was for one member from each area of study to be on each major committee. Second, that there should be one student on each committee and the student should have full voting rights. Third, that all

---

[55] Monash University Archives MON 480 Box14, paper: R Selby Smith 'Future Development of the Faculty' 11 November 1969.
[56] Paper given by Professor Richard Selby Smith to special staff meeting, 3 November 1966.
[57] Ibid.

committees should be open and observers should be able to attend. The Dean was to chair the Faculty Board, the Faculty Board executive, the Planning and Development Committee, the Board of Examiners and the Student Status Committee. The Dean was to nominate the chairs of all other committees such as the DipEd, BEd, research, and higher degrees committees.

John Theobald observed of the changing committee structure a move from 'participative democracy to representational or indirect democracy'.[58] The staff meeting had been the main body for information exchange and decision making but this had given way to committees taking the decisions and reporting to Faculty Board. To prevent staff meetings becoming ones at which the Dean simply provided information, an experiment was tried in 1970 and John Fyfield, an excellent chair and a much respected staff member, was asked by the staff to chair the meetings.[59]

The posts of Associate Dean and Sub-Dean were created in 1969. Prior to this Selby Smith had named a professor as Acting Dean whenever he was away. The Associate Dean took on this role, acting in place of the Dean if the Dean was away, and the Sub-Dean was a new administrative post, dealing with students' admissions and much of the academic administration.

In 1969 the numbers of full-time students taking the various method subjects were as follows: History 216, English 187, Geography 73, Mathematics 69, Economics 64, Science 55, Primary Teaching 40, and Commercial Studies 8. It was also a bumper year for Modern Languages. In terms of method staff, David Murphy took Classics, Leo Duffy Commercial Studies (taken over from Ian Allen),[60] Norman Dobson History, and David Davison Mathematics. Helping in Commercial Studies from 1969 was Joan Taylor (nee Sandy)[61] who took it over from Leo Duffy and also helped in measurement work.

In 1970 the Bachelor of Education committee recommended a change from the way subjects were offered, from one subject over a whole year embracing three terms to making subjects units on a semester system, meaning first and second half-year units. All subjects were then so divided. It was

---

[58] Minutes of Staff Meeting 1 October 1969.
[59] Minutes of Staff Meeting 4 February 1970.
[60] D Ian Allen had been first lecturer in Commercial Studies, a high school teacher of Commercial Studies, and Olympic rower. He completed an EdD at Berkley, California and then took posts at Simon Fraser University, Canada before returning as principal of the Preston Teachers' College and then taking a senior post in the Department of Education. He was a visiting lecturer to the faculty in 1976.
[61] A notable educationist, who had been executive officer of the Victorian Commercial Teachers Association but was to take on many other roles.

a time when BEd was expanding both in terms of students and in terms of subjects being offered. The increasing proliferation of subjects became a concern to the BEd committee, and so they restricted the number of subjects being offered to six BEd units for each of the areas save for Area 5, which was allowed 12 units.[62] In all 21 BEd subjects were offered in 1970.

In this period the faculty achieved its first doctorates: J R Lawry (1968), followed by Bob Bessant (1971), J R Clough (1971) Frank Coulter (1971), Lindsay Mackay (1971), and Dick White (1971).

There were other important developments too, with some staff receiving major research grants from various funds: Musgrave, Dunn, Fensham and the Elwyn Morey Centre being the main recipients. Some staff like Lindsay Mackay had received grants earlier, notably from ARC.

Industrial action by secondary school teachers associated with the Victorian Secondary Teachers' Association (VSTA) threatened to boycott teacher-training supervision which added to the worries of the DipEd coordinator, who was already desperate to find sufficient places in schools for the DipEd students.

In 1970 there were 385 full-time DipEd students and 198 part-time. BEd numbers had risen to 226 (part-time), MEd to 66, with 8 students enrolled for the PhD.

Curriculum Laboratory

The Curriculum Laboratory from the outset had trouble working out what its role should be. The hoped-for vision never really eventuated. It was a storehouse for materials to be borrowed, mainly by students for the practicum aspect of their DipEd. Unfortunately its annual funds ($3,600 in 1970) proved inadequate to deal with the requirements of each of the methods for their books, films, tapes, and other curricula materials.[63] It was also supposed to be an important display space for educational materials and resources, and there were hopes for an evaluation and development role. It had the task of handling orders for the Main Library, but there was debate as to what other functions it should have in relation to the Main Library. When Hilary Webster left to become principal of Jane Franklin Hall at the University of Tasmania, her assistant Meigs Ghent became manager.

---

[62] Minutes Faculty Board 15 July 1970.
[63] Monash University Archives, MON 480 (276) Document on the Curriculum Laboratory 16 June 1970, and later a paper prepared by Professor P W Musgrave on the Curriculum Laboratory 24 August 1970.

Group 70

Given the young faculty and an enthusiastic staff it was natural to look for experimentation and ways of making the DipEd a better course. Traditionally there had been many criticisms of DipEd courses around Australia. These criticisms were spelled out in a three-day seminar held by the National Union of Australian University Students (NUAUS) in December 1967 at the University of Melbourne. Overall the DipEd in Australian universities was considered to be too shallow, too much was attempted in the time available, there was a tension between academic subjects and the practical preparation for teaching, the courses were pitched at first year undergraduate level despite the disparate background of students and the courses were conservative and allowed little original thinking. The staff themselves seldom employed imaginative teaching methods, there was too little small group work, the practical teaching component was inadequate, there was little applicability of the philosophy, sociology or psychology taught in education and in general little attempt was made to facilitate the transition of full-time students to full-time teachers. The survey of such students also suggested the teaching methods employed by DipEd teachers were not exemplary.

The idea to have an experimental group came mainly from Peter Fensham with the strong support of John Fyfield, who became the coordinator of the experimental course. Fensham foreshadowed the move in a report to the Acting Dean after his 1968 trip overseas during which he had been impressed by the integrated and team teaching schemes at Chelsea College London and Ohio State University in Columbus. Fensham felt the present structure of the DipEd was far from ideal.[64] A small group of staff worked on the concept over the next year and finally proposed a pilot plan to the faculty in July 1969.[65] Much thought was given to how time should be allocated. There were frequent planning meetings and circulars, and there were meetings with principals of schools in which the students would undertake teaching practice.

Fyfield headed the team of staff who volunteered to participate in this experimental course, called 'Group 70' as it was initially offered in 1970. Others in this team were Peter Fensham, John Cleverley, Alan Trethewey, Hugh Batten, Terry Hore, Ann Shorten, Dermot Lyttle and Andrew Spaull.

---

[64] Monash University Archives MON 531 Box 44 Report by P J Fensham to S S Dunn Acting Dean, 11 November 1968.

[65] Monash University Archives MON 531 Box 44 Circular from the Dean to all staff 18 July 1969.

The program was to consist of a small group of students and staff arranged 'in a way as to facilitate integration of subject matter and an inter-disciplinary approach to the study of education and teaching.'[66] The innovations related to the deployment of staff in a flexible way to engage students with their discipline, and to the scheduling of time to the various parts of the course. About 80 students was considered a manageable number, in contrast to the 380 full-time students in the usual DipEd. This also meant altering the diversity of demands at different times of the year, for example giving attention to teaching methods before the first period of teaching practice.

Twenty-eight students were selected from the English and history methods of teaching and 52 students from science methods. Half a dozen staff were to have major involvement in the experimental group, and about another dozen staff had a part-time role. Initially the group planned three 'blocks' – with the first block devoted to preparation for school practice, as well as workshop sessions and sessions of micro-teaching. Micro-teaching was very much in favour in this period and was used extensively in many of the method subjects. Block II chiefly examined issues in education as illuminated by psychology, sociology, history and philosophy. Block III was designed to allow for student interests, with them taking two electives from a wide range offered. The emphasis was on a team approach, on a more integrated course, closer contact between staff and students and flexibility – the scope to adapt to changing interests or situations.

The course was evaluated by HERU, although there had also been internal evaluation conferences of staff and students. Those working in Group 70 stated that it was easy to agree on procedures and to adapt and modify them with the help of flexible scheduling. The major difficulty noted was that the style of teaching (working closely with other staff in teams) was not attractive to all staff. While most liked the integration, others favoured more specialisation. There were also problems in coping with the regulations as existed, and also with accommodating part-time students. While there were areas that needed improvement, the staff involved generally found the experiment highly successful.

HERU in their report said that a formal comparison of Group 70 with the traditional DipEd course was not possible. HERU found most students were satisfied with the course as a preparation for teaching, most felt the workload was well spread and nearly all liked the flexible timetable used. The electives,

---

[66] J A Fyfield 'Group 70: An Innovation in Teacher Preparation in the Monash University Faculty of Education' *General Journal*, VCTA Vol 9 1969–70, December 1970, pp. 25–28.

which comprised the final six weeks of the year, were also popular. The main criticism related to a lack of consensus by students on the aims of the course itself, and a continued problem with aspects of the teaching rounds.

There were 48 male students and 32 female students in Group 70. Fifty-two undertook maths/science methods and 28 English/history methods.

Group 70 did not enjoy unanimous staff support. Dr John Hunt was concerned about aspects of the proposal. He felt that the students selected for the experimental group had no option but to join and that they came in unaware of the issues involved and so unable to make an informed choice. He was also concerned that pulling maths and science students into this group meant withdrawing them from academic association with the full range of DipEd students. He was keen for students to become aware of the different disciplines applying to education. Others in the faculty felt it was a form of streaming or grouping. Fyfield responded by stating that selecting the student by the group they belonged to was an administrative decision, not streaming by principle, indicating that there would be choices within the course for students to make.[67]

Despite some staff misgivings, those involved were very happy with how the year went, and with the positive evaluation it received from HERU, it was agreed that the experiment should continue in 1971. They were joined by others, with Professor Peter Musgrave wanting to set up another similar sized group with similar aims. So in 1971 there were two 'experimental' groups. The Musgrave group, known as Group B, consisted of a selection of students from the non-science/maths method students. The large range of methods meant that the method subjects had to stand alone, with integration and close cooperation only possible in the foundation subjects. Initially Group 70 consisted of a mix of students from Science, Maths, History and English Methods, but the History and English Method staff found the arrangement unsatisfactory and so after 1970 withdrew. Group 70 continued beyond 1970 but as a science/maths group only. The Musgrave Group B only lasted for one year, 1971.

Faculty business

By 1970 the business of the faculty had become much larger – there were committee reports to receive, recommendations to send to the Professorial Board and decisions from them to comment on, formal procedures involving

---

[67] Monash University Archives MON 531 Box 44, Letter by J A Fyfield, 21 May 1971 and Comments on Proposals by John Hunt 19 May 1971.

students in higher degrees, appointment of examiners and so forth. The Faculty Board meetings were becoming longer, bogged down by all these administrative requirements. It was agreed to have a 'starred item' policy for Faculty Board meetings. The Dean would star items he felt required discussion and at the start of the meeting any member could ask for any item to be starred. The starred items were discussed but all the rest of the agenda items were then formally passed. This enabled discussion to be concentrated on important items rather than routine or procedural ones about which there was no real controversy.

It is interesting to note that it was only in this period that equal pay for women teachers in Victoria came in. This commenced in January 1971 but for budgetary reasons was phased in over four years.[68] The faculty was to play a significant part in improving the lot of girls and women in education in the next decade.

During this period there was concern that this large education faculty had reached its limit. It had almost reached saturation point in terms of taking DipEd students, with 500 full-time students looking like it would become a quota. Studentship numbers were growing and Monash University had an increasing pass rate, so for 1970–72, it looked as if a crisis was looming.[69]

The faculty had played an important part in contributing a large number of qualified teachers to Victorian schools. The studentship system was a key to this of course, but in these early years Monash attracted many able applicants for teaching. The teacher shortage was such that in 1970 the Department of Education implemented the International Teaching Fellowship Scheme, the brain child of Dr Lawrie Shears, to bring in a hundred teachers from the UK, Canada and the USA. These were in the maths and science field and the scheme meant free travel for the teacher plus an establishment allowance and a re-establishment allowance on return to their home countries.[70]

Peter Fensham had also gathered together from all over Australia scholars involved in research in science education in one way or another. An informal seminar was held in the faculty in 1970 and this resulted in 1971 in the formation of a body: The Australian Science Education Research Association.

---

[68] This was a decision of the Victorian Teachers' Tribunal.
[69] Monash University Archives MON 480 Paper on the Role of Universities in the Education of Teachers, R Selby Smith February 1970.
[70] *Age* 14 October 1970.

Administration

Selby Smith took great care over the appointment of staff. Many were often surprised that after either a casual approach from Selby Smith, or an application for a post from them, they would receive a call to come and have a chat, soon after which they were offered a position. It seemed so quick and easy. However, Selby Smith consulted widely. Where appropriate he would discuss names with education department officials such as inspectors of schools, with principals of schools and with colleagues of the candidate he had in mind. Moreover, before making a final decision he would run the name past the professors of the faculty, and always of a professor in the appropriate department at Monash University: those with history backgrounds, Professor A G L Shaw; psychology, Professor Ross Day; German languages, Professor L Bodi; political science, Professor Herb Feith or Professor Rufus Davis; economics, Professor Don Cochrane; and so forth. Selby Smith, as he did as a school principal, tried to get a mix of staff in terms of backgrounds and age and he also strongly backed people he felt had potential. On this he was often proved right, judging by the number of staff who completed doctorates after their appointment, or who produced significant research and publications. In addition, a notable few went on to chairs or senior posts in other universities or advanced colleges.

The Monash University system was for each faculty to have in it a representative of the academic registrar to handle the academic administration within it. Initially they were called assistant registrars with the faculty name following this designation but this was changed to the title of faculty secretary. Education's first faculty secretary was Russell W Knight who started duty in January 1966. The faculty secretary had a secretary and this office handled the administration not undertaken by the Dean's office. After Knight, Richard B Osborn became faculty secretary from January 1970. Osborn, who had come to Monash from the University of Melbourne, was a highly decorated airman from the Second World War.

The general office and other administrative staff were under the Dean. At this time photocopying was cumbersome to use and certainly not economic, so there was reliance on secretarial assistance and copying by duplicators – either the Roneo or Gestetner types, or small spirit duplicators like the Fordigraph. First, the material was typed on to thin wax stencils. The duplicator then pushed ink through the stencil onto blank paper. Multiple copies could be run off in this way. Academics who tried to do their own duplicating inevitably ended up covered in black ink. Frances Boyle in the office became a duplicator specialist and thanks to her, there were many satisfied and clean-handed academics.

A succession of very capable women (it was inevitably women at that time) headed the general office and supervised the secretarial staff. There was Mrs Campbell, and then Mrs Frida Greenway followed by Ms Bev Schneider. The growing staff meant more demands on secretaries and the duplicator and other means had to be found – the professors surrendered part of their own secretary's time to other staff. The demands for material to be typed and run off for the growing number of courses increased markedly up until computers were able to make an impact.

Staff also came to know the industrious cleaning staff headed then by Mrs Molly Jewell.

The year of 1971 brought great sadness with the death of Hilda Mayberry, the former secretary to the Dean (1963–1970) and a much loved person.[71] In her memory staff subscribed to having a painting placed near the Dean's office and dedicated to her. A work by the artist John Waterhouse was purchased.

Faculty representative on University Council

Monash University's constitution enabled each faculty to elect a member of the University Council, and that person could not be a member of the university staff. Education initially was represented by Emeritus Professor Wilfred Frederick, a former Dean of Education at the University of Melbourne and before that headmaster of Wesley College.[72] An experienced and able educator, Frederick was a well-known and respected figure, and a good friend of Selby Smith. Professor Frederick's term ended ended in 1970, and he stood again for election.

The anti-involvement in Vietnam movement and the student unrest which had engulfed Monash University meant there was a lively and critical atmosphere within the university. Some staff, led by Denis Phillips, approached the prominent trade union leader Bob Hawke (R J Hawke) and asked him to stand for this position to represent the faculty. To everyone's surprise he agreed. Hawke won, and Frederick stepped down. Selby Smith was not amused. The result of this election received widespread media coverage. Selby Smith, being gracious, held a special drinks evening at the

---

[71] Hilda Mayberry died from cancer on 20 September 1971. The plaque on the painting stated 'A friend to all the staff'.
[72] He was elected unopposed in July 1966.

staff club to give Mr and Mrs Hawke the opportunity to meet staff. It proved to be a riotous event. The gregarious Bob Hawke drank everyone under the table, and Hazel kept her end up chain-smoking cigarettes. One member of staff was found next morning asleep in the toilet of the staff club. Bob and Hazel in their jovial informality were an incongruous contrast to the reserved and ethereal Richard and Rachel Selby Smith.[73]

At first Hawke was not a regular attender at University Council meetings, something which the Vice-Chancellor drew to the attention of the Dean.[74] Hawke's presence on the council generally became beneficial and as he was a respected figure from the left, it meant that any council actions against the radical student left could not be painted as being politically motivated. Hawke was becoming an increasingly major national figure, not only as president of the ACTU, but as a potential parliamentarian and even prime minister. In 1973 he resigned from the council as he had become a member of the board of the Reserve Bank of Australia and also national president of the Australian Labor Party.

Departure of the Dean

In November 1970 the Dean, Richard Selby Smith, called all staff (including secretarial, clerical and technical) to a special staff meeting which he assured them would only take 15 minutes. It was an ominous notice and rumours abounded as to what it might mean, but most guessed he would be resigning. For a popular dean such a prospect was widely mourned. He was held in high regard, as well as affection by all. Selby Smith announced he was to take up an appointment as principal of the new Tasmanian College of Advanced Education.

He had established the Faculty of Education well but had a sense that someone with a different range of skills was now appropriate. He also enjoyed a challenge, and had a special fondness for Tasmania, being a keen fly fisherman and bushwalker. Matheson also suspected that his inability to achieve certain aims (such as the concurrent degree) had disappointed him.

Selby Smith was suitably farewelled by the staff, who told their favourite Selby Smith stories and gave speeches full of gentle digs at his effervescent manner. He finished at Monash at Easter in 1971. The staff was keen to mark his contribution and they made two requests. One was that the new education building to be named after him, and the other that he be granted

---

[73] The author was present at this event.
[74] Monash University Archives, MON 496 Minutes of Staff Meeting 2/71, 7 April 1971.

an honorary degree. The Vice-Chancellor Matheson was supportive of both these suggestions, but they were not to be. The Naming of Building Committee of the University responded negatively and pointed out that only the names of persons deceased or retired could be considered. The staff protested that the law building had recently been named the David Derham School of Law, and that Sir David Derham had certainly not died or retired but had gone on to become Vice-Chancellor at the University of Melbourne. The protest was to no avail and to make matters worse there was no honorary degree given either. It was not until many years later in 1989 that, thanks to the efforts of Professor Peter Fensham (then Dean), this oversight was rectified and he was made an Honorary Doctor of Laws. The snubs to Selby Smith were not personal, since he was widely respected, but they reflected a negative view held about education by certain influential sections of the university.

Selby Smith was principal of the Tasmanian College of Advanced Education from 1971 to 1973, but then moved to become professor of education and Dean at University of Tasmania (1974–78). He was awarded the OBE in 1981 for services to education and died in 2005.

Selby Smith's achievements were significant. He had founded a Faculty of Education from scratch that was quickly operational, educating teachers through the DipEd and offering useful teacher professional development courses in BEd and MEd. He established the first PhD program offered by an education faculty in Australia. It was also first in having its own building, and in being a multi-professorial faculty. By any standard it was the biggest education faculty in Australia, and research reports and publications indicated it held a leading role among Australian educators. In a period when the Martin Committee suggested there was a 'lack of a well-thought out plan for the education of teachers', Selby Smith responded with a coherent vision shaped by his beliefs on what teacher education should be about.[75] He employed research-oriented scholars who would set a strong research agenda as well as training teachers 'appropriately'.

It was a time of transformation for teacher education internationally. Teacher training had developed out of the practically based teachers' colleges

---

[75] Paper on Role of Universities in Education of Teachers in Victoria, Monash University Archives, MON 480, by R Selby Smith February 1070. Tertiary Education in Australia (Martin Committee Report) Vol. 1 Government Printer Canberra, 1964. Selby Smith also drew attention to other significant reports about teacher education: UNESCO Expert Report on Teacher Education 1968, Teachers and Youth Leaders (McNair Committee Report) HMSO 1961, High Education Report (Robbins Committee Report) HMSO 1963. It was a period when teacher education was being addressed.

with a primary school orientation. A classics degree sufficed to teach in secondary schools. Philosophers had long discussed the child and varying forms of education but the application of other disciplines to education was relatively new, as was major involvement in research. Monash's education faculty was well set up to be part of this transformation. It was unencumbered by old traditions and was given terms which placed it on an equal basis with other faculties at this new university.

Staff of 1966[76]

Kenneth James McAdam (1920–1976) had trained as a primary teacher, served with the RAAF during World War II, and then completed a BA (Hons) with a psychology major, then a DipEd and BEd. After teaching he worked as a psychologist with the Victorian Education Department until 1956 when he went to Africa. There he worked as an educational psychologist, becoming reader in psychology at the University of East Africa, Kampala, Uganda. In 1963 he became senior research fellow at the Institute of Education at the University of Ghana, but when Europeans were expelled he sought a post at Monash – opting to take a senior lecturer post in education teaching educational psychology rather than a post with the psychology department. He commenced at the faculty on 1 October 1965. A popular member of staff, he was committed to educational psychology rather than psychology and proved an excellent teacher. He also wrote many articles about his research during this time. He completed his MEd while at Monash, but serious ill-health curtailed his career. He retired in 1975 and died one year later, aged 56.

John George Radvansky (1924–2007), a Hungarian baron, commenced studies at the Nadon University, Budapest which were interrupted when war broke out. After serving with the resistance, he escaped to Western Australia and completed a BA (Hons) in philosophy. He then came to Victoria, trained as a teacher, and for the next ten years taught at a number of secondary and technical schools. He then became a lecturer in education (philosophy) at the University of Melbourne. He completed an MA in philosophy at Melbourne, and was described by his supervisors as one of the 'most memorable students

---

[76] The biographical information has been derived from the Monash University staff files held in the Monash University archives. Therefore, some of the careers of people post-Monash are not dealt with. It is of interest to note the salary levels in 1966 – professors were on $10,400 a year, readers (associate professors) $8,600 a year, senior lecturers in the range of $6,500–$7,600 a year and lecturers in the range $4,800–$6,300 a year. Initial appointments were for three years and then if approved were tenured positions requiring retirement at age 65. The senior lecturer post was regarded as the career grade.

2.8 Ken McAdam.
MUA IN-7438

we have ever had'. He was appointed as a senior lecturer at Monash, commencing in February 1966. His wife had a senior post at the Main Library of the university. He possessed a fine mind. John Radvansky was a much loved character in the faculty. A brilliant philosopher, his strong accent revealed his Hungarian origins and his eccentric behaviour had elements of the aristocracy from which he was descended. He often erupted into loud vocal outbursts, such was his enthusiasm, yet he would also enter the study of a colleague for a chat, stand there in thoughtful silence and after a few minutes leave the room. He left Monash at the end of 1971 to take a position as principal lecturer at the Tasmanian College of Advanced Education.

Brian Philip Sureties trained as a teacher and worked with the London County Council. He completed a BA (Hons) majoring in English at London University, then came to Tasmania where he completed his MA in poetry in high schools and then embarked on a London PhD. He became deputy headmaster of Burnie High School (a matriculation school) and then in February

1966 came to Monash as a senior lecturer specialising in English Method. He was also to follow Selby Smith to Tasmania when he returned in February 1971. He was remembered at Monash for the sad loss of his entire library while he was on study leave, when the faculty moved to its new building.[77]

Raymond William McCulloch was Sydney born and completed a BA (Hons) in classics, then completed his DipEd and an honours course in psychology. He taught with the NSW Department of Education until 1946 when he began working for the Commonwealth Department of Labour and National Service as a psychologist and expert in vocational education. In 1953 he was appointed chief psychologist and superintendent of special schools for the Tasmanian Department of Education, publishing many articles, pamphlets and books on psychological and vocational issues, while also lecturing in psychology at the University of Tasmania. In 1960 he became superintendent of research and special education in Tasmania, and also lectured at the University in educational administration. In 1963 he was a UNESCO consultant working for a short time in Northern Rhodesia. He was appointed senior lecturer in September 1965 and became head of the educational administration area of the faculty – which grew in number and prestige under his guidance. He became well known internationally and while not making a major research contribution, was a creative thinker. He was promoted to associate professor. He retired at the end of 1980.

Hugh D Batten had completed a BSc and DipEd from the University of Melbourne, and taught in Victorian state schools (University High School and Glenroy High School) before completing his BEd and becoming a lecturer in education at the Secondary Teachers' College. At the college he lectured in both Science Method and Instructional Materials and Equipment. He was a pioneer in the use of educational media and was appointed to the Monash education faculty in February 1966. He specialised in science method and educational media, widening this to a keen interest in micro-teaching. In 1970 he took a specialised course on micro-teaching at Stanford University, and in 1974 was seconded part time to the Schools Commission. In December 1974 he resigned from Monash to become head of the Department of Educational Resources and Development at Lincoln Institute, a body he later came to head.

John F Cleverley, originally a primary teacher in NSW schools, became a lecturer at Wagga Wagga Teachers' College, and then a teaching fellow at the University of Sydney, before his appointment as a lecturer at Monash.

---

[77] The university gave him an *ex gratia* payment of $3,500 to help cover the loss of all his books.

2.9 Associate Professor Ray McCulloch.
MUA IN-7439

He completed a BA at Sydney University, then an MEd, and his PhD on an aspect of NSW education history was completed in 1967. He wrote extensively on educational history issues and published a number of books. At Monash he worked mainly in HET and history. He returned to the University of Sydney in June 1972.

Lindsay Mackay, a BSc BEd from Melbourne, completed his PhD in 1971 while a staff member at Monash. He had taught physics at Northcote High School before becoming a lecturer at the Secondary Teachers' College. In his BEd he had topped the Measurement course. He was also seconded part-time to ACER for research work. On top of his knowledge of physics and other sciences he became known as a first class researcher, especially in the area of test construction and educational measurement, and his evaluation of the PSSC course was notable. He lectured in test construction and evaluation and in science curriculum. He was engaged in many major research projects while at Monash, as well as his evaluation of the Tertiary Entrance Examination Project, the Core Curriculum Project, and others. He attracted funding for many projects. He was promoted to associate professor in 1975, but resigned in February 1980 to become executive secretary of the Victorian Institute of Secondary Education.

Staff of 1967

John Fyfield started off as a secondary school teacher. He had a Bachelor of Science from Melbourne and taught in the country where he completed his BEd by correspondence. He became foundation principal of a new high school at Robinvale, a newly developed soldier settlement area, where he made his mark. At 35 years of age he was the youngest secondary school principal. After seven years at Robinvale he was promoted to Portland High School. The Department of Education regarded him as not only one of their youngest principals but one of their most outstanding.[78] R Selby Smith, in his capacity as a member of the Commonwealth Committee on Science Laboratories for Schools, visited Portland to inspect a private school. He knew of Fyfield's reputation and sought him out for a meeting. He had also read Fyfield's recent article in the *Australian Journal of Education*.[79] After a pleasant chat over afternoon tea Selby Smith told Fyfield 'there must be a place for you at Monash'. Next week he sent a letter offering Fyfield a post in the education faculty. In a confidential memo Selby Smith described him as 'a most lively and interesting man'. It was a shock to Fyfield and a difficult choice, as he had an assured career in the Department of Education. However, he accepted, and so began a rich and rewarding career at Monash University, which was to continue well after Fyfield's formal retirement.

Fyfield worked in a variety of fields in the faculty: educational administration, measurement, principles of teaching, educational thought and mathematics (he wrote a successful *School Dictionary of Mathematics*, which was published in Australia then re-printed in the UK and Canada). He pioneered research on education in the People's Republic of China, including political socialisation and Chinese education. He published the book *Re-educating Chinese Anti-Communists* (Croom Helm, 1982) and co-wrote with R P Tisher *Beginning to Teach*, a two-volume research study published by the Australian Government. A trusted figure, he was the

---

[78] Discussion with Dr Lawrie Shears former Director General of Education.
[79] J A Fyfield 'The Crisis in Valuation: With Special Reference to the State System of Education' *Australian Journal of Education*, Vol 9:1, 1965, pp. 55–64.

administrative head of two areas within the faculty, served as Sub-Dean, and was sought after as a chairman. He was also an important mentor to staff. He died on 31 March 2013, aged 91 years.

2.10 John Fyfield.
MUA IN-6303

John Richards Lawry, a BA (1954) and BEd (1961) from the University of Melbourne, was a secondary school teacher and then lecturer at the Secondary Teachers' College Melbourne from 1958. He then became a lecturer in education at the University of Queensland (1961–1967), before taking a position as a senior lecturer in Education at Monash. He completed his PhD on the history of education in Queensland soon after coming to Monash. From 1970 to 1973 he was also warden of Roberts Hall at Monash. A key historian, he organised public lectures and seminars and also compiled a significant oral history of retired educators of note. His special interest was 19th-century public education systems. At the end of 1973 he left to become Dean of Education at the Gippsland Institute of Advanced Education at Churchill. He then became Dean of Education at Burwood

State College and from 1978 head of the School of Secondary Education, Victoria College (Rusden Campus). He retired in 1989.

Gerald J Johnston, described as a gifted teacher, had a keen interest in political science and came to take that method subject at Monash, as well as work in the social sciences area as a political scientist. With a BA and MA (majoring in political science) from the University of Tasmania, and a Melbourne BEd, he was first a teacher of English and Social Studies in Tasmanian schools, then lecturer in Education at the University of Tasmania, where he was also liaison officer for the Department of Education. From 1964 to 1966 he was a lecturer at the Hobart Teachers' College.

Mary Nixon (1922–2013), a senior research officer with the ACER, also came in as a senior lecturer, and served a term as head of the psychology area in the education faculty. Nixon had nearly completed her doctorate on the classification skills in young children at Melbourne. Her special interest was in concept formation and the cognitive processes. She had a BA (Hons) and an MA majoring in psychology from Sydney. She had been a lecturer at the Sydney Teachers' College and a senior tutor in psychology at the University of Sydney. Nixon was to take a role with the Child Study Centre and was active as a psychologist, becoming president of the Australian Psychological Association, 1971–72. She was awarded the AM in 1994 for service to the psychology profession. With her main interest in psychology, she was disdainful of some aspects of the education faculty. Mary died in 2013.

Dr Paul Gardner AM was a teacher in the Victorian state education system from 1961 to 1966. He was appointed as a lecturer in the Faculty of Education at Monash University in 1967, and became the faculty's first reader in 1975. During his 36 years in the faculty, he taught at all levels and chaired several faculty committees. He served as Editor of Research in Science Education from 1990 to 1994. Overseas appointments included being an Imperial Relations Trust fellow at the University of London, a Fulbright Senior Scholar at Stanford University, a visiting scholar at the University of British Columbia and Queen's University (both in Canada) and a visiting professor at the Hebrew University of Jerusalem and the Weizmann Institute of Science. Prior to his retirement in 2002, he served for two years as the convener of the steering committee of the university's Research Graduate School. His main field of research was in educational psychology related to science education, attitude measurement, language difficulty and the structure of knowledge. Beyond the university, he was active in promoting human rights, opposing racism and fostering interfaith relations, which led to his appointment as a Member of the Order of Australia in the 2008

Australia Day Honours List. He is currently a member of the Victoria Police Human Research Ethics Committee. He retired in 2005. On retirement he made a generous bequest to the Faculty of Education, in recognition of his time at Monash and to thank Australia for providing his parents refuge from Nazi persecution. It will be known as the Dr Paul Gardner Memorial Fund and is most likely to be used for scholarships to support students.

2.11 Dr Paul Gardner.
Tony Miller, MUA IN-650

Norman H Dobson had already lectured in Social Studies Method, but when he became full-time in 1967 was mainly engaged in taking History Method. He later became the first Sub-Dean of the faculty and was a highly competent administrator. Dobson had been an ordained Methodist minister, and indeed he retained his ministerial licence in the Uniting Church during his time at Monash. He was sometimes called upon by fellow staff to officiate at observances for them, as well as some staff funerals. He had also completed a BA and DipEd pre-war, and then post-war a BEd and in 1964 an MEd. He taught at Carey Grammar School from 1947 to 1966 as senior History and Social Studies master, as well as senior house master.

He also had a number of divinity subjects. He was an examiner for the Schools Board for History and Social Studies. He retired aged 62 years at the end of 1980. Sadly ill-health plagued his early retirement and he died soon afterwards. A popular member of staff, he gave meaning to the post of Sub-Dean. Dobson died in April 1991.

Coming for a short term was an experienced English educator, **Dr John Leese**, who had been Secretary of the Yorkshire Teachers' College Board.

Merrill S Jackson trained as a primary teacher and also completed the Special Teacher's Certificate before teaching in primary schools and special schools. He did a BA (Hons) at Melbourne majoring in psychology and then an MA on the oral development of 11-year-old children. He served as a psychologist and guidance officer with the Victorian education department, then became a lecturer in psychology at the Melbourne Teachers' College and then Geelong Teachers' College. He completed his PhD at Monash in the area of word association in trainable mentally retarded children. He was to work in the Child Study Centre, in the Krongold Centre,[80] take courses in remedial education, and play a key role in the special education area of the faculty. He left at the end of 1974 to become reader in education at the University of Tasmania.

Denis Phillips had a BSc and Dip from Melbourne, adding an MEd in 1961. He taught science in Victorian high schools and was active in the Science Teachers' Association before becoming a tutor in education at the University of Melbourne. He was also a keen philosopher, and undertook a PhD at Melbourne on the ideas of John Dewey and evolutionary thought, gaining the degree in 1968. At Monash he taught History of Educational Thought and took philosophy subjects at the BEd and MEd level. He soon became a prolific writer and one of the leading philosophers of education in Australia. He wrote an influential book called *Theories, Values and Education* (Melbourne University Press, 1971) and followed it with two more: *Holistic Thought in Social Science* (Stanford University Press and Macmillan 1976) and, with John Cleverley, *From Locke to Spock* (Melbourne University Press 1976). He left Monash in September 1974 to take a post as professor of education and philosophy at Stanford University, California – a most prestigious appointment. He retained his links with Monash on frequent visits including a spell as visiting professor for the summer school course in 1979.

---

[80] Situated within the Faculty of Education, the Krongold Centre provides a variety of educational and developmental psychological services, in particular to children, adolescents and their parents.

A lively lecturer and entertaining member of staff, he participated actively in faculty matters.[81]

Phyllis M Scott was originally a kindergarten teacher who became director of the Lady Gowrie Kindergarten and Child Study Centre from 1942 to 1952. She then became a Research Fellow at the University of Queensland, and completed a BSc, MA and PhD (1968) at the University of Columbia, New York. She also worked with the National Institute of Mental Health in Maryland, USA. She came to Monash in 1967 as a senior teaching fellow and was appointed a lecturer in 1968.

Her career at Monash in the Faculty of Education was unfortunate, in that although she did valuable research on pre-school and early childhood, especially concerning Aboriginal children, the unreliability of sustained grant income meant she was often forced to have periods of work without pay. The faculty was unable to support her by filling in the gaps. She received grants from the Children's Commission, the Creswick Foundation, the Lady Gowrie Centre, the Australian Pre-School Association, the Buckland Foundation and the Van Leer Foundation. She began as a research fellow, later becoming a senior research fellow, but as she did not have a tenured lecturer post her situation was precarious. Lacking the necessary support from the faculty for her pre-school research she took up a post in Queensland in 1975. Her departure was a loss to the faculty as she had achieved much.

Staff of 1968

James A Wheeler was a major force in language teaching in Australia. He completed his BA (Hons) at Melbourne. Coming first place in both German and French, he was able to add these to a repertoire which already included Italian and Indonesian. He also completed his DipEd there and became a very successful teacher of Modern Languages – teaching mainly at University High School and Essendon High School. The professor of Germanic studies at Melbourne described Wheeler as the best teacher of German he had seen.[82] He became a method lecturer in Modern Languages at the University of Melbourne's Faculty of Education and was completing an MA when he was appointed to Monash University. A brilliant linguist and teacher, he was also active in the Modern Language Teachers Association, and earned many awards and distinctions himself. He took

---

[81] His skills included those of a magician/conjurer, which were used to good effect at the Child Study Centre and to entertain staff.
[82] Reference for J A Wheeler by Professor Samuel, re: his application to the Monash post. Personal file of J A Wheeler, Monash University Archives.

Modern Language Method at Monash, and later widened his work to take in TESOL and LOTE programs. This included a large grant to introduce the postgraduate Diploma in TESOL. Wheeler was also effective in using micro-teaching in his method work.

Wheeler worked actively with a group to assist gay Catholics, editing a newsletter, and arranging social and religious events. This was important work at a time when the acceptance of gay people was not as it is today and there were special difficulties with the Catholic church.

Terence Hore commenced duty in December 1968 as a lecturer. Originally a teacher in the UK, he completed a BA at Alberta Canada, then an MA and a doctorate both majoring in educational psychology also at Alberta. He had earlier worked in Australia (1960–63) with the National Fitness Council and married an Australian woman. He joined the faculty at Monash to work in the area of psychology and proved a valuable member of staff. In 1973 he transferred to a post in the Higher Education Research Unit (HERU), and became director. He remained director, with the rank of professorial fellow, until his retirement in 1997. Hore was an effective leader of an important team which undertook many projects in the university – often difficult ones – and gained universal respect.

Gerald Burke[83] had a BCom and DipEd from the University of Melbourne and was a teacher with the Victorian Department of Education from 1962 to 1965, mainly in the field of economics. He became a senior teaching fellow in the Department of Economics at Monash from 1965 and commenced his PhD before joining the education faculty as a lecturer in 1968. He completed his doctorate in 1972 on the supply of secondary teachers and began a significant career focusing on the economics of education. Burke became a senior lecturer (1975–86) and then associate professor before becoming a professorial fellow in 2000.

He taught at all levels in the faculty and carried administrative responsibility, including chairing various faculty committees. He was always known as a helpful member of staff and related well to others. He had two periods as a committee member of the Staff Association of Monash University, part of the Federation of Australian University Staff Associations prior to the formation of the National Tertiary Education Union. An expert on issues of teacher demand and supply, and work and education, in 1975–76 he was seconded to the Department of Education in Canberra and was there at the fall of the Whitlam government. In 1985 he was seconded as a visiting

---

[83] For Gerald Burke's recollections of his time in the faculty, see Chapter 9.

fellow to the Centre for the Study of Higher Education at the University of Melbourne.

In 1992 he was instrumental in establishing with colleagues from the Faculty of Business and the ACER the Centre for the Economics of Education and Training at Monash (CEET), and became its executive director. His research and publications were in the finance of education and the relation of education to the economy. Among his publications were *Teachers and the Economy* (Deakin University 1985) and some 70 reports, chapters in books, and articles. He had many consultancies and grants including from the ARC, the Australian National Training Authority and state and national government departments. He was appointed chair of the Victorian Qualifications Authority in 2004, the Victorian Registration and Qualifications Authority in 2007, Skills Australia in 2008, and the Australian Workforce and Productivity Agency in 2012. He retired in 2008 after a record 41-year period of service to the faculty. A greatly respected figure.

2.12 Gerald Burke.
Claude Sironi, Education Faculty

Dermot Lyttle, BA (Hons), came to the faculty as a senior teaching fellow and held this post as well as temporary lectureships until he left in 1977. With expertise in English and philosophy, he had taught in Victorian schools 1961–67 and was English master at Trinity Grammar School. In the faculty he taught History of Educational Thought and Method and Practice of Teaching English. He also served as deputy warden at Roberts Hall. After Monash he spent some time at Preshil School, becoming principal. He also wrote the book *Preshil Uniquely Different* (Kew: Preshil, 2002). He now teaches at Alia College.

Staff of 1969

Keith F Hudson was a much loved member of staff who came initially as a casual appointment in the early days of the faculty to assist students with speech issues. In 1969 this work was formalised when he was appointed a senior tutor. He was to help many students over the years with speech difficulties, and often staff as well. A former actor of note, mainly in radio, he had a magnificent voice which was accompanied by immaculate dress and manners. Sadly serious dementia brought his early retirement on grounds of disability in May 1986.

Alan Gregory AM, BCom, DipEd, MEd (Melb), PhD (SFU), who had been lecturer in Economics Method from 1965, became a full-time lecturer in 1969. He became involved in the social science area of the faculty and later in teaching Curriculum Theory and Development at the Masters and MEd level. He served two terms as Sub-Dean. He also served on two ministerial enquiries, including the Victorian Enquiry into Teacher Education, and served on the Government Long Term Planning Committee. He became a member of the Order of Australia (AM) in 1989 for services to education and the community. Founder of the faculty choir, he left in 1990 to become master of Ormond College at the University of Melbourne. While at Monash he wrote many books on economics and economics method, and later became the writer of institutional histories including the Royal Melbourne Hospital, Melbourne High and Lord Somers Camp and Power House.

Staff of 1970

Brian J Spicer, a BCom and DipEd from Melbourne, started his career as a geography teacher at Niddrie and Footscray High Schools. He then became method lecturer for geography at the Secondary Teachers' College and also at the education faculty of the University of Melbourne. He was also undertaking an MA in geography. He came to Monash to take the Geography Method subject, but proved versatile and embarked on many other projects, often with other staff members. He also completed his PhD while on the staff. He became Sub-Dean and was an active committee man. He was involved in some major research projects, including one with Lindsay Mackay dealing with the children of servicemen and their educations overseas and in changing venues. He took voluntary early retirement in July 1995 and moved on to various consultancies in Asia and Southeast Asia.

English-born **Frederick R Perry** started his career as a primary teacher, with special qualifications in teaching the deaf. He served in the Royal Navy, then came to the Univeristy of Melbourne where he did a BA, then BA (Hons) in psychology, followed by an MA in psycholinguistics. He worked at the Victorian School for Deaf Children 1959–62 then joined the 'psychology and guidance' section of the Victorian Department of Education. A lively person, he worked mainly with the deaf and he became a lecturer at the Training College for the Deaf.

At Monash he was known as a friendly person with an entertaining manner, and a good teacher. He completed his PhD while on the staff at Monash. He joined the special education area and also worked closely with the Krongold Centre, as well as teaching in the special education advanced course for BEd and MEd. He left Monash in January 1975 to become director of advanced studies for the Institute of Early Childhood Development.

Valma (Val) R Hawkes was a Tasmanian graduate, BA, MA, who became a tutor in political science at the University of Tasmania. She had also taught in Tasmanian schools and worked in both the Hobart Technical College and the Curriculum Centre of the Education Department of Tasmania. Hawkes joined the faculty in January 1970, putting her expertise in political science to good use in the social science area. A popular member of staff, she resigned in January 1974 to return to a post in Tasmania.

Brian Bullivant commenced his career at Monash as a senior teaching fellow. From the United Kingdom, he served with the Royal Air Force during the Second World War, then trained as a teacher and also completed a major in anthropology at Birbeck College. He represented Britain in the Melbourne 1956 Olympics and was in the final of the kayaking events. He remained in Australia, completed a BA at Melbourne, and taught in Victorian secondary schools. He completed an MA in anthropology at Monash, then in 1975 his doctorate, a first-ever ethnographic study of a school in Australia, later published by ACER as *The Way of Tradition: Life in an Orthodox Jewish*

School (1978). In 1973 he published *Educating the Immigrant Child: Concepts and Cases*. He became a senior lecturer (1989) then reader (1993). As well as pioneering anthropology of education and qualitative research methodology, Bullivant undertook research and consultancy for various governments and agencies. He had a number of significant publications including *The Pluralist Dilemma in Education: Six Case Studies* (1981) and *Getting a Fair Go: Studies of Occupational Socialization and Perceptions of Discrimination* (1986). He developed theories of culture, ethnicity and Australia as a multi-ethnic society, and their impact on schooling and curriculum. He also served as co-director of the Centre for Migrant Studies at Monash. He published extensively in journals and supervised many research degree students. He regarded Dr Phillip Aspinall, Archbishop of Brisbane and Anglican Primate of Australia, as one of his most outstanding doctoral students. He retired in 1994. He died on 24 November 2013.

Staff of 1971

Stewart C Sykes came to the faculty as a senior teaching fellow in the area of psychology. Originally a primary teacher with expertise in special education (TPTC and TSpTC) he completed an MA in psychology at the University of Melbourne. He was a remedial teacher with the education department and then a research officer for the curriculum and research branch. His special field was learning disabilities. He undertook his PhD at Monash in specific reading disability – a study of its nature and associated perceptual characteristics. He became a lecturer in special education in 1974, senior lecturer in 1978 and then in 1988 director of the Krongold Centre. In 1991 the Krongold and Elwyn Morey Centres were amalgamated into the Monash Institute for Child and Adolescent Studies and Sykes as an associate professor became the director. Of kindly disposition, he assisted many children and young people with disabilities in his career at Monash. He took early retirement at the end of 1996, but continued in private practice as a psychologist.

Theodore H MacDonald, a Canadian always known as 'Theo', was skilled in mathematics and one referee stated that 'he can teach mathematics to a stone'. The faculty was soon to discover it had a true eccentric in its ranks. A McGill graduate in science, he completed an MA in mathematics at South Carolina and a PhD from Glasgow. He had held posts in the West Indies and the South Pacific as well as at Raymond College, Stockton, California. A specialist in models of mathematical cognition, he often

2.13 Dr Brian Bullivant.
Education Faculty

appeared to be in a world of his own, and while he attended staff meetings, he would use this as an opportunity to update his writing. He was rather an isolate as a staff member.

While visiting a DipEd student in Pentridge Prison, he famously explained to prisoners the mathematics of safe combinations! MacDonald was notorious for sleeping in his office overnight, where he also kept his organ. His stay at Monash was short-lived as he left in January 1973 to head the School of Education at the University of the South Pacific, Canberra College of Advanced Education. He did not remain long in that post either – he seemed to have an insatiable wanderlust. Described as erratic, he never seemed to achieve a satisfactory post. He ended up at London Metropolitan University and died on 11 March 2011.

Richard T White had been a research student in the faculty (and from 1970 a teaching fellow) but was appointed a lecturer in 1971. A BSc and BEd from the University of Melbourne, he was a science teacher in Victorian schools and became in 1967 Executive Officer for Physics with the VUSEB.

He had a keen interest in how students learned and was attracted to the theories of internationally known psychologist Robert Gagne. His PhD thesis was entitled 'Learning graphical skills in Kinematics'. He embarked on research involving processes of learning meaningful subject matter and developing more effective teaching in science and mathematics. He became an associate professor in 1976, and also held important consultancies with UNESCO. He got the opportunity to work with Gagne as visiting professor at Florida State University. On the retirement of Ron Taft in 1981, White took the Chair of Education in the psychology area of the faculty. As the later chapters will reveal, he went on to become Dean of the faculty for two terms from 1994, and then Pro Vice-Chancellor of the University in London in 2000, from which he retired in 2001. He was made an Emeritus Professor of the university.

Russell D Linke (1948–1995) came from South Australia, and he completed his BSc at Flinders University in biological science. He was an important early doctoral candidate who proved a brilliant researcher. His gentle sense of humour amused all and he always seemed to be about the place. After completing his PhD in the field of higher education he returned to Flinders University, where he was a research fellow in the School of Medicine. He became director of planning for the Tertiary Education Authority. He then held a post at DEET where he was mainly responsible for a two-volume report titled 'Performance Indicators in Higher Education', which established his reputation as an international authority on the topic. He became Dean of Education at Wollongong, then returned to Flinders as Deputy Vice-Chancellor before taking a post as professor of higher education at the University of Melbourne. He died unexpectedly in Rome in September 1995 while attending a conference on higher education. He was 47 years old.

Chapter 3

Consolidation

1972–1980

There was a seamless transition of Dean from Selby Smith to Syd Dunn. While Dunn lacked Selby Smith's charisma and charm – indeed, he had a speech affliction – he was well liked and respected. While Selby Smith's strength was in initial teacher training and as a superb administrator, Syd Dunn was research-orientated and was not that familiar with the initial teacher training side of education. Dunn promoted curriculum-based research, encouraging the method staff to undertake research in teaching with applicability to the schools. In terms of research he was also a brilliant networker. It was an appropriate change of emphasis for a faculty that had after that first careless rapture of succeeding in initial training, warmly embraced a research approach and a teaching role concerned with post initial training.

In 1970 there were 385 full-time students taking DipEd and 198 part-time students. The BEd had 5 full-time students and 226 part-time students, the MEd 3 full-time students and 63 part-time students, and there were 14 enrolled for PhDs, 6 being staff members. In all the faculty had 894 persons enrolled as students, an EFTS[1] of 706. This increase meant that the faculty projection for 1976, which had assumed 970 student persons and an EFTS of 744, had to be increased to 1119 persons and 847 EFTS. By 1971 the DipEd numbers (full-time) had increased to 410 students, with 47 part-time and 22 were doing the DipEd Tertiary.

DipEd

1971 was a testing year for the organisers of DipEd, with the demand for places in Victorian institutions likely to exceed the supply, and hence a need to impose quotas. This high demand caused particular problems with

---

[1] Equivalent Full-Time Students.

teaching round placements. Admissions for DipEd for the three universities then involved (Melbourne, Monash and La Trobe) were handled by the organisation VUAC (Victorian Universities Admission Committee). In this process 514 students placed Monash as first preference, 451 of them Monash graduates. Of these 317 were studentship holders and 71 were on Commonwealth scholarships.[2]

In selecting students for the DipEd, VUAC were first to consider those who declared Monash as their first preference. After this the appropriateness of their undergraduate degree in terms of teaching methods was considered, especially in relation to the places available. If other criteria were required it was decided on academic merit. This formula disregarded first year results and then gave priority to those with honours degrees, and then compared the number of points scored in the final two years of their course (High Distinction and Distinction: 3 points, Credit: 2 points, Pass: 1 point).[3] From 1971 results in DipEd had been only Pass (P) or Fail (N) with the previous gradings used by Monash dropped (HD, D, C, P and N).[4]

During 1971 debate continued about the form of the DipEd course – the Group 70 experimental course had continued in 1971, and for 1972 what was to be? There was the continuation of Group 70, known as Group B or the Fyfield group – comprised now of necessity of only Science/Mathematics Method students, Group 2 (Musgrave) with Humanities and Social Science Method students, Group D was for the part-time students, with Group A comprising the rump or the rest of the students. There were strong divisions of opinion about the merits of having groups, of whether it was streaming, or how theory and practice could be best brought together. Phillips, Hunt and Cleverly brought their thinking to these issues, as did the proponents of the groups. Special staff meetings were held to debate the issues. At one of these it was finally resolved that: 'The DipEd committee be invited to consider the practicability of smaller groupings of staff and students in regard to planning the 1972 mainstream course'.

One consequence of having DipEd 'groups' was the demise of MUFESSA – Monash University Faculty of Education Staff and Students Association, which had been the focus of social events involving staff and students.

The submission to the AUC for the 1973–75 triennium, prepared in 1970, brought to the faculty's attention the significant increase in the number of studentship holders which would mean a significant increase in DipEd

---

[2] Monash University Archives MON 61 Minutes Faculty Board 17 February 1971.
[3] Monash University Archives MON 61 Minutes Faculty Board 17 February 1971.
[4] Monash University Archives MON 61 Minutes Faculty Board 15 April 1971.

3.1 Claude Sironi's Faces of 1970.
Claude Sironi, Education Faculty

numbers in the future.[5] This raised not only questions of handling the likely increase of DipEd students and finding teaching practice places for them, but also the whole balance of the offerings by the faculty. Syd Dunn raised the issue of the balance between DipEd, BEd and higher degrees. It was eventually agreed that Monash should take into DipEd a number of new students equivalent to the number of Monash graduates who wished to take the course.[6]

The faculty based its projections on the estimate of 26 per cent of the first year intake being potential DipEd students, and that 60 per cent of these would complete their first degree satisfactorily.

---

[5] In 1966 there were 504 studentship holders among first year undergraduates, in 1969, 539 but by 1970 this had become 725. It was recognised that by 1970 the Faculties of Arts, Economics and Politics, and Science had reached their maximum intake of first year students (Minutes of Faculty Board meeting 15 April 1970).

[6] Minutes Faculty Board meeting 15 April 1970b.

In 1973 a quota had to be imposed on DipEd numbers, which was 500 EFTS. BEd too had a quota for 1973, of 210 EFTS. In 1974 the total EFTS was 1086, DipEd numbers were 561, BSpecEd 28, BEd 221, MEd 230 and PhD 46.[7]

From the outset John Theobald had taken on the onerous task of the placement of students in schools for teaching rounds. Matching students, their methods and subjects and schools, while also trying to give them an experience of different types of schools over their teaching rounds, was a highly complex task. As numbers had expanded it was felt that the DipEd program needed its own coordinator. John Theobald was appointed to this post in 1974 and he held it until his retirement. A highly efficient administrator, Theobald made a major impact on the faculty in this role.

It was decided that as from 1975 Method and Practice of Primary Teaching would no longer be offered. This was made with regret, as from the outset there had been a method course available for the training of primary teachers, and the much longed for concurrent degree had mainly primary teachers in mind. Dr Lawrie Shears had initially taken the subject, and then when he became director of education it was taken over by staff from Burwood Teachers' College. The college was now to offer its own DipEd and so to help Monash in this way was considered inappropriate.[8]

In 1974, of the 476 DipEd students, 430 had a Monash first degree, 293 were on Department of Education studentships and 61 were on Commonwealth scholarships. The dominant first degrees held were a BA (237), BSc (124) and BEc (65).[9]

From time to time there were issues with students. On one occasion a female student was accused of plagiarism. The evidence against her was compelling. She had to appear before Dr John Theobald and the Dean, Professor Peter Musgrave. On both occasions she resorted to offering herself as a means of resolving the problem. Both gentlemen were unaware of what had been suggested to them. Observers to this spectacle found it hard to contain their amusement. While failing the subject in question, she went on to grander things, becoming the partner of an international tennis star.

---

[7] Monash University Archives MON 61 Minutes Faculty Board 6 March 1974.
[8] Monash University Archives MON 61 Minutes Faculty Board 3 July 1974.
[9] Reports prepared by Elaine Atkinson 1973–1976, Monash University Archives MON 480 (294).

Government changes

Changing governments affect universities. The Whitlam Government of 1972–75 meant an expansion of the education faculty. It had made university tuition free, assumed more of the funding of universities, and also provided generous research funding. A number of projects were started within the faculty in this period. There was also the setting up of the Education Research and Development Commission. State governments changed the status of the teacher training colleges and the technical colleges, making them autonomous from the education department, which meant they were keen to appoint more qualified and experienced staff as they moved to being tertiary institutions. The faculty lost many valuable staff members: Alan Trethewey, Hugh Batten, John Lawry, Fred Perry and Lindsay Mckay to name a few.

'Difficult financial times' became a constant – to the extent that staff wondered when there had ever been good times. The 1979 budget for the faculty was only .3 per cent better than 1978 and when allowing for inflation, it was effectively a reduction. As a consequence some one-year appointments could not be renewed. The issue also arose of trying to find funds to pay for some staff seconded from the Department of Education. The Vice-Chancellor helped with an additional $68,000.

There was a further complication to financial management when from 1979 the faculty was no longer allowed to carry forward uncommitted funds. This meant in ensuing years mad rushes of spending towards the end of the year – stocking up on duplicating paper and so forth. It was even suggested that the science lab use surplus funds to buy additional supplies of Au.[10]

Other courses

An important move was the introduction of the Bachelor of Special Education degree, first put forward in 1973. There was a great need for training of teachers both generally to be aware of the children with special needs, as well as specialist training for teachers working directly with such children. The coursework in BEd continued, attracting keen interest from teachers, who typically came in after school for the late afternoon classes. In 1974 the number of BEd and coursework subjects offered by each area were as follows: Area 1: 12, Area 2: 10, Area 3: 12, Area 4: 10, Area 5: 14, Area 6: 8 and Area 7: 10. Adding to the coursework offerings of the faculty from 1975 was a graduate Diploma in Education Psychology. Much planning

---

[10] The elemental symbol for gold.

and discussion had gone into this course and it was backed up by a strong teaching team. In 1977 a new degree was created, the Master of Educational Studies (MEdStud) – a coursework degree that also required a project or minor thesis.[11]

This important development was to alter the balance of courses, with a swing over a few years to this course from the BEd.[12] It was to be an additional degree to the thesis degree (the Master of Education). While initially discussed in 1971 it did not come to fruition until 1978. It replaced the option of doing the MEd by coursework. It was seen as a worthwhile professional development degree for teachers, and the pre-requisite was four years of training. By 1983 there were 400 students taking the degree, 36 per cent of the faculty EFTS of 1,100. The projects were part of the degree, with two examiners (excluding the supervisor), and if the standard was high enough a candidate could move to a PhD. There was a corresponding drop in BEd numbers with the new MEdStud, from 357 students in 1978 to 181 in 1982.[13]

It was announced that from 1972 the university would operate on a semester system.[14] This had partly come in response to Professor Don Cochrane's report on year round teaching.[15] The Faculty Board had been lukewarm about the proposal initially as it did not suit the arrangements for DipEd.[16] However, a semester system proved far more convenient for BEd and MEd courses, as most subjects suited the semester size.

Social events

There were frequent social events for the staff. Soup luncheons brightened up the dreary Melbourne winters. Melbourne Cup Day featured a chicken and champagne lunch in the staff room with the technical staff providing TV for the race – special hats were usually abundant. Morning teas celebrated special events such as retirements, and there were social evenings. One featured a night of cocktails created by Maurie Balson (pre.05 awareness), on another a melodrama was performed, and there were sing-songs from the newly formed faculty choir, including such memorable nights as 'Finding

---

[11] Monash University Archives MON 61 Minutes of Faculty Board 6 July 1977
[12] Monash University Archives MON 61 Minutes of Faculty Board 17 February 1971.
[13] Monash University Archives MON 565 Minutes Faculty Board 3 November 1982.
[14] Monash University Archives MON 496 (20) Minutes of Staff Meetings 14 May 1971.
[15] Cochrane was Dean of the Faculty of Economics and Politics.
[16] Monash University Archives MON 61 Minutes of Faculty Board 17 February 1971.

the Lost Chord' which spotlighted Victorian songs. Even visiting scholars participated. Ned Flanders, with his deep bass voice in *Joseph and his Amazing Technicolour Dreamcoat*, is particularly well remembered. Of others, Lawrie Bartak recalls:

> I well remember the peak of my performing career when I played the ironwork created by the noted musical instrument maker, Peter Tucker, as a soloist with the Faculty choir in the Anvil Chorus. The high point of the evening was at supper when the Dean did a double take and said he hadn't recognised me during the performance but now realised who I was.[17]

The choir sometimes sang at special events such as the university commencement service and a Christmas carol concert in the Religious Centre which continues to this day. They even gave concerts at homes for elderly citizens. The choir brought all sections of the faculty together: academic, general, technical staff, visiting scholars and graduate students.[18]

From time to time social cricket matches were played with other departments or faculties. Andy Spaull and Dick White were leading lights in these games. There were matches against the sociology faculty. One day, when education played engineering, there was laughter from the engineering ranks when they saw the opening bowler for education was female. The laughter changed after Claire Warren, who worked in the Curriculum Laboratory, took two wickets in her first over – she was a fast bowler for Victoria!

Art

It was Monash University policy to allow a small percentage of building costs to be used for 'Arts and Embellishments'.[19] Among the works acquired was a piece by a talented student at Brighton High School, Dominic De Clario, called *Cityscape*. De Clario became a recognised artist and professor of visual arts at Monash University. The faculty also obtained a watercolour of the Monash playing fields by the Hon. Sir John Bloomfield, the Minister of Education who established Monash University, and was also an able water-colourist.[20]

---

[17] Dr L Bartak to the author 6 April 2012.
[18] Staff from other parts of the university often joined in too.
[19] MON 496 (21) Minutes of Staff Meeting 4 October 1972. The members at this stage were Mary Nixon, John Fyfield, Alan Gregory and administrative officer Maureen Elms.
[20] Sadly both paintings have disappeared from the faculty.

Faculty Board

The governing body of the faculty, Faculty Board, was a large and cumbersome body. There was representation from University Council, other faculties, the library, other education faculties, teacher union bodies (of both government schools and private schools), and representatives of the Department of Education, the independent schools sector, and Catholic schools. Internally there were categories for teaching fellows and tutors, students, lecturers senior lecturers and professors. Given this vast array of categories, the membership was constantly changing. In 1971 for example, four DipEd groups meant four student representatives. There were too many changes over the year to detail but staff well recall various external members who made notable contributions – be it Dr Tom Coates of Wesley College ensuring the grammatical correctness of all motions passed, Alice Hoy representing Council while always wearing a hat, the bored disinterest of Professor Owen Potter of engineering, the keen support of Dr Lawrie Shears from the Department of Education. While generally the board was supportive of the faculty (it tended to rubber stamp basic decisions) it had its moments of conflict. There were sometimes general issues raised. In determining the quotas for 1971, the staff-student ratio of 1:16 emerged. One Faculty Board member, Professor Goldman from La Trobe, said this figure was disgraceful and worse than the figures in teachers' colleges where there was no expectation of research.[21]

Sometimes differences between sections of the faculty would emerge in debate on an issue – and these were often contentious. There was also a Faculty Board executive empowered to act and attend to urgent matters in between meetings of the full Board.

The university seemed to take a very legalistic view of Faculty Board. In 1978 there was a congratulatory note in the minutes stating A M Rice has been awarded the PhD degree. This met with a rejoinder from J D Butchart, the academic registrar, stating 'Surely you mean that Mr A M Rice has satisfied the requirements for admission to the PhD degree'.[22]

Experimenting with the DipEd

Evidence from internal studies had shown the value of early immersion into teaching practice in teacher training. So in 1976, as an experiment, teaching

---

[21] Monash University Archives MON 61 Minutes Faculty Board 15 October 1970.
[22] Monash University Archives MON 480 Letter from the Academic Registrar to the Faculty Secretary 13 September 1978.

3.2 Cast of *The Mill Girl*: Robyn Small, Dick Gunstone, Cath Henderson, John Fyfield, Ron Laura, and Mavis Kelly, 1976.
Education Faculty

practice was introduced early – two days a week between 22 March and 7 May (seven weeks). This was followed by the usual two three-week teaching rounds during the rest of the year.[23] Sadly, while helpful to the students, the placement schools did not react favourably to this arrangement and so the usual pattern of three, three-week teaching rounds resumed in 1977.[24]

There continued to be uncertainty both nationally and within the faculty as to the numbers appropriate for initial teacher training. The Partridge Committee had suggested that DipEd quotas be reduced but the Tertiary Education Commission in 1978 warned that numbers should only be reduced 'with extreme care'.[25] Begun in 1978 (but reporting in 1980) were two enquiries into teacher education. There was a Commonwealth-appointed body, the National Inquiry into Teacher Education, chaired by Professor Auchmuty, and the Victorian-appointed Victorian Enquiry into Teacher Education, chaired by Mr Justice Austin Asche. (Alan Gregory was a member of the Victorian Enquiry.) Both committees received an abundance of quality submissions which in retrospect provide a 'state of the art' report

---

[23] Monash University Archives MON 565 Minutes of Faculty Board 1 October, 1975.
[24] Monash University Archives MON 565 Minutes of Faculty Board 6 October 1976.
[25] Monash University Archives MON 565 Minutes of Faculty Board 3 May 1978.

on teacher education of the time, but sadly little was done to implement the recommendations of either committee, despite being favourably received.

It was a period of reports, with the Williams Report on Education and Training and the Partridge Committee report also at this time.

DipEd Tertiary

The DipEd Tertiary, which had operated so effectively with about 20 university staff each year, was no longer offered after 1977.[26] The relevant minutes state that 'the original structure and balance of the course had become difficult to sustain'. Much of the demand for the course (especially from Monash University staff) had been met and as HEARU had become firmly established it was taking on much of the need of staff for help with teaching, curriculum and assessment. There was sadness at seeing the demise of what had been a successful program. HEARU itself had become well established and in 1980 a review of it by the Professorial Board concluded 'since its inception HEARU has made a real contribution to the Monash community in a number of ways'.[27]

In-service education

Many of the academic staff were involved with in-service education for teachers and others such as psychologists, parents and so forth, but this was usually on an ad hoc basis – responding to invitations from community groups and schools. A more formal arrangement came in 1978 with the establishment of what would become the Monash Teachers' Centre. Discussions with teachers, inspectors and principals from the area, and from schools Monash was associated with, resulted in meetings convened by Lawrence Ingvarson that talked about a Monash Teacher or Education Development Centre.[28] Meetings were held with representatives of all types of schools in the inspectorates of Caulfield, Oakleigh, Scoresby and Waverley as well as the education department regions of Knox and Frankston. A constitution was drawn up and a committee elected. The intention as outlined in the constitution was to provide professional development support for teachers, facilitate cooperation between faculty and school communities, hold conferences, meetings, seminars and workshops for teachers, and also to be an

---

[26] Monash University Archives MON 496 Minutes of Faculty Board 7 September 1977.
[27] Monash University Archives, MON 480 HEARU annual report 1980.
[28] Monash University Archives MON 480 (695) Monash Teachers Centre 1978–1982.

informal meeting place for teachers. Rex Thompson from Monash High School was the first chairman of the centre, and the group applied to the Department of Education for the secondment of a teacher to work there as well. An opening soiree was held on 27 November 1978.

Another development in the late 1970s was the formation of MATE – the Monash Association for Teacher Education. This was a further attempt to develop closer relations with the schools the faculty was linked with – both those in propinquity and also schools hosting Monash students for teaching practice. To give MATE more teeth, they were given three representatives on the DipEd Committee.[29] To not have voting rights was seen as being simply tokenism.[30]

Curriculum Laboratory

A report to Faculty Board outlined the main purposes envisaged for the Curriculum Laboratory.[31] It was to have a display function for curricula materials and materials from method lecturers; a workshop function for students to create materials to use in schools (transparencies, tapes, displays); a storage and loan function of materials for students, and to store higher degree theses and research papers; an information function on curricular materials, bibliographies, indices etc. provided by method staff; and finally an evaluation function, maintaining a file of evaluations and evaluating new materials.[32] A committee was set up to supervise the Curriculum Laboratory with Alan Gregory as chairman and Meigs Ghent as manager. The development of the lab being promising, it was decided that a lecturer should be appointed to head it. Following advertisements, Brian Carroll (an American) was appointed in 1974. He lasted only a few months and then left to take up a position at the Ballarat Institute. In 1976 Dr Floyd Ausburn, a graduate from the University of Oklahoma, was appointed.

The Curriculum Laboratory changed its name to the Educational Materials Centre and then again to the Educational Services Centre[33] under Ausburn.

---

[29] Monash University Archives MON 565(15) Minutes of Faculty Board 7 November 1979.
[30] Monash University Archives MON 61 Minutes of Faculty 7 November 1979.
[31] Monash University Archives MON 61 Minutes of Faculty Board 17 February 1971.
[32] Monash University Archives MON 61 Minutes of Faculty Board 21 April 1971.
[33] Monash University Archives MON 496 Minutes of Faculty Board 17 April 1974 and 1 March 1978.

In July 1977 the idiosyncratic Meigs Ghent resigned. Despite not liking her job she did it with brilliant efficiency. A classics graduate with a strong interest in theology, she had an excellent command of English and delighted in correcting the grammar and spelling of some of the academic staff. A kindly person, a row of champagne bottles in her back office signified the birthdays of various staff members.

She also instigated some of the best hoaxes experienced by the faculty. With the arrival of Maureen Elms as an administrative officer, there was a noticeable increase in accountability and efficiency. Meigs Ghent sent around a circular which purported to come from Maureen, indicating that academic staff would in future be required to sign a time-book noting their arrival and departure each day from the faculty. This caused a storm of protest with a stream of angry academics seeking immediate audience with the Dean. Ghent recalls many incidents of interest during her time in the faculty, including, memorably, a couple making love on the front counter of the Curriculum Laboratory.

Library

Funds for the library, which had in the early years of the faculty been generous, suddenly became insufficient. The devaluation of the Australian dollar in 1977 had a devastating effect on library finances. Overseas books and periodicals became much more expensive, and the library suddenly had a deficit of $166,000. The situation was to worsen as journals, especially in the medical, science and engineering areas, became much more expensive. Slowly and painfully cuts had to be made and the concept of all major periodicals and journals in a field being obtained was now questioned. From then on there were tensions in the library committees (the General Library Committee and the Main Library Users Committee). Often education had to team up with the arts and law faculties to diminish the cutbacks inflicted by the medicine, science and engineering faculties.

Research

There were many research grants in the early 1970s. Eltham College involved Lindsay Mackay and John Fyfield in a school evaluation, Shirley Sampson had a major project from the Schools Commission on sex roles, and Lawrie Bartak had a grant from the Turner Trust for work on autism. Lindsay Mackay coordinated a number of projects which involved many of the staff of the faculty: the Country Education Project, the Core

3.3 Seminar techniques. From left: Dr Denis Phillips, Dr John Cleverley, John Fyfield, and John Clift.
MUA IN-1645

Curriculum Project and an evaluation of the College of Nursing. In 1979 there were 213 enrolments for research degrees and in 1982, 193. About 60 research degree candidates had graduated each year at this period, and the faculty was able to give between three and six research scholarships each year.[34]

It was not until 1970 that the university collected and published a list of research and publications by staff. The 1970 edition was a duplicated document, as were the next two years' editions. It was not until 1973 that the research report comprised a properly printed booklet. Between 1967 and 1975 the following staff or soon-to-be staff members were awarded doctorates: John Lawry, Dick White, Lindsay Mackay, Diana Davis, Andy Spaull, Ron King, Merrill Jackson, Geulah Solomon, Fred Perry, Paul Gardner, Leo West and John MacArthur. There were others who went on to significant careers elsewhere: Bess Deakin, Bob Bessant, Jim Clough, Russell Linke, Geoff Beeson,[35] Russell Docking, Barry Fraser, Lesley Johnson and Kay Paterson.

---

[34] Monash University Archives MON 61 Minutes of Faculty Board 5 May 1982.
[35] Beeson went to Rusden State College, then to a chair at Deakin University and finished his working career as Pro-Vice Chancellor of Deakin.

The Faculty of Education section for 1970 showed 102 papers or articles, by 32 staff. There were many articles relating to the schools board (VUSEB) and school subjects, featuring work on science education by Hugh Batten, Lindsay Mckay, Peter Fensham and Paul Gardner. Social science was represented by John Hunt, Alan Gregory and Brian Spicer.

There were a number of significant books. Peter Fensham assembled the papers given out at the seminar series celebrating the Universal Declaration of Human Rights and printed them in as a book called *Rights and Inequality in Australian Education*.

Dick White was very interested in the writings and research of the famous psychologist Robert Gagne. Among his writings was research on learning hierarchies. White was keen to give a proper statistical base to Gagne's hierarchies, which he did, publishing the results in the journal *Psychometrika* in 1973.[36]

Organisation of the faculty

In April there was a long discussion about the organisation of the faculty and the roles of the Dean and that of department heads. The Dean had delegated the head of department role to the area heads and chairman of committees. John Hunt raised concerns about the active and creative role of ordinary staff members in the decision-making process, and said that the Planning and Development Committee, which had assumed a major role in the faculty, excluded representatives of many staff.[37] As the Dean reported to the staff in March 1973, 'areas were treated as quasi-departments and staffing was on the basis of the expected EFTS in each area.'[38]

A working party looking at the committee structure of the faculty pointed out that there were two main groups of committees: committees of Faculty Board and advisory committees to the Dean. Such was the tradition of democratic governance in the faculty that many were not aware that many of the committees were only advisory committees – meaning that the Dean need not accept their recommendations. The committees of Faculty Board were Faculty Board Executive, Higher Degrees Committee, BEd and Advanced Course Work Committee, Bachelor of Special Education Committee, Diploma in Education Committee and the Diploma in Educational Psychology Committee. The committees that were advisory to the Dean were Planning

---

[36] Richard White 'Monash University Faculty of Education 1969–1999', unpublished paper.
[37] Monash University Archives MON 496 (20) Minutes of Staff Meetings 5 April 1972.
[38] MON 496 (21) Minutes of Staff Meetings 7 March 1973.

and Development, Resources, Research and Publications, Conference Travel, Research Grants, Minor Works, Educational Materials Centre (formerly Curriculum Laboratory), Computational Services and Overseas Study Leave. Two other committees seemed to be outside these two groups: the Krongold Centre Committee and the Pre-School Committee.

The faculty agreed to remain non-departmental, and that 'decisions should where possible be delegated to the Area or Committee responsible'.[39] The areas remained the basic unit for staffing and for organising subjects, courses and student supervision.

There was a strong move towards a more democratic form of governance and to diminish the dominance of the 'God Professor'. Aside from Professor Neale, this had support from the other professors in the faculty. A minor matter gave the faculty some encouragement: the Faculty of Arts sent a notice around to other faculties with a proposal that they elect their own Associate Dean. Previously the Dean had made such appointments, and this proposal gave staff the opportunity of participating. There was also the implication of a non-professorial appointment. The faculty enthusiastically supported this move, which gave it heart that the university would countenance greater participation of non-professorial staff in governance.[40]

The increasing size and complexity of the faculty posed a strain on the administration, so it was decided to create the post of Sub-Dean. Norman Dobson, who was in charge of History Method, was appointed the first Sub-Dean and as a competent administrator he shaped this important role.[41] The Sub-Dean was to deal with academic enquiries, course matters, selection of students, assisting part-time students, enrolment of students, as well as being an ex officio member of every faculty committee – this last to ensure a knowledge of what was happening in the faculty.

The pressure on the general office for secretarial help was growing with increased staff and it was felt by some that typing for research was being neglected.[42] The ink duplicators were still the main source of copying, with use too of thermofax copiers.

In that period there was limited access to the one University computer, which had a memory of 3,200 kilobytes. Most students and staff resorted to the use of calculators or even logarithm tables for their statistical work. For

---

[39] Monash University Archives MON 61 Minutes of Faculty Board Appendix A 19 April 1972.
[40] Monash University Archives MON 565 Minutes of Faculty Board 5 September 1979.
[41] Monash University Archives MON 496 (20) Minutes of Staff Meeting 4 August 1971. He was appointed initially for twelve months ending 30 June 1972.
[42] Monash University Archives MON 496 (20) Minutes of Staff meeting 5 April 1972.

typing out work, there was the major advance of the golf-ball typewriter with some correction facilities but it was still a long way from word processors.

Staff meetings continued, and with an elected chair, but staff were getting used to the change in the role of the staff meeting, with Faculty Board and faculty committees assuming the main administrative roles. Brian Spicer questioned the effectiveness of staff meetings, describing them as 'non-decision making, ineffective and ill-attended'.[43]

In December 1974 Lindsay Shaw took over as faculty secretary. Shaw was a very experienced administrator whose quiet manner hid a highly competent person. With the departure of Vin Masarro to a post at the Gippsland Institute of Advanced Education, Mrs Lee Chessman became an administrative assistant in the Faculty Secretary's office. Chessman had previously been secretary to Professor Taft.

Dean

In March 1975 the Dean, Professor S S Dunn, announced he was being seconded to the Commonwealth Department of Education to be the first full-time chairman of the Australian Advisory Committee on Research and Development in Education. With his extensive knowledge of what was happening in research throughout Australia, Dunn was an ideal choice as chairman.[44] He was respected and had a capacity to network and bring researchers with common interests together. He had also encouraged bringing research into the classroom. With his quiet efficiency he had been a popular and successful dean. The Faculty Board in recording its appreciation noted his wisdom, knowledge and experience.[45] Dunn initially took leave to take this appointment but later formally resigned from Monash, and staying in the new post until his retirement.

It proved difficult to find a successor. None of the professors in the faculty seemed keen. There were few applicants for the position and the selection committee could not agree on any of them being suitable. Musgrave was Acting Dean until he went on study leave and was followed by Ron Taft. After protracted negotiations, Professor Peter Musgrave was persuaded to take the position. He did so with some reluctance. Musgrave had been in the faculty since 1970 and was head of the social foundations area. He was

---

[43] Monash University Archives MON 496(20) Minutes of Staff Meetings 2 June 1971.
[44] Technically Syd Dunn only resigned as Dean, but not from his chair. He took a year's leave of absence in case his new post did not work out. However, he did not return to the faculty.
[45] Monash University Archives MON 61 Faculty Board meeting 5 March 1975.

a renowned scholar with an international reputation and a prolific writer. While Musgrave was not at ease relating to people, he was keen to work well with people. He regarded administration as irksome and attempted to resolve each task as speedily as possible, which was sometimes not the most appropriate action.

Direction of the faculty

In 1976, as the faculty was seeking a new dean, there was an acknowledgement articulated by the Planning and Development Committee (P & D) that there had been a shift in emphasis toward higher degree work. At this stage a third of the faculty's teaching resources were devoted to DipEd, a third to BEd and advanced coursework and a third to higher degree work. Of the total EFTS in 1976 of 1223 about 500 came from DipEd, 220 from BEd, 120 from BSpecEd and 380 from higher degrees.

In 1979, looking ahead to the 1982–84 triennium, Faculty Board resolved that the faculty would continue its present direction with more weight given to research and further professional training. There was a prediction of an EFTS of 1150 (recognising a further reduction in DipEd numbers by 10 per cent) and the hope too of establishing an Educational Services Centre which would offer professional training. It also resolved to support the Centre for Migrant Studies within the Faculty of Arts.[46]

The University Commission visited the university in May 1980 and this enabled the faculty to put its case. It was pointed out to the UC that the faculty was somewhat different from other such faculties because of the much higher proportion of graduate students, particularly PhD candidates. It also pointed out that the large number of fixed-term appointments (12 since 1977) was detrimental to the faculty, with serious consequences to its supervision of research students. The members of the University Commission asked what effects the research in the faculty had on schools. They made favourable comments about the faculty's efforts to assist disadvantaged students.[47]

Associates and fellows

Two honorary categories were available for the faculty to accord recognition to scholars and give them an office and access to university facilities: associate

---

[46] Monash University Archives MON 565 Minutes of Faculty Board 7 March 1979.
[47] Monash University Archives MON 61 Minutes Faculty Board 16 July 1980.

3.4 Dr Pierre Gorman CBE with his 'hearing ear dog',
Paul (an Airedale Terrier).
MUA IN-671

of the faculty and fellow of the faculty. A notable associate was Dr Pierre Gorman, a world authority on persons with disabilities and especially deafness. Gorman was engaged initially as a lecturer in special education but later took a senior research post supervising a major research project the faculty had (examining the value of the work preparation centres that had been set up by the federal government to assist young people with mild intellectual handicaps in finding employment). Gorman was a person with private means and usually anonymously donated his salary back to the university. After the research project was completed he became an associate and in this role he proved a valuable staff member, taking courses and supervising higher degree students. Gorman was born deaf, or as he would describe it 'profoundly hearing impaired'. He was the first deaf person to graduate from the University of Melbourne and the first to gain a doctorate from Cambridge University. He was fortunate in his ability to lip read and also speak. While his accent was unusual, he lectured and spoke and many people were unaware of his disability. Gorman also served on the Vice-Chancellor's Committee, dealing with disability issues on campus and on the board of the Alexander Theatre. Later he was made a fellow of the faculty.

Syd Dunn, after he retired from his chairmanship of the ERDC, was also made an associate.

While the title of 'fellow of the faculty' had existed for some time to recognise distinguished scholars the first fellow to be appointed was Emeritus Professor W F Connell (1916–2001). Bill Connell had been an important force in Australian education and was Dean of Education at the University of Sydney from 1955 to 1976. He had both a masters and a doctorate and was involved in the history of education and comparative education. Well known internationally, his presence in the faculty was not merely honorific. He was sought after for advice, supervised some students and continued his writing and research. He completed a mammoth *History of Education in the Twentieth Century* as well as *Reshaping Australian Education*. In fact his writing was recognised by the award of a Doctor of Letters from the University of London during his time at Monash University. A popular figure, he became a familiar presence in the faculty for some years until ill-health intervened.[48]

University Council

Una Hodgson served the faculty well as its representative on council but retired in 1978, with Max Oldmeadow taking her place. He was a former method lecturer in history, and had been a federal member of parliament for the Dandenong area, where he was greatly respected. He was at the time principal of Chandler High School. No one knew the faculty better than Oldmeadow, who was an experienced and wise educator.

In the 1980s it became the custom for a 'state of the art' report to be given to Faculty Board on various topics. In March 1982 a report was given by Dr Shirley Sampson on 'Women and Education'.[49] She reported that nine members of staff were involved in advanced coursework programs in studies relating to the education of girls and women. In the DipEd there was a component in all streams relating to the education of girls and women. Sampson also referred to the list of research publications in this area and the funding the faculty had attracted. She also mentioned how staff had

---

[48] Minutes of Faculty Board 6 October 1976. Professor W F Connell (1916–2001) OBE 1978, PhD Lon., Hon D Lit (Ed) Lon., Hon D Litt (Ed) Syd., MA Illin., MA MEd Melb., FASSA, FACE, foundation editor of the Australian Journal of Education (1957–1972).

[49] Minutes of Faculty Board 3 March 1982.

served on various outside committees, and also been involved in in-service education program. A new health and human relations course was also proposed, which had arisen from courses on women. Sampson discussed the gaps that still existed in some studies. There were factors precluding women from posts in educational administration. There was a serious drop-out of girls from science subjects in year 11. She also referred to the priority given to education for girls by the Schools Commission report, and that an action/research working party had been set up. What Dr Sampson did not outline was her own role. From 1975 until 1977 she was chair of the Premier's Committee on Equal Opportunity in Victorian Schools. (R J Hamer was Premier at the time), and her report was fully accepted and implemented by the Education Department. She had also been a member of some key committees relating to women and education, such as the Victorian Advisory Council on the Status of Women (1978–82) and the Schools Commission Working Party in the Education for Girls (1981–84). From 1982–84 she was chair of the Ministerial Advisory Committee on Women and Girls to the Minister of Education (R Fordham) and from 1987-88, chair of the Personal Development Curriculum Frameworks Committee for the Ministry of Education.

3.5 Dr Shirley Sampson
Claude Sironi, Education Faculty

VISE

Prior to Monash, with only one university in Victoria, entrance to it (matriculation) was determined by student results at the matriculation examination. The courses, rules and regulations for this were set down by the Schools Board of the University of Melbourne. It had representatives of the schools on the board as well as university people, and it also set up a series of standing committees which determined the course and requirements for each subject. Again school representatives as well as university personnel were on these standing committees. The chairman of each was the chief examiner for the subject. With the arrival of Monash University, and later La Trobe, it was necessary for this arrangement to change. Accordingly a new body was set up called the Victorian Universities and Schools Examinations Board (VUSEB). This was an independent body but with representatives of each of the universities, as well as school and teacher representatives, and a similar system to the standing committees organised courses and exams for each of the subjects. Education faculty staff at Monash had a keen interest in this body and many were actively involved. It was often held that the courses and requirements at the year 12 level set the framework for the rest of the school curricula so there was a keen interest, especially from method staff, many of whom were actively involved as examiners and committee members. With different ideas prevailing and varying governments, this body changed over the years. In 1976 a new body called the Victorian Institute of Secondary Education (VISE) replaced VUSEB. At one stage Professor Peter Musgrave was chairman of the body, and Associate Professor Lindsay Mackay left Monash to become its executive director. At that time the body was called the Victorian Curriculum and Assessment Authority (VCAA).

Summer teaching

In 1977 there was discussion in the faculty about the prospect of a summer teaching program. At that time the whole university closed down after the October–November examinations and commenced again in late February–early March of the following year. It was suggested that the faculty have a summer semester of teaching offering subjects at the BEd and MEd level.[50]

While there was no apparent legal barrier to such a development, the university met the proposal with considerable coolness. When the law faculty also expressed interest, via the Dean, Professor Gerard Nash, the

---

[50] Monash University Archives MON 480 Box 14 Faculty Board Minutes 2 March 1977.

university became more cooperative.[51] Not all staff within the education faculty were enthusiastic about the proposal but there was general support for the experiment to be given a trial. It was felt that teachers, who were the main clients for the BEd subjects and MEd coursework, would find the idea appealing, as they would not have to rush in for late afternoon/evening classes after a busy day at school. They could also enjoy something like the experience of being a full-time student, as they would be at the campus each weekday in January. Library facilities would be more available to them. The proposal that there be teaching every weekday in January was to ensure there was a course time at least equal if not in excess of that of a normal 13-week semester. It was envisaged that staff who participated would have reduced loads or even some free time during the rest of the year as compensation. Each area of the faculty agreed to offer a subject and so initially seven subjects were offered for January 1978. In the end only six subjects were actually offered, with numbers being insufficient for the seventh. Eighty-three students were enrolled and 36 of them took two subjects. Alan Gregory and Andrew Spaull coordinated the program, both of whom had witnessed summer schools in operation in North America.

HERU completed an evaluation of the summer semester program.[52] The report concluded that the program had been highly successful with the quality of the subjects offered considered equal in standard to 'normal' BEd and MEd subjects. The students who took the course were highly motivated, and they made much more use of the library. On the negative side the intensive teaching meant some students wished for more variety in the means of presentation and staff found the correction load a burden. Some staff felt there was not proper compensation in the time allowance given during the rest of the year. Overall the student experience was found to be 'profitable and enjoyable even if exhausting'.[53] The BEd committee resolved in June to continue the summer semester in January 1979.[54]

---

[51] Monash University Archives MON 480 Box 14 Letter from Prof Gerard Nash to Alan Gregory 23 May 1977.
[52] Monash University Archives MON 480 Box 14 Dr T Hore to Dean 27 July 1977.
[53] Monash University Archives MON 480 HERU Report by N S Paget and T Hore April 1978.
[54] Monash University Archives 480 BEd Minutes 26 June 1978.

New building extension

Construction was expected to commence on the major extension to the existing building in May 1975 and take 12 months to complete. In July 1974 tenders had closed for the additions to the Child Study Centre and plans for the Krongold Centre were in their final stage. Both projects were plagued by industrial issues and rapidly escalating building costs. These meant considerable delays. In the case of the addition of a fourth floor to the Education Building, the project had to be reduced to two-thirds of its original size to cope with the costs. This resulted in an odd looking top floor that was out of kilter with the rest of the building, and the inability to extend the lift to the additional floor. Occupancy was also delayed by over a year.[55]

Occupying the additional space on the top was the Centre for Research into Aboriginal Affairs. Dr Eve Fesl, the director of the centre, had close links with the faculty both academically and socially. The proximity gave rise to useful collaborations in research.

Status and reputation of the faculty

By the late 1970s it was clear that Monash's Faculty of Education was well established as the top in Australia and one with a growing international reputation. With six professors and an academic staff of over 60, its very size made it formidable, and the multi-professorial appointments ensured a breadth of scholarship across the main disciplines relevant to education.

The Vice-Chancellor, Professor Ray Martin, in a letter to the Dean, Professor P W Musgrave, in May 1979 reported with some surprise that after interviews with Professor Dunbar, chairman of the Universities Council and Professor Peter Karmel, chairman of the Tertiary Education Commission 'there is no doubt in my mind that the Monash Education faculty is very highly regarded in those quarters'.[56]

Statistics were also revealing. In 1978, of the masters theses candidates there were 142 at the Monash education faculty out of an Australian total of 501, meaning Monash had 28 per cent. Masters by coursework figures were similar and of the 209 PhD candidates, 52 candidates or 25 per cent were at Monash. The figures also showed that 74 per cent of the staff at Monash had doctorates, compared to 62 per cent at Macquarie University, 56 per cent at University of Sydney, 35 per cent at University of Melbourne, and 58 per cent

---

[55] Monash University Archives Minutes of Staff Meeting 7 May 1973.
[56] Monash University Archives, Letter from Vice-Chancellor (Ray Martin) to Dean of Education (P W Musgrave) 7 May 1979.

3.6 Top: Andy Spaull, Keith Hudson, John Fyfield, Warren Mellor. Bottom: Maurie Balson, Floyd Auburn. Claude Sironi, Education Faculty

3.7 Stairs that led nowhere – the result of cutbacks while building was in progress.
Tony Miller, MUA IN-3635

in the Monash arts faculty.[57] There had also been stability of staff at Monash with only six departures in the last four years. Those leaving went to prestigious appointments such as Denis Phillips to Stanford and others to chairs or senior posts in the Advanced Colleges.

The faculty could also boast strength across a wide range of disciplines relevant to education, whereas other education faculties usually showed strength in one field only, such as the University of Melbourne's dominance in Australian education history.

---

[57] Monash University Archives, 'The Status of the Education Faculty' by P W Musgrave 1 February 1979.

Using the measures of the US Social Science Citation Index, Monash had 14 entries in 1975 with other Australian universities scoring as follows: Macquarie 7, Sydney 7, Melbourne 7. There was a similar pattern for such figures for the rest of the 1970s.

Monash also had the lead in terms of books published by staff. One book, edited by one staff member with contributions by other staff members, drew a review in the *American Education Research Journal* by the distinguished American psychologist Lee Cronbach of Stanford University:

> The fact that each of the authors is associated with Monash University, either as a Faculty member or graduate student, bespeaks a vigour of enquiry into curriculum that few American universities could match.[58]

Another element which had a major impact was the visiting lecturer program. The faculty, like other faculties at Monash, appointed a visiting professor every second year. In this period the visiting professor program brought some famous names to the faculty. There was Professor G H Bantock[59] from the UK in 1971, Dick Ripple from the USA in 1975, Robert Gagne from Florida in 1976[60] and Vid Peczak and David Layton from Leeds in 1977. Others included Ulf Lundgren, an eminent Scandinavian scholar and Marvin Wideen from Simon Fraser University in Canada, who later with Dick Tisher published a book on research in teacher education. The visiting lecturer program meant there were overseas visitors coming at least once a year, and often more. Each area took it in turn to nominate a scholar and this proved highly stimulating to staff, able to bring to Monash scholars of merit in their field. This had been achieved by keeping an academic staff post vacant, and added to this were any salary savings gained from delays in appointments. Some visitors came for only a few months, some for longer. Sometimes they paid their own airfare; sometimes the fund was able to provide this as well as salary while they were here. As well as the immediate benefit of having such scholars at Monash, it also meant that over the years there grew a network of scholars all over the world who were familiar with the education faculty at Monash University. While most of the scholars were from the USA and UK, there were some from Scandinavia, the rest of Europe and Asia.

---

[58] *American Education Research Journal* 12:2, 1975, pp. 211–213.
[59] An eminent British educator and author of amongst other works *Education in an Industrial Society*.
[60] Robert M Gagne (1916–2002) internationally famous for his work on the conditions of learning and a pioneer of the science of instruction during World War II.

An instructive example is the visit of Robert Gagne. Gagne was aware of the work Dick White had done in furthering Gagne's research. It was a tribute to White that Gagne came to Monash, as he was a person much sought after given his strong international reputation. During Gagne's visit a group of research students were working on aspects of Gagne's learning theory. One was Andrew Mackenzie, who had been granted a two-year fellowship by the ERDC to undertake research. Mackenzie recalls this period with great satisfaction. His work resulted in an article in the prestigious US journal *American Education Research Journal* – an Australian first for a research student.[61]

John Fyfield took a group to China in 1978.[62] This was a group of high powered educators and they were fortunate in the opportunities they were given. Fyfield negotiated with Chinese authorities who surprisingly gave him permission to interview former Chinese leaders who had been deposed and who were being 're-educated' in prison. He returned in 1979 to conduct interviews with a series of these former leaders, including the brother of the last Emperor of China, and this resulted in a book.

In 1979 the faculty had an EFTS of 1266. These student numbers comprised (in EFTS terms), 242 in research higher degrees, 472 in coursework higher degrees, and 552 in courses other than higher degrees. This showed the changing balance of the faculty.

To bring the faculty back to earth, there was criticism of the faculty and its courses by radical students in the student newspaper *Lot's Wife*. An article described the DipEd as a 'boring ritual' and the faculty 'of the established, by the mediocre, for the middle-class'. It went on to complain that 'each year the same hotch-potch is served up for the unwilling to consume and disgorge at the whim of their assessors'.[63] On a positive note the writer noted a 'De-schooling group' set up within the faculty. Even some staff were cynical about DipEd, as Mary Nixon wrote to Ron Taft in 1973: 'Don't expect anyone to take DipEd seriously, except the young...'[64] This was not a view held by most staff.

---

[61] Andrew Mackenzie became a highly respected school principal in South Australia and in Victoria, at the time of writing, Hume Anglican Grammar School. Discussion with Mackenzie on 14 March 2012.

[62] Fyfield had previously been to China with a mainly University of Sydney-based group under ex-Monash staff member John Cleverley.

[63] *Lot's Wife* 16 October 1972.

[64] Monash University Archives, MON 75 Ron Taft's papers, Mary Nixon to Ron Taft letter dated 8 May 1973.

Staff

In 1972 John Radvansky departed for Tasmania and Dick White and Paul Gardner were promoted to senior lecturer. New staff were Alex MacKenzie (psychologist) and John Watt (philosopher), teaching fellows Lawrence Ingvarson and Ann Shorten, and senior teaching fellows Kathie Forster, Win McDonell, Kay Brown and Barry Fraser. New part-time method lecturers were Dick Gunstone (Physics), Ray Anderson (Biology), David Murphy (Classics), Barry Lay (Commercial), Tom Seabourn (Social Studies) and Bruce Worland (Music).

Salaries for lecturers in this period were in the range $8,698 to $11,982 and for senior lecturers $12,268 to $14,308.

Ron King, who had made an impact in his work in educational administration, was appointed to the chair of education at Wollongong University.[65]

In April 1972 the appointment to a new chair was announced: Dr R J W Selleck[66] from the education faculty at the University of Melbourne. Richard Joseph Wheeler Selleck had been a senior lecturer in the Faculty of Education at the University of Melbourne. He had been a primary teacher in Victorian schools 1954–57, and then was in the curriculum and research branch of the Department of Education 1958–1961. In 1962 he was appointed a lecturer in education at Melbourne. He had completed a BA and BEd, and in 1962 won the Pitman Prize for the history of Australian education. He had a Nuffield Fellowship in 1968 which he held at the Institute of Education at the University of London, and a PhD from the University of Melbourne. His book *The New Education 1870–1914* (Pitman, London, 1968) was regarded as a significant piece of landmark research dealing with the 'New Education' movement in Britain. He also published *English Primary Education and the Progressives 1914–1939* (Routledge and Kegan Paul, 1971) and wrote many articles on Australian education history, becoming editor of *Melbourne Studies in Education*. At the University of Melbourne he was the junior member of an impressive team of education history scholars: Bon Austin, Edgar French, Gwen Dow, and Steve Murray-Smith. Selleck was to have a major impact in the faculty. He would soon build a staff team that would rival Melbourne's.

Two years later in 1974 it was announced that the sixth chair of education had been accepted by Professor R P (Dick) Tisher. It had been desired that the chair be in the field of teaching and learning, and Tisher met this

---

[65] Monash University Archives, MON 61 Faculty Board Minutes 5 March 1975. Sadly King, a successful professor, developed a form of cancer and died in 1976, aged 43 years.

[66] For Richard Selleck's recollections of his time at Monash, see Chapter 9.

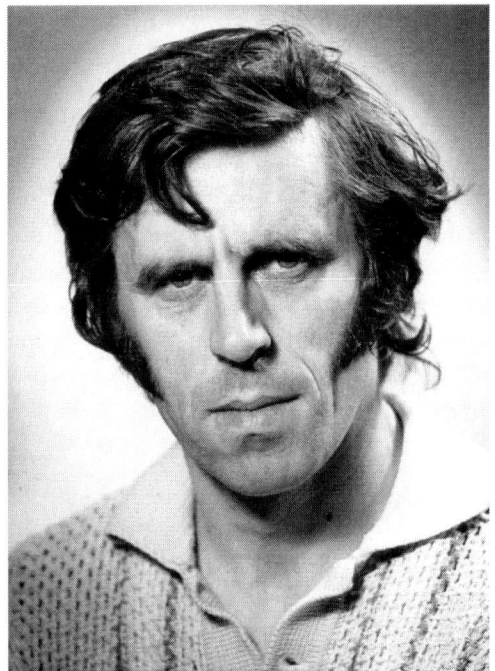

3.8 Professor R J W (Dick) Selleck, 1972.
MUA IN-258

requirement. Tisher came from the University of Queensland where he had been a reader in education. Previously he had taught in secondary schools and been a lecturer in education at the Armidale Teachers' College. He had a BSc (Hons) from Sydney; he completed an MSc in 1952, a BA at the University of New England with first class honours in education and in 1968 a PhD at the University of Queensland. Tisher's research was on the nature of the teacher-learning process, studies on the effects of different teaching strategies on pupil growth. Tisher headed Arca 4 of the faculty: 'education – practice – general studies'.[67] Among his many publications were:

Beginning to teach Vol.1: The Induction of Teachers: A Bibliography and Description of Activities in Australia and the U.K., a research report on stage 1 of the Teacher Induction Project and *Beginning to Teach Vol. 2: The Induction of Beginning Teachers in Australia.* There was also *Teacher Induction: An Aspect of the Education and Professional Development of Teachers.*

---

[67] Dick Tisher was to remain in the faculty for 16 years before being approached to become executive chairman of VCAB in 1990.

Here, finally, was the achievement of having a sixth chair – long the aim of Selby Smith in his vision for the faculty.

There were a group of resignations from the faculty, all of whom had made notable contributions. Hugh Batten went to the Lincoln Institute; Merrill Jackson went to the University of Tasmania; Fred Perry to the Institute of Early Childhood Development; Alan Trethewey, a foundation member, to be Dean of teacher education at the Toorak Teachers' College;[68] Dr John Lawry to become head of the School of Teacher Education at Gippsland Institute of Advanced Education at Churchill; Lindsay Mackay to become executive secretary of the Victorian Institute of Secondary Education (VISE); Alec MacKenzie to be director of student counselling at the University of Western Australia; and Ron Laura to the chair of education at the University of Newcastle.[69] Theo MacDonald also resigned.

Serious health problems forced the premature retirement of Ken McAdam in March 1975.[70] A greatly respected teacher and psychologist, McAdam had made a significant contribution to the faculty and his death in October 1976 was greatly mourned. In the same month the faculty was also sad to learn of the death of foundation staff member Henry Schoenheimer. Schoenheimer was a key person in the early days of the faculty and a much loved character. These deaths hit those who knew them hard.

New staff appointed in 1975 to psychology were Lawrie Bartak, an expert in autism, and Dr Gil Best, an audiologist.

General staff

Among the general staff (later called professional staff) were not only secretarial workers and administrative officers but also a range of technical staff who became important in the life of the faculty. Peter Tucker was a fabricator and worked in metal, making models as well as undertaking a range of technical duties. From his reasonably equipped workshop he even managed to make an anvil for Lawrie Bartak to bang in the faculty choir's rendition of Verdi's *Anvil Chorus*. John Gipps, who ran the science laboratory, was very skilled and also ran courses for science students. Graeme Wallington was a specialist in audiovisual and arrived in 1973 along with the photographer Claude Sironi, whose role changed as technology developed. Sironi was

---

[68] Minutes of Faculty Board 6 October 1976.
[69] Monash University Archives MON 61 Minutes of Faculty Board 5 March 1980 and 6 September 1978.
[70] Monash University Archives MON 61 Minutes Faculty Board 5 March 1975.

known for his effervescent helpfulness. Later came Gordon Perkins from Telstra with skills in IT and with computers, who became an important part of the faculty.

3.9 Professor Dick Tisher.
MUA IN-5901

As rapid changes in technology occurred this group had a special role in helping staff make the best use of the new developments. In early 1970s, the main tools used were the slide projector, movie projector, ink and spirit duplicator, tape recorder, calculator and early form of overhead projector. The professional staff were helpful as well as flexible in attending to the infinite variety of staff needs, whether for lectures, talks or research.

The secretarial staff provided stability. The staff grew in 1975 with the arrival of Bev Schneider and Heather Phillips (from the English department). Schneider and Phillips were to serve the faculty well. Schneider took charge of the general office. Phillips with her cheerfulness was helpful in many capacities and remains in the faculty 38 years on.

Method staff

A distinctive feature of the faculty in its first 15 years was the willingness to appoint to full-time tenured positions specialists in 'methods' – the method and practice of teaching a specific subject. This was true of History (Norm Dobson), English (Henry Schoenheimer, Brian Sureties, then Diana Davis), Economics (Alan Gregory), Geography (Brian Spicer), Modern Languages (Jim Wheeler), Mathematics (Theo MacDonald, Ken Clements and later Dudley Blane) and Science. Science was especially blessed for in addition to the method lecturers were tenured staff with special expertise and interest in science education – John Theobald, Paul Gardner, Dick White, Peter Fensham, Lindsay Mackay, Hugh Batten and later Dick Gunstone. Full-time staff in charge of methods had a distinct advantage over part-time lecturers who normally had a principal responsibility to a school.

Full-time method staff had the opportunity to pursue research interests, to write in their fields and to establish international links. This most of them did. They were also able to offer courses of advanced methods of teaching in their subject speciality at the BEd and Masters coursework level. They also supervised research work by students in method areas. Many of these lecturers were also active in subject associations which were influential with teachers, the Department of Education and curriculum setting bodies, at the national as well as state level. The subject associations were especially strong in the 1960s and 1970s, for example the Victorian Commercial Teachers Association owned its own building and conducted a large publishing business as well as undertaking professional development in the economics and commercial field. The lecturers were supported by part-time method tutors, usually teachers seconded from Department of Education schools. There were some remarkable people who took this role, for example Ian Harrison, Garry Bell, John Brooke and Marli Wallace in Economics Method; Joan Sheen, Eleanor McCoy, Ann Feehan and Tom Comerford in History Method; Ray Anderson, Cathy Shannon, Colin Oates and Eric Friedman in Science Method; David and Doug Clark and David Davison in Maths Method; and Ann Badger in Social Studies Method. The existence of so many full-time method staff softened the blow when the Department of Education ended free secondments of teachers to the faculty.

Review committee of university governance

In 1978 there was a university committee of enquiry into university governance and administration. Late in 1980 this committee was asked to look at arrangements in the Faculty of Education. This was prompted by Professor Neale. In particular: should areas of study in the Faculty of Education be deemed to be departments and the heads of areas to be chairs of departments?

The process was off to an ominous start when the Monash Review Committee rejected a request that a faculty member should be added to the committee to review the faculty's government.[71] Faculty Board endorsed a motion from the faculty staff that 'The Faculty resolved to express to the Vice-Chancellor and the chairman of the Committee of Review its opinion that it is carrying out well its functions of teaching and research and that there is no need to deem its areas to be departments for any purpose.'

The Review Committee took a conservative and legalistic approach to the question and recommended to Council 'that the arrangements adopted in the Faculty of Education should be brought into conformity with the requirements of "Statute 2.3 –The Faculties".' The committee described the election of area heads as a 'radical development'. The committee stated that these heads 'must bear the responsibilities of chairmanship', unless they were on sick leave or study leave.[72] It was a setback to the more democratic approach that the faculty had embarked on.

The council ordered the faculty to comply with university requirements. A special meeting of the faculty resolved to inform the Vice-Chancellor 'that the members of the Faculty consider his prohibition on consultation with the Faculty in the recent matter of the governance of the Faculty intolerable and not conducive to the best interests of the good health of the University.'[73]

Conclusion

The faculty could take great pride on the continued high standards in the DipEd. Good students (they had sound academic backgrounds and most were keen to pursue teaching as their vocation), well run courses, competent staff and close links with schools all meant a professional training which was greatly respected and admired by the students and by the schools these students were to teach in. A thriving DipEd had underpinned the success of the faculty. During the 1970s there was a large number of new staff appointed and economies of scale gave great scope for imaginative appointments.

---

[71] Monash University Archives MON 61 Minutes of Faculty Board 7 May 1980 and 25 June 1980.
[72] Monash University Council Papers 1981 Volume 2, Meeting 6–10, p. 1543 C412/81.
[73] Minutes of Special Meeting of the Faculty of Education 15 December 1981.

In this period the emphasis in the faculty had swung strongly towards research and post-initial training, with large numbers enrolling for research degrees. The books and publications coming out of the faculty were being noticed overseas. This was further enhanced by the large number of visiting scholars and also the regular attendance by Monash staff at key international conferences and seminars in their field.[74] The faculty was on the map internationally.

Staff of 1972

Ann Rosemary Shorten, although she became a senior tutor in 1972, had commenced with the faculty in 1969 as a tutor in History Method. A graduate from the University of Melbourne – BA, DipEd, BEd and MEd – she had a remarkable career. She was at first a teacher in the Victorian Department of Education, later becoming principal of Collingwood Girls High School. In 1965 she was a lecturer in education at the University College Townsville. She was actively involved in History Method in the faculty and in 1976 assumed a role in the administration of teaching practice for DipEd, as well as teaching at the BEd level. She became a continuing lecturer in 1976. She then completed her doctorate in 1976 on the topic 'The Imperial Validity and Maritime Education in Australia 1869–1923'. She then completed an honours law degree (LlB), winning, among other prizes, the Supreme Court Prize in 1985. She also practised as a barrister. She taught at all levels within the faculty and as well as her role in teaching practice, as school executive officer she held administrative posts including that of Graduate Studies Advisor (formerly known as Sub-Dean). She published widely in historical and maritime fields as well as on education and the law. She was promoted and on taking early retirement in 1996 held the rank of associate professor. A much respected figure she died on 5 April 2014.

Martin Sullivan came as a senior teaching fellow from Kelvin Grove Teachers' College. A graduate of the University of Queensland and teacher in Queensland schools, he had a keen interest in industrial history as well as the history of Queensland education. He completed his doctorate at Monash supervised by Dick Selleck, and in his words 'fell on his feet', as the history group within the faculty gradually assumed a leadership position in

---

[74] Dr Dick Gunstone in his 'Outside Studies Programme Report' of 1981 noted that the visiting scholars also meant that institutions overseas were keen to receive visits from Monash scholars. Monash University Council papers, 1981, Vol.2, p. 1664.

Australian education history. Sullivan with Selleck edited *Not So Eminent Victorians* (1984) and with Andrew Spaull *A History of Queensland Teachers Unions* (1989) and *Men and Women of Port Phillip* (1989). Sullivan left Monash in 1998 and has primarily been an independent historian since.

3.10 Eleanor McCoy, Dr Ann Shorten, Ann Feehan, and the Dean, Professor Peter Fensham, 1986.
Richard Crompton, MUA IN-660

Marilyn Goodall, BA (Melb) BEd MEd (Monash), formerly a teacher in secondary schools, held temporary lectureships in the faculty before taking a fixed-term lectureship in 1983. A specialist in reading and learning disabilities, she worked in psychology and within special education in the faculty and was a much valued member of staff. She resigned in 1984 to take up a position at Methodist Ladies' College.

Ronald Charles King had been a part-time teaching fellow from 1970. He had a BCom and BEd from the University of Melbourne and had also completed a major in psychology. He completed an MA from La Trobe and then a PhD at Monash in 1972. He had worked as a psychologist in charge of the South Melbourne Psychology Centre and also with the psychology branch of the Department of Education. His research interests were in the social dynamics of family life and the school as an organisation. He joined the faculty as a lecturer in 1972, becoming senior lecturer in 1975. He worked in the educational administration section of the faculty. He had an engaging personality and was an excellent teacher, and had widespread interests. He was appointed as professor of education at the University of Wollongong in 1975. Sadly King developed a serious illness and died a few years after taking up the appointment.

Lawrence C Ingvarson was appointed a lecturer in 1972. Perth born and educated at the University of Western Australia and an MA in educational psychology from the University of London. He had been a science teacher in WA schools and a physics teacher in London. His research was in teacher–pupil interaction and classroom behaviour. He became a lecturer in education at Stirling University in Scotland, where he met John Theobald, who was on study leave from Monash. He was attached to Area 4 and developed an interest in continuing education and worked with the Monash Teachers' Centre. He was promoted to associate professor in 1997 and resigned early 2001 to take up a position as research director of the Teaching and Learning Program at ACER. He became recognised for his research on teacher professional development, teacher quality, teaching and leadership standards, assessment of teacher performance, performance pay, school improvement and the evaluation of educational programs, and has published widely in these areas. He has played a major role in the development of teaching standards in Australia, working in collaboration, for example, with the Australian Science Teachers Association, the Victorian Institute of Teaching, the NSW Institute of Teachers and Teaching Australia. He was a member of the Ministerial Advisory Committees for the Victorian Institute of Teaching (2000–2001) and for the TAFE Development Centre (2002–2003), and a member of the Advisory Council for the National Institute for Quality Teaching and School Leadership. With Steve Dinham and Elizabeth Kleinhenz, he developed a national standards framework for the teaching profession for the Ministerial Council for Employment, Education, Early Childhood Development and Youth Affairs. The same team also produced a report on teacher quality for the Business Council of Australia titled 'Teaching Talent: The Best Teachers for Australian Schools'.

Alexander James MacKenzie, known as Alec, was a graduate from the University of Western Australia majoring in psychology. He became a lecturer in education at the University of New England, Armidale and was an experienced psychological counsellor. He taught in Western Australian schools (1956–1960) and was a counsellor for the Department of Education of Western Australia. His special fields were verbal learning, personality and abilities. He worked in the psychology area of the faculty. He left in 1979 to take up a post as director of counselling at the University of Western Australia.

Diana F Davis had a BA from the University of Melbourne with majors in English and psychology. She also completed a DipEd, BEd and an MA thesis degree in English on Australian literature. She won the Dwight Prize in Education. She taught in secondary schools and became a lecturer in English and psychology at RMIT. She became a teaching fellow in 1968 then in 1979 a senior teaching fellow, serving in both English method and psychology sections of the faculty and becoming a lecturer in 1972. She completed her doctorate at Monash in the field of social psychology. She served on the National Committee on English Teaching in 1974, and became head of English method. In 1980 she was described as 'one of the best known and regarded academics in the field of English education in Australia'. She published extensively and also had a heavy supervision load. In December 1988 she resigned to become professor of education at James Cook University Townsville, and is now an adjunct professor of the Australian National University, Canberra.

Staff of 1973

John T McArthur, a senior teaching fellow was a BCom DipEd graduate from the University of Melbourne. He became a teacher of commercial subjects and history in Victorian high schools. He completed his BEd at Melbourne and then his MEd at Monash in which he specialised in educational administration. He became a research fellow in 1974, working on the School Library Project. He completed his PhD at Monash in 1975 on educational administration, teacher socialisation and pupil control ideology. He published widely – at first mainly statistical works and then work in educational administration. He became a lecturer in 1976, then senior lecturer. He had a close working relationship with Ray McCulloch; together they built up an excellent section and attracted many senior educators, and also good staff like Ron King and Judith Chapman (who both went on to chairs). He received a number of large research grants and also wrote several articles of significance, as well as publishing 'The First Five Years of Teaching: their effect on pupil control Ideology and commitment to teaching' (1980) and substantial research on nursing education. His quiet reserved manner hid a formidable intellect. He was seconded to the Australian Education

Council in 1983 and was so well regarded he resigned in June 1985 to take the senior executive post in that organisation.

Margaret Gilchrist did a BA (Hons) with a double major in psychology at Melbourne (1949) followed by an MA on interpersonal attraction and personality and then a doctorate, also at Melbourne, on the relation of some personality and ability variables to creativity and academic achievement (1970). A tutor, then lecturer in the psychology department at Melbourne, she became a senior lecturer in the education faculty. She was the author of many articles and some jointly with Ron Taft. She was appointed to Monash in July 1973 as a senior lecturer in educational psychology. Highly intelligent, she taught and supervised in this field and also published. She took early retirement at the end of 1985.

Norman C Nettleton, a New Zealander with medical studies and a degree in psychology from the University of Otago and a postgraduate diploma in science became an assistant lecturer in psychology. In 1970 he took an appointment as a research assistant in psychology in the Department of Psychology at Monash University. He undertook an MSc on ear and hemispheric asymmetry and was appointed a lecturer in education in the special education area in 1973. He became senior lecturer in 1983. He continued an active role in psychological research, and was coordinator of the Diploma in Educational Psychology. He took early retirement at the end of 1996.

Andrew D Spaull, from La Trobe valley, completed an MCom (1966) and DipEd (1965) at Melbourne and taught in Victorian secondary schools. He was a tutor in economic history at Melbourne, and in 1968 became a lecturer at the Monash Teachers' College. He did historical research at this stage on brown coal and on John Monash. He was appointed a senior teaching fellow at the education faculty in 1969 and then in 1973 became a lecturer. He completed his PhD in 1972 on teacher unions. A prolific writer, he published many books and articles in the area of labour history, education history, education and policy. In the education faculty he taught in a range of fields as well as supervising many thesis students. His books include: *Teachers in Conflict* (with Bob Bessant; 1972), *Politics of Schooling Pitman*, (with Bob Bessant; 1976), *Australian Education in the Second World War* (1982), *A History of the Australian Education Council 1938–1986* (1987), *A History of the Queensland Teachers Union* (with Martin Sullivan; 1989) and *John Dedman: A Most Unexpected Labor Man* (1998). A much respected historian, he became a senior lecturer and then a reader. A stroke stopped his outstanding academic career and ill-health forced his retirement in 2003. A hearty character, he was a gregarious teacher and a lively presence in the faculty.

Shirley Neta Sampson was first appointed as a senior teaching fellow. She had a BA and DipEd from the University of Western Australia and had taught in schools in WA, Tasmania and Nigeria. She became senior history mistress at Firbank CEGGS and was an examiner in Year 12 Australian history. She became a lecturer in social foundations at Monash Teachers' College in 1970. During her period at Monash she completed her doctorate in the Faculty of Arts (Sociology) on the sex role orientation of adolescent girls, and became a lecturer from 1974, tenured from 1983 and a senior lecturer in 1984. She taught in the faculty at all levels and pioneered courses in gender in education and the education of girls and women. She supervised many students at masters and doctoral level and played a major role in research relating to the education of girls. She also received many major research grants for her work. She wrote extensively, including the books *Initiatives to Change Girls' Perceptions of Career Opportunities: An Evaluation* (1983), and with Gilah Leder *Educating Girls: Practice and Research* (1989). From 1975 until 1977 she was chair of the Premier's Committee on Equal Opportunity in Victorian Schools and her report was fully accepted and implemented by the then Department of Education. She had also been a member of some key committees relating to women and education: the Victorian Advisory Council on the Status of Women (1978–82), the Schools Commission Working Party in the Education for Girls (1981–84), and from was chair of the Ministerial Advisory Committee on Women and Girls (1982) and the Personal Development Curriculum Frameworks Committee (as chair; 1987–88). She died in October 2007, aged 80 years.

Robin Small had a BSc in physics and mathematics from the University of Canterbury (1965), New Zealand, then undertook a BA in philosophy and an MA with first class honours (1970). He became a lecturer in philosophy at the University of Canterbury in 1969. He came to the ANU in 1970 on a doctoral research fellowship with a special interest in the concept of man in existential philosophy. In the faculty his teaching and research was in education philosophy. He resigned in 2003 to take up a post in New Zealand at the University of Auckland. He is now a professor and a senior staff member of the School of Critical Studies in Education. His books include a study of Karl Marx's contributions to educational thought, a survey of the phenomenological tradition and several works on the thought of Friedrich Nietzsche. He later moved on to work in ethics.

Jeffrey S Kaiser came to the faculty in 1973 on a two-year fixed-term appointment. A graduate from the State University of New York, he taught business education and maths in schools before becoming involved in educational administration. His doctorate from New York was on general system theory and the beliefs formation systems of administrators as functions of mindedness. He was an administrator in the Board of Cooperative Educational Services in New York. He lectured in educational administration in the faculty. He wrote articles on school finance. He returned to the USA after his term ended in December 1975.

Staff of 1974

Richard Gunstone began professional life as a science and maths teacher for 12 years with the Victorian Department of Education (BSc Melbourne, TSTC), and was heavily involved with the Science Teachers Association of Victoria. He was part-time seconded to the faculty as a methods person (1971–73), did a BEd and took a contract lectureship in science education (science and physics methods) in 1974. He did a PhD while working full time, became an associate professor and then in 1995 professor of science and technology education. He nominally retired at the end of 2005, and is still very active in research and writing as an emeritus professor today. As well as sabbaticals at LRDC (U Pittsburgh), Leeds and U British Colombia, he also worked extensively in Philippines, Korea, Southern Africa, Spain, London, and in later years for the European Commission. His research funds include 15 ARC Discovery grants. He has recently completed editing the first Encyclopaedia of Science Education for Springer. He is a life member of the Science Teachers' Association of Victoria and a fellow of the Academy of the Social Sciences in Australia.

Pierre P Gorman became a lecturer in the faculty in the field of special education in 1974 but had served part-time since 1972. A graduate of the University of Melbourne in Agricultural Science (1949) and Education (DipEd), he was the first deaf person to graduate. He completed a PhD at Cambridge University, the first deaf person to do so. He developed (with Paget) the Paget-Gorman sign system, which is still in use today. He also worked as librarian at the National Institute for the Deaf in London. He had a remarkable capacity to not only lip-read (in French as well as English) but also to talk and lecture. As well as teaching in the special education area he was involved in some major research projects within the faculty, including one on the evaluation of the work preparation centres for young people with mild intellectual disabilities which were funded by the Commonwealth Department of Social Security. He also served on various Monash committees, including the board of the Alexander Theatre and the

Vice-Chancellor's Committee on Disability. He was privately a generous benefactor to the faculty and Monash University. After he formally left a full-time post he became an associate and then a fellow of the faculty and retained a keen and active interest, including teaching in higher degree courses and supervising students. He was helped by his loyal dog, Paul (a champion Airedale) who became well known on campus and was described as Pierre's 'hearing ear dog'. He was also busy outside the faculty in various causes, helping libraries, promoting an awareness of people with disabilities, remaining active with his old college at Cambridge, taking visiting professorships overseas and being a generous benefactor to the Baillieu Library at the University of Melbourne. He was honoured with a CBE and the University of Melbourne gave him an Honorary Doctor of Laws. He gave the occasional address at this graduation ceremony. He also established a charitable trust, the Gorman Foundation, which was set up to promote an awareness of people with disabilities in the community.

Brian Frank Carroll, a Canadian with a BA (Carleton) and Master of Library Science (University of Western Ontario) came in 1974 to be lecturer in charge of the Curriculum Laboratory. He was head librarian at the York Resource Centre in Toronto and had much experience in new technologies associated with libraries. His stay was short-lived as he left in February 1976 to be Director of Curriculum Resources at the Development Library at the Ballarat College of Advanced Education.

McKenzie Alexander Clements (known as Ken) was lecturer (1974–1975) and then senior lecturer (1976–1982) in the Faculty of Education at Monash University. Before arriving at Monash, Ken taught mathematics in four Victorian schools. He was in charge of mathematics education in the faculty and brought great energy to this job. He was also a competent historian and gifted teacher of mathematics who wrote some significant articles on Victorian education history. After leaving Monash early in 1982, he taught at Prince Alfred College in Adelaide (1982–1983) while simultaneously completing theological training at Tabor College. He worked in India in 1984 and 1985, before resuming his academic career at Deakin University (1987–1993), then becoming professor of education at the University of Newcastle (NSW). Between 1997 and 2004 he was professor of education at Universiti Brunei Darussalam and since 2005 has been a professor in the mathematics department at Illinois State University. Since leaving Monash, Clements has served as a consultant in India, Japan, Malaysia, PNG, South Africa, Thailand, the United Kingdom and Vietnam. He has also contributed much to the international mathematics education literature, having written or edited 24 books and more than 200 articles. With Nerida Ellerton, he co-authored a UNESCO book on mathematics education research and in 2012 Springer published their book *Rewriting the History of School Mathematics in North America 1607–1861*. Clements has co-edited three international handbooks on mathematics education and is an honorary life member of both the Mathematical Association of Victoria and the Mathematics Education Research Group of Australasia.

Alan M Rice a BA (Hons) Monash and TPTC (Burwood), taught in Victorian primary and secondary schools (1965–1972), and became a teaching fellow in the politics department at Monash. He undertook an MEd thesis on political decision-making, the pluralist world and political socialisation. He was appointed a lecturer in the faculty in 1974 to work in politics of education with the social science group. He completed his doctorate and was actively involved in research in the politics of education and Asian education and published in these areas. He set up an Asian Education Centre within the faculty. He was promoted to senior lecturer in 1984. He took a voluntary separation in April 1999.

Geoffrey Neale Molloy was originally a physical education graduate from the University of Melbourne, and taught in Victorian and later Canadian schools as a physical education teacher. He did an MA and BEd in Alberta, Canada, and then a PhD on age, socio-economic status and patterns of cognitive ability. He worked as an associate professor at Arcadia University in Nova Scotia, with research interests in learning theory, child development and behaviour modification. He was appointed as a lecturer in the psychology area in 1974, then senior lecturer and became an associate professor in 1993. He published in his research area.

Clifford A Wilson joined the faculty in 1974 in the psychology area. A graduate from Sydney (BA and MA), he later completed a PhD in the USA. His special field was psycholinguistics, and he developed a Language Abilities Test which became widely used. He lectured at Toorak Teachers' College and in the USA taught at the University of South Carolina. He also had a strong involvement with a Christian group and his books and publications in response to the book the *Chariot of the Gods* became bestsellers. He was much sought after as a speaker on this area. He became a part-time senior lecturer but resigned in 1980 to take up posts in the USA.

Staff of 1975

Lawrence Bartak was a Melbourne graduate, obtaining first class honours in psychology in his BA and MA. He became a tutor at the University of Melbourne (1961–65) before moving to London where he was a lecturer in the Department of Child Psychology at the University of London and honorary psychologist at the Maudsley Hospital. His research interests were in the cognitive characteristics of austistic children and he wrote extensively on this field. He took appointment in the faculty in 1975 as a senior lecturer. He completed his PhD in 1977. He had an active teaching and research career, continuing his special work on autism, achieving an international reputation and teaching in the special education area. He became director of the Krongold Centre in 1996. He retired in 2003.

Gilbert Best was a graduate in speech pathology and audiology. He completed his MSc at Purdue University, Indiana, and then his PhD in 1970, also at Purdue in the field of speech science and disorders of communication. He was an associate professor of special education at the University of Nebraska at Omaha, and then became a lecturer in the School of Speech Science at the Lincoln Institute. He came to Monash in 1975 as a senior lecturer. He had an active role in the final stages of the building of the Krongold Centre and then in its early management. He also coordinated the Bachelor of Special Education degree. His research interests centred on the effects of hearing loss (conductive deafness) on language, learning and behaviour in pre-school and early school-age children. He served as chairperson of the Centre for Migrant Studies and as Sub-Dean during the deanships of Professors Fensham and Aspen. He retired in 1996 after 21 years in the faculty.

Warren L Mellor, a graduate of University of Sydney (BA DipEd), taught in NSW secondary schools and became a lecturer in education at the University of New England. In 1973 he completed an MEd at the University of Oregon. He worked with the ERIC consortium, and completed his PhD at Oregon in 1975. He took a senior lectureship in education administration with special interests in the management of educational institutions, organisational innovation and information flow. During his time at Monash he played a key role in the education administration area. He also held a consultancy in Paris at the International Institute for Educational Planning and became involved in advising in developing countries. He resigned in 1992 to take up a consultancy post in Asia. He became Director and UNESCO representative to India, Bhutan, Maldives and Sri Lanka.

Stafford Kay, an American, was a graduate from the University of Wisconsin at Madison (MS 1965, PhD 1973). He became a lecturer in educational policy studies in 1973 at Kenyatta University in Kenya. He also had interests in social foundations of education and comparative education. He served in the Peace Corps (1966–68). He was appointed to a lectureship in social foundations, and was later promoted. He was also Warden of Deakin Hall (the library there is named after him). He resigned in 1980 and returned to the USA where he worked first for the Phelps Stokes Fund, a non-profit organisation which assisted minority groups with education, and was director of the Washington Office. After 16 years with Phelps Stokes in 2002 he became director of programs and administration for the National Council for International Visitors and was director of the information exchange and management systems. He died in October 2012.

Staff of 1976

John Wyn Owen, known as Wyn, was Welsh and had a BSc and Diploma in Physical Education, and a second BSc with first class honours in psychology. He taught in schools and then served with the Royal Navy during World War II. He became a lecturer in education at the University of Hull, and then to Makerere College at the University of East Africa. A senior lecturer, his main interests in psychology were in concept formation, thinking and reasoning. He joined the faculty in 1976 as a senior lecturer and served with Area 1, taking a role in both teaching, supervision and administration. A quietly spoken scholar, he was well respected by staff and students. He took early retirement in 1988.

Peter Edwards joined the faculty in 1976. A graduate from Claremont Teachers' College in Western Australia, he taught in WA schools and graduated BA (1964) BEd (1968) from the University of WA. He then graduated MA (1972) and EdD (1974) from the University of British Columbia with his special interest in reading. He became a lecturer in curriculum studies at Canberra CAE where he developed his expertise in reading and also published a spelling list. He came to Monash and was involved in the special education area and was soon promoted to senior lecturer. He took early retirement in 1989 and went to the USA.

Philip A Greenway, born in Britain, was a graduate in psychology from Edinburgh University (MA first class honours), and then completed his PhD at the University of Louvain, Belgium in physiology and psychology. He then did postdoctoral work in Pennsylvania. He taught at the University of Aberdeen. His main research interest was in the field of the psychology of learning. He had a wide range of publications in learned journals. He became a lecturer in 1976, and senior lecturer in 1978. He retired at the end of 2011.

Dominica Nelson was originally a primary teacher, teaching in aboriginal communities in Queensland, then travelling widely in Italy before returning to Australia to work in adult literacy with the Council of Adult Education. From 1976 to 1980 she came to the faculty and taught 'language across the curriculum' at both DipEd and MEd levels. She went on to work with migrants and refugees and she also wrote in this area and in adult literacy. Cancer stopped her passionate career in 2001.

Floyd B Ausburn, a graduate from the University of Oklahoma, trained as an opera singer, then as a teacher, completing his BA and MEd at Northeastern State University. He then moved to educational technology and he completed a PhD in instructional technology at Oklahoma. He became coordinator of media services at the University of Oklahoma and in 1976 was appointed to the faculty as lecturer in charge of the Educational Materials Centre (formerly the Curriculum Laboratory). He taught educational media at various levels, including a course on educational television at the masters level. A popular member of staff, he resigned in 1987 to sail his yacht in the South Pacific with his wife Lynna. He eventually returned to the USA.

Staff of 1977

Jeffrey R Northfield had a Bachelor of Agricultural Science and a BEd from the University of Melbourne and was a science teacher with the Victorian Department of Education from 1962–1968. He then lectured at the Secondary Teachers' College before becoming a lecturer in Science Education at the Riverina College of Advanced Education. He was appointed as a senior teaching fellow at Monash in 1973, becoming a lecturer in 1975. He completed his PhD at Monash on 'New Science Courses and Teachers', was active with the Science Teachers Association and became involved in evaluation of the science curriculum through the project ASTEP. He served on the Biology Standing Committee and was involved in examining. He was appointed an associate professor in 1990. Prolific in research and writing, he achieved 114 publications, 8 books, and 16 chapters in books and many research papers. Professor Fensham described him as 'an outstanding teacher, exceptional teacher educator and valued educator'. He became Director of Teacher Education in the faculty and was also a key person in the group of science educators at Monash which achieved international recognition. He was also a participant in the PEEL project, another project of international significance. He was appointed a professor and head of the Peninsular Campus of the faculty in 1995. His practical common sense and easy going style helped remove barriers until ill-health forced his early retirement in 1997. Sadly this popular and well respected colleague died from cancer in May 2004. The faculty instituted a Jeff Northfield award for research on teaching in his honour.

Howard Brown, after a BA (Hons) degree majoring in geography, completed his DipEd (1968) and then taught at Kew High School. In 1972 he was seconded to the education faculty as a part-time method tutor in geography. He later completed a BEd and a Master of Environmental Science. He became method lecturer in geography in 1977 but with the end of secondments returned to Doncaster High School in 1980. A much respected member of staff, he was frequently asked for advice and to undertake special projects for the faculty. He came back to the faculty in 2002 as a tutor and then in 2004 assumed the post as administrative officer for the PEEL project, a post he held until 2012. His wife, Jenny Brown, also a Monash graduate, has also had a long career in the faculty.

Dr Ronald S Laura, American born, attended Harvard University, Cambridge University (St John's) and Oxford University (Brasenose) (PhD). He was a philosopher with keen interests in health and fitness. Laura came to Monash to take a position in educational philosophy. In 1978 he was appointed to the chair of education at the University of Newcastle. During his time there he developed special interests in the philosophy of health education, with a companion interest in the ramifications of our technological lifestyle as it impacts on the human body and spirit. He has been active in the Philosophy of Education Association of Australasia including terms as president, and served as Dean of the Faculty of Education at Newcastle where he remains the senior professor. He has published widely in his fields.

Staff of 1978

Gilah C Leder[75] was a graduate of the University of Adelaide (BA and DipEd) and of Monash University (MEd and PhD). Her doctoral thesis was on fear of success and sex differences in participation and performance in mathematics. Her main research interests were in mathematics education, gender, affect, and exceptionality. After teaching at secondary schools, at the

---

[75] For Gilah Leder's recollections of her time at Monash, see Chapter 9.

Melbourne State College and working for the faculty as a tutor in mathematics method, Leder gained a tenured lectureship in 1978. She was promoted to associate professor in 1988 and resigned in 1994 to take up a chair in education at La Trobe University.

Leder served as president of the Mathematics Education Research Group of Australasia (1994–1998) and the International Group for the Psychology of Mathematics Education (1999–2001). She was a fellow of the Academy of the Social Sciences in Australia, a life member of MERGA, and is currently an adjunct professor at Monash University and professor emerita at La Trobe University. She was awarded the 2009 Felix Klein medal in recognition of her contributions to mathematics education, nationally and internationally.

Leder published widely and served on the editorial board of national and international mathematics education and general education journals. In 2013 she was awarded the Career Research medal of the Mathematics Education Research Group of Australia. Recent publications include: 'Looking for Gold: Catering for Mathematically Gifted Students Within and Beyond ZDM', in *Towards Equity in Mathematics Education: Gender, Culture, and Diversity* (2012), 'Taking Stock: From Here to the Future', in *Research in*

3.11 Dr Gilah Leder.
Claude Sironi, Education Faculty

Mathematics Education in Australasia 2008–2011 (2012), *Stepping Stones for the 21st Century* (2007) and *Beliefs: A Hidden Variable in Mathematics Education?* (2002).

Staff of 1979

Judith Dorothy Chapman commenced her education at the University of Melbourne with a BA majoring in English and history. A teacher in Victorian schools (1970–76), she did her Doctorate in Education at the University of North Carolina on the competencies of Victorian secondary school principals. She joined the faculty as a lecturer in 1979 in the educational administration area. She taught in these courses, continued her research and published widely. She was promoted to senior lecturer and then in 1993 to the chair of education at the University of Western Australia. In 1998 she was appointed Dean of Education at the Australian Catholic

3.12 Professor Judith Chapman AM.
Richard Crompton, MUA IN-656

3.13 Peter Gronn.
Claude Sironi, Education Faculty

University and after her term ended in 2003, remained as a professor. In addition to her writing in educational administration she published in the area of life-long education. In 1999 she was made a Member of the Order of Australia.

Staff of 1980

Peter Christian Gronn, a BA (Hons) Melbourne in history and political science (1968), DipEd (1969), taught in Victorian technical schools. He completed his BEd at Monash (1973) and became a lecturer in politics at Burwood State College (1974–79). He completed his PhD at Monash (1979) on the politics of school management with a comparative study of three school councils. His thesis was noted as a significant contribution to research in the educational administration area. He was promoted to senior lecturer in 1985, served as group head in 1991, and was promoted to associate professor in 1995. He was also Associate Dean (Teaching) (1999–2000), and Associate Dean (Development) (2002–2004) and was granted a personal chair in June 2003. He resigned in February 2007 to take up a chair in Scotland as professor in public service, educational leadership and management at the Department of Educational Studies, University of Glasgow (2007–2008). He then became professor of education at the University of Cambridge, where he was head of the Leadership for Learning academic group (2008–2011) and then head of faculty. He is an academician of the Academy of Social Sciences, a fellow of Hughes Hall, Cambridge, and a fellow of the Royal Society of the Arts and the Australian Council for Educational Leaders.

Peter Gronn is a leading international scholar in government and non-government school systems and in educational and school leadership. He is the author of about 130 publications. His most recent book is *The New Work of Educational Leaders* (2003). He has also undertaken biographical research on the famous Australian educator Sir James Darling. In 2005–2006 Gronn acted as a consultant to the Australian Council for Educational Research on the project 'Standards for School Leadership' and in 2006–2007 he co-authored the Country Background Report for Australia, which formed part of the OECD international project on school leadership.

Margaret N Brumby had a BSc from the University of Melbourne. She then worked in the Walter and Eliza Hall Institute laboratories and completed a Master of Science in the Cancer Research Unit and a DipEd from La Trobe University. She completed her PhD at Surrey University in the UK. She came to Monash first as a postdoctoral fellow and senior tutor in 1980, and in 1983 was lecturer in charge of biology, science and health education. A noted scientist, she was also well versed in bioethics and learning styles. In 1987 she was appointed general manager of the Walter and Eliza Hall Institute. She was later made a Member of the Order of Australia for services to medical research and education.

Joanne Deppeler began a Masters of Educational Studies, part-time in 1980 at Clayton. She completed her first subjects with Dr Lawrie Bartak and Gilah Leder while concurrently giving the occasional lectures and supervising student practicums in special education. She then went on to complete her thesis under Gilah Leder's supervision in 1982 and soon employment in a number of fractional research assistant and lecturing appointments in what was then referred to as Division 7: Special Education. In 1988 she was re-located to the Henry and Dinah Krongold Centre and under the then Director Stewart Sykes continued teaching in both the Postgraduate Special Education and psychology programs, delivering interventions directly to students in schools and to teachers in development partnership projects. She completed her PhD in 1994. In 1997, after more than 15 years of continuous one-year contracts in the Faculty of Education her appointment along with the appointments of a large number of female colleagues was converted to tenure as a result of the Higher Education Contract of Employment (HECE) Award. Joanne continues as an academic in the Faculty as an associate professor. Since 2010 she has held the position of Associate Dean Higher Degrees Research. In 2012 she was the recipient of the Dean's Award for Excellence in Innovation and External Collaboration and nominated for the Vice-Chancellor's Award for Excellence in the same category for her ongoing research in partnership with education systems in Australia and in many international contexts.

John Gipps, who had a BSc and MSc, was officially termed a 'professional officer', working in the faculty from 1972 until 2013. He initially ran the science laboratories at Clayton campus, adding in 1999 those laboratories at Peninsula. He prepared materials for the science staff and presented sessions in practical science to students. He later advised Monash students in schools. He was also involved with the Philippines Australia Science Education Project (1990–91) and chaired the faculty OHS&E Committee in 1996 and 2005. He was involved in courses in environmental health (1998) and, with Jeff Richardson, was in charge of courses in computer control and interfacing. His specialties were environmental chemistry, colour in chemistry demonstrations, computer-interfaced science experiments, teaching about human evolution and teaching science in primary schools. He also authored 29 articles in refereed publications and had papers presented at over 70 conferences on science, mathematics and computer education.

Chapter 4

Special education

The faculty had been divided up into 'areas' that grouped together staff with similar interests or backgrounds. Initially those with special education interests were housed within Area 1 (psychology). Professor Marie Neale requested that an extra area, Area 7, be created to cater solely for special education. The request was granted and Professor Neale became Area 7's head.[1]

In a paper presented to the Planning and Development Committee in February 1971, Professor Neale argued for the establishment of a centre which would conduct research in special education, and prepare a diverse range of specialists to work with exceptional children and with specific problems in children's learning. Monash was the only Australian university with a chair in special education and it also had appropriate staff for such a centre. Neale envisaged something different to the existing Elwyn Morey Child Study Centre, which did accept some children with various disabilities, but only in a limited way. Neale's conception was far broader.

The Australian Universities Commission (AUC) had also mentioned the importance of special education in its Fourth Report (May 1969).[2] The Senate Standing Committee on Science and Arts had recommended to the AUC that there should be a university department in special education in each state. Vice-Chancellor Louis Matheson asked the AUC in 1972 for additional funds for Monash to devote to special education.[3] Professor Peter Karmel, chairman of the AUC, indicated to Matheson that the commission would address the issue of special education in its Fifth Report.[4] Matheson wrote to the Dean, Professor Dunn, to stress how important it was for the

---

[1] Monash University Archives MON 486 (62) request to P & D 29/10/70.
[2] Monash University Archives 486 (62) Proposal to Planning and Development Committee by Professor M D Neale, 9 February 1971.
[3] Monash University Archives MON 486 (62) Letters 23 February 1972 and 1 March 1972.
[4] Monash University Archives MON486 (62) Letter from Professor Peter Karmel to Louis Matheson 3 May 1972.

faculty to have such a program. Matheson indicated that while the main responsibility of the faculty was to train teachers, arising from that task was the need and opportunity to develop teachers who could teach children with various kinds of disability.[5] However, he was cautious, and warned that if too much was attempted, the area's limited resources might be overwhelmed.

The Dean also warned Professor Neale that 'our clinical activities must be for teaching and research and we are not equipped to give a community service'.[6] Therein lay the issue of future contention: the community need for assistance even in the simple forms of assessment and diagnosis was great, not to mention in ongoing treatment, and while this would fit well with training of special education teachers, and for research by staff, there was a limit.

Faculty Board discussed the matter and noted the faculty's limited facilities of space, personnel and resources. The board was keen to ascertain how many non-graduate teachers needed training in the field, and also to look at training psychologists to work in schools. What was called the Curriculum Laboratory in the new building was being re-imagined as a possible area for special education.[7] The mere fact that Monash had created a chair in special education had focused attention on the occupant and created pressure to solve the deficiencies in the area. Neale referred to the 'enormous frustrated segment of the community aware of the short comings of existing services...'[8] Professor Neale saw the faculty having to respond in various ways: sensitisation to individual differences at initial teacher training, postgraduate training in specialised courses such as a diploma, bachelor or master's degree, and research in higher degrees. Neale herself was keen on providing a diagnostic and clinical service directly to children and parents.

In 1972 there were only two courses available in Victoria to train teachers in the special education field. There was a Trained Special Teachers' Certificate at the Melbourne Teachers' College, which was an extra year course added to the Diploma of Teaching Primary (or the TPTC), and a course offered at the Glendonald Training Centre for Teachers. The former offered work with the blind, physically handicapped, remedial and intellectually retarded

---

[5] Monash University Archives MON 486 (62) Letter from the Vice-Chancellor to the Dean on 5 April 1972.
[6] Monash University Archives MON 486 (62) Letter from Dean 6 April 1972.
[7] Monash University Archives MON 486 (62) Letter from the Dean, Professor Syd Dunn to the Vice-Chancellor 24 April 1972.
[8] Monash University Archives MON 486 (62) Letter from Professor Marie D Neale to the Dean of Education 17 May 1972.

children, and the latter obviously worked with deaf or hearing impaired children.⁹

There was a need to provide special education teachers and especially to extend and broaden their professional competence in comparison to what those teachers in Victorian schools were currently trained for. There was also the need to upgrade the competence of the general teacher to cope with the many problems they would face in regard to special education in the mainstream classroom.¹⁰

Neale saw the proposed centre as preparing specialists for the various disciplines concerned with the developmental needs of children. She sought to cater for exceptional children including those with intellectual disabilities, learning disabilities, brain injuries (neurological dysfunction), physical disabilities (such as cerebral palsy, orthopaedic anomalies, vision and hearing problems), emotional disturbances, and the gifted.

A disagreement between Professor Marie Neale and the faculty arose by March 1973. This came to a head with a letter from Professor Neale to the Dean, Professor Dunn, in which she outlined with some passion her hopes and aspirations but expressed concern at the 'lack of principles which guide our staffing arrangements'. She also stated 'for three years I have tolerated the manner in which my specialist skills have been negated while being delegated to work as tutor in this or that psychology course, or fill in for sections of BEd work...' Professor Neale expressed considerable frustration at her situation.¹¹

In a long letter in reply, Professor Dunn outlined the reality of funding and staff – deriving as it did from students, courses or special grants.¹² He outlined the staffing that accompanied the calculations from EFTS and courses and pointed out the problems of getting additional staff. Much of Professor Neale's work was orientated to special education and there were insufficient student numbers to attract substantial funds from EFTS. Dunn pointed out that the Child Study Centre and work in special education had to be funded, and the faculty relied on what it obtained from the AUC via the University as a whole. He also pointed out that originally the work

---

[9] Monash University Archives, MON 486 (62) Report by Fred Perry 9 June 1972. The terminology may not be that used today.

[10] MON 496 (19) Paper by M D Neale and S S Dunn 'The Development of Special Education and the Centre for Child Study and Special Education' 2 February 1972.

[11] Monash University Archives MON 338 Staff file Professor M D Neale, letter to Professor S S Dunn 19 March 1973.

[12] Ibid. Professor S S Dunn 27 March 1973.

in special education was not envisaged as a separate area but part of the psychology area of the faculty. He said 'I know that there is a gap between your expectations and the reality that has occurred in special education, but I also believe your expectations have been unrealistic and take insufficient account of how a university functions'.

There were also considerable outside demands on Professor Neale, who would be awarded an OBE in 1979 for her dedicated service to exceptional children and made a Member of the Order of Australia (AM) in 1989 for services to education and particularly to children with special educational needs. She was eagerly sought after to serve on various committees and enquiries as it was a period when there was increased recognition of the issues in special education. She was a warm and generous person as well as a gifted communicator. She was the only person in Australia to hold a chair in special education at that time. Some of these difficulties spilled over to the staff who had teaching and research obligations in the faculty as well as demands in the field of special education. Passionate about her field, Professor Neale gave the faculty teaching and research needs a lower priority.

There was a general increase in community awareness of the issue of 'special education'. One manifestation of this was setting up a ministerial committee of inquiry into special education in Victoria. Professor Neale was asked to be a member, the only non-government person on the committee (the majority being from the education sector).[13]

Neale was persistent in her quest for a centre of special education. She clearly identified the need and her hopes were supported by many parents and others caring for children with special needs. There was formal endorsement for her cause from the AUC and bodies like the Senate Committee on Science and the Arts. The charismatic professor was able to attract much interest in her work, and gained the support of the Department of Education and various benefactors.

Finally, the centre was able to be set up on the receipt of a substantial donation from Dinah and Henry Krongold, initially of $100,000, later increased to $150,000. This attracted for building purposes a 4:1 subsidy from the Commonwealth Department of Social Security (initially it had been a 2:1

---

[13] Vice-Chancellor Professor Matheson was cross that Professor Neale was appointed to this committee without reference to the university. Monash University Archives MON 486 (62) Letter from J A L Matheson to the Alan Scanlan, Assistant Minister for Education, 30 November 1972. Mr T L W Emerson chaired this committee.

4.1 Model for the Krongold Centre. Professor Marie Neale with Dinah and Henry Krongold.
MUA IN-1635

subsidy but the rapid inflation brought this generous revision).[14] The process to achieve a designated building was slow and fraught with problems, mainly from inflation, which meant a serious escalation in building costs as the centre was being planned. The initial architect report estimated a total cost of $490,000. The firm of John Scarborough was used again, but a key role was played by Alan Scott, the Monash University architect. The building was to include a hydrotherapy pool, a gymnasium, a lift, an experimental laboratory, a creative room, a play room, social and domestic training areas and a diagnostic testing room, as well as offices for the director, lecturers and tutors.[15]

After much debate and discussion, it was finally decided that the faculty would offer a specialised course: the Bachelor of Special Education, a

---

[14] Monash University Archives MON 61 Faculty Board Minutes 2 October 1974.
[15] Monash University Archives MON 480 (269) Architects Report on Krongold 14 March 1974. Members of the committee included the Dean, Hugh Batten, Fred Perry, John Theobald, Professor Neale, E C Snell, Dr T N Adamson, as well as the university architect Alan Scott, university buildings officer L N Meares, and Ken Atkins).

4.2 John Mooney, Executive Officer of the Krongold Centre.
Education Faculty

two-year course, commencing in 1974.[16] The AUC recommended extra funds for Monash University for special education.[17]

In July 1975 the Acting Dean (Peter Musgrave), in a statement to the Planning and Development Committee, said it seemed 'the Krongold Centre will develop more along the originally intended lines as a laboratory type institution involved in research, diagnosis and assessment rather than as a school'. A committee under Professor Neale (as chair) was set up, made up of faculty representatives, Krongold himself and representatives from other parts of the University including the professor of paediatrics and the university finance officer. An inaugural meeting was held on 5 November 1975.[18]

In what John Mooney describes as one of the most successful entrepreneurial ventures in education history, Marie Neale and T L W (Les) Emerson, Director of Special Services, Department of Education, combined to achieve a remarkable centre. Neale's charisma, her talent for vividly communicating

---

[16] Monash University Archives MON 480.
[17] Monash University Archives MON 61 Faculty Board Minutes 3 July 1974.
[18] Monash University Archives MON 535 (Box 47) Krongold Child Training Centre document by P W Musgrave, Acting Dean 15 July 1975. Also, minutes of meeting 1/75 of the Krongold Centre Committee.

the needs of exceptional children, and her ability to attract the support of the community combined well with the wise instincts of Emerson, who saw the need and the ways in which a contribution could be made. Neale attracted the funding from the Krongold family and support from key people such as the Vice-Chancellor. Emerson provided the full-time secondment from the Department of Education of a teacher who would be the main supervisor (called the Executive Officer), a domestic science teacher, an infant teacher trained in social education, and an array of part-time secondments: a physiotherapist, a speech pathologist, a physical education specialist and an occupational therapist. In addition he arranged for leave on full-pay for a number of teachers to undertake the Bachelor of Special Education course. The Department of Education gave leave to over 67 students (on full pay) to undertake the Bachelor of Special Education. It was a very generous provision and gave the idea some reality. He pointed out that these secondments would have to be reviewed annually, as he was subject to the will of politicians.

At the second meeting of the committee, in March 1976, the Vice-Chancellor suggested that the Prime Minister be asked to perform the opening ceremony. This was agreed to.

With the Prime Minister Malcolm Fraser in attendance, the official opening of the Krongold Centre attracted national interest. During this period student activism at Monash was at its most violent stage. The opening was a dramatic event. Present was John Mooney who was at the time Executive Officer of the Krongold Centre. Here is his account of the events:[19]

> There was great expectation in the air on Monday, 23rd August, 1976. The opening of the Krongold Centre had finally come. A large number of parents and preschool children were busily involved in a series of afternoon clinic programs. The official opening was to take place in the Alexander Theatre. There was great excitement that the Prime Minister of Australia, Mr Malcolm Fraser, would be the guest speaker and would officially declare the centre open.
>
> At 3.00 pm, the official party made their way into the Alexander auditorium and the official guests stood to welcome them. There was an ominous feeling in the air as a large number of people had gathered to protest about the Prime Minister's presence on the campus.

---

[19] John Mooney, who became principal of the Emerson Special School, kindly supplied this information at the request of the author in 2012.

As the opening ceremony proceeded, it became more and more difficult to hear the proceedings because of the deafening sound that was coming from the protestors gathered outside of the main doors to the right of the stage. The doors were being battered and rammed. The audience were becoming increasingly alarmed and distracted when it appeared that the besieged doors were threatening to give way.

Members of the Prime Minister's security staff took steps to ensure his safety on stage. I was sitting in the front row of the audience and was becoming concerned that the parents and students in the Krongold Centre could be at risk. I managed to leave the Alexander Theatre by an alternative route and ran to the Krongold Centre by gaining access to the ring road at the front of the Educational Faculty. When I gained access to the Krongold Centre, I found that a number of protestors had barricaded the parents and children in the teaching rooms. Protestors stood guard at the door to prevent parents or children leaving. Fire reels had been accessed and were in readiness to prevent the official party from entering the building.

A number of the official party tried to access the Krongold by walking along the muddy slope adjacent to the rear fence of the Elwyn Morey Child Study Centre. They were pursued by a number of protestors and fell to the muddy ground in their full academic dress.

I noted that the senior organisers of the protest group did not appear to be Monash students. On a humorous note, I noticed that one female protestor was sitting in the middle of a large maiden hair fern that I had borrowed from the office of Norman Nettleton for the opening. This plant was Norm's pride and joy. When I asked the protestor not to sit in the middle of the maiden hair fern, she told me that I was interfering with her rights of where she wanted to sit. I explained to her that I had the plant on loan and I asked her to respect the property of other people. She, in turn, approached the leader of the protestors who was organising the positioning of his group to ensure that no official party members could enter the building. He approached me and stood nose to nose with me. I told him that my request to his colleague (he used the word 'comrade') was reasonable.

I asked the protest leader how he felt about locking parents and pre-school children with disabilities in rooms without any access to water and toilets. I also asked him if he would do this to members of his own family and was he proud of doing this to people who were very vulnerable.

A consultation took place between protestors. I stood my ground in the middle of the Krongold foyer. He returned to me and looked me straight in the face. He told me that he and his colleagues were leaving the building. I thanked him for his understanding.

The Prime Minister did not attempt to enter the Krongold Centre. It was too dangerous. It was a day that I will never forget. The parents, children and staff still celebrated the opening of this wonderful centre. We were so appreciative of what Dinah and Henry Krongold had done for children with disabilities in Victoria. We were disappointed that this wonderful day did not achieve the fullness of what it offered. However, nothing detracted from what Monash University and the Krongold family had achieved.

4.3 Opening of the Krongold Centre. From left: Vice-Chancellor Professor W. A. G. Scott, Mrs Dinah Krongold, Mr Henry Krongold, and Prime Minister Mr Malcolm Fraser.
MUA IN-1640

Professor Ron Taft, who was Interim Dean at that time, reports that the official party departed the Alexander Theatre for a grand afternoon tea, unaware of the plight of Malcolm Fraser who demonstrators had forced to hide in the basement toilets. The Prime Minister's security officer was unable to summon help from the local police for some time – not until the Prime Minister was able personally to convince them that the distress call was genuine. The violence of the demonstration and the plight of the Prime Minister attracted considerable publicity and the point and importance of the Krongold Centre itself was lost.

The first graduates from the Bachelor of Special Education course completed their course at the end of 1975 (see photograph). By 1976 the Krongold Centre and the related Bachelor of Special Education course were thriving. The Dinah and Henry Krongold Child Training Centre came fully into operation in 1977. It was described as a diagnostic and therapeutic centre for exceptional children and children with learning disorders.

In addition to the Bachelor of Special Education, the Krongold undertook major assessments of children with special needs and over the 1976–78 period gave help and training to over 700 children – a remarkable achievement. John Mooney, the Executive Officer of the Krongold Centre, not only had the expertise and training in special education but was a capable administrator. He went on to make a major contribution as principal of Ashwood Special School (1986–1997) and then as principal of Emerson School (from 1998).

As Neale went overseas it was Dr Gil Best, a senior lecturer in the faculty with special interests in audiology, and John Mooney as Executive Officer who oversaw a large portion of the first three years of the Krongold Centre's operation. They had an excellent staff, seconded from the Department of Education. These were Sandra Heeps, Marie Green, Michele Klimovics, Don Cowell and Leanne Briggs. A large number of faculty staff were actively involved in the development of programs: Dr Lawrence Bartak, Dr Gil Best, Dr Stewart Sykes (later director of the centre), Dr Merrill Jackson, Dr Peter Edwards, Dr Norm Nettleton, Dr Cliff Wilson, Mrs Jenny Wise, Mr Brian Thompson, Mr Ken Clements and Mrs Judy Mitchell. A number of therapy staff were also there: Mr Peter Bourke, Mrs Mel Hunt, Mrs Marilyn Wood and Mr Nathan Slowo. Rosemary Martin worked in a secretarial capacity, and Sister Pam Forsyth was Nurse Administrator. A key role was also played by Judy Matthews – nominally secretary to Professor Neale, but shouldering a heavy burden with all the work of the Krongold as well as the diverse activities of the energetic Marie Neale.

4.4 Dr Gilbert Best (left) and audiologist Dorothy Moore, test hearing at the Krongold Centre.
Claude Sironi, MUA IN-7410

4.5 Dr Stewart Sykes.
MUA IN-640

T L W Emerson OBE retired as Director of Special Services in the Department of Education in 1976. This was noted with great regret by Faculty Board.[20] Emerson was not only a greatly respected figure in special education but his support for the program at Monash in securing seconded staff and seconding teachers to do the course was fundamental to its success. Emerson's enormous contributions to Victorian education were acknowledged by the naming of the state's largest special school, located in Dandenong, as the Emerson School. Emerson died in November 1985.

Conflict intensifies

In May 1979, Dean Professor Peter Musgrave issued a document titled 'Future Development of the Krongold Centre'. It had emerged from a report of the sub-committee established to review the Krongold Centre. It reviewed the issues facing the centre, the withdrawal of full-time study leave on full pay for Department of Education teachers from the Bachelor of Special Education course, the numbers involved in that degree, whether the practicum was best taken at the Krongold during the second year of the course, and the number of teachers seconded to the centre from the Department of Education. It also outlined the sources of funds – from the faculty, from the Vice-Chancellor, from the Department of Social Security – and brought to light a likely significant shortfall, especially given general tightening of finances and the change in the Department of Education's policy on secondments.

Professor Neale reacted badly to this document, seeing it as an attack on her and her policies. She regarded it as a personal smear that negated the services she rendered and gave a false view of her role. She appealed to the Vice-Chancellor, complaining of her treatment by a 'kangaroo court' and saying that she was 'politically clobbered, physically exhausted and spiritually shattered'. Such a reaction was a surprise to the Dean and the review committee, who were primarily concerned with the grim realities of the situation. The end of secondments was to be a real blow to the Krongold Centre and ultimately was to be the end of the full-time Bachelor of Special Education course. The essence of the BSpecEd remained despite these restrictions, and later there was courses offered at the masters level. As Lawrence Bartak, Head of Area 7, stated in 1978, they needed to 'provide

---

[20] Monash University Archives, MON 496 (19) Minutes of Faculty Board 5 May 1976.

a practical and realistic response to an acute and unprecedented change of policy by the Department of Education'.[21]

Professor Neale was so incensed at the BSpecEd becoming part-time that she resigned as chair of its committee. She told the Faculty Board that the modifications to the degree 'did not accord with the original plans and that the educational context of the course had changed'. She added that 'she was unable to accept that the part-time degree is the same as the full-time degree'.[22] The staff of the area were more realistic and knew that with the end of free secondments by the Department of Education, which affected students as well as staff, the full-time degree was no longer possible. They aimed to achieve the same goals and standards in the part-time degree.

In 1979 the Krongold had to face a cutback of staff seconded from the Department of Education, leaving only three full-time teachers with the part-time services of another three.[23] The Vice-Chancellor used his fund of bequests to keep the nurse administrator, the media technologist and some paramedical staff. There was also the problem that few full-time students were now available during the day.

The tabling of the Fourth Annual Report of the Krongold Centre to the Faculty Board in 1980 gave an opportunity for special education lecturer Dr Lawrie Bartak to draw attention to the Krongold's holding of 'seminars and workshops with other organisations in which other appropriate staff members of the Faculty had not been invited to participate or even being informed'. Bartak expressed misgivings about the adequacy of the Faculty Board's relationship with the Krongold and at the 'serious lack of consultation between the centre and the rest of the Faculty'.[24] There was clearly a rift between Professor Neale and the special education staff within the faculty. Professor Neale took exception to the statements by Bartak, feeling there had not been any serious lack of consultation as she had informed the Dean and the Vice-Chancellor about the workshops she held. While Professor Neale's lack of agreement with the statement was noted, the Dean clarified that 'it did not imply that the Faculty Board agreed with the opinions she had expressed.'[25]

---

[21] Monash University Archives, MON 565 Minutes of Faculty Board 1 November 1978.
[22] Monash University Archives MON 565 Minutes of Faculty Board 2 May 1979.
[23] Monash University Archives MON 565 Minutes of Faculty Board – Third Annual Report of the Krongold Centre 20 October 1979. Sister L J Groom was the nurse administrator and Mr G C Harris was the media technologist.
[24] Monash University Archives Minutes of Faculty Board 5 November 1980.
[25] Monash University Archives Minutes of Faculty Board 6 May 1981.

Marie Neale was more engaged in the practical side than in research; she did not extend her earlier work on developing tests (such as the Neale/Schonell reading tests that she had created earlier in her career). Her colleagues in Area 7 explored their own interests in the field.

Neale was frequently overseas attending seminars and conferences, and while her appearances and talks at such bodies brought attention to the Krongold and the faculty, she tended not to use these gatherings to promote the research being undertaken at Monash by her colleagues. She spoke brilliantly when reporting on case studies of children she had diagnosed and arranged programs for.

Professor Neale remained at loggerheads with many in the faculty, including staff in Area 7 over her role and that of the Krongold. In March 1982 the new Dean, Professor Peter Fensham, together with the Vice-Chancellor, brokered a peace when she became a research professor for exceptional children, with funds for her to continue her work and research. This gave her the chance of being at arm's length from the faculty. The cost of this was the faculty losing access to the Krongold facilities for teaching special education. The Krongold under Neale was separated from the faculty. To complicate matters, it became clear that a new role for the centre was needed as there were significant policy changes at state and federal levels, with funding consequences. There was a massive shift to 'mainstreaming' and 'integration'.

The university convened a special committee to review the Krongold Centre in 1986, having in mind Professor Neale's retirement at the end of 1987. Professor N W Murray chaired this review; Dick White was also a member. A parent representative from the Krongold Centre, Karen Ekberg-Sands, also served on this committee and delivered a minority report, but the majority report won the day and their recommendations were accepted.[26]

The latter years of Neale's time at Monash coincided with this swing by governments to a mainstreaming approach to children with special needs. This was contrary to Marie Neale's emphasis: she retained her interests in assisting children with special needs with diagnosis and the prescription of specific appropriate programs. She was not alone in holding this view, but it was at odds with what both state and federal governments were then financing.

---

[26] Monash University Archives MON 480 folders 35 & 36 Krongold Centre Review Committee report March 1987. Ekberg-Sands minority report reflected the concerns of some parents at the implied criticism of Professor Marie Neale.

Professor Marie Neale retired at the end of 1987 and despite her differences with the faculty she had achieved much and many children and parents were to be ever grateful for her work.[27]

In September 2001, Professor Neale together with Henry and Dinah Krongold attended a special event to celebrate the Krongold Centre's 25th anniversary. At this event Henry Krongold said 'the vision we shared with Professor Marie Neale has provided us with an object of love and perpetual motivation'. Professor Neale said the centre had 'transformed and extended the range of our work for children with special needs'.[28]

The Krongold today

Since 2001, both the Krongold Centre and the Elwyn Morey Centre have maintained a very high quality community service for children, adolescents and occasionally adults with special needs. The applied work of these centres has been enriched by a renewed emphasis on research and clinical and applied professional training within them. This has stemmed from the appointment of Professor Dennis Moore as professor of special education and Director of the Krongold Centre. Moore has very ably facilitated the growth and development of both centres in recent years with particular emphasis on research. The Elwyn Morey Centre, which started many years ago as a kindergarten program within the Faculty of Education under the guidance and creative enthusiasm of Associate Professor Elwyn Morey, went on to develop inclusive programs for children with special needs. Later, it became a specialised early intervention centre with the help of its current directors Rosalind Patterson and Diane Chandler, both highly qualified and experienced consultant teachers, in association with its then chair, Dr Lawrence Bartak. The Krongold Centre has likewise continued to provide research, consultancy and training facilities for psychologists, teachers and other professional staff and has continually adapted to up-to-date policies on inclusion of children with special needs in mainstream schools.

---

[27] Professor Marie Neale died on 20 December 2011, aged 89 years.
[28] Monash University Archives, Monash University Memo 12 September 2001.

Chapter 5

Good times

1981–1988

The budget razor

The 1980s was a difficult decade for universities. Universities in Australia had become more susceptible to the whims of changing governments as well as changing economic circumstances. In 1980 Monash University's budget was reduced by $300,000 and the education faculty had to bear a cut of $100,000 – one third of the total university cut! The Vice-Chancellor urged the faculty to delay filling the vacant chair caused by Ron Taft's retirement. Faculty Board expressed concern over the cuts and the deleterious effect they could have, especially so given the present staff-student ratio, which compared unfavourably with the rest of the university and with other universities. It also argued that while the TEC had recommended reduced initial training places, this did not necessarily apply to all institutions. The Faculty of Education also had a higher proportion of staff on fixed-term appointments compared with other faculties and other universities. On top of this was the loss of secondments. It all meant an increased workload for existing staff. In particular there was a need for a core of continuing appointments to maintain basic faculty responsibilities in the method area.[1] The concerns about this situation expressed by both the staff and the Faculty Board were simply noted by the University Council.[2] The principle enunciated by Louis Matheson at the founding of the faculty, that education would be treated the same way as other faculties, had been seriously eroded.

---

[1] Monash University Archives, MON 61 Minutes of Faculty Board 10 September 1980.
[2] At the meeting on 5 November 1980.

Losing secondments

The news came after a meeting with the Department of Education at which they declared that from 1980 there would be no unpaid secondments of teachers to educational institutions.[3] Howard Brown, who was seconded as a method lecturer in geography, recalls that there were 42 teachers seconded by the Department of Education to Monash in the late 1970s – the equivalent of 14 full-time teachers – and they were all sent back to their schools in 1980. This was far from a purely financial blow – the faculty lost people who were at the chalkface in teaching students the subject they were assisting in at Monash and who also took back to the schools ideas and developments they absorbed in the faculty. The culture of secondment had created close relationships between the faculty and the schools, to the benefit of both.

The then Director-General of Education, Dr Norman Curry, was sympathetic to the universities and to the secondment of teachers, but pressure was being applied to the department by the government. As Curry stated in a letter to the Dean: 'we do want to encourage universities to use such staff but constraints have been placed on us by the Department of Management and Budget.'[4] The cost of these secondments was high and on-costs to the basic salary were very high – 25 per cent for such teachers compared with the usual 7 per cent.[5] Various other arrangements were tried but did not really succeed, and on-costs by 1987 had risen to 31 per cent. There was much talk of the 'highly valued contributions' these teachers made and the 'abiding influence the Ministry has which will be lost'.[6]

The years 1980–81 saw three significant retirements: Ron Taft, Ray McCulloch and Norm Dobson. Selby Smith had a policy of appointing a wide variety of staff according to multiple criteria, including experience. These three retirements represented experienced staff that he had appointed. Taft brought an established reputation in psychology that enhanced the standing of the faculty. Ray McCulloch, as an experienced and successful education administrator, brought experience as well as erudition, which gave credibility to the faculty's offerings in educational administration. Norm

---

[3] Monash University Archives, MON Minutes Faculty Board 4 July 1979.
[4] Monash University Archives, MON 480 Letter from Dr Norman Curry Director-General of Education to Professor Peter Fensham, Dean of Education, 27 March 1985.
[5] Monash University Archives, MON 480 Letter from Professor Peter Fensham Dean of Education to Dr Norman Curry Director-General of Education 19 November 1984.
[6] Monash University Archives, MON 489 John Theobald, coordinator of DipEd to Ian Cathie, Minister for Education 7 June 1985. The on-cost figure was to reach 47 per cent in 1988: it included holiday pay loading, long service leave, payroll tax, Workcare, superannuation (21.5 per cent), and administrative costs of 3.4 per cent.

Dobson, an experienced teacher of history and social studies, also brought his capacity for efficient administration, as shown by his work creating the office of Sub-Dean.

Eventually Taft's chair was advertised. Richard T White, more commonly known as Dick White, was appointed to the chair. While some in the psychology area viewed him as a science educator and learning theorist, he was a member of the Australian Psychological Society and had published extensively in the leading psychology journals; his background made him ideal for a chair in education in the area of psychology.

Dean

In 1981 the issue of the deanship arose again, as Professor Musgrave, who had taken the post with some reluctance, was unwilling to take a further term.[7] He had been a successful dean.

An appreciation of Musgrave and his role as dean was well expressed by another dean, Professor Dick White. He wrote the following tribute upon Musgrave's death in 2011:

> Peter Musgrave came to the chair of sociology in education in 1970, when the Faculty of Education was in its youth – a time of excitement, growth, and burgeoning research.
>
> Peter was well suited to the time: his scholarly interests were broad, and his aim was to integrate diverse fields into a comprehensive sociology of education. This breadth enabled him to be an effective leader of a vigorous group of scholars who covered a wide spectrum of fields, in politics, economics, sociology, and comparative education.
>
> Peter was a prolific scholar of international renown. The Monash library holds 29 of his books, and he wrote hundreds of articles. His output was a model for his colleagues to follow, and was a factor in Monash having the pre-eminent faculty of education in Australia. Peter did much to encourage research among his colleagues. He was assiduous in attending research seminars, whatever the topic, where he made frequent, helpful, and positive contributions.
>
> As well as research, Peter was active in teaching and supervising research students. Administration was less to his taste, though he was

---

[7] Monash University Archives MON 61 Minutes of Faculty Board 4 March 1981.

competent at it. A few years after he had come to the faculty, the Vice-Chancellor prevailed on him to be Pro-Vice Chancellor. Peter moved to the 'Castle,' but within a week he was back in the faculty, having found that managing the parking committee and similar tasks was far from what he wanted to do.

Peter did not seek to be Dean, but when the mantle fell on him in 1977 he accepted it as a duty, which he discharged with integrity, fairness, and tolerance. Actually, for someone who was not eager to be Dean, it was not a bad time to have the job. His predecessors, Selby Smith and Sid Dunn, had established sound systems of administration; he had strong support from colleagues. Consequently Peter did not find the deanship as onerous as he might have feared. He continued to have time to write, teach, and attend seminars. He was a visible, and respected, Dean.

Eventually, after much delay and negotiation, Professor Peter Fensham was persuaded to take the post, which he did on 1 January 1982. There followed one of the most significant deanships in the faculty's history. It was a difficult time; a period of economic stringency. The difficult financial times meant that no appointments would be made with a result that there was a disproportionate number of fixed-term appointments. Despite this Fensham was to have a major and enduring impact on the faculty. While he was to complete his term as dean in 1988, he did not retire until the end of 1992. In 2005 the new science laboratories built on the fourth floor were named in his honour.

Faculty governance

The Monash Review Committee's rulings set back the faculty's plans to move to more democratic governance involving non-professorial staff. The report irked the faculty. Participation of non-professorial staff had worked well and the majority of the professors, while keen not to be seen to shirk their responsibilities, were happy with these arrangements. Only Professor Neale, who had been one of the instigators of the governance review, was not happy with non-professorial appointments to key positions.

The terms areas, divisions and groups were employed for many years in the history of the faculty, when the faculty was only at Clayton. They were really the same thing: quasi-departments, the basis of which came from the way the original Diploma of Education course was structured in 1964, with its four 'foundation' subjects.

These grew into seven divisions. They were:

1. psychological studies
2. social and comparative studies
3. historical and philosophical studies
4. research and evaluation in curriculum-specific subjects and teaching
5. curriculum studies in theory and practice of specific subjects
6. educational administration
7. special education.[8]

The divisions were more commonly known by their numbers.

These 'quasi-departments' elected members to key faculty committees, but as they were not formal departments they did not have budgetary functions or in university terms, legal status.

The question of how best to govern the faculty remained an issue – various forms of reorganisation were put forward in 1984 and 1985; the Dean suggested a structure of three groups, while John Hunt proposed a four-group structure. Hunt's proposal saw a group comprising all the psychologists; another group for social science, educational administration, studies and social science methods; a third for history, English, languages and philosophy; and a fourth comprising staff involved in physics, biology, science, science methods, curriculum and evaluation studies.

The Dean had sent a document around for reorganising the faculty. As well as the change of areas to divisions to John Hunt's four groups, the chair of level committees was to be appointed by the Dean on the advice of all staff. There were to be four elected staff representatives from each group on the all-important Planning and Development (P&D) Committee. This was all to come into effect from 1986.

There was much discussion of the proposed reorganisation, and at a staff meeting the following resolution was carried:

> Staff confirm their continuing commitment to the system of maximum individual autonomy in teaching and research, both for reasons of academic freedom and for reasons of morale and quality of work. As corollary where group decisions are taken they be made within a participatory structure.[9]

---

[8] Monash University Archives MON 496 Minutes of Staff Meeting 17 October 1984.
[9] Monash University Archives MON 496 Minutes of Staff Meeting 6 March 1985.

5.1 Four Deans: Professor Peter Fensham, Professor Peter Musgrave, Professor Syd Dunn, and Professor Richard Selby Smith. Christmas Party, 1981.
MUA IN-260

It was a period of significant change in every way – technology especially – and there were seemingly endless government committees or commissions all requiring responses. These included the National Advisory Committee on Computers in Schools report (1983), the Victorian Participation and Equity Program, which represented a new thrust from the earlier emphasis on transition from school to work, and the Blackburn Report on secondary schooling.

Administration and staff matters

The faculty was well served by good administrators under faculty secretary Lindsay Shaw, who, while quiet and retiring in manner, was effective and well informed. He was supported by a succession of competent assistants: Lee Chessman, Vin Massaro (who went on to very senior administrative posts) and Margrette (formerly Waldron) Fairbanks. Fairbanks was not only a competent administrator – she joined in fully with the life of the faculty generally, be it the choir or social events, during her 21 years there.[10] She was a key administrator as deputy to the Faculty Secretary. As such she had heavy responsibilities as the Faculty grew and she serviced many of the main committees. She confessed to being bored sometimes with some

---

[10] Margrette Fairbanks was at the faculty from May 1980 until October 2001.

5.2 Margrette Fairbanks.
Claude Sironi, Education Faculty

of the committees. She recalls 'I remember being bored in Staff Meetings and writing my own version of faculty minutes (unpublishable) in my head, watching Ailsa knitting her family history, Wyn Owen slowly munching on an apple trying to chew quietly, Marie Neale sitting directly in front of Peter Musgrave and embarassing him with a show of legs and cleavage, and others sneaking in late to sit in the back row against the wall, or to just nod off! Dave Murphy held court at the front desk.[11] Other notable general staff were Elaine Scott (1969–1990), Pat Sharples,[12] Connie Stuart (1970–1987), Lee Chessman and Val Newson, who followed Hilda Mayberry as secretary to the Dean in 1970 until her retirement in 1990. Others of note were Jean Shaw, Daphne Attwood, Judith Marks, Kath Kinnear and Janine McAlpine. Sharon Cook (née Butler) resigned for family reasons in 1988 after 14 years in the faculty, having commenced as a young junior in 1974 – her work dealing with student enquiries was especially valued. The highly

---

[11] David Murphy had been a plasterer who worked on the Menzies Building. When he retired at supposedly 65 years, he confessed that he was actually 10 years older. His wife was head of the faculty cleaning staff.

[12] Pat Sharples died in May 2010.

5.3 Lindsay Shaw, the Faculty Secretary, was also a benefactor to the library, donating a large collection of Australian children's books, with rare books librarian Susan Radvansky (left) and Brenda Niall (right), 1981.
Richard Crompton, MUA IN-6966

competent Bev Schneider headed the general office, supported by Heather Phillips and two sisters who ran the duplicating: Frances Boyle and Hazel Evans. There were other too, like the warm-hearted Margaret Morgan.

The retirements of Gilchrist, Musgrave, Selleck and Shaw marked the start of a series of retirements, unsurprising, given the age structure of the faculty. When Shaw retired, he was the third Faculty Secretary (or Assistant Registrar as they were sometimes called), and it was stated that the faculty owed much to him for his 'great administrative skills and judgement and for his willingness to serve the Faculty in so many ways'.[13] Shaw was followed as Faculty Secretary by Sue Aspinall. Aspinall had previously worked in

---

[13] Monash University Archives, MON 49 (22) Papers to Staff Meeting Faculty of Education, 29 May 1986.

administrative posts in the arts and engineering faculties, and with the University Council Secretariat. She had also been seconded to the State Board of Education in 1985.

There was a significant group of new staff appointed in 1983: Margaret Brumby to Group 5, Glenn Rowley to Group 4, David Bennett to Group 6, Chris Sharpley to Group 1 and Lesley Hardcastle (who had been a full-time secondment), to Group 5.

There was an important breakthrough in the malaise over new appointments when four continuing lectureships were appointed. These were all to be highly significant: Dr Shirley Sampson, Ann McDougall, Peter Gronn and Glenn Rowley. On the downside, Michael Norman, Helen Smith and Helen Praetz all resigned. Sampson's appointment was welcomed as she was a pioneer of education for women and girls, and had previously been on a fixed-term contract. Ann McDougall, who came from Melbourne State College, had computer education expertise; Peter Gronn came into educational administration and Glenn Rowley, a respected lecturer from La Trobe University, came into a key research advisory role.

Wyn Owen took over as Sub-Dean from July 1982 to September 1982 and then John Fyfield returned to the post until June 1983.

Barbara Lewis, who had been foundation director of the Elwyn Morey Child Study Centre, resigned in April 1986 after 20 years of service. Barbara Lewis was a quiet, unassuming director who was experienced, highly competent and coped well with the demands of running a normal kindergarten at the centre as well as satisfying the research needs and investigations of faculty staff. She was replaced by Margaret Moody (assisted by John McCarten and Jennifer Young).[14]

Another significant loss was Diana Davis, who had achieved so much in English method and in the faculty generally. Davis was appointed in late 1988 to the Foundation Chair of Language, Arts and Education at James Cook University, Townsville.

Connie Stuart resigned in 1987. Stuart was secretary to Group 2, one of a formidable group of highly competent people who were professorial secretaries with responsibilities to the administration of the groups. There was Lee Chessman followed by Judy Marks for Group 1, Lorraine Elliott for Group 3 and Pat Sharples for Group 4 and Group 5, and later, Cath Henderson. Graham Wallington (technician) and Lorraine Elliot (secretary to Group 3) retired in 1988.

---

[14] Monash University Archives MON 496 (22) Minutes of Staff Meeting 18 February 1987.

An Honorary Doctor of Laws was awarded to the faculty's second Dean, Professor S S Dunn.[15] There was celebration too when Pierre Gorman was awarded a CBE in the honours list. Both Dunn and Gorman were associates of the faculty. Bill Connell continued as a fellow. The setting up of a Victorian government Long-Term Planning Committee, announced in August 1980, comprised three Monash names: Alan Gregory, Don Cochrane and Mitchell McKenzie.

Razor gang

There was uncertainty about the effect the reintroduction of university fees for second degrees and higher degrees would have on enrolments, with a reduction in enrolments to somewhere between a half and a third of current numbers forecast. The earlier abolition of fees had caused an upsurge in higher degree enrolments, especially among women, and married male teachers took advantage of this as the absence of fees meant there was not a toll on family finances.[16]

In the period when there were no fees there was a surplus of applicants for masters degree courses, so not all of them could be admitted. With the re-introduction of fees, the faculty soon stopped meeting target enrolments. Further cuts by the Commonwealth government 'razor gang' meant the abolition of two bodies – the Curriculum Development Centre (CDC) and the Educational Research and Development Committee. The faculty had enjoyed close links with both of these federal bodies.

In 1981 the faculty had 274 EFTS in DipEd. For DipEd Psych there were 39, BEd 80, BSpecEd 49, MEd Studies 498, MEd by minor thesis 27, MEd by thesis 138, and PhD 51, with a total faculty EFTS of 1125.92.[17]

In 1982 staff who left were not replaced and there was a 7 per cent reduction in the faculty budget.[18]

In-service training

There had been various forms of in-service training made available by faculty members. This was in addition to the formal courses and the efforts

---

[15] Monash University Archives MON 61 Minutes Faculty Board 2 November 1983.
[16] This point was made by Margrette Fairbanks in a communication to the author, 16 April 2012.
[17] Monash University Archives MON 496 folder 246, 10 August 1983.
[18] Monash University Archives MON 61 Minutes of Faculty Board 15 July 1981, and 9 September 1981.

5.4 Mordialloc High School students Jason Dennis and Reena Flemington with Dr Diana Davis, 1986.
Richard Crompton, MUA IN-637

of individuals to respond to requests from schools and groups to speak or give advice.

While starting in 1979, in 1981 this was formalised into what was called the Monash Teachers' Centre. The intention was to make the faculty's human and material resources available to local schools and schools with Monash connections, and to provide opportunities for teachers to meet away from their workplace. On its committee of management were local teachers, principals, inspectors and faculty representatives, with faculty member Lawrence Ingvarson playing a key role. During 1981 there were 3,000 people participating in centre activities. The Department of Education had seconded primary teacher Lois Johnson half-time to help run the centre. When Johnson arrived, the centre was given an extra lift. She was a gifted organiser but was also excellent with people. The centre became so busy that Johnson had to serve full-time from 1984. The centre catered for the professional development needs of teachers, with curriculum days, meetings with overseas educators, workshops, courses in teaching techniques and forums on curriculum issues such as the Blackburn Report, computers in school and multiculturalism.[19] For the 1985 program Johnson reported that of the 3,000 participants in centre activities, 1,253 were primary teachers, 728 post-primary and 1,094 others. Graham Lee was chairman for a period, and also principal of Monash High School. He later moved to Blackburn High. When Lois Johnson relinquished this position to return to schools she was accorded a farewell lunch by the staff. The first course served was teddy-bear biscuits, a symbol of the hospitality she had dispensed.

Parent-Teacher Education Centre

A successful centre in the 1980s in the faculty was one inspired by Associate Professor Maurice Balson. Balson, a psychologist and foundation member of staff, was a charismatic figure and as a lecturer had the gift of translating psychological concepts and ideas into understandable terms to his audience. He was well-versed in the areas of psychology relevant to teaching, parenting and children. He embraced an Adlerian framework, which was offered to masters degree students in Individual Psychology Part I, II and III. Over 200 students undertook these courses at the masters and doctoral levels over four years. Much sought after to talk to teacher and parent groups, Balson established the Parent-Teacher Education Centre. The centre began with a seeding grant from the Vice-Chancellor and some 1,300 people attended its launch in Robert Blackwood Hall. Dame Elisabeth Murdoch supported the concept and donated $50,000 to the centre.

The centre offered six-week courses to parents, teachers, pre-schools and community health centres. MEd students were involved in these courses, acting as counsellors, co-counsellors and group leaders. In its first year the centre presented over 120 seminars to community groups, while over 300 parents and teachers attended courses there. The centre had administrative staff and a committee comprised of faculty members, school teachers and parents. The centre flourished for a number of years but relied much on the skill and enthusiasm of Maurie Balson, who retired in 1994. The Adlerian Society of Australia was launched from this centre. The new Dean, Professor David Aspin, considered parent education irrelevant to the wider faculty and withdrew support. The centre moved from Monash and was replaced by a community-based centre.

---

[19] Paper by Lawrence Ingvarson on the Monash Teachers Centre, October 1985.

Methods

The end of 'free' secondments from the Department of Education was a setback. The faculty had enjoyed a high reputation for its work in the various teaching methods. This was particularly true of economics and commercial education, which was extended to include the new Legal Studies subject. The faculty was the first place to offer Method and Practice of Teaching Legal Studies (in 1974). In 1972 there had been 100 students taking economics method but by the 1980s the figure had dropped to the 30s. The commercial method attracted smaller numbers. There had been a number of strong secondments in this field – people like John Brooke, Marli Wallace, Wilbur Courtis and Anita Forsyth in Economics; Leo Duffy and Ron Craven in Commercial Studies and Zenon Starnawski and David Brisset in Legal Studies.

David Brisset, for example, did his DipEd at Monash, became a secondary school teacher in 1970 and returned in 1977–79 as a method tutor in Commercial Studies, and then in 1981 became method lecturer in Legal Studies – a pioneering post which he held successfully until 2003 when he retired both from this post and teaching in secondary schools. An outstanding teacher, many generations benefited from his skills. John Brooke became a high school principal then moved into chartered accounting, becoming one of the state's leading insolvency accountants. In retirement he became a notable farmer, mayor of his shire and a key member of state water boards in central and western Victoria. Marli Wallace became a leading figure in education and vocational training, holding many nation-wide consultancies. Anita Forsyth was yet another figure who would make a major contribution to the faculty.

The economics and commercial group had strong links with the Victorian Commercial Teachers Association (one of the most successful of the subject associations).[20] Monash had a first in offering advanced method work in these areas at the masters level. Other methods could also boast outstanding staff: Lesley Hardcastle and Lesley Farrell in English, Eli Brererton in Geography, Ann Feehan, Anne Barber and Joan Sheen in History and Ian Mitchell and Ray Anderson in Science. The synergy with the profession and with subject associations was of crucial importance in establishing a culture that embraced research into practice. For example, the Australian Association for the Teaching of English established the position of 'research

---

[20] This organisation owned its own premises and conducted an extensive publishing business as well as an active professional development programme.

officer', an honorary position held first by Brother Kevin King (St Kevin's College) and then by Diana Davis.

Mathematics

There had been a strong mathematics group within the faculty, well served by the foundation method staff (who were part-time), but it was given more strength with the full-time appointment of first Theo MacDonald and then Ken Clements. Clements was multi-talented and an energetic staff member who gave great life to mathematics. During the early part of his eight years at Monash, Clements began to wonder about the possibility of establishing a national mathematics education research association, with annual conferences and a journal. In 1976, John Foyster (of ACER) and Clements established the Mathematics Education Research Group of Australia (MERGA). The first annual MERGA conference was held in the Rotunda theatres at Monash in 1977, with over 100 mathematics educators in attendance. Clements was keynote speaker at the 35th annual MERGA conference, held in Singapore in 2012. Walking around the Monash corridors in the late 1970s were young scholars interested in becoming fully qualified mathematics education researchers. Among these were Barbara Clarke, David Clarke, Doug Clarke, Phil Clarkson, Gilah Leder, Charles Lovitt, Anne Newman, Dianne Siemon, and Ross Turner – all of whom were young, impressive and destined to make a huge impact on mathematics education, not only in Victoria, but also in Australia and indeed across the world.

Clements recalls the Faculty of Education during his time (1974–1982) as an amazing place to work. As a young scholar he found himself rubbing shoulders, every day, with internationally recognised and extraordinarily active scholars like Peter Fensham, Syd Dunn, Dick Selleck, Peter Musgrave, Ron Taft, Marie Neale, Dick White, Dick Tisher and Ailsa Zainu'ddin. The very impressive science education group included Elaine Atkinson, Peter Fensham, Paul Gardner, John Gipps, Dick Gunstone, Lindsay Mackay, Jeff Northfield, Dick Tisher and Dick White. At that time, many top-flight international science educators visited Monash, and he well remembers when Peter Fensham asked him if he would nominate a top international mathematics educator to be invited to visit Monash. Clements suggested Dr Alan Bishop (then at Cambridge University) and Bishop and his family came to Monash for the second half of 1977. He remembers Bishop's wonderful contributions at Monash at that time. Of course, years later, Alan would move from Cambridge to become professor of mathematics education at Monash University.

Northfield had a keen interest in teacher research, and in 1983 he and Dick Gunstone took a Year 7 science class for the whole year in order to explore how children learn in the classroom. Northfield repeated this in 1993, taking a Year 7 science and maths class. It was a bold thing to do. He received with Ian Mitchell a major ARC Research grant in 1995–97 and again in 1998–2000.

When Clements left, Dudley Blane came from the UK. Stillwell from the mathematics department had made an important contribution to the education faculty but he surrendered this link to move full-time into mathematics. Gilah Leder joined the faculty in mathematics, marking the start of a noteworthy career. It was estimated that 38 per cent of mathematics education research in Australia occurred at Monash. In 1983 there was five PhD students and nine MEd students doing maths research, and in DipEd there were 60 students taking Basic Mathematics.[21] In 1984 Leder and Blane proposed having a Mathematics Education Centre, which they were to bring to fruition.[22]

TESOL

A major breakthrough came in 1988 when the faculty received a major grant for Jim Wheeler to inaugurate the postgraduate Diploma in TESOL (Teaching English to Speakers of Other Languages). It was a significant grant since it provided, for starters, for a fixed-term lecturer. The lecturer appointed was Christine Riddell.

The MEd subject Methods and Practice of TESOL was offered to 40 students in two classes, one taken by Christine Riddell and the other by a sessional lecturer from Footscray TAFE. Jim Wheeler was overall supervisor. There was considerable conviviality and bonding between all 40 students with a roster drawn up for catering for refreshments during the morning break. It was high-pressure teaching and learning but was much appreciated by those students for whom a place couldn't be found in the regular semester classes. All TESOL classes were capped at twenty students and were always over-subscribed (i.e. more students than places).

The faculty also provided a coherent MEd studies program in TESOL for a group of Chinese students. In first semester 1988 at least seven students

---

[21] Monash University Archives MON 61 Minutes of Faculty Board 7 September 1983.
[22] Monash University Archives MON 496 Minutes of Staff Meeting 8 August 1984.

specialising in TESOL enrolled. The students, chosen from universities throughout China, had superb English according to Wheeler, although they had never before been outside China.

Multiculturalism

Another key area was what was then called 'multiculturalism' – a term Dr Brian Bullivant coined but which he later felt inappropriate. Bullivant, who had become a reader in 1982, was a pioneer in the field and active with the Centre for Migrant and Intercultural Studies that had been set up at Monash. He was chairman for a number of years and also research coordinator. The two key founders of the group were Bullivant and Professor Michael Clyne from linguistics. Others involved were Dr Gil Best, who served on the Centre for Migrant Studies, English method lecturer Diana Davis and languages methods lecturer Jim Wheeler. There was a 'multicultural' component in the DipEd as well as an elective, and there were opportunities for further study in the field at coursework and research degree levels.[23] Bullivant became a key figure in the multicultural movement. He wrote extensively on the area of ethnic groups, cultural pluralism and race. His main research interests were applied cultural anthropology, and he also undertook comparative studies in race and interethnic relations, as well as developing models of ethnocultural pluralism. Bullivant regarded much of what the faculty did as pedestrian and self-defeating and tried to point out new approaches, especially new approaches to research rather than quantitative ones. The faculty was a major figure in promoting work in what was then called 'multiculturalism'.

Historical work

There remained a strong historical group in the faculty. Ailsa Zainu'ddin led a women's studies group that looked at the history of education for women, with participation from people like Marj Theobald. Professor Dick Selleck led a strong history group in the faculty with Andy Spaull, Marty Sullivan and Ailsa Zainu'ddin. This group had an impressive list of publications in the history of education area, and also (for the Victorian Department of Education sesquicentenary) organised the Historic Schools Society of Victoria, which among other things produced *School Days*, a publication of extracts from the school readers, school paper and other departmental

---

[23] Monash University Archives MON 61 Minutes of Faculty Board 3 November 1982.

publications.[24] In terms of courses offered, Sullivan covered the colonial period of education up until 1872, Selleck covered from 1872 to 1920, and Spaull covered from 1920 until the Whitlam dismissal in 1972. Zainu'ddin offered courses in South-East Asian education as well as education for women. Later Selleck and Spaull offered a key subject entitled History of Public Policy, which attracted much interest.

Marj Theobald recalls chatting to the librarian at the Institute of Education Library in London, and, the name of Selleck coming up. Theobald explained that Selleck held a chair at Monash. The librarian exclaimed with surprise 'so that's where he went! The assumption being that someone who produced work of that quality had to come from Britain!

Project for Enhancing Effective Learning – PEEL

A project that was to prove a major breakthrough in educational thinking and practice was the PEEL project which emerged from research by some Monash scholars and soon developed into a major team project. Research in 1980 by Dick Gunstone and Dick White on aspects of learning by first-year physics students[25] revealed poor quality answers to what was considered elementary physics that shocked the researchers. Other projects also suggested that despite lessons which appeared successful, many students had little real understanding of what they were supposed to have learned.

One of these was a coursework masters research project focused on chemistry learning, which was undertaken by Ian Mitchell, then a full-time high school teacher and later a method lecturer in chemistry and a full-time staff member. Another contemporary research student in science education, John Baird, investigated metacognition – how learners understand and control their own learning – in both his thesis studies.

Initially, the link between Baird's research on metacognition and the growing number of studies of the nature of science students' understanding was not realised. Then in 1984 Mitchell presented his masters research at a science education research conference. Baird, later a lecturer in biology and biology method at the Melbourne College of Advanced Education, also presented a paper. Mitchell immediately saw the link to Baird's metacognition research and worked with him to put their ideas into practice in a two-year

---

[24] Monash University Archives MON 61 Minutes Faculty Board 8 September 1982.
[25] R F Gunstone and R T White 'Understanding of Gravity', in *Science Education*, 65, 1981, pp. 291–299.

5.5 Historians of education: Dr Ailsa Zainu'ddin, Professor R J W Selleck, Dr Andrew Spaull, and Dr Martin Sullivan.
Richard Crompton, MUA IN-7406

project at Mitchell's school, Laverton High School.[26] Mitchell and Baird led the group, but others in the Monash science group were also involved.

The project involved students being trained in the skills of learning with the aim of finding approaches to enable more effective and lasting learning. Recognising that ability was not intelligence, and that skills appropriate to the subject needed to be mastered by students, they aimed to achieve metacognition development in the study. From the very beginning the project embraced other subject areas as well as science, an inspired decision as the participating teachers were hearing many very helpful ideas across subject areas.

The challenges PEEL was tackling proved to be complex, and the first few months were very difficult. There were problems in getting students used to actually thinking rather than copying and memorising teacher notes.

---

[26] John Baird and Ian J Mitchell (eds) *Improving the Quality of Teaching and Learning: An Australian Case Study – the PEEL Project*, Monash University Printery, 1986.

5.6 PEEL consultants John Baird and Ian Mitchell, 1986.
Tony Miller, MUA IN-6399

Active learning was more tiring and demanding for them. Addressing these problems proved stimulating for the teachers and this action-research project had an impact on the teachers taking it as well as the students; the teachers became more metacognitive about their teaching and learned to change and improve their strategies.

At the end of the two-year project period the staff involved refused to allow it to end. It continued at Laverton High and two years later began to spread to other schools, nationally and then internationally. While each of the PEEL groups operates autonomously, there are networks, meetings, a journal, conferences and short courses to help participants share experiences. Much writing has emerged from the project both in terms of articles by PEEL participants for teachers and schools as well as articles by academics on the significance on learning and metacognition thinking. This project is still ongoing and has had a major effect on pupils and teachers as well on learning theory. It was an unfunded initiative that started from a team of education faculty people.[27]

PEEL continued to be successful and in the Australia Day Honours list of 2011, Ian Mitchell was awarded the Medal of the Order of Australia (OAM) in recognition of his leadership role with PEEL.

Equality of opportunity

Questions of equal opportunity for men and women and especially improving the situation of girls and women in education were often at the forefront and in 1984 a faculty committee comprising Margaret Brumby and John Theobald looked at the situation from a staffing viewpoint. They found that at the senior level women had a representation of 7:38. At lecturer level it was a more equitable 8:9; at the tutor, teaching fellow level it was 19:5. They noted that university policy in regard to any appointment was 'the best person for the job'. There was a problem of gender imbalance at senior levels and less likelihood of females contributing to leadership and decision making. It also noted that women in the faculty had attracted sizeable research grants and were well represented on major committees. A later committee was also set up comprising Margaret Gill, Ann Shorten and Rosamund Winter.[28]

Technology

The technical staff were very useful members of the faculty, helping the academic staff with their teaching, research and other events such as public seminars. The 1980s saw rapid changes in technology. With $70,000 set aside for equipment, the faculty was able, thanks to careful stewardship, to afford to buy a colour television set and also a word processor for the general office. The word processor was operated by the faculty research typist, who had to undertake special training, and academic staff were amazed that their research could be 'kept' on this new machine. The original one used was a Wang. A problem arose later as technology changed and early processors became obsolete. How was one to retain the earlier work which had been typed in to the machine? The 1980s really saw the effects of changing technology. There were the consequences of the microchip revolution. Colour TVs were now affordable for schools, there were new concepts like telematics,

---

[27] Rosamund Winter reports that in 2014 the PEEL database is still significant and regularly searched by current students.
[28] For Rosamund Winter's recollections of her time at Monash, Chapter 9.

5.7 PEEL in the primary classroom.
Claude Sironi, Education Faculty

5.8 Ian Mitchell working with primary students on a PEEL project.
Claude Sironi, Education Faculty

ergonomics, digital video and audio, micro computers, computer-generated graphics, AUSSAT satellites and teleconferencing. This created enormous problems for the faculty – the new equipment was quickly obsolete and more new equipment had to be purchased. The equipment had to be maintained and in-service training was urgently required so people knew how to use the new technology.

General interests

Contemporary issues were responded to by the faculty, whether major reports such as the Blackburn Report and the issue of integration in schools, or 'state of the art' reports where Faculty Board heard from different staff members each meeting about their work. Some of these were John McArthur on nurse education, Gil Best on hearing loss in children, Judith Chapman on the principalship, Wyn Owen on teacher stress, Diana Davis on language and English, and Shirley Sampson on affirmative action and equal opportunity.

In 1981 Diana Davis reported to Faculty Board about the major changes in language teaching over the last ten years – how foreign languages had changed from just French and German to a wide range now. There were also sizeable numbers of students doing higher degree work in languages. In the DipEd there was language across the curriculum, a requirement for all students in all streams. There was a range of language options now in DipEd electives and courses in second language and bilingual education.[29]

In the 1980s the two secondments in Modern Language Methods were due to return to their schools because they had received promotions. Jim Wheeler decided to make more use of sessional staff. There had always been a sessional tutor in Indonesian since that language was made available in Modern Language Methods. In the 1980s there were students whose languages were, besides the 'traditional' French, German and Indonesian, students with undergraduate qualifications in Chinese, Italian, Japanese and modern Greek. Accordingly sessional tutors were engaged to give tutorials on Friday afternoons after the Friday morning two-hour lecture/seminar class. The sessional tutors were all outstanding practising teachers of the language concerned and were released by their school principals to undertake the work. Considerable organisation was required: the teachers had to be found – not so difficult because outstanding teachers in any language were well known. They had to be first informally approached, then the school

---

[29] Monash University Archives MON 496 Faculty Board Minutes 7 July 1982.

principals formally requested to grant time off. The tutors were briefed on the Modern Language Methods course. Contracts were offered and signed. Friday afternoon was Modern Language Methods afternoon in the faculty because the rest of the faculty, like the rest of the university, were not keen on Friday afternoon sessions.

An important development occurred in 1981, when Victoria College was formed by the amalgamation of a group of Teachers' Colleges – Burwood, Rusden and Toorak together with the non-TAFE part of Prahran College. This formed a college of 5,500 EFTS with 7,600 students (65 per cent of whom were in teacher education) and 750 staff.

The field of educational administration was a specialty that was taken up by many within the Victorian teaching service. The masters courses expanded rapidly. Ray McCulloch headed this area of the faculty. In the early years he and Ron King offered most of the courses with King specialising in innovation and change. When King left Warren Mellor came in as a Senior Lecturer later joined by John McArthur.

The initial popularity of courses in educational administration came from a push in North America, where there was a certification of school administrators, together with the expansion of administrative posts within the schools and school systems. People keen on such careers better equipped themselves by obtaining qualifications in this field. The course attracted large numbers of students, many of them teachers in senior positions in schools. Ray McCulloch was respected as an experienced administrator with functional expertise. Mellor took over the work in innovation and change, but added forecasting and planning and his own areas of expertise. McCulloch, an experienced administrator himself, brought wisdom, while Mellor had a doctorate in the field, was well versed in modern developments and was keen to develop links with Asia. (Mellor was to go on to senior education posts with UNESCO). There was a demand from many Asian nations for such courses, although Monash proved slow to respond. John McArthur was another key member of the team and he also had IT and computer expertise. Permanent appointments came with Judith Chapman (1980) and Peter Gronn (1981), both of whom were to go on to prestigious chairs. Use was also made of shorter term appointments, and people of the calibre of Michael Norman and Allen Hulls (RMIT) helped. Hulls, who was deputy principal of RMIT, also completed his doctorate in the faculty under Mellor. There were a series of short term appointments to fill gaps for staff on leave, so the team had Jeff Kaiser, Ean Seaton, Mac MacPherson and the experienced administrator Michael Norman. The courses attracted principals and vice-principals from Victorian schools, some of whom continued on to doctoral studies, and some overseas students also undertook doctorates in this field.

When Ray McCulloch retired in 1981, Warren Mellor became Head of the educational administration group. Monash was first in the field but it set off courses in other institutions and the Department of Education also set up its own Victorian College of Educational Administration in Geelong.

The extent of staff's research interests and involvement with outside bodies is illustrated by one staff meeting in 1986, at which it was noted that five staff members had received ARC grants, five had received Monash Research Fund grants, there were two postdoctoral fellows (Dr Hannah Arzi and Dr Marjorie Theobald), Judith Chapman was doing work for the National Conference of Secondary Principals and the State Board of Education, Diana Davis was involved with the Australian Student Project, Gerald Burke with the Centre for Higher Education at the University of Melbourne, Jeff Northfield was doing work for the Regional Board of Education, Stewart Sykes was involved with integration and the relevant Department of Education taskforce and Dick Tisher was doing work for the Australian College of Nursing.[30]

DipEd

In March 1988 Dr John Theobald relinquished his appointment as DipEd coordinator. He had been in poor health with a chronic back problem for some time. He had administrative responsibility for the DipEd since the outset and he coped with the complex problems of rapidly expanding numbers and finding places for these students in schools, while also ensuring all students had appropriate experiences in these schools. For example, he always tried to provide students with a mix of school placements, high school, private school, technical school and even country school. His broad outlook also meant work with the method staff and those providing courses in the foundation subjects, not to mention addressing the needs of individual students. Theobald was a masterly organiser and a person of wisdom and kindness. His contribution to the faculty had been enormous.

Dr Jeff Northfield took over from him in a restructured post which combined the functions of coordinator with chair of the DipEd Committee itself, and he was to be called Director of the Diploma in Education. While the

---

[30] Monash University Archives MON 496 Minutes of Staff Meeting, 9 April 1986.

move made sense, the DipEd committee were miffed it was done without reference to them.[31]

During the 1980s the 'quality' of the DipEd students seemed to deteriorate – with many finding teaching less attractive. As Margrette Fairbanks reflected 'the move to higher degrees coincided with the time that DipEd lost some of its status and from an administrator's perspective appeared to cause a rift or hierarchy to emerge among the academic staff'.[32]

BEd

In 1982 Dr Paul Gardner,[33] chair of the Bachelor of Education Committee, reported to Faculty Board on what he called 'the rise and fall' of the BEd. In 1974 there were 57 subjects offered in the BEd taken by 565 students. Following the decision in December 1977 to offer the coursework MEd Studies degree, enrolments in 1978 were 357 and by 1981 they had dropped to 181.

The degree had functioned as a means of professional development for teachers without the requirements of a thesis or a major project. It also served as an avenue for entry into the masters thesis degree. There was the suggestion that with the MEd Studies degree coming in, the BEd should be abolished. However, there was still a demand for BEd, and the summer term was to be offered for a fifth time with 63 students taking the six subjects. There were also plans to consider non-graduate entry into the BEd – for example for experienced teachers who had a TPTC or TSTC.[34]

The DipEd Psych continued – serving the interests of those wishing to complete their psychology qualifications in order to be eligible for registration. Most of those who took the course were to work in educational settings as counsellors, guidance officers or social workers.

MEd Studies

There was a review of the highly successful Master of Educational Studies course. Wyn Owen chaired the committee of review.[35] The purpose was to

---

[31] Monash University Archives MON 496 (22) Minutes of Staff Meeting 13 April 1988; Simon Marginson *Monash: Remaking the University*, St Leonards, NSW, Allen and Unwin, 2000.
[32] Margrette Fairbanks, communication to the author 16 April 2012.
[33] For Paul Gardner's recollections of his time at Monash, see Chapter 9.
[34] Monash University Archives MON 61 Minutes of Faculty Board 3 March 1982.
[35] Monash University Archives MON 496 Minutes of Staff Meeting 6 June 1984.

be a coherent course to develop interest in education through coursework and independent study. It was to be a one-stage degree with six subjects plus an independent study. The independent study or project was either to involve a research investigation, construction or development of a curriculum and curricular materials, or a critical literature review. Guidelines were developed for the projects, including a suggested word length of 10,000 words for a single project and 20,000 words for a double project, with a maximum of 60,000 words. There were division advisors for the project, and while normally the supervisor would not be an examiner, they were now not excluded from examining. If an MEd Studies student showed a research orientation and a demonstrated research capacity they were not excluded from going on to the PhD. The introduction of the MEd Studies degree was especially important in that its central research project encouraged teachers in the classroom to explore problems central to their practice. While becoming familiar with the current theories in their teaching disciplines, teachers had the opportunity to road-test theories and their practical applications in their own school contexts. PEEL was one such example; Peter Durkin's exploration of James Britton's language-teaching principle was another. In addition, MEd Studies classes contained both secondary and primary teachers and administrators. While the latter were certainly in the minority, the opportunities for exchange and cross-fertilisation were beneficial and in many cases stimulated a broadening attitude change.

John McArthur did much to involve students who were interested in nursing education within the MED Studies degree. He was also engaged in research on nurse education, which became a specialty of the educational administration area of the faculty.[36] It was a loss to the faculty when John McArthur resigned in 1985 to take up a position of Chief Executive of the Australian Education Council, as it was then called – a national body comprised of the Ministers of Education of the states and the Commonwealth.[37]

Higher degrees

Chris Reynolds had undertaken a study of higher degree students in the Faculty of Education from 1966 to 1985, and as part of this did a survey with Helen Chan. He found that 87 per cent of such students were in employment while studying, that higher degree study was predominantly a part-time experience. He found students rated their supervisors highly and that the

---

[36] Monash University Archives MON 61 Minutes of Faculty Board 4 July 1984.
[37] Monash University Archives MON 496 Minutes of Staff Meeting 5 June 1985.

outcomes were intrinsic in nature. There seemed to be a genuine commitment to scholarship. The student did feel a lack of recognition and the need for networking. Reynolds felt the part-time student lacked a collegiate feeling that was experienced by the small group of full-time doctoral students. The high academic standing of the faculty had attracted students.[38]

In 1982 there were 114 students enrolled for MEd by major thesis and 79 PhD candidates. The MEd by coursework and minor thesis had been replaced by the MEd Studies, and was being phased out from 1978. In this period between 50–60 research degree candidates graduated each year. It showed the strong research component of the faculty. MEd Studies enrolments had risen to 360 EFTS. The MEd Studies was not envisaged as a research degree, although the MEd Studies had a project requirement, and for this there were two examiners who could not be the candidate's supervisor.

Rapid advances in technology provided problems for the Research Committee. Glenn Rowley, who had undertaken the important role of research advisor since 1984, warned of the move to personal computers and by 1989 there were 90 in the faculty with more to come. Rowley reported that during 1988 he had 322 appointments with students seeking advice for their research with statistical analysis or the use of computers.[39] Not only was Glenn Rowley an important advisor to a host of research students on their research methodology, but aided by Sharon Fitzgerald, he helped with statistics and in the days before Windows, helped with early computers running on DOS.

The Research Committee set the requirements for research degrees, approved admissions to candidate, helped link students with their topics and the selection of a supervisor and looked after the progress of the student. Sometimes the overseas qualifications of candidates had to be assessed. The committee gave extensions of time, dealt with problems candidates had, approved changes of supervisor and ultimately arranged for the examination of the thesis. There were sometimes issues arising from conflicting reports by examiners to resolve. The committee was mindful too of any investigation that could be intrusive of the subjects, such as students in schools, although a formal consideration of ethical questions was in the 1980s in its infancy; the bureaucratic requirements from ethics committees were yet to come. In 1984 the Director-General of Education sent out a memo of guidelines for

---

[38] Monash University Archives MON 496 (22) Minutes of Staff Meeting 5 November 1986.
[39] Monash University Archives MON 497 Research Committee Minutes 3 May 1989.

research in schools and researchers were now required to obtain permission for such school projects from the Department of Education.[40]

There had been concern with the rapid growth of higher degree work, of the apparent lack of difference in some cases between a minor thesis and a major thesis for the MEd. More significantly there was also concern at a lack of difference between a major thesis and a PhD thesis in some notable cases. This issue was raised with the Research Degrees Committee and Musgrave and Hunt were asked to draw up a statement on the matter. They responded: 'The essential difference between a Master's and a Doctor's thesis lies in the quality and is difficult to define... essentially a doctoral thesis is expected to make a significant contribution to a particular field of study. In particular, that would appear to entail greater mastery of a fields, greater originality in posing the research problem and greater sensitivity in identifying theoretical and possibly practical implications.'[41]

In terms of length the general rule of thumb was for a masters thesis to be about 60,000 words and a PhD thesis 100,000 words. The Assistant Registrar B D Shields in a memo said that the university recommended 120,000 words as a maximum for a PhD thesis.[42]

Dean Professor Fensham sent a memo to the Research Committee in 1987 drawing attention to the 'Faculty's high output of research, but the relatively low awareness of this in the education system as a whole'.[43] In the same year it was reported to the committee that in 1986 there had been 100 research projects undertaken, 15 books produced, 19 reports and 121 published papers in refereed journals.[44]

Paul Gardner, chair of the Research Committee, did a summary of major research projects gained by the faculty during the period 1985–87 and found that grants totalled $447,600. In this period had been 35 PhDs completed, and 37 masters thesis degrees. Staff had 189 publications in refereed journals, authored or co-authored 28 books, edited or written chapters for 104 books, written 22 refereed and published conference papers, published 36 monograph reports and 75 'other' publications.[45] A further report

---

[40] Memo No.4 4 June 1984 from Dr Norman Curry, Director-General, Education Department of Victoria.
[41] Monash University Archives MON 498, P J Musgrave and F J Hunt Research Degrees Committee minutes 29 June 1983.
[42] 21 June 1983 as reported to Research Degrees Committee meeting 29 June 1983.
[43] Monash University Archives MON 497 Research Committee Minutes 19 June 1987.
[44] Monash University Archives MON 497 Research Committee Minutes 5 November 1987.
[45] Monash University Archives MON 496 P L Gardner, chair Research Committee June 1988.

5.9 Mrs Ruth Webster and her supervisors Dr Glenn Rowley and Dr Chris Sharpley.
Richard Crompton, MUA IN-656

undertaken by former staff member John Fyfield in 1988 showed a similar pattern.[46] Fyfield gave a detailed report of each staff member, showing their current research and recent publications. It was an impressive report which confirmed the pre-eminent position of the faculty in educational research in Australia.

Special education

The faculty's involvement in special education continued. This related to children requiring exceptional teaching and teaching children with impairments and disabilities. Courses were offered at the bachelor and masters level as well as the specific Bachelor of Special Education course. The BSpecEd, although originally catering for 80 EFTS, now had 45 EFTS and had been a part-time course since 1970. There was a steady demand for the course, and students comprised about 62 per cent teachers from mainstream schools and 27 per cent teachers from special schools. The staff members in this field

---

[46] John Fyfield 'Research and Researcher in Education', Clayton, Vic., The Faculty of Education, Monash University, 1988.

were undertaking research in giftedness, middle ear problems, borderline psychotic children and autism.[47] However, there was a strong move externally away from the traditional way of assisting children with special needs. This was exemplified by the Victorian Ministerial Review of Education Services for the Disabled (1984). This report saw the current system in the state as complex, fragmented and firmly based on the principle of categorisation. This review emphasised the right to educate all children in regular schools, and no one was to be categorised because of a disability. What became called 'integration' represented a major departure from current practice.[48] There was concern expressed that devolution of responsibility for children with special needs to the mainstream school meant teachers who had to deal with this were not properly equipped.

In May 1987 Dr Lawrence Bartak produced a paper setting out how the Krongold Centre could be 'renegotiated' back to the faculty. He spelled out the initial intention for it to be a clinical facility for the preparation of people in special education. He recommended forming links with the Queen Victoria Medical Centre and the Elwyn Morey Child Study Centre so that expertise could be pooled. He pointed out that the practicum was a core component of the Bachelor of Special Education. From 1987 students in the BSpecEd were required to complete 45 days of practicum. He said faculty staff would undertake clinical work in the Krongold. Staff were to be sought from the Department of Education and from the Queen Victoria Medical Centre.[49]

Budget

In 1982 the faculty faced a budget cut of 7.5 per cent on the previous year which also meant a cut in EFTS from 1,240 to 1,100. The faculty was not helped by having a $50,000 of unspent funds from the previous year, which it was not allowed to carry forward. This all had an adverse effect on staffing, with 10 positions vacant and the faculty having to restrict itself to fixed-term appointments. Planning for the 1985–87 triennium showed no new developments.[50]

The budget for 1984 was determined at $3,562,421 with extra grants of $70,000 for equipment (TVs and word processing), and a further $7,500

---

[47] Monash University Archives MON 61 Minutes of Faculty Board 7 September 1983.
[48] Monash University Archives MON 61 Minutes of Faculty Board 4 July 1984.
[49] Monash University Archives MON 496(22) Minutes of Staff Meeting 3 June 1987.
[50] Monash University Archives MON 61 Minutes of Faculty Board 5 May 1982.

for research. A deficit was expected for the year.[51] The faculty was allocated $3.6 million for 1985, some $70,000 short of estimated needs. One of the problems of the faculty budget was the incremental increases which were built into staff salaries, which meant that unless extras funds were provided for these increments, the faculty would be worse off in real terms. Unexpected resignations gave some salary savings to ease the problem. Budgetary problems continued throughout the decade; 'incremental creep', promotions and retirements added to the problem as did equipment obsolescence. While some large ARC grants in 1987 helped, many planned appointments of new staff could not proceed. There was encouragement to recruit fee-paying overseas students but this was not a move favoured by staff.[52] The view of most staff was that there was a 'better way to help people in other societies', than to extract fees from them.[53]

Costs became a constant issue. The problem also arose of how to cost staff who were seconded to outside positions. Gerald Burke prepared a paper on this which showed that the following had to be allowed: payroll tax 6%, workers compensation 1.4%, superannuation 14%, long-service leave allowance 2.5%, and the annual holiday loading which applied then, 1.34%. This meant a total of 25.34% had to be added on to the salary cost of any staff member seconded. When later the Department of Education did their arithmetic to estimate the cost of teachers seconded from them to the faculty the result was even more horrendous.

The university library became a major issue in this period. There was concern at the state of library funding, which had meant a drastic reduction in the number of journals purchased. The escalating cost of books and periodicals, especially from overseas because of the state of the Australian dollar, meant a drop in real terms of funding for the library. A substantial cut in periodicals as well as reduced book purchases resulted.

Numbers

In 1981 the faculty had 274 EFTS in DipEd. For DipEd Psych there were 39, BEd 80, BSpecEd 49, MEd Studies 498, MEd by minor thesis 27, MEd by thesis 138, and PhD 51 with a total faculty EFTS of 1125.92.[54]

---

[51] Monash University Archives MON 61 Minutes of Faculty Board 2 May 1984.
[52] Monash University Archives MON 496 Minutes of Staff Meeting 9 October 1985.
[53] Monash University Archives MON 496 Minutes of Staff Meeting 7 October 1987.
[54] Monash University Archives MON 496 folder 246, 10 August 1983.

In 1982 there were for BEd 181 students compared with 565 in 1976 (reflecting the introduction of MEd Studies in 1977). For 1982 there were 445 enrolments for masters by coursework, 215 for research degrees and 440 enrolments for 'other than higher degree'. The strong research-degree enrolments were maintained over the last five years. Between 50 and 60 research-degree candidates had graduated each year.

The introduction of HECS also came with a change of funding formula, with student numbers being a key factor. In addition to that, the Commonwealth devised a weighting system that assigned different sections higher or lower weighting, and more or less funding accordingly. Medicine, for example, was given a high weighting on the basis of the high cost of educating a medical student, but education was disadvantaged.

In 1984 the Commonwealth Tertiary Education Commission (CTEC) decreed that full-time students at all levels would all count as 1, whereas previously higher degree students had counted as 2. This had a major effect on the education faculty because of its high proportion of higher degree students.

The faculty in 1985 had 80 staff (67 EAS), but there were only three of them under 40 years of age.

The Dean, Peter Fensham, in 1985 saw the faculty developing as one initially concerned with the preparation of secondary teachers.[55] It soon became the largest supplier of secondary teachers in Victoria, helping to meet the teacher shortage crisis which had afflicted state education. In 1975 the faculty produced 600 DipEd graduates. It then moved to provide further education opportunities for teachers and also research experience. By the second decade the 'Faculty became established in Australia as having a pre-eminent and quite distinctive role in research'.[56] With the expansion of the school system slackening, and much of the demand having been satisfied, 1985 saw a falling off in DipEd numbers (to about 300 a year), although the demand for continuing professional development and for research degrees continued.

In 1983 the Academic Registrar J Butchart tried to reactivate the naming of chairs and he asked the Dean to call his own chair the Ian Clunies Ross chair of education. What had been Syd Dunn's chair, now held by Professor Dick Tisher, was to be called the K S Cunningham chair, and what had been Professor Ron Taft's chair was to be called the Fred Schonnell chair of

---

[55] Monash University Archives MON 496 (22) Dean's Annual Report to Council for 1985 P J Fensham, Dean Faculty of Education.
[56] Ibid.

education. However, the use of the names soon lapsed and thirty years later has been forgotten.

Council

Max Oldmeadow resigned as faculty representative on the University Council in May 1984 to take a post as a commissioner on the new Victorian Education Services and Arbitration Council.[57] Win McDonell was elected to the position. McDonell was an outstanding mathematics educator who had worked in this area in the faculty but had gone on to take a senior administrative position in VISE. She was married to Dr Jack McDonell. Formerly in physics but later director of the Centre for Continuing Education (housed in the faculty); he had also been warden of Deakin Hall.[58]

The Vice-Chancellor Professor Ray Martin indicated he would step down in 1987. Martin was the second vice-chancellor of Monash University but his relations with the faculty had not been close.

There was a push in this period for the universities to take full-fee paying students from overseas. The ECOPS faculty had accepted full-fee paying overseas students from 1986, and medicine from 1987. A committee was set up to discuss this option. The Victorian body, VPSEC (Victorian Post-Secondary Education Committee) had pushed for tertiary institutions to market courses to overseas students.[59]

Visiting professors

In 1983 came Professor Michael Apple from Wisconsin, Ned Flanders from Berkley, Abraham Blum from Israel, David Shipstone from Nottingham and Tony Edwards from the UK. In 1985 there was Professor Richard Shavelson of the University of California, Professor Ference Marton of the University of Goteburg and Professor Gaalen Erickson from the University of British Columbia. Douglas Barnes from the University of Leeds came as a visitor in 1986 as did Peter Robinson from Bristol. They were all distinguished names well known in the literature.

---

[57] Monash University Archives, MON61 Faculty Board Minutes 2 May 1984. Max Oldmeadow OAM (1924–2013) served on Monash Council 1978–1984; he retired as principal of Chandler High School with Department of Education in 1982. He was MHR for Dandenong 1972–75 and he co-authored with Henry Schoenheimer *The Human Adventure* – a very popular school history book.

[58] Dr J A McDonell was housed in the education building at Clayton and had close links with members of the faculty including being in the faculty choir. He died on 10 August 2012.

[59] Monash University Archives MON 496 (22) Minutes of Staff Meeting 6 August 1986.

Social life

The social life of the faculty continued – morning tea was still an important daily gathering at which departures and arrivals were celebrated. Social events continued – Melbourne Cup Day was always special with hats worn for the champagne and chicken lunch. The faculty choir continued and evening events were held. There was always much collegiality and fun among staff. Ken Clements recalls the following incident:

> One staff member had recently acquired his PhD and some colleagues were amused when they noticed that his Melbourne phonebook entry had "Dr" added to his name. So, one night, they rang the staff member's home and, using an absurd fake accent, led a conversation that went something like this:
>
> *Staff*: Is ze doctor there pliz? Zis is urgent. My vife is about to have a baby, and ve need a doctor. It is velly urgent.
>
> *New PhD*: Oh... ah... I am a doctor, but I am not a medical doctor.
>
> *Staff*: It is velly important that you come right now. Zis is my address... [some phony address was given]. I zink that my house is close to where you live.
>
> *New PhD*: Oh no, I can't do this – you'll have to find a medical doctor.
>
> *Staff*: But zis is velly important. Please come now... Ze baby will definitely come.

For the 1982 Christmas festivities, a list of suggested 'state of the art' papers was distributed: 'The art of office management' by Lawrie Bartak; 'A cognitive map of research funding criteria', a joint paper by Dicks Gunstone and White; 'My overhead projector transparency masterpieces' by Peter Fensham; 'Hisnher'snits' by Shirley Sampson; 'It's not my period' by Andy Spaull and/or/neither Marty Sullivan. Staff were also urged to use up unfinished casks in offices as they would go off after Christmas.

1987

The tough tines experienced by the faculty became very wearying. Dean Fensham in his report to University Council in 1987 said that the 'sense of chronic constraint and neglect I experienced is more apparent in 1987 than in any of the previous 20 years I have been at Monash', and this was at a time when the *Times Higher Education Supplement* had ranked the faculty as one of the top three outside the UK.[60]

It was a period too, when the shortage of teachers suddenly officially evaporated and the Victorian Department of Education announced they would need 1000 fewer teachers, despite continuing shortages of Maths/Science and Commercial Studies teachers. DipEd enrolments fell as a consequence. Higher degree students were now required to pay, as Dawkins stated that 'students who enrol in higher degree courses could afford to pay them.'[61]

Chair

It was finally agreed that Professor Musgrave's chair should be filled. In preparing for its advertisement the Dean made notes of the area in which the chair was to be filled. He said that the social sciences area in education was one of the three central planks of foundation studies in the faculty. He drew attention to the leadership of the faculty at the masters and doctoral levels and in research:

> The fields of study assume even more prominence than they would in situations where the main activity is initial teacher education.[62]

Fensham pointed out that educational administration and management also formed part of this group. There were now four chairs in the faculty, one being lost when Fensham became Dean and another when Marie Neale took a research chair in 1982. The faculty had 80 staff members (an EAS of 63), 7.9 per cent of whom were at the level of professor, reader or associate professor (for Monash overall the figure was 15 per cent).

Appropriate advertisements were placed for the chair in what was now called 'Group 2' – an amalgamation of the social foundations division and education administration. It had 15 staff: 1 reader, 10 senior lecturers, 2 lecturers and 2 tutors. The courses run by these staff members represented 315.6 EFTS – a quarter of the faculty's student body. John Fyfield was the group head. Two non-professorial staff were elected by the group for the selection committee.

---

[60] Dean's Report to Council for the 1987 Academic Year. The *Times Higher Education Supplement* 23 January 1987 – it stated 'outside Britain Monash University is the surprise rival to Stanford and Harvard'; this was in regard to the 'best department in research and teaching'.
[61] Monash University Archives MON 496 Minutes of Staff Meeting 7 October 1987.
[62] Monash University Archives EA 162/1/2 17 July 1985.

5.10 Peter Fensham (wicketkeeper) and Professor Marie Neale (bat). Professorial Board cricket match, 1982.
Richard Crompton, MUA IN-2289

Previous to this it had been agreed within the faculty that the views of the staff of an area or group should be considered when making such appointments. There was a recognition though that the shared decision-making principles embraced by the faculty was at odds with the procedures imposed by the university for such matters as chair selection.[63] The custom had become for the selection committee to give shortlisted applicants the chance of giving a seminar in the faculty so that the views of the staff involved could be ascertained.

All this was done. One of the candidates was Millicent Poole, who had an impressive résumé and list of publications and came recommended by many, including Professor Peter Karmel. However, the group did not want Poole for the chair. The members felt her interests were more akin to Group 4 than Group 2. Despite this strong expression of opinion, Millicent Poole was appointed to the chair. It was hardly a good start for her in the faculty.

---

[63] J A Fyfield in a report on Chair Selection Procedure Minutes of Staff Meeting 6 August 1986.

5.11 Professor Millicent Poole.
Tony Miller, MUA IN-665

However, she applied herself strenuously to her duties and endeavoured to break down this barrier.

Millicent Poole was a Queenslander, with degrees from the University of Queensland, University of New England and Kelvin Grove Teachers' College. She completed her MA at the University of New England, and her PhD at La Trobe University titled 'Linguistic, Cognitive and Verbal Processing Styles: a social class concept'. Poole taught at La Trobe and then Macquarie University, where she became an associate professor. She was prolific in her research and publications. Her books included *Mosaic Melting Pot: Cultural Evolution in Australia* (1979) and *Cultural Life Possibilities: Australia in Transition*. She went on to either write, co-write or edit 27 books. She undertook research on human learning and development and the role of education in that process. She was concerned with socialisation of cognitive styles within social class contexts. She was also involved in a number of cross-cultural studies. Poole was active in educational organisations, including serving on the executive of the Australian Council for Educational Research, and was editor of the *Australian Journal of Education*. After her time as chair of Group 2 finished, she became Pro-Vice Chancellor (Research) at the Queensland University of Technology, Deputy Vice-Chancellor at the

Australian National University, and then Vice-Chancellor of Edith Cowan University, WA.

Dawkins

More and more universities were subject to the influence of the Commonwealth Government. While Monash University was founded by the Victorian Government, very soon the power of the Commonwealth through its funding became evident. The universities were no longer institutions of value in themselves as places of scholarship; increasingly they were expected to service social and economic goals. Universities were required to contribute to the national economic well-being, provide new ideas and a more educated workforce and serve an innovation and entrepreneurial function as well. Universities as well as working with industry had also to reflect models of efficiency and productivity. The major reforms associated with Minister John Dawkins[64] especially affected Monash University and had major consequences for the education faculty. Dawkins became the minister responsible for high education, but in a new expanded portfolio called the Ministry of Employment, Education and Training. The Department of Education was now the Department of Employment, Education and Training (DEET).

A green paper issued in July 1988 entitled 'High Education – a discussion paper' signalled many of the major reforms that were to come. Among these reforms were the reintroduction of university fees and the HECS system, and also the abolition of what had been called the 'binary system', with the universities and the colleges of advanced education all to become part of one university system. Dawkins stated 'in its place would be a system of higher education where institutions define their teaching and research strengths in agreement with the Commonwealth and are funded accordingly'.[65] This latter move precipitated what Simon Marginson called a 'frenetic round of mergers and upgradings'.[66]

Dawkins wanted fewer but larger institutions, competitive tendering between them and better targeting, as well as more responsive decision-making.

---

[64] John Dawkins (1947–) was a Member of Parliament from WA (1974–75, 1977–1994) for the ALP. In 1980 he was Shadow Minister for Education became Minister for Finance in the first Hawke Government in 1983. In the second Hawke Government (1984–87) he was Minister for Trade, and in the third Hawke Government (1987) Minister for Employment, Education and Training, an important new portfolio. In the Keating Government of 1991 he became Treasurer before resigning in 1994.

[65] Media release by the Hon. John Dawkins MP, 9 December 1987.

[66] Simon Marginson *Monash: Remaking the University*, St Leonards, NSW, Allen and Unwin, 2000.

At the time the Commonwealth was paying 85 per cent of the funding for tertiary institutions.

There was much debate on the Dawkins issues among staff and Simon Marginson, from FAUSA, was asked to speak to a staff meeting about the matter.[67]

In Victoria this meant that the technical colleges of advanced education and the teachers' colleges were all to become universities. The Victorian Government had brought in a system where all the technical advanced colleges became part of the umbrella organisation the Victorian Institute of Colleges (VIC), where a central body administered degrees and the constituent colleges had reasonable autonomy. The various teachers' colleges were brought together under the umbrella organisation of the State College of Victoria (SCV). So each college had as its title State College of Victoria – Toorak, SCV – Burwood, SCV – Rusden (the college adjacent to Monash), or SCV – Frankston (the former Frankston Teachers' College). This system had worked very well. All these constituent colleges faced a major upheaval in trying to comply with the Dawkins reforms.

Tribute from *The Times*

Meanwhile the faculty in the 1980s continued to enjoy the high status it had experienced in the 1970s. The DipEd staff were in high demand with the subjects associations, not only in Victoria but Australia wide. There were also international consultancies to UNESCO in South-East Asia and with the ASEAN nations. The research and publications list remained impressive, with a large number of scholarly books and articles in esteemed journals, as the annual research report bore witness. In 1987 the *Times Higher Education Supplement*, as was its custom, undertook a survey of education faculties in the UK, and as part of this they surveyed scholars within them to determine the 'most desirable places to work' outside of the UK. Three places stood out: Harvard, Stanford and Monash. As the survey stated 'Monash University in Australia was the surprise rival to Stanford and Harvard'. While it was widely stated that Monash had the 'best' education faculty in Australia, this was formal external recognition of the high status the faculty enjoyed.[68]

---

[67] Monash University Archives MON 496 Minutes of Staff Meeting 13 April 1988.
[68] *Times Higher Education Supplement* 23 January 1987.

5.12 Dick White, Dick Selleck, Marj White, Joan Northfield, Jeff Northfield, and Trish Pettit.
Claude Sironi, Education Faculty

Staff of 1981

Michael John Norman joined the faculty as a temporary tutor but soon became a lecturer in educational administration. A BA DipEd BEd MEd from Melbourne, he also had a Bachelor of Divinity and was an ordained Methodist minister. His educational expertise was in curriculum design and contemporary values. He also taught in the Department of Education before becoming principal of Box Hill Grammar School (later called Kingswood College) 1963–71. He then worked in the education faculty at Melbourne, and in 1973 became principal of St Pauls School Woodleigh. He also acted as a consultant to the Schools Commission and to the Methodist Church. He was known as an excellent administrator and educational innovator. He left the faculty in 1982 to become Director of Curriculum at the Victorian Department of Education.

Reynold John Sinclair Macpherson (known as Mac) took up a fixed-term lecturership in 1981. A New Zealander, he had trained as a primary teacher with a speciality in remedial teaching in Auckland, and then worked in Scotland as a remedial teacher. He completed a BA (Open University), DipEd at Reading, and then an MEd Admin at the University of New England on role conflict and the role of deputy principal in senior high schools. He completed his PhD at Murdoch University on peer consultancy – principal triads and whole school developments in government secondary schools.

He taught in WA and became an education officer with the Department of Education. He was involved in INSET in WA. He worked in the educational administration area of the faculty, His time at Monash was extended but he resigned in September 1984 to take a post at the University of New England.

Anita Forsyth, a BEco and DipEd from Monash, completed her MEd in the faculty and became well known as an outstanding teacher of economics. In 1981 she was seconded to the method staff to teach economics, becoming full-time in 1999 and a senior lecturer in 2006. In 2003 she was accredited as a Victorian Department of Education school reviewer. In 2011 she was invited by the DEECD to conduct an analysis of specialist school reviews which culminated in the publication of a government report entitled 'Analysis of Specialist School Review Reports: 2009 and 2010'. She is a life member of the Victorian Commercial Teachers Association (VCTA), having served on the board for 20 years and edited the economics section of the association's journal *Compak* for 22 years. Forsyth has written a number of text and curriculum materials which promote the role and importance of economics and business curriculum, pedagogy and assessment, including the chapter 'A Role for Economics Education in the 21st Century' in *Teaching the Social Sciences and Humanities in the Australian Curriculum* (2011). Since 1999 she has been the Chair of the VCE Economics Examination Setting Panel and Chief Assessor. Across 2011–13 she was appointed by the Australian Curriculum and Assessment Authority (ACARA) to advise and write the economics and business Australian curriculum for the foundation to Year 10 levels.

Valina Rainer had a BA from the University of Sydney and an MA from Melbourne in philosophy. She taught philosophy at the State College of Education Melbourne and then in 1981 joined the faculty as a senior tutor and in 1986 as a lecturer. In the faculty she taught philosophy and courses in History of Educational Thought. In 1991 she left to take a post at La Trobe University.

Staff of 1982

Dudley Blane was at Cambridge before taking the mathematics education position vacated by Ken Clements in 1982. He had visited Monash earlier as part of a Defence Fellowship research project looking at the problems of children from British military families that paralleled the work of Monash staff Lindsay Mackay and Brian Spicer in the same area. He obtained his a PhD from the University of London in 1978 while still serving as an education officer in the Royal Air Force. During his first year he became head of Richardson Hall. He obtained a substantial grant from CRA to set up the Monash Mathematics Education Centre in the faculty and was also active on the committee of the Mathematics Association of Victoria (MAV) including a stint as their President. With John Fyfield he edited a mathematics dictionary. After leaving Monash in 1995 he went on to complete 16 years as a full-time international education consultant working for several aid agencies, including the World Bank, the Asian Development Bank, AusAID and the European Union and in less developed countries, mainly in Pakistan, Bangladesh, Indonesia and Northern Cyprus.

Staff of 1983

Margaret Brumby was appointed as a lecturer in 1983 although she had been a senior tutor and postdoctoral fellow in the faculty since 1980. She has a BSc and MSc from the University of Melbourne, a DipEd from La Trobe University and a PhD from University of Surrey in the UK, completed in 1979. She had also been a senior research assistant in cancer research at the Walter and Eliza Hall Institute (WEHI). She was also involved in HSC biology and science. Her main research interests at Monash were in developing critical scientific thinking. She left Monash in 1987 to take up a senior administrative post at the WEHI as general manager. She was administrative head of what is the flagship of Australian medical research first under Sir Gustav Nossal and then Professor Suzanne Cory. She was made a Member of the Order of Australia for her services to medical research. She retired from her post at WEHI in 2007.

Glenn Rowley completed a BSc in mathematics in 1962 then did his DipEd, BEd and was a high school teacher in mathematics. In 1972 he completed an MA in Toronto in the area of measurement and evaluation and went on to complete his PhD in 1975. He taught at the Ontario Institute for Studies in Education (OISE) at the University of Toronto and Michigan State University. From 1975 he held a position at La Trobe University in evaluation and measurement, research methodology and statistics. He soon had achieved an enormous list of publications in his field. He came to Monash as a senior lecturer in 1983, becoming an associate professor in 1990. He maintained his high rate of research activity and became an important figure as a research advisor to thesis and doctoral students. He served as Associate Dean and undertook much committee work. A genial person, he gave considerable help to generations of research students. In February 2002 he left to become general manager of the Victorian Curriculum and

Assessment Authority, and after retiring from this post he undertook part-time work with the Australian Council for Educational Research. He also became editor of the *Australian Journal of Education*.

Lesley Elizabeth Farrell, a BA (Hons), DipEd and MEd all from Monash, later completed her PhD in linguistics on the topic 'Written discourse organisation of Vietnamese and Chilean VCE students in social studies and humanities'. She had taught in Victorian secondary schools before joining the faculty to work in English method. She became education officer of the Victorian Association for Teaching of English in 1987, and in 1990 left Monash to become lecturer in language and literacy at Deakin University. She returned in 1993 as lecturer in English language, literacy and TESOL. She gained accelerated promotion to senior lecturer and in 2001 was promoted to associate professor. She resigned in 2008 to take up a post at the University of Technology, Sydney.

David Monash Bennett held a BA (Hons) from Melbourne with a UK teaching diploma. After war service he taught in secondary schools and then joined ACER where he was a research officer and later chief research officer. He was widely engaged in testing, developing materials, publications, aids and educational research. In 1970–72 he was principal of the innovative ERA School at Donvale, a progressive school founded by the Educational Research Association. In 1973 he became a full-time member of the Schools

5.13 Lesley Farrell.
Education Faculty

Commission, taking an active role in its work. He also served on many other educational bodies such as the Curriculum Development Centre and was a visiting fellow at the Education Research Unit at the ANU. An innovative thinker, he was a popular member of staff. Sadly Bennett's stay at Monash was short; ill-health forced his resignation. Bennett was also noteworthy as a grandson of Sir John Monash, after whom the university was named. He died on 1 May 1984, at the age of 59.

Christopher F Sharpley was a graduate from Bendigo Teachers' College and he then taught for five years in Victorian schools, including a one-teacher rural school. He then completed a BA and an MEd with first class honours at the University of New England. He also completed diplomas in psychology and school counselling at the University of Queensland. He completed his doctorate at the University of New England and in 1979 was awarded the university medal. His research was in children's learning processes and the study of individual differences. He was appointed to Monash University in 1983. He was known as an outstanding teacher and also maintained a high research output – by 1986 he had 28 articles in refereed journals and chapters in books. He was founding director of both the Centre for Stress Management and Research and the Stress Management and Counselling Clinic at Monash University. He was promoted to associate professor in 1991 and then resigned from Monash in June 1997. He became a professor of psychology at Bond University and then Dean of the Faculty of Health Sciences and Medicine. He retired in 2004 and is currently professorial research fellow in psycho-oncology at John Flynn Hospital and adjunct professor of physiology at the University of New England.

Dr Lesley Hardcastle, a Monash graduate (BA DipEd and M Ed Studies, then PhD), was a key figure in English method, but with qualifications in social psychology became involved in issues affecting marginalised people, with research into people suffering from drug and alcohol addiction as well as offenders. She became a Research fellow in the Centre for Mental Health and Well-being at Deakin University.

Staff of 1984

Colin William Evers, BA (Hons) from the University of Sydney, he completed a LittB from the University of New England and also pursued education studies. His doctorate at Sydney in the area of philosophy was on the epistemological and semantic bases of the philosophy of education, and the contrasting approaches in Australia, the UK and North America. His thesis was regarded as a major contribution and secured brilliant reports and his subsequent writings gave him an international reputation. He became a senior lecturer in 1989 and associate professor in 1993. He taught in the philosophy area of the faculty, and continued a rich output of publications. He resigned in August 2000 to take up a chair in education at the University of Hong Kong. He then became professor of educational leadership at the University of New South Wales.

Monica Louise Slattery came to the faculty as a tutor in psychology and principles of teaching in 1984. She had trained first at Rusden State College with a Diploma of Secondary Teaching then a higher diploma and a BEd. She also did a psychology major at Swinburne, and a Graduate Diploma in Counselling at Gippsland. She also completed an MEd Studies in the faculty. A teacher of English in Victoria and NSW, she became a tutor at Gippsland Institute. She was promoted to senior tutor in 1985 at Monash and then lecturer in 1987. Among other interests she was manager of the Australian Triathlon Team in 1992. She became heavily involved in the DipEd year. An activist, she promoted student interests and brought an innovative approach to teaching and learning. Illness plagued her later years in the faculty but she managed to complete her PhD before her death in October 1997.

Jennifer (Jenny) Elizabeth Brown completed her BA (1968) and DipEd (1969) at Monash before commencing as a secondary teacher of geography. Whilst on family leave in 1982 she was offered the opportunity to visit DipEd students on their teaching placements. The following year she was appointed to a casual position as a tutor in geography method, later becoming part-time lecturer. She worked with Jeff Northfield in the pioneering school-based program, teaching the foundation units in partner schools to students who opted for a term-long teaching practice placement. During this time she completed her MEd Studies. She was a member of the research and writing team for Lessons for All – a four-year evaluation of the VCE implementation 1989–1992. Brown was course advisor and course coordinator of the Graduate Diploma of Education and then both DipEd and the double degree (BEd) courses based on the Clayton Campus. Throughout her time at Monash, Brown was on the exam setting panel for VCE Geography for a number of years and maintained a strong association with the Geography Teachers' Association of Victoria (GTAV). She continued her association with the faculty as a member of the school review team until the end of 2012. A capable administrator as well as teacher, Brown was a much respected figure in the faculty.

5.14 Jenny Brown.
Claude Sironi, Education Faculty

Staff of 1986

Vicki Lorraine Lee completed a BA in psychology and then an MA and PhD at the University of Auckland. Her doctoral topic was 'Discrimination and production of speech in children: an experimental analysis'. She tutored at the University of Auckland in psychology and completed postdoctoral research on the effects on spelling of training children to read. She became a lecturer in education at the University of Newcastle in 1984 and was appointed to Monash in 1986. In 1985 she had published 11 papers and the book *Beyond Behaviourism*; Dr E F Segal of San Diego University described her research as having made a major impact on the future direction of academic psychology. She became a senior lecturer in 1990 and a reader in 1996. In 1990 she was awarded the medal for excellence by the Academy of Social Sciences in Australia. She continued her prolific writing and research at Monash, despite a disc injury. She resigned in August 2001.

Lawrence Bernard Angus had a BA and Diploma of Teaching from the University of Adelaide. He later completed a Graduate Diploma in Educational Administration, and then at Deakin University an MA and PhD (an ethnography of a Catholic Brothers school as part of Australian society). He was a teacher in South Australian and Victorian schools 1971–1982. He became a sociology lecturer at Deakin University before being appointed to the Monash education faculty in 1986. He taught at all levels and undertook research; one project was on improving the quality of Australia's schools. An energetic member of staff, he became head of the Social, Administrative, Comparative and Policy Studies Group from 1991 to 1995, and was promoted to associate professor. He was Associate Dean (Staff) in 1999. In 2002 he resigned to take a senior professorial post at the University of Ballarat. His publications include some 16 books and reports and over 50 refereed book chapters and articles in academic journals. His scholarship and contribution to equity research and ethnographic methodology have been internationally significant. He has a record of using ethnographic research to pursue questions about the embeddedness of social and cultural norms and equity relations in institutional structures, social attitudes and conventional practices.

Staff of 1987

Terri Seddon was born in England and held multiple degrees: BSc (Newcastle), PGCE (Bristol), BA (Macq), DipEd Stu (STC), and PhD (Macq). She joined the faculty on a fixed-term lectureship in 1987, became senior lecturer in 1992 and associate professor in 1996. In 2000 she was appointed to a chair of education at Monash. Her research focuses on educational restructuring and the politics of educational work in schools and in post-compulsory and adult learning spaces. Recent studies explore the nature and implications of partnership work, changes in governance and the effects of intercultural engagements on knowledge and innovation. She is currently co-editor of the World Yearbook of Education. Seddon was research assessor on the Social, Behavioural and Economic Sciences panel of the Australian Research Council College of Experts (2005–7) and a member of the Research Evaluation Committee for ERA 2010. She has been engaged in many funded research projects and held several consultancies both overseas and in Australia. She has published extensively in her field, exploring the pattern of identities, relationships and cultures orchestrated through education, across time and social spaces. Some of her recent books are *Educators, Professionalism and Politics: Global Transitions, National Spaces, and Professional Projects* (2013), *Learning and Work and the Politics of Working Life: Global Transformations and Collective Identities in Teaching, Nursing and Social Work* (2010) and *Reshaping Australian Education: Beyond Nostalgia* (2000).

Jill Robbins completed her masters at Monash and later her PhD, in which she focused on young children's thinking in relation to natural phenomena. Her research interests included young children's thinking, early childhood science and technology, mathematics in preschool, and intergenerational learning. She was a senior lecturer within the faculty and from 2007 to 2010 course advisor for the Bachelor of Early Childhood Studies. Over her time at Monash, she has taken a leading role in the development of early childhood from a small 'niche' course in the 1980s to one of the current flagship areas within the faculty, with undergraduate and masters courses, as well as PhD students, across three campuses. Robbins has a commitment to social justice, and her prolific committee involvement has included serving as Chair of the Faculty Equity and Diversity Committee in 2007. She has also been a member of the Disability Contact Network since its inception, as well as the Monash Inclusive Practices Committee. In the past she has served on the Monash University Exclusions Appeals Committee and on Faculty Board, the Faculty Staff Committee, and the Faculty Course Directors' Committee, as well as many others. Robbins retired at the end of 2010 but remains an adjunct senior lecturer within the faculty.

Staff of 1988

Neville John King came to the faculty as a lecturer in educational psychology in 1988. He had been a lecturer in the Department of Psychology at the Phillip Institute of Technology. He had a Certificate of Education, a Diploma of Physical Education and a BA (Hons) from the University of Tasmania. He taught in Tasmanian schools and later completed a PhD at La Trobe University: a mediational analysis on biofeedback-induced control of peripheral temperature. He was a member of the Australian Psychological Society. He was a specialist in children's phobias and behavioural problems of children. He published extensively both before and after his time at Monash. He was promoted to senior lecturer in 1989 and associate professor in 1993. He took early retirement in 2007.

Michael Buxton served as a lecturer, mainly in the History of Educational Thought, and also completed his DipEd, BEd and PhD at Monash. He then served for 12 years with Victorian Government Planning and Environment agencies and with the Victorian Environment Protection Authority. He formerly headed the intergovernmental process for developing Australia's National Greenhouse Strategy. In 1998 he joined RMIT as a professor. He was an elected Victorian local government councillor and mayor for 10 years and a member of the Upper Yarra Valley and Dandenong Ranges Authority for six years. Buxton heads a research team which has investigated the nature and extent of contemporary peri-urban regions in Australia; identified future patterns of socioeconomic, environmental change in peri-urban landscapes; and developed scenarios for future land use and management based on 'business as usual', interventionist and deregulated options.

Chapter 6

Silver jubilee and amalgamations

1989–1999

6.1 Faces of 1990.
Claude Sironi, Education Faculty

The silver jubilee was a prime opportunity for the faculty to engage with its alumni. As part of the 1989 celebrations, the Monash Education Alumni was set up. One of the association's first acts was to create a scholarship fund to assist research students. The scholarships of $250 each were named in honour of Peter Fensham, who had completed his term as dean the previous year and who had made such a significant contribution to the faculty. In 1989 the fund was $6,500, with the intention to award six $250 scholarships annually.[1] The alumni, under the guidance of Dr Paul Gardner, organised a rich program of activities. During 1989 talks were given by the Hon. Joan Kirner (Victorian Minister for Education), Dr Barry McGaw (Director of ACER) and the Hon. Barry Jones (Federal Minister for Science and Technology).[2] In 1990 McGaw was made an honorary professor of the faculty.

Dean

Fensham gave notice of his intention to step down as Dean in early 1988. Many hoped Dick Selleck would be willing to take up the position as he was widely respected by the staff and his help was frequently sought by all staff, not just those from his area or group. Selleck, however, was not disposed towards an administrative role and health issues were also a concern. Dick Tisher was leaving the faculty to take up the senior post at VCAB. Neither Dick White nor Millicent Poole was interested. While the internal appointments before had been successful the faculty also felt an outside appointment would be fitting. No professors of the faculty applied for the position of Dean when it was first advertised in June 1988 and at this round no appointment was made. While there were appointable candidates, none had sufficient staff support. The post was re-advertised but this time the process was assisted by written invitations and personal phone calls to some prospective candidates. David Aspin, professor of education at Macquarie University, applied for the position. Aspin was no stranger to the faculty, having come as a visitor twice before, and his work in philosophy was known to faculty philosophers Small and Evers.[3] The second interview, involving five candidates, took place in early November 1988. Aspin received overwhelming support from staff and was appointed.

Review of the faculty

Soon after becoming Dean, David Aspin proposed a thorough review of the faculty – by experts external to the faculty and to the state. The review was intended to examine existing programs, courses, research and the character of the faculty. Various international and interstate names were put forward

---

[1] Monash University Archives MON 493 Research Committee Minutes 31 May 1989.
[2] Dean's Annual Report to Council, Council Papers Monash University, 1990, p. 402.
[3] See biographical details of Professor David Aspin in staff section at the end of this chapter.

to do this review.[4] These included Jill Maling (Deputy Vice-Chancellor at the University of Western Sydney), Professor Kevin Marjoribanks, (Deputy Vice-Chancellor of Adelaide) and Professor Alan Cumming (Dean of the school of education at the University of Technology, Queensland). Aspin prepared terms of reference for such a review and spelled out the procedure to be followed.[5] This proposal generated much discussion as it came at a time when the faculty was facing amalgamations. These would definitely affect the faculty but there was uncertainty as to how they would happen and what the consequences would be. The planned review did not eventuate, the key external scholars being unavailable, and although the project lapsed it had set in motion much thinking within the faculty. Some years later (in 1994) there was a review with Michael Norman, Dianne Bradley, Rick Shavelson and Vaneeta Zigouras (Principal of Westall Secondary College).

Doctorates in education

An early initiative of the new Dean was to present a paper to the Research Degrees Committee proposing two further doctorates. One was to be a higher doctorate in education styled a DLitt (Education). This was modelled on a similar degree recently introduced at the University of London. Most other Faculties at Monash had higher doctorates. Arts had the DLitt, Engineering had a Doctor of Engineering, Medicine had the MD and Science a DSc. One of the problems for education having one was that an EdD or Doctorate of Education was common in the USA and was regarded as of lower standing than the PhD. The second doctorate proposed by Aspin was aimed at teachers and other professionals to enhance their training and experience.[6] Aspin was insistent that there was parity of status between the PhD and EdD degrees.

This was much debated in the faculty – some remained sceptical because of their view of the American EdD as being second class to the PhD. In July 1990 there was a special staff meeting to discuss the EdD degree. It was revealed that Canberra would approve the degree's doctoral status. Dawkins' White Paper on Education in 1989–90 had proposed such professional doctorates. The 'market' was seen as potential high-fliers in education in

---

[4] Monash University Archives MON 496 (22) Minutes of Staff Meeting 19 April 1989.
[5] Monash University Archives MON 480 folder 40 The Dean (David Aspin) to P&D 13 March 1989.
[6] Monash University Archives MON 496 (22) Minutes Research Degrees Committee 12 July 1989, paper prepared by Professor David Aspin 8 June 1989.

6.2 Professor David Aspin, Dean of Education.
MUA IN-592

Australia rather than overseas students. Eventually the proposal went through all the stages for approval: staff meetings, the PhD and Scholarships Committee, Faculty Board, Professorial Board and finally Council.[7] It was a triumph for Aspin to have carried the proposal through all stages and in record time.

The Doctorate in Education program would comprise two foundation courses, elective courses, an integrative seminar in a chosen area of concentration, two methodological/research courses plus a thesis of about 52,000 words. The 'concentrations' intended for 1991 were higher and tertiary education and primary and secondary education.

A further track program was outlined by Terri Seddon. This was to be in the field of education, social change and policy. Research subjects would be required, and subjects from social, economic, political and historical perspectives on education. Jeff Northfield foreshadowed a track related to

---

[7] The first EdD was conferred on Eileen Sellars in October 1994. The Dean at the time lamented that David Aspin, who had brought in the EdD, was interstate and unable to be present for this event.

the professional development of teachers and specifically one on science and mathematics education. Paul Gardner put forward a possible track on curriculum issues in science, mathematics and technology education.[8] Other staff proposed appropriate tracks from their fields of expertise.

Growth

In addition to 'normal' activity – the frenzy of the DipEd year, the rush of teachers from schools for 4.30pm coursework degree classes, the collegial group of thesis students lingering after morning tea – there were further developments. One was the growth of centres, for example in the educational administration area Judith Chapman initiated a 'School Decision Making and Management Centre'. The centre had an initial grant from the Vice-Chancellor of $14,000 in 1987 but after that became self-funding. Among the activities of the centre was the holding of a national seminar in 1989 in conjunction with DEET (the Department of Employment, Education and Training) on 'Improving the quality of Australian schools', informed by the OECD report 'Schools and Quality'. David Istance from OECD attended and the proceedings were published by ACER. The centre was also involved in training programs for UNESCO and seminars were held for senior officers of the Indonesian Ministry of Education. Judith Chapman was director of the centre and Vern Wilkinson was executive officer. In 1991 the centre's income was $233,166.

The Centre for Science, Mathematics and Technology Education had also become self-funding. The centre was engaged in seminars, national projects, conferences, grants from the ARC and PASMEP, and also attracted overseas visitors. In 1990 income associated with the centre's research and development activities was in excess of $600,000. The Centre for Human Stress Management and Research received a grant of $42,779.

The Professional Development Centre, formerly the Teachers Centre, a faculty initiative, continued with Alan Gregory then Dudley Blane as director and Joan Szalman as executive officer. When Peninsula Campus came on board, their South Pacific Centre for School and Community Development, started in 1988, became part of the faculty. There was also Maurie Balson's thriving Parent Education Centre.

---

[8] Monash University Archives MON 496 paper 27 June 1990 Minutes of Staff Meeting, 4 July 1990.

The offerings in the language area had also expanded with Jim Wheeler's DipTESOL developed into a masters degree in TESOL and the addition of a Diploma of Asian Language.

Method work continued to be hampered by the lack of secondments from the Department of Education and the high cost of the university paying for the time of such teachers. Some limited funding from the Commonwealth and the university helped to pay for secondments. By 1992, Jeff Northfield, the director of DipEd, had to write to the Victorian Minister for Education, with great regret, to say the faculty would not be renewing secondments for 1993 due to 'continuing financial cutbacks to the faculty and the high on-cost charges'.[9]

Summer school

The faculty had run successful summer schools during the January period from 1978 until 1983 but lack of staff availability led to their demise. However, in 1989 with low numbers a concern to the faculty a working party recommended the re-establishment of a summer semester program. Dr Robin Small was appointed the coordinator, and while it was originally intended to offer subjects in both the BEd Studies and MEd studies courses, there were insufficient numbers to justify the former. In 1990 there were 95 students (102 enrolments) for the five subjects offered. Overall it was regarded as highly successful despite the problem of the 6pm closing of the Main Library and the issue of parking.[10]

Constraints

In his report to University Council in 1989, the Dean, David Aspin, wrote of the 'increasingly severe set of constraints': reduced resources, insufficient student numbers and the requirements of the University's Strategic Management Plan.[11] Major changes had taken place and the old academic collegial approach had given way to a new managerial approach, with money and numbers driving things rather than academic interests.

Another constraint was the decision of the Victorian Ministry of Education to only allow student teachers to be supervised by what they called

---

[9] Monash University Archives, MON 498 Letter from Jeff Northfield Director of DipEd to the Minister, 2 October 1992.

[10] Monash University Archives MON 496 (22) Minutes of Staff Meeting 13 June 1990, report by Dr Robin Small.

[11] Dean's Annual Report to Council, Monash University Council Papers 1990, p. 402.

'advanced skills teachers', who would be expected to supervise such student teachers as part of their normal duties. This meant they would no longer receive any extra payment.[12]

In February 1990 staff was informed that smoking at the university was no longer permitted in any areas of the buildings or in university vehicles. The only areas excluded from the ban were the non-communal areas of the halls of residence or flats.

Tiananmen Square

Margrette Fairbanks recalls an incident after the dramatic events of 3–4 June 1989 in Tiananmen Square in Beijing:

> During the Tiananmen Square crisis when we had about twelve Chinese students with us, I became aware that one of their number was reporting back on the actions of the others to authorities in China. Those of us closely involved were warned to be cautious about how we related to all of them. It appeared that they would not be able to attend their own graduation ceremonies, which upset them. So we arranged for a mock graduation in one of our large rooms downstairs with a curtain backdrop, hired academic wear, with Claude Sironi taking photos of them with rolled up "certificates" presented by the then sub-dean Gil Best. I also had an evening at my home for them that they brought food for us all. I know Gil and Dawn Best were there, not sure about who else. Peter Fensham also took them to stay overnight at his holiday house (and his next door neighbour's) at Phillip Island. His wife and I also went along. The Chinese students cooked, and we took them to see the penguins. Afterwards one of them played a two-stringed bow instrument beautifully and we taught them Waltzing Matilda!
>
> Dawn and Gil Best also had the students for dinner and bravely gave them a Chinese meal.

Research

Each year brought new research grants for staff projects. In 1987 Fensham, White and Gunstone secured a Program Grant, the only one given in the field of education by the Australian Research Grants Committee. In 1989 there

---

[12] Ministry of Education document, 18 September 1990.

was $700,000 from the Victorian Health Promotion Foundation to Peter Fensham and Jeff Northfield for the 'Health in Primary Schools Project'. Jim Wheeler received $30,000 from DEET for professional development of language teachers. (This funded a series of four-hour Saturday seminars which were well attended by language teachers.) Laurie Angus and Judith Chapman received a research grant of $40,000 for their work on the organisation and administration of Australian schools. Shirley Sampson received $11,000 for her work on girls and physical education. Paul Gardner, Gilah Leder and Dick Gunstone received $20,000 from the Academic Development Fund for research on science, mathematics and technology education. Stewart Sykes received grants for his work in the Krongold Centre.

Status and strengths

Despite the continuing difficulties of constant change, budget cuts and shortfalls, and reorganisations for financial efficiency, the faculty's reputation remained high. Dean Aspin, was able to inform the Vice-Chancellor, Mal Logan, of specific areas in which the faculty had won national and international recognition for excellence in research, and he pointed out that on the criterion of internationally refereed journals, 'this Faculty is per staff member per annum, second only to the Faculty of Medicine in this University and leader in the field internationally, being one of the top three or four internationally'.[13]

Paul Gardner detailed the research strengths, which covered five fields, plus a category he called 'developing strengths'. The five main fields were educational policy and administration, the social context of education, the processes of teaching and learning, educating individuals with special needs, and historical and philosophical studies. 'Developing strengths' included the development of a graduate school of education, health education, new conceptualisations of technology education, distance education, early childhood and primary education, education and the promotion of social justice, education and the interface between industry, commerce and community, and foundational research in educational theory.[14] Science education was also a well-established and internationally recognised strength.

---

[13] Monash University Archives MON 497 Letter from the Dean (Aspin) to the Vice-Chancellor (Logan) 13 June 1989.
[14] Ibid.

6.3 Faculty of Education Study Group. From left: Dr Ian Mitchell, Professor Dick Gunstone, Professor Alan Bishop, and Chris Penna.
MUA IN-6187

6.4 Education's stall at the Great Australian Science Show 1992.
Claude Sironi, Education Faculty

Staff

There was a move to appoint a postgraduate coordinator to ensure research students' needs were being met satisfactorily. In 1989, there were 99 PhD students, 36 MEd and 511 MEd Studies enrolled in the faculty.[15] Frances Boyle and Hazel Evans, sisters who ran the faculty duplicators, resigned in July 1989. It was a signal that a new age of technology had arrived, with the photocopier replacing the messy duplicators. Professor Marie Neale's chair in special education remained unfilled.

Sue Aspinall, who was Faculty Secretary, left in late 1988 and in April 1989 she became manager of human resources at Flinders University in South Australia. She was followed in her post in December 1988 by Viv Kelly. Other retirements were Carolyn Grbich and Valina Rainer. At the end of 1989 John Hunt retired. A great stalwart of the faculty, he had made an enormous contribution. The normal celebratory carry-on for a retirement was notably missing in the case of John Hunt, who in a farewell message to staff indicated that his contractual responsibilities to Monash were at an end. He stated:

> Such occasions are usually marked by some form of celebratory activity. For me the occasion is not generating much in the way of celebratory feelings or dispositions. A number of factors, such as the mixed nature of the experience at Monash, the negative as well as the positive aspects of changing formal relationships, the uncertain prospects for concerns that seem to me to be important, and the depressing commercialisation and trivialisation into which higher education is being directed, dispose me to a wake as much as to a celebration. All things considered, the time is not much of a one for reflecting on the past or dwelling on the present, or on what might have been.'[16]

Hunt had been a productive member of staff – founding and shaping the social foundations section of the faculty, promoting the cause of sociology and the social sciences in schools and as well as an administrative load, he supervised many students. He also published several books and key articles. His final book was published after his retirement in 1990 – sadly a further work in retirement could not find a publisher. Some staff felt Hunt was not well treated by the faculty and this is partly reflected in his reflections of his time at Monash.

---

[15] Lesley Wilcoxon report to Research Degrees Committee 12 July 1989.
[16] The Faculty of Education Newsletter December 1989.

During 1990 Professor Poole took a year's leave of absence, seconded to Griffith University in Brisbane, to undertake a special project.

Departures in 1990 were Professor Dick Tisher, who became chair of the Victorian Curriculum and Assessment Board (VCAB). Tisher had been asked to take this position. Alan Gregory left to be Master of Ormond College at the University of Melbourne. Long-serving and well-regarded secretary Pat Sharples also resigned, and research secretary Elaine Scott retired because of ill-health. At the end of the year came the early retirement of John Theobald due to ill-health. A morning tea was held to farewell John Theobald in November 1990. A foundation member of staff and the foundation coordinator of the DipEd since 1974, John's influence in the faculty had been enormous. Along with a key role organising teaching practice was his role in DipEd and in making the 1969 building possible. A clear, well-organised teacher. his lectures had been appreciated by many generations of students as was his matchless administration of the DipEd course, including the difficult task of teaching-round placements.

6.5 Four Deans: Professor David Aspin, Professor Syd Dunn, Professor Peter Musgrave, and Professor Dick Selby Smith.
Claude Sironi, Education Faculty

Funding

The faculty's financial position was adversely affected by the reductions in university funds in both 1990 and 1991. The difficulties it sustained during these years were exacerbated by the move on the part of the university to introduce and apply to all faculties the 'Relative Funding Model' imposed by the Commonwealth Government, in which different levels of funding were assigned to each of the faculties. Under this new formula about a third of Australian universities would have their funding reduced and in the case of Monash it meant a 2.95 per cent reduction for the 1991–93 triennium.[17] It was felt the implications would hurt the education faculty.[18]

In 1990 the faculty faced a 5.67 per cent reduction in the budget, and carried forward a deficit. The cutbacks meant 'the Faculty was unable to pursue initiatives'. In 1991 the situation was worse, with a 10 per cent reduction, and the trend continued with a 6 per cent reduction in 1992.[19] There was discussion of not filling the vacancies created by the resignation of Millicent Poole or of five other staff retiring at the end of 1992.[20]

While it had been agreed to fill Dick Tisher's chair, the budget deficit of $80,000 from 1989 meant that appointment was delayed to allow time to clear the deficit.[21]

1991

Performance indicators had arisen as an issue in 1987 with an Australian Vice-Chancellors Committee report – which raised questions of numerical appraisal, teaching and curriculum, student progress rates, research output and professional services.[22] Performance indicators became an issue in the 1990s, especially following a listing in the magazine *The Bulletin* of its ranking of faculties in Australian universities.[23] In 1991 the rankings for education showed Monash education faculty as number 1, followed by the University of Queensland, the University of Sydney and the University of Melbourne. The rankings showed other Monash faculties rankings as

---

[17] Relative Funding Model, Department of Employment, Education and Training, ACT, June 1990.
[18] Monash University Archives MON 489 Minutes of Interim Management Committee, 13 September 1991.
[19] Monash University Archives, MON 496 Minutes of Staff Meetings.
[20] Monash University Archives, MON 496 Minutes of Staff Meetings 19 June 1991.
[21] Monash University Archives, Chair of Education file, 27 March 1990.
[22] Monash University Archives MON 496 Minutes of Staff Meeting 9 February 1987.
[23] *The Bulletin* 26 February 1991.

6.6 Paul Gardner, David Aspin, the Hon. Simon Crean MP, Minister for Science and Technology, and Gilah Leder in Dean's Conference Room, 1990.
Claude Sironi, Education Faculty

Arts: 2, Engineering: 5, Law: 2 and Medicine: 2. Understandably there was much discussion about these rankings and their validity. One academic, Murray Print from the University of Sydney, wanted to open up the whole issue of performance indicators.[24]

In 1991 the faculty had an impressive 694 higher degree students (483 of them part-time) and 1050 'other than higher degree students (410 of them part-time), giving a total student number of 1744.[25]

In 1991 Viv Kelly, who in a short time had proved an effective Faculty Secretary, transferred to the central administration to fill a gap there. This move exacerbated faculty feelings towards the university administration and they said so,[26] even though the move had been Kelly's choice. Kelly had been a successful administrator.[27] There was disquiet among the staff regarding changes taking place in the university sector and the administration of the university. At another staff meeting the 'managerial style'

---

[24] Murray Print, University of Sydney, to David Aspin, Dean (undated letter) probably March 1991.
[25] Monash University Annual Report, 1991.
[26] Monash University Archives MON 496 Minutes of Staff Meeting 10 April 1991.
[27] Viv Kelly was later to marry Dick Selleck.

of the administration had been criticised.[28] This came on top of an unsuccessful meeting of staff with the Vice-Chancellor Mal Logan, with staff expressing their dissatisfaction with this meeting.[29] Clive Vernon followed Viv Kelly as Faculty Secretary;[30] Vernon was to be followed in 1993 by John Duncan.

Jim Wheeler had health problems which forced his early retirement in 1991. Wheeler had carried a heavy burden for many years overseeing all the language methods and pioneering a raft of courses dealing with TESOL and other languages. A brilliant linguist, Wheeler was to spend much of his retirement in Thailand.[31]

In August 1991 Poole gave notice of her resignation to become Pro-Vice Chancellor (Research and Advancement) at the Queensland University of Technology.[32] Poole had not had an easy time at Monash, and while carrying her administrative responsibilities she also continued her outside work with the Australian Journal of Education, some key committees and was highly productive with her research and publications.

Ilana Snyder was awarded the AARE prize for the best PhD in Education in Australia.

1992

Evers, King and Molloy were all promoted to associate professor and Terri Seddon became a senior lecturer. Ann McDougall received the Vice-Chancellor's award as a Distinguished Teacher.[33] In 1992 the position of 'student support officer' was created with Ms Rosemary Viete offering literacy and oracy workshops, setting up peer-support groups and giving help to overseas students.

Fensham retires

The end of 1992 was significant for the faculty as one of its brightest lights retired – Peter Fensham. Fensham had been accorded a dinner to note his term as Dean when he stepped down in 1988, with many speeches of tribute together with a note of humour, especially having a dig at Fensham's

---

[28] Monash University Archives MON 496 Minutes of Staff Meeting 19 September 1991.
[29] Monash University Archives MON 496 Minutes of Staff Meeting 27 September 1991.
[30] Vernon later became manager of Student Admissions and Records.
[31] Monash University Archives MON 496 Minutes of Staff Meeting 21 August 1991.
[32] Monash University Archives MON 496 Minutes of Staff Meeting 21 August 1991.
[33] Monash University Archives MON 496 Minutes of Staff Meeting 26 October 1992.

6.7 Viv Kelly.
Claude Sironi, Education Faculty

overseas travel. Paul Gardner said: 'Stand on any street corner in any city anywhere in the world and sooner or later Peter Fensham will pass by.' He was a popular professor and a very successful dean, known for his dynamism and his support of colleagues. With PhDs from both Bristol and Cambridge, Fensham was one of Australia's foremost science educators, with a particular interest in chemical education. From a readership in physical chemistry at University of Melbourne, he moved to Monash in 1967, to be the first professor of science education anywhere in the world outside the USA. He led a strong research group for 25 years among which his own interests ranged from equity in education generally to conceptual learning in science. His focus shifted to the role of science education in the issue of equity. He had much experience with UNESCO of working in developing countries and was visiting professor in a number of leading overseas universities.

Fensham was the first nationally appointed president of the Australian Science Teachers Association (1972–74). He was involved with science teachers in every Australian state and served on curriculum committees and reviews about many aspects of science education. In the early 2000s he was made patron of the Science Teachers Association of Victoria.

He founded the Australasian Science Education Research Association (with help from Dick White and Lindsay Mackay), the second-oldest body of its kind in the world. He is perhaps best known for his seminal 1985 paper 'Science for All' and the many projects he has worked on since to make that vision of schooling a reality.

Within the faculty he had helped establish the areas, extended the opportunities for more democratic leadership, developed exchanges with overseas universities, coped with the problems of the Krongold Centre and revamped the visiting scholars program. He also managed to persuade Dawkins to provide 5000 HECS-free places for teachers.

Fensham played a major role in the developments of the curriculum reforms recommended to the Victorian Government by the Blackburn Report in 1985, leading to the creation of the Victorian Certificate of Education. He was the author of several well-known books of science education, including *The Content of Science* (with Gunstone and White), *Defining an Identity for Research in Science Education*, and *Developments and Dilemmas in Science Education* (1988). In 1998 he was awarded the Distinguished Researcher Award of the North American Association for Research in Science Teaching. Important was his work with others in the faculty and his encouragement of their research, making Monash one of the most eminent centres for science education in the world. A modest man, he was always keen to help others. He has worked in many overseas countries and continued a long association with UNESCO and with IOSTE. In 2003 he was national visiting professor at Kobe University in Japan. He served on the TIMSS Advisory Group for Science and has been a member of the Science Expert Group of the OECD's PISA project since its inception.

Upon his retirement he moved to Queensland and became an adjunct professor at QUT. At the end of 2003 he was appointed Science Education Ambassador for Queensland. In 1986 he was made a Member of the Order of Australia, AM 'in recognition of service to the community and to education'. His departure was a significant one for the faculty as he had been a wise and effective Dean and the faculty benefited from the high status in which he had been held. He was made professor emeritus in honour of this.

Amalgamations

The Dawkins changes meant the reinstitution of full fees. Government funding would be more selective and competitive. Institutions had to find additional sources of funding, including charging overseas students, which resulted in the replacement of the binary system of tertiary education in favour of larger multi-campus institutions. The Vice-Chancellor Mal Logan was close with members of the Hawke Government, notably John Button, Paul Keating and John Dawkins, and became a key unofficial but powerful advisor to the ALP on higher-education issues.[34] Most Monash staff saw their university, like the University of Melbourne, as substantially a single-campus institution that grew in stature with age and with the performance and reputation of its staff and students.

However, Vice-Chancellor Mal Logan and Peter Wade (who was responsible for the financial management of the university), together with a group in University Council, had a different vision. They were concerned about the university becoming stagnant and complacent, especially as its once young and enthusiastic staff aged. The education faculty itself at this time had a number of older staff who were senior lecturers.

An atmosphere of confusion and turmoil prevailed, the staid university structure facing massive change as it was forced to embrace a corporate structure.

From 1989 to 1992 the faculty faced continuous uncertainty as mergers and amalgamations were floated and discussed. Over this period rumours were rife around the university and undoubtedly damaged some of the negotiations. There was a certain arrogance by some at Clayton, who felt these mergers imperilled their guardianship of the educational pantheon.

While Logan as Vice-Chancellor pushed the 'big picture', the actual negotiations, which were protracted and sometimes acrimonious, were conducted by his deputies. Firstly by Pro Vice-Chancellor Professor John Hay, then by Professor Robert Pargetter and later by Professor Ian Chubb. For the education faculty it took at least five years for these mergers to come to fruition. Much of the discussion of and negotiations regarding possible future mergers and amalgamations were carried out by an Associated Amalgamations Committee, made up of a small number of staff chaired by Professor Dick White, whom the Dean had asked to take on this difficult task. The Interim Management Committee was set up to be a forum for the whole faculty, with a similar role and function to the former Planning and Development Committee.

Over this period Monash University changed radically, becoming corporate in approach and embracing new programs fitted to this new age, with a major expansion of the whole university over a number of campuses. This

---

[34] Graeme Davison and Kate Murphy, *University Unlimited: The Monash Story*, Crows Nest, NSW, Allen and Unwin, 2012.

expansion was to go beyond amalgamations and mergers to new campuses, including overseas ones. The term 'Greater Monash' was employed and as Davison and Murphy state, Greater Monash conveyed 'a sense of global vision, chauvinistic pride and vaulting ambition!'[35]

Officially the Gippsland Institute of Advanced Education joined Monash University on 1 January 1990, the State College of Victoria Frankston having amalgamated six months earlier. The story is more complex than this, but for the education faculty, the effective mergers came first with Frankston (or Peninsula) –as Gippsland at first had an 'affiliation' status with Monash University as a college, the faculty was not affected for some time. Some background to both of these institutions is appropriate.

6.8 Gippsland Campus.
MUA IN-6549

Frankston

The 1950s saw a rapid expansion in teacher training, including in the neglected area of primary teacher training. The inadequate one year for the primary teacher was extended to two and there were a number of new

---

[35] Ibid. p. 219.

teachers' colleges opened – Geelong (1950), Toorak (1951), Burwood (1954), Coburg (1957) and Frankston (1959). Frankston opened with Warwick Eunson as principal in an old house known as 'Struan', a historic home from 1903 on what was called the Struan Estate. A new building for the college was created at the corner of McMahons Road and Hastings Road Frankston. When Eunson left to become principal of the Melbourne Teachers' College in 1962, G A Jenkins replaced him. The college opened with 109 students. It specialised in early childhood and primary teacher training.

The college had adopted the seahorse as its emblem, appropriate for a bayside campus. Formality was encouraged: everyone was addressed as Mr or Miss and beards and red dresses were discouraged. Buildings were added to the original house and by 1962 there were 425 students and 34 staff. Woodhouse described this early period as one of 'student conformism and quiescence' in which a 'strong sense of community' prevailed.[36]

From 1963 the two-year Trained Primary Teachers Certificate (TPTC) and Trained Infant Teachers Certificate (TITC) were both phased out, to be replaced by a three-year Diploma of Teaching (Primary).

A major building program began in 1972. The site was transformed by extensive plantings of native trees and shrubs. A twin four-storey tower block housed a new library and resource centre. A new theatre, a library and a student union building were added. The theatre became an important resource for the local community.

In 1973–74 the college severed its close connection with the Department of Education and became part of the State College of Victoria (SCV). As the State College of Victoria at Frankston it became a degree-granting institution.

The year of the Whitlam dismissal, 1975, was a year of turbulence and student unrest and dissent.

From 1977–1982 Dr Graham Trevaskis was the principal at Frankston. A former primary and secondary teacher himself, he had undertaken advanced study and had been professor of education at the University of Papua New Guinea before heading to State College, Ballarat in 1976.[37]

Following initial talks with Caulfield Institute of Technology in the early 1980s, the college became the Frankston campus of the newly-formed

---

[36] The source of much of this material was from the book by Fay Woodhouse, *Still Learning: A 50 Year History of Monash University Peninsula Campus*, Sydney University Publishing Company, in 2008.

[37] After amalgamation with Chisholm, Trevaskis became Associate Director of the Institute.

Chisholm Institute of Technology in 1982. Some who studied at Chisholm Caulfield thus ended up with Monash degree certificates on their graduation.

The Peninsula campus occupies and still uses the former stately home of the 'Struan' Estate.

One of the problems with all the amalgamations was that the 'game' was played out at senior level, the vice-chancellors or college heads negotiating, without consultation with the staff who would be most affected. At one stage it appeared Monash University would amalgamate with Victoria College, which would have had an enormous impact on the education faculty. While this did not eventuate, the possibility of merging with Rusden State College (which was located very near Monash on the other side of Blackburn Road) seemed real, and David Aspin the Dean was told it was going to happen,[38] on top of the amalgamations with Frankston and Gippsland. At the time the Monash/Chisholm amalgamation created the second-largest university in Australia.

The reality turned out to be amalgamation with what had been Frankston Teachers' College/ State College of Victoria Frankston/Peninsula Campus of Chisholm Institute of Technology. Frankston Teachers' College like other such colleges was generally staffed with highly competent teachers skilled in passing on their knowledge to the young primary-teachers-to-be. A research orientation was never part of the job description, yet staff at such colleges were always keen to be up to date and so attended conferences and professional development courses at universities and elsewhere. They were also usually well-versed in the ways of the Department of Education and its schools. So a merger forced on the college without consultation posed a threatening scenario. The working world as they knew it was to be no more. It was expecting a lot for these people to readily fit in with the staff of an education faculty like Monash, which had a strong orientation toward research and publication. Dick White, who was actively involved in the negotiations, in his memoirs has stated:

> The two halves had different procedures and different traditions. Funding at Frankston had been based on contact hours while in both the old and the new Monash it was based on student numbers and research performance. Consequently, courses at Frankston involved high student contact and staff did no research. Some people who held senior positions at Frankston lacked the academic qualifications that

---

[38] Minutes Interim Management Committee 7 November 1990.

were expected for promotion or even appointment in a university. All of these matters had to be addressed sensitively and sensibly.[39]

The situation was made worse by the fact that in the previous merger when Frankston became part of Chisholm, it had to simultaneously face staff cutbacks and redundancies. The Monash merger with Chisholm Institute of Technology was completed during 1989, becoming official on 1 July 1990. By this time it was offering more than just education courses; there were others including nursing and art and design.

There were some positives as some of the Peninsula staff were well known to Monash people. Some like Dick Trembath had undertaken research and a higher degree with the faculty, and he and others like Ray Anderson, Tony Townsend and Elizabeth Mellor had doctorates – many had embraced research as being part of their academic life.

From the mid-1970s, many staff at Frankston realised that pre-service teacher education was changing and to possess a higher degree would be a necessity in the times ahead. When the School of Education at Chisholm was drawn into Monash most of its remaining staff had gained higher degrees.

In June 1990 the staff at Clayton were informed how the merger between the University and Chisholm Institute of Technology would affect the faculty. Clayton would be called the School of Graduate Studies. The Frankston part of Chisholm was to be called the School of Early Childhood and Primary Education (SECPE). An expanded Faculty Board would govern the two schools, although the Dean, Associate Dean and Faculty Registrar at Clayton would hold these positions in the new structure. The Dean would also be head of the SGS at Clayton and the head of SECPE was to be head of the School of Education at Frankston.

For the moment the four teaching and research groups within the SGS (Clayton) continued. The Dean was now to be advised by the new Interim Management Committee consisting of the Dean, Associate Dean, the Professors, the Head of SECPE, and one staff member from each of the two schools. The Assistant Registrar or Faculty Registrar would service the committee.[40] The Interim Management Committee (IMC) was set up to act as a kind of executive for the broader faculty. The head of each of the component schools was to be a professor.[41] Initially the work and discussions on amalgamation involved the School of Graduate Studies, Clayton and

---

[39] Richard White 'Monash University Faculty of Education 1969–1999', unpublished paper.
[40] Monash University Archives MON 496 (22) Minutes of Staff Meeting 13 June 1990.
[41] Monash University Archives MON 489 (216) IMC Minutes 12 December 1990.

Peninsula, for although Monash University College Gippsland was now affiliated, for a while it operated autonomously. It was not until November 1991 that the head of the SGS Clayton (Dick Selleck) met the head of the School of Education, Gippsland (Len Cairns) to discuss integration.[42]

For the faculty this really meant joining with the Peninsula or Frankston section, which had been SCV Frankston/School of Education, Chisholm. The amalgamation with Gippsland was different – it was not a total merger initially; the Gippsland Institute of Advanced Institution became established as a University College of Monash University, on 1 July 1990 – and was called Monash University College Gippsland. So initially this link with Gippsland did not directly affect the faculty. For a while there were just the two locations for the education faculty – Clayton and Frankston (Peninsula). In August 1990 a staff meeting was attended by staff from SECPE (Frankston) as well as from SGS (Clayton).

The Dean's establishment was 'detached' and was to comprise the Dean, the Dean's secretary, the Assistant Registrar, the Assistant Registrar's secretary and half of the time of the Associate Dean (Research). The cost of the Assistant Registrar was transferred from the university to the faculty budget with the new title of Head of Administrative Services. The title had originally been Faculty Secretary; it then became Assistant Registrar (Education).[43] It was decided that for the moment the present group structure would remain. From 1994 for two years, group heads would be any staff member elected by their group; the professor would assume other roles. The head of each of the component schools as well as group heads would be members of the Planning and Development Committee (P & D). There were to be three course-related committees. One, for the undergraduate and pre-service level, would cover the Grad DipEd, the BEd and Bachelor of Teaching, a second would comprise the postgraduate coursework degrees – the other graduate diplomas, the other BEd and coursework masters. The Research Degrees Committee would administer the MEd by thesis, the PhD and the EdD. The new post of School Executive Officer would replace that of Assistant Registrar (Education) and this person would now be part of the Dean's establishment. For Clayton, Professor Dick Selleck was head of the School of Graduate Studies.

The post of Assistant Registrar, previously called Faculty Secretary and held by Clive Vernon, then went to John Duncan in February 1994. His stay

---

[42] Monash University Archives MON 489 (217) IMC 15 November 1991.
[43] Monash University Archives MON 497 Minutes of Staff Meeting 17 February 1993.

was short and in August 1995 Peter Yates from the Faculty of Economics and Politics took over. In 1998 Peter Lawford, formerly Registrar of Education at RMIT, was selected 'from a strong field of applicants'. Lawford was to have a long term in a role which changed considerably. With the change in the culture of the university, the Faculty Manager as he was to be called became a significant post in faculty governance. Originally the Faculty Secretary had been regarded as the representative of the Academic Registrar in the faculty. Indeed for a time the post was called Assistant Registrar (Education), and the Academic Registrar showed his authority by frequently rotating the holders of the office to other faculties, to the annoyance of the faculties. The role had been mostly an academic one with appropriate administrative duties, assisted by two other staff, an assistant and a secretary. Financial matters for each faculty were not elaborate and only minor matters were handled within the faculty, with major financial issues dealt with centrally. This was all to change as the university became more corporate so the post became a significant managerial one, dealing with all administrative matters and now complicated financial and planning matters. The Faculty Manager soon had a group of at least three people who dealt with the financial issues, as well as other staff members handling the academic and administrative issues.

The Vice-Chancellor in a memo in 1990 stressed the need to develop research strengths at the School of Early Childhood and Primary Education at Frankston and to increase research production and the number of research students at the SGS.[44] A noteworthy program at Peninsula was the overseas-trained teachers program in early childhood which enabled those with qualifications not recognised in Australia to be upgraded.

Professor Anderson from Frankston stated that contact hours had been reduced at Frankston in order to free staff for research.[45] The amalgamations brought other problems with some from other faculties confirming their attitude to education as an area in a university. The Dean of Medicine, reacting to Frankston programs, felt a reference to a Certificate of Massage was 'surely a joke', and went on 'I am very concerned at the mickey mouse courses in nursing', and asked for a Standards Committee to be set up to 'save us from this embarrassment'.[46] The nursing and massage sections at Frankston became part of the Faculty of Medicine.

---

[44] Memo from Vice-Chancellor to Faculty of Education 15 November 1990.
[45] Monash University Archives MON 496 Minutes of Staff Meeting 20 October 1993.
[46] Letter from Robert Porter, Dean of Medicine to Peter Darvall, Dean of Engineering, 6 November 1990.

6.9 Ray Anderson.
Education Faculty

Gippsland

What became Monash University College Gippsland began as the Yallourn Technical School in 1928, set up to train State Electricity Commission of Victoria workers for the Yallourn Power Station. It became Yallourn Technical College in 1958. The Gippsland Institute of Advanced Education (GIAE) took over college courses after it was formed in 1968 at its location at Churchill. At Churchill the institute was bizarrely located in the midst of the stark Hazelwood Power Station with views of more industrial plants at Yallourn interspersed with farms and a tranquil countryside. As the road meandered through both rural tranquillity and industrial activity, one beheld a campus in 63 hectares of grounds with a large Binishell immediately taking one's attention. A Binishell is a large reinforced concrete dome shaped and lifted into place during construction by air pressure which is applied to a flexible membrane underlying the wet concrete and reinforced steel. Its inventor, architect Dr Dante Bini, directed the construction of the Binishell in December 1979. It was demolished in 2009.

The founding director in 1968 was Dr Max Hopper and by 1975 the institute had schools of engineering, applied science, visual arts, education, business and social sciences. It also pioneered distance education and introduced external studies to students living throughout the region. Distance education soon developed into a major operation with quality materials available to the students.

The first step in the merger of Monash and Gippsland came in January 1989 with the announcement that the two councils had agreed that the Gippsland Institute of Advanced Education should become an affiliated institute of Monash University from 1990.[47] Mentioned was the desire for Monash to extend into the distance education mode which had been successfully undertaken by Gippsland. Both institutions promised 'vigorous co-operation'. So Gippsland became Monash University College Gippsland.

In recent years the campus has undergone substantial expansions and upgrades of its buildings: Science and Engineering (1986), Information Technology (1994), a two-level library (1997), Gippsland Education Precinct (2006) and a new auditorium completed in 2008, replacing the iconic Binishell.

Eventually the amalgamation with GIAE was to go ahead and an official ceremony was held on 24 February 1989. Dr Len Cairns was the head of school at Gippsland. Cairns had a reputable academic history including his doctorate and time on the staff of the education faculty at the University of Sydney.

Coping with the amalgamation changes

Many problems and issues arose over the links with Gippsland and Peninsula. One was a concern as to whether the degree testamurs would state the campus of origin on them, or just refer to Monash University.[48]

There was an outward courtesy about it all. At the first meeting of the newly constituted Faculty Board in November 1990, the Dean, David Aspin, 'expressed his pleasure at welcoming so many colleagues to the meeting from the SECPE'.[49] The Peninsula campus also said they would make an office available for visiting Clayton staff.

When the three component parts of the faculty were called together in May 1993 to develop a strategic plan, there was a feeling that it was not a serious exercise for Clayton as they had the upper hand. Len Cairns, representing Gippsland, prepared a paper outlining his own vision as well as

---

[47] *Sound*, the official Broadsheet of Monash University, 1:89 24 January 1989.
[48] Monash University Archives MON 496 Minutes of Staff Meeting 21 August 1991.
[49] Monash University Archives MON 496 Minutes of Staff Meetings 7 November 1990.

posing questions that needed to be answered.[50] Cairns felt his submission 'fell on deliberately deaf ears', and even key issues like future chairs were not debated.[51] Cairns painted what he saw was a grim picture of the faculty in 1993 – an ungainly three-campus structure, a weak financial position, with much rhetoric but little forward thinking and the need to 'shed cobwebs'. He also had some positive suggestions as he visualised the future of what the bigger faculty could be.

As Dick White commented in his reflections, 'the schools recognised that although the merger was not the choice of either group it was an accomplished fact and that it was important to make the best of it.'[52]

Deputy Vice-Chancellor, Ian Chubb, in setting out his 'Visions of the Future', showed enrolments for pre-service courses in education across the three campuses of Monash University's Education faculty.[53]

Enrolments in Pre-Service Courses Monash Education Faculty

	1990	1993
SGS (Clayton)		
DipEd	221	188
SCEPE (Frankston		
B Teaching Primary	122	83
B Teaching EC	41	35
BA/B Teaching	–	18
Grad DipEd	–	27
SOEG (Gippsland)		
B Teaching Primary	64	45
Dip Teaching (Distance)	2	1
BEd Secondary	16	30
DipEd (Secondary)	78	53

---

[50] Len Cairns, 'Future of the Faculty of Education – Some Issues for a Strategic Plan' 17 May 1993.
[51] Letter from Len Cairns to Margaret Gill 26 July 1994.
[52] R T White Memoirs of the Faculty of Education, Monash University p. 20.
[53] Monash University Archives MON 496 Minutes of Staff Meeting, School of Graduate Studies 18 August 1993.

Chubb tried to address the vast array of different courses and degrees offered by the three campuses. He outlined too the various types of pre-service courses, for example the Gippsland BA and teaching double degree or the BEd/BTeaching double degree which would enable a teacher to be registered as a primary and secondary teacher. There was a double degree for training language teachers. He also pointed out that the demand for these courses greatly exceeded the number of places available, and that there was a growing number of students in education courses who were not teachers, such as nurses and state emergency workers. Chubb also required the faculty to spell out its 'Vision for the Future' in 1993. Chubb set out suggestions for targets: the continuing steady development of postgraduate programs, the development of a wide range of teaching modes (distance, telematics, open learning), flexibility to allow professional development activities to be integrated into ordinary programs, for some international content to link in with Asia, to have the highest quality of teaching at all levels, and to broaden the teaching programs to take account of the increasing demand for learning in a variety of contexts. He foreshadowed that there should be a policy for fee-paying students, a points system for credit for professional development courses, and the development of more distance-mode courses. Chubb expressed the desire for more research output from SOEG and SECPE and to aim for higher degrees for all full-time members of staff by 1998.

It was hoped four new professors would be appointed by the end of 1995, with at least one chair at SECPE and SOEG. There was a structure put forward of what committee would act across the three locations, and which would be Faculty Board committees and which 'committees of advice' to the Dean (such as on Outside Studies Program).

The Dean, David Aspin put the Chubb vision to the staff. Staff were expected to implement these targets and to respond quite specifically – in the case of research, for example, to increase by 1998 the number of publications by 25 per cent, conference participation by 20 per cent, conference papers by 25 per cent, applications for research grants by 50 per cent and total funds awarded by 50 per cent. It was a big ask for a faculty that was already highly productive. In adjusting to the new arrangements of the amalgamations, the Clayton component prepared a report on how the new School of Graduate Studies (SGS) was to be constructed.[54]

One consequence of the Dawkins reforms was that since 1988 there were 36 tertiary institutions, and an elite group of universities set up an organisation

---

[54] Monash University Archives MON 496 Minutes of Staff Meeting 20 October 1993.

called the Group of Eight (Go8) consisting of the top universities in Australia: Sydney, Adelaide, Western Australia, Melbourne, Queensland, Monash, NSW and the Australian National University. The Group of Eight would issue statements and its leaders would hold regular meetings. Logan attached great importance to Monash being part of this group.[55] In the 'Vanstone' era, the Group of Eight were aware of the clawback of funds from the universities following 1988, and acknowledged the policies that laid emphasis on equity, access, growth in student numbers and uniformity. They felt more emphasis needed to be given to diversity, quality and international competitiveness. They were also critical of the Relative Funding Model devised in 1990, which had the same basis for funding of every cognate discipline, with the former CAEs and the former universities treated equally, with insufficient acknowledgement of research.[56] Treating all universities equally was what they called a 'recipe for higher education mediocrity'. As David Walker warned in *The Independent* of 16 May 1996, everyone cannot be excellent.

1993

In May 1993 Professor David Aspin indicated that he would not seek re-appointment as Dean. In a letter to the Vice-Chancellor, Aspin stated it had been a 'privilege to serve Monash University', but he warned 'as has been always been the case, the opportunities for growth and expansion within Education are available, but to grasp them and take fullest possible advantage of them will continue to prove challenging.'[57] They were difficult times with cutbacks and problems with numbers which combined with more intense lobbying from staff competing for grants, promotions and key positions. Matters were complicated too by the faculty being over three locations, each campus proud of their own traditions and achievements. David Aspin in a paper reflecting on his period as Dean has stated:

> The position of Dean in any university is complex, variegated and difficult. As Dean one has to attend to the needs and interests of a range of different constituencies, between which there are always going to be tensions and stresses. One has to attend to the decisions and

---

[55] Monash University Archives MON 480 Vice-Chancellor (Logan) to the Deans 14 June 1996.

[56] Monash University Archives MON 480 Vice-Chancellor (Logan) to the Deans, 14 June 1996.

[57] Letter to the Vice-Chancellor Professor Mal Logan, by Professor David Aspin, Dean of Education, 23 May 1993.

requirements of a range of other agencies and persons to whom one is answerable, some external, some internal to the university.

Aspin, who was a good speaker, had been much sought after to talk to schools and conferences. Anita Forsyth found Aspin not only a kindly Dean but noted that the students found him an inspirational lecturer.[58] He was a prolific letter-writer – many staff appreciated his personal notes when they achieved a grant or had a publication accepted. Aspin had maintained his research and scholarship during his time as Dean. At the end of his term there was considerable pressure on Professor Dick Selleck to take the position. This was widely supported within the faculty and a view strongly held by the Vice-Chancellor. Selleck, while always willing to do his bit in terms of administration, was unwilling to take on the deanship. It was not his style to be an administrator; he was a historian with a brilliant research record, and furthermore his health was not good and so he understandably declined.

Dick White, in a short paper reflecting on his time as Dean, recounts:

> Although staff of the Faculty of Education at Monash University endorsed with enthusiasm David Aspin's appointment as Dean in 1989, reduced funds and uncertainties over possible amalgamations made his task difficult, so that by 1993, the last year of his five-year term, there was little or no support for him to have a second term. When in the middle of the year the professors of Education at Clayton informed the Vice-Chancellor of this, he concurred. The question then became what now?

Unusually the position was not advertised. Following a meeting between Deputy Vice-Chancellor Ian Chubb and Dick Selleck, Ray Anderson and Len Cairns (representing the three component schools of the faculty), Professor Dick White was appointed Dean for a two-year term from February 1994. White insisted the post be advertised in 1996. Margaret Gill reflects that at the time 'there was very little effort amongst the faculty professoriate to advertise widely or internationally for a new Dean'.[59] White knew the faculty well, having been a doctoral student and then an academic who was steadily promoted through all the ranks to professor. Over a period of two decades he had developed an international reputation for his research.

---

[58] Anita Forsyth interview 20 June 2012.
[59] E-mail to the author.

6.10 Justice Sally Brown, Debbie Corrigan, and Rosamund Winter at the launch of *Lessons for All: Evaluation of the VCE Implementation* by Jeff Northfield and Rosamund Winter, November 1993.
Claude Sironi, Education Faculty

White had firm views as to the role of an education faculty in a university. He had a strong research focus and was unyielding in his pursuit of these goals.

White had worked closely with his secretary Cath Henderson in his role as head of Group 1 (Psychology). Henderson was highly competent and knew the faculty well and White was able to arrange for her to go with him as secretary to the Dean.[60] Vera Maschette had been the previous secretary to the Dean. Dick White was keen to maintain the contact between the Dean and the staff that had so characterised the early days of the one-campus faculty. In the days of Selby Smith, Dunn, Musgrave and Fensham you would always see the Dean at morning tea to hear news, exchange some views and feel you were in touch. With three campuses, attendance at morning tea was sadly diminished. White had the idea of a monthly newssheet called the Dean's Diary. This was mainly extracts from his diary, but it also included news, publications he had that could be borrowed, and comments on people. It was a warm informative diary that helped with communication and tried to get all staff feeling they were part of the one faculty. White felt the need

---

[60] Monash University Archives MON 480 folder 31.

in difficult times to reassure staff and to better communicate with them. The diary was sent out by email for the first time, heralding a new era.

The launch of the book *Lessons for All* edited by Jeff Northfield and Rosamund Winter in November 1993 was a notable achievement. It represented an important evaluation of the VCE; it was a team effort instigated by Jeff Northfield that included 11 faculty members writing from their special perspectives. Northfield mentored and encouraged less experienced staff. It was also a successful publication by the new APress press, a faculty enterprise started at the suggestion of Rosamund Winter with strong support from Dick Selleck (then Head of School), which provided an opportunity to publish work by faculty members. It had to be self-supporting, a hard ask, and as a result of indifference from the faculty, it wound up after about four years.

Centres

By 1993 several centres were operating on the various campuses of the faculty and it was regarded as timely to review how they operated. Professor Dick White proposed that centres should have a committee of management; they should meet 3–4 times a year; prepare an annual budget and report to the Head of School, who would appoint the Director. White also pointed out that all assets of centres belong to the faculty. He wanted the Dean and Faculty Management Committee kept informed by the staff running them of their activities. He proposed a levy of 10 per cent on each centre to go to faculty funds. Centres were to be subject to review and their funds monitored by the faculty. These recommendations were supported and became guidelines.[61]

In 1998 eight centres were listed. The Professional Development Institute, previously the Centre for Continuing Education (with Michael Kupsch as Director), the Centre for the Economics of Education (Gerald Burke), the Centre for Health Education and Social Science (Philip Edwards), the Krongold Centre for Exceptional Children (Lawrence Bartak), the Centre for Science, Mathematics and Technology Education (Richard Gunstone), the South Pacific Centre for School and Community Development (Tony Townsend), the Monash Centre for Stress Management and Research (Daniela Guidara) and the Centre for International Education (Fazal Rizvi). The Asia Pacific Education Centre had been disbanded.[62]

---

[61] Monash University Archives MON 480 (folder 38) Discussion Paper on Centres 2 December 1993.

[62] Monash University Archives MON 501 R T White (Dean) to Personnel Services 4 November 1997.

The Centre for International Education proved highly successful. The field was a new one and had instant appeal. The centre fitted the move of the university to become more international. Cultural issues, cross-cultural exchange, cultural borrowings together with the role of new technology were part of the centre's work. MEd enrolments in a course in international education, expected to be around 25 students in the first year (1998), had 130. As enrolments in other masters courses had declined this was important for the faculty to maintain numbers. The course and the centre's research and consultancy activities catered for an important newly emerging field, with international officers from schools, TAFE colleges and other institutions taking the course. After Rizvi left Monash to become PVC (International) at RMIT, Simon Marginson became Director.

Dick White prepared a proposal to establish a Key Centre for Quality Learning and Teaching. The proposal was refereed by leading international scholars who testified that the faculty contained scholars who had carried out pioneering work in this field. However, the university did not even put the proposal forward to DEET; only proposals from Engineering and Science were put forward. It was clear to White that the way the requirements were worded (it required an 'industry partner' and education was not defined as an industry) meant it was unlikely a key centre would ever be placed in Education.[63] A similar thing happened earlier in the very first round of these key centres when Canberra gave priority to setting up one up for mathematics and science education, but Monash University did not want its first key centre to be in education. What seemed a certainty was not allowed by Monash to proceed and so was not submitted. Ironically Fensham was asked by Canberra to choose one of the other applications.[64]

The Elwyn Morey Centre continued. In a 1993 report there are details of the early intervention program which supported families and provided an integrated pre-school program for three- and four-year-old children who were developmentally delayed. There were two full-time pre-school teachers, two kindergarten assistants, a part-time speech pathologist, and a clinical psychologist (who was the Director). The centre, together with the Krongold Centre, was part of the Monash Institute for Child and Adolescent Studies (MICAS). The centre was used as a placement for special education students (both bachelor and masters students) doing a practicum and it was also used

---

[63] Monash University Archives MON 480 (folder 48) R T White to Professor Peter Darvall Deputy Vice-Chancellor 22 November 1994.

[64] Fensham chose the Curtin University of Technology, which was awarded the centre.

as practicum experience for undergraduate students of education, medicine, psychology and speech pathology. Dr Lawrence Bartak was the Director and Dr Stewart Sykes was Director of the Krongold. Bartak was also president of the Intellectual Disability Review panel set up by the Minister for Community Services.

Ray Anderson, who had been head of Peninsula since the amalgamation, left in May 1994 to take up a post in Hong Kong. It was noted how assiduous he had been in defending the interests of his colleagues at Peninsula and Dick White said that, 'we valued his wisdom, calmness and integrity'.[65]

6. 11 Jeff Northfield speaking at a Faculty Day 1997.
Claude Sironi, Education Faculty

Northfield was offered the post of professor and Head of School at the Peninsula campus. He was a reluctant applicant. He stated: 'It appears that there is a staff view at Peninsula expressing a preference for a Head without a Clayton background and therefore I am not confident that I could gain widespread support in the position'. Northfield was nevertheless persuaded to accept the position and he took it up in 1995.[66] Peninsula stalwart Dick Trembath postponed his planned retirement to act as Head of School until

---

[65] Monash University Archives, Education Faculty Dean's Diary May 1994.
[66] Monash University Archives, letter from Jeff Northfield to Mr S Harrison Personnel Section 16 December 1994.

Northfield took over. Northfield took up the challenge of his new post quickly and soon gained the strong support of the Peninsula staff. Dick Trembath remarked that everyone soon loved Jeff, as he was not only highly competent but thoughtful and caring. In August 1995 he prepared a discussion paper on 'Moving Forward' which he sent to staff. He lamented the loss of up to nine academic staff in 12 months, and the loss of this experience and expertise. He said 'some academic staff feel pressure to alter their roles to fit a "university culture"' but urged them to maintain quality teaching and to 'wait for opportunities that fit in with your own interests'. [67]

There was no doubt that the Peninsula staff felt vulnerable. Sentiments expressed by a different section of Peninsula could equally have applied to education. Professor Phillip Steele, Head of the Peninsula School of Computing and IT, wrote to the Pro-Vice Chancellor (Peter Chandler):

> Monash Peninsula has a number of outstanding staff and a number of excellent academic programs. It is already conducting some high quality research that is recognised not only within the greater Monash but also nationally and internationally. However, it cannot be denied that Peninsula is somewhat vulnerable and it is viewed by some Monash staff and some potential Monash students as the least attractive of the Monash metropolitan campuses.[68]

In his report to University Council in June 1994 in his first year as Dean, Dick White said that the Faculty of Education was in a good state, with the demand for its courses strong and the quality and quantity of its research outstanding. However, there were now 155 students in DipEd compared with 500 a few years earlier, reflecting the general reduction in teacher numbers. The quality of the DipEd seems to have been sustained given an exit survey undertaken of the 1994 DipEd group. Asked whether they would recommend other students to do their DipEd at Monash, 71 per cent strongly agreed, 26 per cent agreed and only 3 per cent were undecided.[69] Masters candidates both for coursework and theses had built up to 182, and there were 70 doctoral candidates. White reported that 42 academic staff had published 13 books, 53 chapters in books, 82 articles in refereed journals, 29 other

---

[67] Monash University Archives MON 480 (folder 43) Jeff Northfield, Head Peninsula School of Education to all staff, 16 August 1995.
[68] Monash University Archives MON 480 (folder 43) Professor P Steele to Professor Peter Chandler 15 March 1995.
[69] Monash University Archives MON 480 Letter from R T White (Dean) to the Vice-Chancellor.

6.12 Peninsula Campus.
Education Faculty

6.13 Peninsula Campus.
Education Faculty

reports and 114 conference papers. It was again a formidable record. Faculty staff had received numerous research grants including six ARC grants, and as White commented in regard to research there were 'promising signs' from Peninsula and Gippsland. White also pointed out that the introduction of fees for graduate students would affect the faculty adversely, since for those taking the course (mainly teachers) there was no direct financial return for completing higher degree studies.

ESC

The Educational Services Centre (ESC) once again became the subject for review. The cutbacks of the late 1990s partially brought this about. The staff operating the ESC had taken packages, and the centre seemed hardly used, with most of the materials locked up and even equipment like the staplers attached to mighty chains – thanks to the engineering wizardry of Peter Tucker, they could not depart their home location. In 1998 the centre was revamped, staff engaged to run it and Ros Winter given an oversight role. It once again changed its name, this time to the Library and Media Resource Centre (LMR). There was a technical librarian (Sue Egan), teacher librarian, audio-visual resources officer (Angela Rye), IT experts and Claude Sironi for audio-visual help. It became once again a library or resource centre for teachers in training. It soon became an important and popular hub for students doing teacher training; it was also highly regarded by the higher degree students.

Chairs

After Millicent Poole left in 1991, the faculty was slow to fill her chair because of budget issues. Peter Fensham's chair had also not been filled. In 1994 approval was given to advertise for a Chair of Educational Policy and Administration and a Chair of Science and Technology Education. The faculty was proactive in seeking people to apply for these chairs and Dick White wrote to a number of potential women candidates drawing attention to the positions. The normal processes took place to fill these chairs, with the complex pattern of forming appropriate selection committees, electing staff representatives, developing preliminary shortlists and then a final shortlist of candidates who gave seminars within the faculty.

The Chair of Educational Policy and Administration was filled by Fazal Rizvi. Rizvi completed his BEd in Canberra, then an MEd at Manchester and a PhD at the University of London in 1984 on 'the fact-value distinction

6.14 Professor Fazal Rizvi.
Education Faculty

and the logic of educational theory'. While initially working in philosophy, Rizvi moved to work in the areas of education, public policy and global studies. Rizvi had spent three years teaching in schools in Australia and the UK and then fifteen years in the tertiary sector, including eight at Deakin University. In 1991 he was appointed associate professor of education at the University of Queensland, and was promoted there to a chair in 1995. Rizvi had published extensively and had developed a strong international reputation in a number of fields, not only in education but also in arts and cultural policy. Between 1993 and 1996 he was a member of the Australia Council for the Arts and was later appointed a director of the Australia Foundation for Culture and the Humanities. His book, *Culture, Difference and the Arts* (published by Allen and Unwin in 1994) is still widely used. His other academic work included research on racism in Australian schools and society, multiculturalism as an educational policy, education and cultural policy, higher education and the politics of Asia–Australia relations, democratic reforms in educational governance, and ethics in educational administration. For most of the 1990s he also edited for Routledge a highly influential international journal, *Discourse: Studies in the Cultural Politics of Education*. At Monash much of his work focused on globalisation and educational policy, an area on which he has published a number of books as well as chapters and articles. Rizvi took up his appointment on 29 January

1996. He left to take up a position as Pro-Vice Chancellor (International) at RMIT, and then went to Illinois as Director of Global Studies in Education and in July 2010 he took a chair at the Graduate School of Education at the University of Melbourne.

For the Chair in Science and Technology Education, there was a keen search for a leader in this field, especially given the work of Fensham and his team in putting Monash's work in this area on the world map. Richard 'Dick' Gunstone was selected as he had a proven and outstanding record in this field. Gunstone was first appointed to the faculty as a part-time lecturer in 1972 in the subject Method and Practice of Teaching Physics. He had a BSc and a TSTC from the University of Melbourne and completed his BEd and MEd at Monash. A teacher in Victorian high schools, he had been method tutor in physics at Melbourne and been active on the Science Teachers Association and as an examiner on the Physics Standing Committee. He had also been associated with the Australian Science Education project and the Australian Science Teacher Education Project (ASTEP). He took a fixed-term lectureship before getting tenure. His PhD on structural outcomes of physics instruction, completed in 1980, was a notable one. He became senior lecturer in 1981 and an associate professor in 1989. He worked in both the secondary and primary areas, particularly with the children's science group, and he also spent a year teaching science to a Year 7 class. He undertook significant research, often with others at Monash (Dick White, Peter Fensham), and his special area was in science education, cognition and metacognition and assessment and curriculum. In his time at Monash up to 1995 he had research grants from 25 projects representing over $1 million in funds. He had written eight books, contributed chapters to 24 books, had 50 papers in refereed journals and written many other publications and conference papers. He became internationally known for his innovative work in science cognition. He also maintained a heavy teaching and supervision load and continued to be active with the science teachers. He was appointed to the Chair of Science and Technology Education in the faculty in 1995. He 'retired' at the end of 2005 after 31 years in the faculty, but in 2013 he still has two ARC grants, is working on two books and is editor-in-chief of the first encyclopaedia of science education. He also had a key role in establishing the John Monash Science School on campus, for selective students, emphasising science. With Gunstone, the faculty had someone who knew the Clayton campus well, who as Associate Dean (Research) had been assiduous in visiting Gippsland and Peninsula, and who was well known and respected by the staff.

6.15 Professor Richard Gunstone.
Education Faculty

Women

Thanks to the example and work of people like Shirley Sampson, Ailsa Zainu'ddin, Ann Shorten and Diana Davis, there was an awareness of the need to ensure opportunities for women as well as for courses and research on women and girls in education. In 1995 the Dean Dick White in a confidential report to the Vice-Chancellor listed the women he had invited to apply for chairs in education. He had approached five for the Chair of Science and Technology – none of whom applied. For the Chair of Policy and Educational Administration he approached fourteen women scholars, and five applied. Two of these were to achieve chairs in the faculty.[70] In retrospect many women felt they did not receive much mentoring or career advice. Some of the female staff felt they could not gain promotion readily at Monash, and so sought posts elsewhere. Diana Davis (James Cook University), Gilah Leder (La Trobe University) and Judith Chapman (University of WA) were outstanding examples of this.

Reflecting on the overrepresentation of males in the 1960s and 1970s in senior posts, White stated 'I believe that this was not through bias in

---

[70] Monash University Archives MON 480 Letter from R T White, Dean of Education to the Vice-Chancellor 27 June 1995.

selection, but because few women had defeated the various obstacles that made it difficult for them to undertake full-time study and acquire doctorates.' For whatever reasons, females were underrepresented in the faculty during those years. White was able to report some improvement by the end of his term in 1999 although equality had not been achieved. By 2007, however, 5 of the 9 professors and 5 of the 12 associate professors/readers were female.[71]

Margaret Gill looking back on this time has commented:

> The perception that the Faculty's culture was one of 'blokiness' remained pervasive, despite academic work in the field of Womens' Studies by people like Sampson and Zainu'ddin or Dick White's invitation to female applicants to apply for advertised chairs.[72]

6.16 Christmas Party, Clayton, 1995. Margaret Gill entertaining.
Claude Sironi, Education Faculty

---

[71] Richard White 'Monash University Faculty of Education 1969–1999', unpublished paper.
[72] Submission by Margaret Gill to the author September 2013.

Gill felt many were simply unaware of how deep-seated this perception was, or why, after being invited, so few women actually applied for chairs. Gill[73] herself, when she became head of the School of Graduate Studies, was reminded by Andy Spaull that she was the first woman in the faculty appointed to a senior management post. In Gill's view, the paucity of women in senior positions was a university-wide issue. Around that time the University created equal opportunity and affirmative action committees in each faculty to consider these matters.

One positive development in 1995 was the establishment of a lively, informal study group titled 'Feminist Readings'. This was an initiative of Georgina Tsolidis and Terri Seddon. The group met during lunchtimes and participants would present papers critiquing different education topics through a feminist prism. The meetings were open to everyone – including, in Margaret Gill's words the 'blokes', some of whom attended from time to time.

Technology

In 1994 all members of staff were issued with their own computers. It signalled the official end to the notion of a typing pool or secretarial assistance – everyone had to be their own secretary now. Previously academics would hand-write letters or papers, have a secretary type them out and present the final product with appropriate formatting and layout. Then there were word processors, which for the secretary replaced the typewriter. Finally came the personal computers. Many found it hard to cope even with much explanation of the new desktop technology. Marty Sullivan wrote to the Vice-Chancellor in response requesting a Mont Blanc pen and a bottle of ink! In the 1990s electronic mail was developed and much was now available online, including the university library catalogue. While the process did not happen overnight, over a few years the changes were massive. All had to learn but some staff did not take up the opportunities provided to learn.[74] There were reports of both technophobia and technoscepticism.[75]

---

[73] For Margaret Gill's recollections of her time at Monash see Chapter 9.
[74] Have added material here from an excellent paper on IT changes by Rosamund Winter. There is a further paper by her 'So long, and thanks for all the fiche; the electronic library – why don't academics use it', paper to the Australian Computers in Education Conference ACEC conference, 1996. In this she shows the slow learning of the new electronic world by many academics and it also shows the magnitude of these technological changes on learning and research.
[75] S Fitzgerald, R Winter and D Yammouni 'Issues for Supporting Flexible Learning', paper for the South Pacific User Support Conference, 1999.

6.17 Jeff Northfield.
Claude Sironi, Education Faculty

1995

The UK Society of Education awarded a prize for the outstanding work on the history of education in the period 1992–1994 to Dick Selleck for his superb book on James Kaye-Shuttleworth. All of Selleck's books had been acknowledged as significant pieces of research. The US Spencer Foundation also recognised the quality of his work. News came that the PEEL book had been translated into Danish.

In 1995 Queensland University of Technology asked the faculty to nominate academics 'who you perceive to have exemplary or notably teaching practice': the four names submitted were Associate Professor Ann McDougall, Associate Professor Margaret Gill, Dr John Loughran and Ms Margaret Gearon. Loughran was also awarded the Vice-Chancellor's award for distinguished teaching. Gill and McDougall had previously held the same award. Vicki Lee was promoted to reader and Terri Seddon to associate professor. Professor Len Cairns was further extended in his appointment as Head of Gippsland.

The Alumni Association continued in their presentation of awards at their annual dinner. Guest speakers included former Monash graduate

6.18 Dick Selleck speaks at a Christmas luncheon for staff.
Education Faculty

6.19 Len Cairns.
Education Faculty

and researcher Dr Barbara Fary, principal of Camberwell Anglican Girls Grammar. In 1995 Chris Sharpley was the speaker. Awards were given to the outstanding student completing PhD, MEd Studies and DipEd. In 1995 the PhD award went to John Loughran, with other awards to Jennifer Betts, Helen Forgasz and Lesley Farrell.[76]

White in 1995 invited all the retired professors home for dinner to meet the new professorial team.

That year saw a number of early retirements of key people: Dick Trembath, Elizabeth Mellor, Brian Spicer, Charles Meyer, Joe Dor, Ian Drake, Dudley Blane and Judith Phillips.

1996

The 1996 federal budget had implications for higher education, with Education Minister Amanda Vanstone's directives causing concern to universities throughout Australia. The imposition of fees and further cuts were all implied by the directive. Margaret Gill, who was Head of the School of Graduate Studies, used this as an opportunity for a thorough review of the school and to look at what she called 'the SGS in a post-Vanstone world'. Gill prepared an initial position paper in September 1996 and the final draft (number seven) was presented to the Planning and Development Committee in November. The process aroused much staff interest and there was a very high response rate to Gill's paper. Most made contributions. Gill expressed the view that the 'Faculty had had a university-wide reputation for looking inward and dwelling on its past prestige and former glories'.[77]

The Australian Council of Deans of Education had recognised an increased demand for trainee teachers in Australia for 1998–2005, so the pre-service component of the faculty seemed secure. The Department of Education was more demanding of the level of professional development it required of its existing teachers. The changing market – the internationalisation of education, the expansion of institutions – contributed to a more complicated scene.

Despite having what Margaret Gill described as 'disestablished' 41 subjects in 1995, 29 subjects were still listed for BEd Studies, 126 subjects listed for masters level and 16 at the EdD level: a total of 171 subjects! This also had implications for staff workloads.

---

[76] The Dorrit Monheit was presented to the student with the most outstanding PhD thesis.
[77] Margaret Gill 'The SGS in a Post-Vanstone World: The Need for Change, a Strategy Paper', 10 November 1996.

There were 41 committees holding an average of 302 meetings a year (excluding university-wide committees); 44 full-time staff were spending much time sitting on committees. Gill proposed a rationalisation and reduction of subjects offered above the pre-service level. She also argued for a core and team taught approach with electives, and the group structure to be replaced by a teaching/study group structure.

Her final report was issued on 10 November 1996. What was special about this project was the high proportion of staff involved and, for the university, the relative speed with which this exercise was undertaken. The report recognised the need for major changes in the faculty, specifically the School of Graduate Studies. It brought proposals to cut costs, increase earning capacity and generate more efficiency in administration. Recommendations were made to cut back committees, trim courses and programs, cater for international students, foster stronger research leadership, use administrative staff more efficiently, expand professional development, develop commercial production of curriculum materials, and as part of the cutback of committees to replace the group structure. Many of these recommendations were implemented.

6.20 DipEd Students Revue, 1996.
Claude Sironi, Education Faculty

1996 budget

With the whole university under financial pressure, comprehensive measures were required. To fund salary increases, long-service leave and early retirements, the faculty needed to cut expenditure by 8 per cent or find new sources of revenue. The Dean made it clear that the faculty had 'to earn a lot more money than we get directly from the government'. It became a definite requirement that all faculties had to earn a substantial proportion of their income. All forms of outside earnings were sought. When Michael Kupsch, director of the Professional Development Institute (set up in 1994), gained a contract to conduct school reviews of 260 government schools over three years, it gave faculty funds a much-needed boost. Another means to achieve savings was encouraging the early retirement of staff. While this involved financial incentives for staff to take the 'package', in the long term it meant salary savings for the university. The early retirement package was first offered in 1994 and proved attractive to staff. It continued to be offered for succeeding years despite warnings from the Dean that there was no guarantee that such a package would be available each year. In his report as Dean to University Council in September 1996, Dick White said that 'instead of retreating intro apathy, staff though annoyed by the cuts, had been active in thinking about how to increase income and reduce costs'. He also reported on the important collaborative work done with other faculties, the creation of double degrees and bridging courses and in terms of external matters the regular holding of the 'Forums on Education' as well as expansion[78] into AVET.[79] In 1996 Monash added a new campus at Berwick which was not to affect the faculty for a few years. Double degrees represented a major development, with the faculty teaching at the undergraduate level at Clayton campus, and the double degrees in Arts and Science gave the faculty an extra 20 EFTS.[80]

Fazal Rizvi took up his chair in 1996, with Gerry Tickell as Associate Dean (Teaching), Dick Gunstone as Associate Dean (Research) and Margaret Gill as Head of the School of Graduate Studies. Rizvi had been very happy at the University of Queensland, but his family wanted him to move to Melbourne. Feeling ambivalent about the chair, he was moved to flippancy at the interview. Noting that the selection committee comprised

---

[78] S Marginson, *Monash: Remaking the University*, St Leonards, NSW, Allen and Unwin, 2000, p. 244.
[79] Monash University Archives MON 484, 2006.12 (34) Dean's Diaries by R T White (Dean) September 1996.
[80] Ibid.

among others Dick Gunstone, Dick Selleck and Dick White, Rizvi joked how his first name, Fazal, was 'Dick' in Farsi.

Upon his arrival, he found a faculty that had a strong focus on teacher education and schools, to the detriment, he felt, of other areas of scholarship such as higher education studies. He also lamented the lack of contact with other faculties and departments around the university, especially considering the able scholars in the faculty, who could well relate to people in their disciplines elsewhere. For example he noted the string of highly competent philosophers who had been in the faculty: Denis Phillips, Ron Laura, Robin Small, Colin Evers, David Aspin and Andre Gallois. However, he did not feel there were close links with other philosophers at Monash. Of course, as Marginson has stated, 'other academics did not always take the study of Education seriously.' Rizvi himself sought closer links with the Monash Asia Institute and Monash Centre for Australian Studies and was appointed to the boards of the Monash Gallery and the Australian Centre for Contemporary Arts (ACCA). Rizvi felt the faculty's narrow focus and the lack of contact beyond made it difficult for it to realise its full potential. He also denounced the unhelpful politics from the remnants of what had been the formal groups.

Dr Stewart Sykes left the faculty at the end of 1996 after a long and distinguished period of service to the faculty, the Krongold Centre and special education. Unfortunately, a rift had spoiled his period in the faculty, so he left with some sadness.[81] Sykes had earlier been recognised for serving in the faculty for 25 years. Presentations of the 25-year award were also made to Paul Gardner, Bev Schneider, Norm Nettleton, Brian Spicer and Dick White. Lawrence Bartak took over from Sykes as Director of the Krongold Centre from 1997.

In 1996 Jill Robbins, course advisor for the Bachelor of Early Childhood Education, travelled to Malaysia to investigate the possibility of linking with Universiti Sains Malaysia in Penang to provide a program for upgrading teachers working in child care settings to degree status. While this did not go ahead, it was the forerunner of later offshore programs offered in Singapore.

Jeff Northfield took the remarkable step of teaching a Year 7 class at Frankston for a year and then co-writing a book (with John Loughran) on the experience: *Opening the Classroom Door.*

---

[81] Monash University Archives MON 480 Letter from Stewart Sykes to Margaret Gill 9 December 1996.

6.21 Victorian Minister for Education Joan Kirner visiting the Faculty of Education. From left: Alan Gregory, John Hunt, Martin Sullivan, Joan Kirner, Gilah Leder, John Baird, Jeff Northfield, and Peter Fensham.
MUA IN 647

At the end of 1996 Professor R J W Selleck retired. Dick, as he was always known, was a great asset to the faculty. A quiet, modest man, he was self-effacing yet no one did more to help his colleagues. His kindly efforts on behalf of others earned him much affection and respect from staff. Under his leadership he encouraged his team to become a formidable group of scholars in the field of the history of Australian education. His own academic work was profound, particularly a book on the New Education movement,[82] and his key work on the great Australian educator Frank Tate.[83] He followed this with a book on the British educator James Kay Shuttleworth. There were other books too, as well as many quality articles, not to mention his meticulous and helpful supervision of many higher degree candidates. While not keen

---

[82] R J W Selleck, *English Primary Education and the Progressives, 1914–1939*, London, Boston, Routledge and K Paul, 1972.

[83] R J W Selleck, *Frank Tate a Biography*, Carlton, Vic., Melbourne University Press, 1982.

on administration he carried a heavy burden in this area. He was made an emeritus professor from Monash University, and also became a professorial fellow at the Centre for the Study of Higher Education at the University of Melbourne. In this role he completed *The Shop: The University of Melbourne, 1850–1939* and with Stuart Macintyre *A Short History of the University of Melbourne*. Both were published in 2003 by Melbourne University Press. Selleck declined a separate farewell, and joined other retiring staff for a dinner at the staff club. Margaret Gill took over from Dick Selleck as Head of the School of Graduate Studies.

1997

This year saw a shift in emphasis from graduate courses to undergraduate courses and notable was the development of double-degree courses. As school enrolments rose there was a growing need for more teachers. An increase in HECS fees had hit postgraduate numbers. For example, research-degree numbers were 126 EFTS in 1996, short of the expected 154 EFTS. DEETYA funding was based on student numbers and research performance. Financial issues loomed large in 1997. The Dean pointed out that unfunded salary increases hit staffing. Each rise of 1 per cent meant fewer jobs in education so staff had to be reduced, yet the amount of work required in teaching and research supervision remained unchanged. Fewer sessional teachers were employed.[84] The Dean set down policy as to what constituted a 'large' or 'small' class in terms of postgraduate courses. If a class was large (defined as over 40 students) some assistance with marking was available; if it was small (fewer than 10 students) it would not count as part of the lecturer's load.[85] Minor issues were hotly debated, such as the academic dress of the EdD.[86] The faculty was stuck though with 'banana' as the official faculty colour. A new Vice-Chancellor took over, with Logan replaced by David Robinson who was Vice-Chancellor of the University of South Australia. Professor David Aspin proposed a centre for his keen interest in lifelong learning, which White as Dean supported. Staff were pleased when Bernard Holkner in November 1997 was given tenure. He had been in charge of IT at Clayton and his strong leadership was noted; his

---

[84] Monash University Archives, Dean's Diary September 1997.
[85] Monash University Archives MON 480, Dean (R T White) to Faculty Executive 13 October 1997.
[86] Monash University Archives MON 480 Memo by the Dean 29 September 1997.

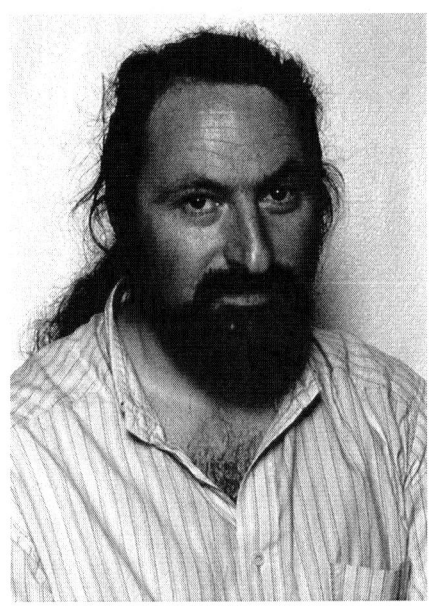

6.22 Bernard Holkner.
Education Faculty

courses enjoyed a 'high level of positive student response'. A month later he was promoted to senior lecturer.[87]

Lawrie Angus, chairman of the Conference Travel Committee, wrote to Dean White to complain about the inadequate funds for conference travel – there was only $1 left in the account! The Dean replied 'I am glad to hear that you have $1 for conference travel. Use it wisely.'[88]

The faculty organised a series called 'Six Town meetings' around the issue of 'The Great Debate – Funding for Australian Schools'. They were held in a range of venues including Geelong High School, Peninsula Monash, University High and Brighton Secondary College and were presented by expert speakers such as Anne Morrow, Simon Marginson, Morag Fraser, Fr Chris Gleeson, Sharon Burrow, Ros Winter and Bishop Michael Challen. The top names of presenters drew good crowds and it was an important contribution to the debate on funding. Marty Sullivan coordinated the program.

In October 1997 faculty sadly reported the death of Monica Slattery. Slattery had been an active force in the faculty for many years, a great friend of the students and founder of the teaching and learning course in DipEd.

---

[87] Monash University Archives MON 480 27 November 1997.
[88] Monash University Archives MON 501 (folder 27) letter 3 November 1997.

6.23 Ann Morrow asking a question at the Great VCE Debate organised by the Faculty. Alexander Theatre, Monash Clayton, 1990.
Claude Sironi, Education Faculty

6.24 Monica Slattery, Mary Nixon, and Sally Kent.
MUA IN-8297

Monica had suffered a debilitating illness for the previous three years. Annette Douglas of Peninsula campus also died and her loss was greatly lamented.

The faculty choir continued with Margaret Gearon directing and Ros Winter again organising, and the annual carol singing remained a key feature.

John Loughran and Julie Landvogt – supervised by Gilah Leder and Richard Gunstone – won the American Education Research Association award for the best dissertation in Teaching and Teacher Education (in 1995 and 1997 respectively). At that time they were the only two winners of this award to come from outside North America.

1998

The problem of an appropriate organisational structure for the multi-campus faculty loomed large. The areas, groups or divisions, as they were variously known at Clayton had worked well. Peninsula even suggested they become an additional group. However, the matter was resolved in May 1997 when the University Council approved the restructure of the Faculty of Education in which its three Schools would be dissolved and the faculty would operate as a single unit. So not only did the groups go, but so did the three schools that had comprised the three campuses of the faculty. This single-unit structure had some uneasy elements, but this was to be the end of re-structuring. There were, however, five academic 'teams'. Another development in 1998 was that staff were to be appraised annually as part of a new enterprise bargaining agreement.[89]

In this year came the sad news of the death of Syd Dunn, second professor of the faculty and second dean. Syd was a much loved figure who made a significant contribution to education both in the faculty and at a national level.[90]

In 1998 Dick White continued as Dean, P I Yates was Faculty Registrar, the Associate Dean roles were taken by Professor Alan Bishop, Professor Richard Gunstone (Research), Gerry Tickell (Teaching), Associate Professor Margaret Gill (Staff) and Professor Fazal Rizvi (International).

The faculty in 1998 gained the services of Simon Marginson from the University of Melbourne, Centre for the Study of Higher Education, as a reader. Marginson was an international authority on education policy and

---

[89] Monash University Archives, Faculty of Education, Dean's Diary May 1998.
[90] Syd Dunn's widow Moira died in January 2013.

6.25 Professor Simon Marginson.
MUA IN-6731

higher education and had also skills in markets in education. He was to play an important role at Monash as an advocate for higher education studies until he returned to the University of Melbourne in 2006. Margaret Gill, after a relatively short but highly effective stay at Monash, retired at the end of 1999.

White took sabbatical leave in 1998, and the Vice-Chancellor Professor David Robinson prevailed on Professor Fazal Rizvi to take the post of Acting Dean. Rizvi had never aspired to be an administrator and as it turned out did not enjoy his seven-month experience. He had, in his own words, 'a year from Hell'. A number of issues coincided to make the year extremely difficult for deans across Australia. The High Court of Australia had made a decision known as 'HECE', concerning Higher Education Continuing Employment positions. The decision meant that anyone who had been in a short-term academic post longer than three years had to be either given tenure or let go. The decision had drastic consequences for universities. Rizvi discovered that there were 35 part-time non-tenured academics in this position in the faculty, which created an immense problem. The numbers only justified the creation of 15 tenured posts, and so a decision was made to 'spill' all these 35 positions, consolidating them into 15 full-time posts that could be demonstrated as essential or strategic to the future of to the faculty. The process to determine the fields of these 15 posts was long and complicated, and Professor Stephen Kemmis from Deakin was called in to give advice on the posts required. In campus terms it meant three positions at Peninsula, two at Gippsland and ten at Clayton. Only a very small number of the 35 contract academics were offered tenure, leaving many others disappointed and their friends unhappy.

The whole operation alienated many people within the faculty and displeased the union, yet the whole process had to be undertaken in three months. Despite strong backing from the Vice-Chancellor David Robinson and others such as Peter Wade, it was not a happy time for the faculty, or for its novice Acting Dean. To make matters worse, there was in the same period a review of both the Krongold Centre and the Elwyn Morey Centre, with a conclusion that the superb facilities and resources were not being used adequately. An audit report on what had seemed the highly successful Professional Development Institute also found that despite the high turnover of over $2.5 million, little of this was going back to the faculty. The audit recommended that the institute either meet a specified income return or be closed. Unable to meet the target, four years later the centre closed. After being the 'Dean they had to have', Rizvi had no taste for faculty administration, and at the end of 1998 he took up a post at RMIT, closer to his academic interests in international education.

6.26 Great Display – a display of Education faculty books, publications and theses at Clayton, 1994.
Claude Sironi, Education Faculty

6.27 Display of Staff Publications, 1994.
Education Faculty

6.28 Professor Richard White, Dean of Education.
MUA IN-6704

Dick White's term as Dean concluded at the end of 1999, and he was appointed as Pro-Vice Chancellor of Monash University London, where he was to spend two years before his retirement. This was located in King's College, London. It was a fitting finale to his distinguished career. White had commenced in the faculty in 1969 as a PhD student. Paul Gardner gave the address at the dinner honouring White.

Conclusion

It is fitting to note Dick White's reflections on the faculty after going from research student in 1969 to lecturer, senior lecturer, associate professor, professor and then Dean in his 30 years in the faculty. In looking at the changes over these years White noted that initially the faculty was comprised of both young and enthusiastic staff – only the Dean (Selby Smith) and Syd Dunn were over 50 years of age. He felt that youth brought both 'energy and enthusiasm and a readiness to try new ways'. By 1985 only three tenured staff were under 40 years of age. Another notable change was the paucity of staff with higher degrees in the early days – by 1999, every appointment required a doctorate. Continued growth in those early days meant ample funds, vacancies to appoint good staff and the expansion of courses and offerings. However, in the late 1970s this came to an end with financial restrictions which meant reduced funds and heavier loads for staff. White noted with approval the changed lot of female staff – a minority in the early years but with their situation improving, albeit slowly, with a vastly improved participation rate by the time he left in 1999. The situation was to improve further for women in the next decade. White lamented that the university used a changed funding formula under the Hawke government in the 1980s, which disadvantaged the education faculty considerably. Funding and other requirements placed the pressure on research as a principal objective.

White also noted the demise of the teaching generalist and of non-academic posts such as the various technicians, photographers and professorial secretaries in favour of administrative officers, which meant academics had to attend to many non-academic duties. Professors had to learn to use their phones! The budget required staff cuts but these were achieved by redundancy and early retirement packages of various kinds.

The faculty had also moved in to an era where education had become highly politicised – and so needed to react to the changing requirements.

Gerald Burke has pointed out there was a good side to these changes:

the growth of general (Professional) staff meant that a fair bit of administrative work in relation to committee and student matters were taken away from academics – or should have been. The provision of computers (and the tech staff to support them) I think really made academics much more productive than if they took their typing to the Faculty typists.

White also commented on the change from the compact unit in one building to the spread over three campuses and the disintegration of the 'collegiality' that was a feature of the first 20 years. Complexity had replaced simplicity in administration. What Dick Selleck called the 'managerial' approach took over from the gentlemanly academic approach of Selby Smith. Selby Smith recruited people he felt were 'good people', especially favouring those who understood schools. He saw research as a natural outcome of what 'good people' would produce, rather than a pre-requisite. As with schools, universities were becoming 'corporate' – a trend which not only continued but became more aggressive.

White's reflections seem shared by most staff who were part of that era. A committee doing a report on the restructuring of the faculty in 1985 observed that 'evidence to hand suggests that this is the best Education Faculty in Australia' and they backed what they called a 'well founded claim' by reference to research and higher degree output and professional autonomy. By 1999, however, the situation had changed dramatically, with both the amalgamations and the change of Monash to an expansionist corporate structure exemplified by the term 'Greater Monash'. These were testing changes which challenged the way the faculty had operated.

Staff of 1989

David Nicholson Aspin was born and educated in England. Upon graduation from his first degree at Durham (BA Hons Classics) he undertook his PhD at Nottingham on 'Mind and Meta-causation'. He taught Classics for three years at Nottingham High School, before lecturing in classics and philosophy of education at Nottingham University and then Manchester University (as a senior lecturer). He was appointed to the Chair of Philosophy of Education at King's College London, a position which he held for ten years, during which time he was also adjunct professor at the London Institute of Education. He was appointed to a chair in education at Macquarie University in 1988 after which he became Dean of the Faculty of Education at Monash University in 1989. After five years as Dean and Head

6.29 A festive morning tea, 1990. Recognisable standing are David Aspin, Dick White, and Dick Selleck.
Claude Sironi, Education Faculty

of the School of Graduate Studies, Professor Aspin returned to a Chair of Philosophy of Education in the Faculty of Education at Monash.

Professor Aspin had served as a visiting professor both nationally and internationally. In 1999 he was awarded the distinction of a visiting fellowship at the Rockefeller Foundation Centre for International Study in Bellagio, Italy. In 2007 he was elected a visiting fellow of St Edmund's College, Cambridge. Aspin has been working for some years on lifelong learning and its implications for learning and teaching in educational institutions. He has published widely in this field and has co-authored and co-edited a number of books, chapters and papers on the concept of lifelong learning and its implications for education policy and practice; he has also authored chapters and papers in the philosophy of education. His many publications include *Quality Schooling: A Pragmatic Approach to Current Problems, Trends and Issues* (1994), *Logical Empiricism and Post-Empiricism in Educational Discourse* (1998), *The International Handbook on Lifelong Learning* (2001), and two symposia for Springer Press: *Philosophical Perspectives on Lifelong Learning* (2006) and *Values Education and Lifelong Learning* (2007). He continues to take an active role in research and scholarship and most recently edited and published a paper in a special issue of the journal *Educational Philosophy and Theory*.

6.30 Alan Bishop.
Education Faculty

Alan Bishop graduated BSc with First Class Honours from the University of Southampton in 1961; he then completed a DipEd at Loughborough College and an MA in Teaching at Harvard University. In 1969 he completed his PhD at the University of Hull. He also gained an MA from Cambridge University. After 1969 he was at Cambridge University as a lecturer in education and a fellow of Wolfson College. Bishop had been an academic visitor to Monash in 1978 and 1985 so knew the faculty and its staff. His appointment to Monash in 1992 was regarded as a great coup for the university. In 2001 he was awarded the Vice-Chancellor's Award for Postgraduate Supervision.

Bishop's research interests are in mathematics education, including the visual aspects of mathematics, concept formation by the deaf, teachers' decision-making, mathematics teacher training and multicultural aspects of mathematics education. His book *Mathematical Enculturation* (1988) aroused international interest. He published 18 books in total and 14 chapters in books, as well as numerous articles. His significant publications quickly established his international reputation as one of the top mathematics educators. Bishop was influential in establishing and raising the professional norms within the discipline of mathematics education, particularly with his involvement in various professional associations and in his editorial roles with key journals including *Educational Studies in Mathematics*.

He was made professor emeritus and on his retirement in 2005 a group of scholars in mathematics education honoured him by publishing a book marking his notable contribution to the field.

Rosamund Winter, a graduate in Arts, Education and Librarianship from the University of Melbourne and former teacher and teacher librarian, joined the faculty in 1989 on a 0.5 contract as the Faculty Research Assistant. Her role was to work with staff who had no external research funding and on faculty-based projects. This extended to work with HDR students, and in 1991, she was promoted to Research Fellow on a 0.85 contract. This contract was later converted to a full-time tenured position. In 1997, with colleagues Claude Sironi, Sue Egan and Angela Pye, she established the Library and Media Resources Centre (LMR) which supported staff and students across all campuses and degrees until it was closed at the end of 2008.

From 2002 to 2008 she was Lecturer-in-Charge of Teacher Librarianship Method, introduced following the establishment of a double degree program with the Faculty of Information Technology. This move was welcomed by the School Library Association of Victoria, as it provided the only on-campus opportunity in Victoria for librarians to gain a qualification in Teacher Librarianship. The Method was discontinued in 2009, aligning with a national trend in the reduction of teacher librarianship courses. The parlous state of school libraries and teacher librarianship training, a matter of some concern to the profession, was highlighted in her Submission to the Parliamentary Committee Inquiry into School Libraries and Teacher Librarians in Australian Schools (Hansard, 2011).

From 1993 to 2015 she was responsible for the verification of the annual HERDC publications data, and worked on the project team for the ERA submissions in 2010, 2012 and 2015. In 2012, with colleagues Raqib Chowdhury and Anna Podorova, she was nominated for the Vice Chancellor's Award (and received the Deans' Award) for Programs that Enhance Learning, for the HDR Seminar Series run annually for many years. From 2004 to 2008 she was Campus Coordinator at Clayton. She has always been an active member of the NTEU, and from 2008 to 2012 was a member of the Monash Branch Committee.

Deborah Corrigan was a Monash student (B.Sc 1978, Dip.Ed 1979) and a current MEd Studies student (graduated 1989) when she began as a part-time tutor (0.6) on contract in the Faculty of Education in February 1988. Deborah was appointed as a tutor in Chemistry Method and Teaching and

Learning in the DipEd program at that time as the Faculty was a graduate school of education located at Clayton. In 1997 Deborah was appointed as a tenured tutor in the Faculty was promoted to lecturer in 1998. In 1999 Deborah graduated with her PhD and increased her part-time fraction to 0.8 as she became the Director of DipEd. In 2001 Deborah was promoted to Senior Lecturer, became full-time in the Faculty and the Director of Pre-service Programs. In June of 2001 Deborah was appointed as Associate Dean (Teaching and Learning) a position she held until 2006. In 2007 Deborah was promoted to Associate Professor in the Faculty and became the Co-Director of the Centre for Science, Mathematics and Technology Education. In September 2010, she became the Deputy Dean of the Faculty of Education, a position she still holds. In 2011 Deborah was given the task to grow the Faculty by starting up the Faculty on the Berwick campus, which in 2014 has grown to 700 students. Her research interests have remained in science (chemistry) education and teacher education more generally. She has worked with King's College – London to continue the work of the combined Monash University – King's College London International Centre for the Study of Science and Mathematics Curriculum. In February 2013 Deborah had completed 25 years service to the Faculty of Education at Monash University. In recent years Debbie has carried a heavy administrative burden in the Faculty.

Margaret Gill was a graduate in arts and education from the University of Melbourne. She was awarded the Dwight's Prize in the Diploma of Education and the Sir Isaac Pitman Prize in the History of Australian Education in the BEd. In 1975 she was awarded a senior research fellowship from the Commonwealth Relations Trust that enabled her to complete an MPhil at the University of Leeds, working with Douglas Barnes and the British Schools Council. Her initial professional role was as lecturer at the then Kindergarten Teachers' College. She subsequently taught in both government high schools and technical schools and in the independent sector. In 1973 she was appointed lecturer in curriculum and teaching at the then Monash Teachers' College, later Rusden State College, where she became a senior lecturer. She was a former president of both the Australian Association for the Teaching of English and the International Federation for the Teaching of English.

She has researched, taught and published in the fields of English curriculum change, literacy education and teacher professional standards and professional development. She was a keen advocate for literacy standards and was critical of politicians who hijacked this agenda for political purposes. Her main research interests included the impact of professional and institutional influences on teachers' work. In 1994 she was appointed an associate professor, received the Vice-Chancellor's Award for Distinguished Teaching and an Order of Australia medal for Services to Education. She became Head of the School of Graduate Studies in 1996. She retired at the end of 1999 but continued as a faculty associate until 2002 in order to complete a major ARC research project on the development of teaching standards for the English teaching profession.

Jane Southcott, BMus (Honours), DipEd (Adelaide), MMusic (London), PhD (Deakin), an Associate Professor in involved in music education. A graduate in Music from the University of Adelaide, she has a MA in music education from London, and a Ph D from Deakin University, on Music in state-supported school in South Australia to 1920. After teaching in schools and colleges he commenced at Gippsland Institute of Advanced Education in 1985 and transferred to Clayton campus in 1990. As well as work in music method she has supervised many students in higher degree work, and also organized a number of performances of reviews and musicals with her students. She received a Special Commendation, Vice-Chancellor's Award for Distinguished Teaching and in 2013 served as an expert witness for Parliament of Victoria Education and Training Committee Inquiry into the extent, benefits and potential of music education in Victorian schools. She explores community music, culture, ageing and engagement in the arts employing both a qualitative, phenomenological approach and quantitative strategies. Her other research field is historical, particularly concerning the development of the music curriculum in Australia, America and Europe. She is a narrative historian and much of her research is biographical. She has written many articles, book chapters and has edited two scholarly works, and has had a strong supervision load. Her research and supervision interests have involved music education and research in music education, music curriculum history in Australia, America and Europe, phenomenological research in Music/Performing Arts and positive ageing community music, positive ageing, and arts and multiculturalism.

Staff of 1990

Ilana Snyder was appointed to a continuing lectureship in 1990, also having completed her PhD at Monash. She was appointed to a chair in education. An expert in literacy, Snyder's research focuses on the changes to social, cultural and educational practices associated with children and young people's use of digital media in school and out-of-school settings. A particular interest is the complex connections between literacy, technology and disadvantage. Australian Research Council-funded projects include two three-year studies: the first examined the relationships between the use of new technologies, pedagogy and organisational change in Australian higher education and the second explored the digital literacy practices of young people in all the domains of their lives. A recent project focused on the use of mobile phones to deliver literacy outcomes to indigenous children in remote communities. Recent books include *The Literacy Wars* (2008) which examines the volatile public debates around literacy education and two collections of essays, co-edited with John Nieuwenhuysen: *Closing the Gap in Education?* (2010) which looks at the education of marginalised peoples and communities in southern world societies and *A Home Away From Home?* (2011) which considers the complexities of international education in globalising times. Snyder is a member of a number of editorial boards and a reviewer for several national and international funding bodies.

Len Cairns was a primary teacher and special needs teacher in NSW rising to a Deputy Master before being seconded to the University of Sydney to teach and administer the first Bachelor of Education Degree in Australia. He left Sydney to become Head of School (at Dean level) of the School of Education at the then Gippsland Institute of Advanced education. Len also taught at the Literacy across the courses for Primary and Secondary teachers and wrote and taught the first Masters course in Reading and Psycholingustics at Sydney and later a new Masters Course at Monash (The Reading Process: Research Theory and Practice) which ran successfully well in to the 2000s. Len's Masters Degree at the University of Arizona was in Literacy teaching, Psycholinguistics and Writing researchLen has extensive experience in Victorian schools as a School Reviewer 1997-2011 and in many DEECD Professional Development courses. He has specialised over recent years in Leadership, and as a developer, theorist and practical researcher in popularising the concept of Capability, Capable Teachers and Capable Organisations. Len has been a founding member in such Teacher organisations as the Primary English Teachers Association, the former Australian Reading Association, The South Pacific Association for Teacher Education (now Australian Teacher Education Association), and has published over a dozen books and numerous articles in his career. Dr Cairns became an Associate Professor and also Associate Dean Development, and formally retired at the end of 2013 but has a retained a role in university development work.

Margaret Mary Gearon first joined the faculty as a senior tutor and research assistant. A BA BEd from Melbourne, she completed an MEd Studies and a Maitrise des Sciences du language from the Sorbonne in Paris. Previously an assistant lecturer at La Trobe University, she was a renowned teacher of languages, making her name as a teacher of French and Italian at Glen Waverley High School. She did much work in the LOTE area for the Department of Education and was a leading figure among language teachers, both in Victoria and in the Australian Federation of Modern Language Teachers Association. She became a lecturer in 1992. Her doctoral supervisor Professor Michael Clyne described her 'as one of the most outstanding language teaching methodologists in Australia'. Wheeler endorsed that and added 'she was a tireless and devoted teacher and lecturer and her work was of the highest standards'. Her thesis was on 'code switching practices of teachers of French in their classroom oral discourse'. She taught in the LOTE and languages area in the faculty, was promoted to senior lecturer and in 2010 took early retirement. She was awarded a commendation from the Vice-Chancellor for her excellence in teaching. She also conducted the faculty choir.

6.31 Dr Margaret Gearon.
Claude Sironi, Education Faculty

Leonie G Kronborg, BEd (VU), MEd (Mon), PhD (Mon), commenced as special education consultant/lecturer in learning disabilities and gifted education to the Krongold Centre in 1990. She established the postgraduate Certificate of Education (Gifted Education) course in 1996 and subsequently taught subjects in gifted education and special education in the Master of Education specialising in gifted education courses. During this time, she was President of the Australian Association for the Education Gifted and Talented Children (AAEGT). Her research interests have included creativity and teaching styles to develop creative students, evaluations of programs which educate gifted secondary students in Victoria, an examination of a leading Extended Curriculum Program at an independent school, and recently the professional development, teaching attitudes, competencies and teaching strategies at selective schools. In 2008 she completed her PhD, which focused on factors contributing to talent development in eminent Australian women and gained an award in 2009 for outstanding doctoral research from the USA (National Association for Gifted Children). She coordinated and developed the Master of Education (Gifted Education) from 2006 and has supervised research students. She was an elected Australian delegate of World Council for Gifted and Talented (2007–2011) and was subsequently elected to its executive. In 2006 she was awarded life membership of the VAGTC, in 2012 she was recipient of the Dean's Award for Teaching Excellence and in 2013 the Vice-Chancellor's Award for Teaching Excellence.

Raymond McDonald Anderson gained his TPTC from Burwood Teachers' College and then completed a BCom and BEd at University of Melbourne. He taught in primary schools 1961–67, and then in Papua New Guinea 1969–1971 at Madang Teachers' College. He completed an MEd at Monash in 1977 and in 1981 a PhD at Stanford University on self-instruction as a method of preparing trainees to apply an inductive teaching model. He became a lecturer at the State College of Victoria Frankston in 1973, became senior lecturer, then head of a department and in 1982 Dean of the School of Education Chisholm. After the amalgamation with Monash he became Head of the Peninsula Campus as a professor. His research interests were in curriculum design and evaluation and in social studies.

William Gerrard (Gerry) Tickell had first come to the faculty in 1985 to help with English method. Tickell, a BA DipEd BEd from Melbourne, completed an MEd thesis at Monash (1974) and became one of the leading educational figures in Australia. Known as an innovative teacher and as a leader of the teacher union movement. Tickell held many posts: schools commissioner, chair of the State Board of Education and member of the National Board of Employment, Education and Training. He was also president of the Australian Teachers Federation; manager of the professional development unit of the Department of Education and before coming to Monash was Director of the Institute of Educational Administration (1989–1993). He was an author, union leader and major figure in policy development in educational administration. He served on the Council of the Curriculum Development Centre. He ran the Swinburne Community School (an alternative school) 1972–77 and was a writer in the field of English. He returned to the faculty in 1995 to work in educational administration and in 1996 became Associate Dean (Teaching), with the rank of associate professor. He retired from the faculty in 1999, having made a significant contribution in his short time.

Elizabeth Jean Mellor had a BA, Advanced Diploma of Education and MEd. She taught in South Australia and then at Wattle Park Teachers' College, and in 1964–66 taught at the University of Alberta Canada. In 1970 she went to New Zealand and became a lecturer at Hamilton Teachers' College. In 1975 she took a post at the State College of Victoria Frankston in the field of child development and education psychology. She completed her PhD at Deakin University in 1990 on the public and private provision of education, health and welfare for poor children in Australia 1880–1980.

Staff of 1991

Marged Goode was one of the early undergraduates at Monash, starting in 1963 in its third intake. She reported that she had a wonderful time but failed. Returning in 1972, she completed a BA with majors in sociology and psychology and became a research assistant to Prof Ron Taft in 1975. She went on to complete the DipEd Psych, one of the first to do so. Following a short stint away, Goode returned in 1976 as a research assistant to Dr Lawrie Bartak. By 1979 she was doing casual teaching in the faculty, and working on other research projects. In 1980 Goode gained her registration as a psychologist, completed her MEd and presented her thesis results at a conference in Lisbon. Goode was away from Monash for the next 10 years, but a fortuitous encounter with Bartak led to her beginning her work as a field supervisor for BSpecEd, and MPsych students – a role she continued in both paid and honorary capacities for the next 21 years. During 2001, Goode worked as locum for Cathie Hughes in the Krongold. She completed her PhD at Monash in 2004. She returned to the Krongold in 2009, supervising students and having a clinical role in the Autism Service until May 2013. She maintains an honorary connection to the Faculty of Education, thus continuing a contact which has spanned 38 years.

Staff of 1993

Elizabeth (Libby) Joan Tudball was a history graduate from the University of Melbourne (BA DipEd) and taught in secondary schools in Victoria, notably at the MacRobertson Girls High School 1976–1989. She became active in the History Teachers Association of Victoria and the Victorian Association of Social Studies Teachers. She was method lecturer in history at the University of Melbourne Institute of Education 1985–1989, and then for Asian studies and social education 1990–1992. In 1993 she came to Monash University working in history and social studies method. She has held many posts including Director of Pre-service Education and Professional Development. She has been a leader of substantial reviews and change in teacher education programs in the Faculty and has served as a School reviewer for the Victorian Department of Education. She has continued active service to the profession as President of the Social and Citizenship Education Association of Australia. In 2013 she as appointed as an advisor to ACARA in the development of citizenship education for the Australian curriculum. She completed her PhD in 2005, and became a Senior Lecturer in 2006.

6.32 Libby Tudball.
Education Faculty

Michael Dyson, a long term resident of the Gippsland region, was Head of School (Education) at the Gippsland Campus and will lead the school in its transition phase to the new regional university, to be known as Federation University Australia. Michael commenced his career as a primary school teacher in New Zealand and moved to Australia in 1978. This was followed by ten years as a primary school principal at Lumen Christi Primary School in Churchill, followed by a number of years working as a learning technologies consultant at regional, state and national levels. His PhD, focused on renewal in pre-service teacher education, was completed in 2004. His research interests are in the areas of pre-service teacher education, holistic education, the educational use of ICT and alternative ways to conduct education in the 21st century. Michael has led a research partnership with the School for Student leadership, also known as the Alpine School, over the last 13 years and has held many leadership portfolios in education. He is on the Editorial Board of the Australian Journal of Teacher Education, the Australian Journal of Computers in Education, Asia Pacific Journal of Education and the Journal of Transformative Education. He is the current president of the Gippsland branch of Australian College of Educators.

Staff of 1995

Chandra Shah was appointed to the faculty in 1995 as research fellow in the Monash University–ACER Centre for the Economics of Education and Training (CEET). He graduated from Imperial College, London with a BSc (Honours) in mathematics. In 1975 he completed a Graduate Diploma in Education at Reading University (UK) before teaching at a high school in Melbourne. In 1988 he was appointed senior tutor and then lecturer in the Department of Econometrics, Monash University, where he also completed a Masters in Economics. He was appointed lecturer in the Faculty of Business and Management at Deakin University in 1992. In 1995 he completed his PhD in econometrics at Monash University. Shah is currently associate professor and mainly works on publicly commissioned research with a focus on the economics of education and training, the labour market, workforce development, migration and social inclusion. He was an associate director of CEET from 2009 to 2010 and the director from 2010 to 2011.

Michael Kupsch, a Monash graduate with a BEc and DipEd, was appointed in 1995 as director of the Centre for Continuing Education. This centre, which was self-funded and based at Peninsula, had been successful thanks to former director Dale Ingamells. On Ingamells' retirement Kupsch was appointed. He had been a commercial teacher in Victorian secondary schools, and then became Education Manager of the Securities Institute of Victoria and National Educational Manager of the Financial Planning Association. The centre changed its name to the Professional Development Institute. Kupsch left the post in 2001 to become Business Manager of the Faculty of Information Technology at Caulfield Campus.

Staff of 1998

Greg R Lancaster commenced at the Gippsland campus on a part-time secondment from the DEECD where he was employed as a secondary physics, maths and IT teacher. He completed a BSc double major in physics and maths at LaTrobe University in 1978 and a DipEd (LaTrobe 1979). He specialised in tutoring physics method and completed a Masters of Teaching focusing on the use of ICT at Monash in 2003. In 2006 he resigned from the DEECD after 26 years to continue in part-time position in the faculty where he worked as a science (physics) educator. Lancaster has played an important role in assisting with project managing and delivery of a number of science education projects including the Science Teaching and Learning (STaL) program for the Catholic Education Office, the development of the web based P-10 Science Continuum and the highly successful Professional Learning in Primary Science (PLiPS) program for the Victorian Department of Education. In 2009 he was appointed as an academic liaison for the John Monash Science School and continues to work in this role to support and strengthen professional relationships between the school and the faculty. His research interests include pedagogies for effective team teaching and the use of flexible learning spaces and applications of new learning technologies to build conceptual understanding in physics. He is assisting in curriculum development and virtual laboratory simulations for the NBN Virtual School of Emerging Sciences.

Richard James Trembath graduated BSc, DipEd from University of Melbourne and taught in Victorian high schools for nine years before spending a year in England as a Commonwealth Exchange Teacher in 1968. In England, he was able to travel extensively as Victorian English-Speaking Union Travelling Scholar. He returned to Frankston Teachers' College and completed an MEd by major thesis at Monash in 1976. He played an active part in the discussions which led to the formation of Chisholm Institute of Technology and the incorporation of this into Monash University. Always interested in science and the teaching of it, for many years he worked on the councils of the Science Teachers Association of Victoria and the Australian College of Educators. In 1978–79 he undertook graduate studies in environmental science and science education at the University of Texas and his PhD was nominated for the outstanding university dissertation of the year. He believes that primary teachers need to have a sound knowledge of the subjects they teach and was a strong advocate for the general studies component of pre-service courses. His research interests include the ways in which people understand and fail to understand scientific explanations. As associate professor he led the School of Education at Peninsula Campus before he retired.

Andrew John Cope, Melbourne-born, moved to Gippsland to take up his first teaching position at a school with only 10 pupils. He had a varied professional background – from classroom teaching, to physical education consultancy, to working with the Catholic Education Office in Warragul, to tertiary teaching at University of Melbourne and finally to the Gippsland Institute of Education. As a senior lecturer he was a great supporter of physical education and was a role model for his students through his own involvement in a range of outdoor sporting activities. He was known as 'Copey', he had a passion for life and the outdoors and he integrated these wherever possible into his teaching. Among his many achievements was the Bachelor of Sport and Outdoor Education at the Gippsland Campus. Single-handed he made this course a reality, against a great deal of opposition, at a time when the ongoing viability for education at Gippsland was in question. This course, now a lighthouse program of Monash University at the Peninsula Campus, only happened because of the inspiration and perspiration of one man. What he loved most was taking students on outdoor journeys, ranging from surfing, kayaking, bush-walking, to cross country and downhill skiing in winter.

He was tragically killed in a car accident on November 16th 2006, aged 56. In 2012 he was posthumously awarded an Australian College of Educators award for his contribution to physical health and wellbeing.

Rosemary Bennett has been from 1998 a lecturer at Peninsula Campus Faculty of Education. Rosemary has brought a range of skills to the pre-service teacher education programs at Peninsula Campus over the past 14 years. She has taught across early childhood and primary education along with contributions to the BSOR course in the area of physical education and health. She has held a number of course leadership positions within the faculty and has strongly supported the development of the international fieldwork placement program in the Cook Islands. Rosemary regularly lectures at Monash's Singapore campus where she has introduced wellbeing and sustainability units as well as innovations in the creative arts. Her qualitative research and publication is in the field of early childhood creativity through music, movement and dance. She became tenured in 2001. Rosemary has a strong commitment to experiential learning and arts-based education.

Simon Marginson, BA (Hons) Melbourne, completed his PhD on the topic 'Markets in Education', which won the Chancellor's Prize and also the Australian Association for Education Research Prize for the best doctorate in education. He worked for the Federation of Australian University Staff Associations, and in 1991 became senior research fellow for the Centre for the Study of Higher Education at the University of Melbourne. He wrote extensively on education policy and published three major books: *Education and Public Policy in Australia* (1993), *Educating Australia* (1997) and *Markets in Education* (1997). He was also the recipient of major research grants. He chaired the editorial board of Australian Universities Review between 1995 and 2000. Offered the chair of education at Griffith University, Dick White urged the Vice-Chancellor of Monash (David Robinson) to secure him for Monash, which was done. In 1998 he joined the Monash University Faculty of Education as reader. He was appointed to a personal chair as of 2000 and directed the Monash Centre for Research in International Education in 1999–2006. He also edited the *Australian Journal of Education* from 2000 to 2005. He became fellow of the Australian College of Education in 1994 and Fellow of the Academy of Social Sciences Australia in 2000. In 2002 he was awarded a five-year Australian Professorial Fellowship on the recommendation of the Australian Research Council (ARC). Marginson returned to the University of Melbourne Centre for the Study of Higher Education in July 2006.

Chapter 7

Entrepreneurial times

2000–2010

With Dick White's move to London, the position of Dean was advertised in August 1999, and a selection committee formed. From a shortlist of four candidates Dr Susan G Willis, Dean of the School of Education at Murdoch University, was selected. Dr Willis had a BSc and DipEd from the University of Western Australia and a PhD from Purdue University. Willis had been a teacher in Western Australian secondary schools, specialising in mathematics, and also held posts in curriculum development before taking a university position. She had been associate professor at Murdoch from 1994, and Dean of Education since 1997. Her research interests were in mathematics curriculum, gender, social justice and education, professional judgement and accountability. She had published eight books and monographs, 38 chapters in books and refereed articles, 12 commissioned research reports, and had large research and development grants. She accepted the appointment in December and took up her post in April 2000. Dick Gunstone had been Acting Dean.[1] While David Aspin and Dick White had helped oversee the transition of the Faculty into a new age and over three locations, it was the new Dean, a fresh face from outside who was to consolidate these moves.

Willis had been at Murdoch University for over 20 years and felt the need of a new challenge. She admired the Monash education faculty, had spent six weeks of a study leave here and became enraptured with the university library and its central role at the heart of the university.

She came to Monash in dramatically changing times. Enrolments were falling and there were consequent financial problems.

Sue Willis was to be Dean for a decade. Entrepreneurship became the catchword of the times. The faculty had to continue to find new sources of funding and attract a wider clientele. The faculty encouraged participation

---

[1] Dick White was suitably farewelled at a dinner in the Banquet Room of the Campus Centre on 6 December 1999 with speeches by Paul Gardner, Peter Fensham and Dick Gunstone.

in double degrees, developed courses at all levels for organisations not just for individuals, offered courses in more than education and took part in an extensive outreach of offerings, especially overseas. In addition it was to be a period of high staff turnover. What had been a bright young vibrant faculty had become an older one and the former bright stars had to be replaced. By 2010 two-thirds of the staff had not been there in 2000. New appointments were an important element of the period Willis was Dean. She warned each selection committee: 'Don't appoint yourself'. She reminded members that they were already here and the faculty did not need more of them. She also rejected the notion that had been a long-standing tradition in the faculty, that staff had to have school teaching experience and that they should know the Victorian education system. Whereas staff had looked at the PhD as the culmination of their academic career, now it was a pre-requisite to start a career and preferably with some publications.

Dean at Council

In an oral report given at the University Council in 2000, the Dean Professor Sue Willis outlined the major issues facing the Faculty of Education. These were, primarily, the need to improve the finances and to 'reinforce and enhance research and professional productivity and reputation'. Willis reminded the Council that while the university was not a business and should not be, there were nevertheless money pressures which meant they had to be more businesslike. She said that some members of the faculty regretted this emphasis and many were not sure how to go about it. She also reminded Council that time spent on sourcing funds took time away from teaching and research. She also recognised that the faculty was expected to be more self-reliant and entrepreneurial. There were problems for the education faculty, as teachers were not high-income earners and so were less willing to pay fees for courses. In the major field of faculty work, which was initial teacher training (at all levels – early childhood, primary, secondary, vocational and adult), DETYA funds were the major source of funds. Willis saw the solution as short courses and award courses. There were possible partnerships with specific groups both in Australia and overseas to provide such courses. Willis reminded Council of the research culture of the faculty and its success in gaining prestigious grants. She was intent it remain a premier research faculty.

7.1 Professor Sue Willis, Dean of Education.
Education Faculty

7.2 Peter Sullivan.
Education Faculty

Chairs

When Willis came in, chairs were held by Aspin, Bishop, Gunstone and Rizvi with Gerald Burke in a special chair as director of his centre. Just prior to her term, appointments were made to two advertised chairs: Terri Seddon and Simon Marginson, both internal candidates (the latter was offered a personal chair). During her tenure a number of additional professors were appointed, including one for the Gippsland campus and two for the Peninsula campus, and two internal applicants were promoted. By the end of her tenure there were eleven professors including six women. These were Gerald Burke, Marilyn Fleer, Jane Kenway, John Loughran, Dennis Moore, Peter Sullivan, Terri Seddon, Ilana Snyder and Margaret Somerville. Arriving soon after were Sue Webb and Mike Askew.

Selection committees

Willis has an impact on the procedures of selection committees. She insisted all discussion of candidates had to be based on documentation tabled or circulated: applications, CVs, reports from referees and so on. Unsubstantiated gossip about candidates was not permitted to be brought into the discussion. As mentioned earlier, she felt there had been a tendency for staff to appoint people very like themselves. It was a different era; no longer could someone with good school teaching experience and some academic promise come on board and achieve a doctorate as a culmination of their career. It was now important to have a doctorate and preferably some research publications on entry.

Administration

With the abolition of groups or areas, governance centred on portfolios. Associate Deans held these responsibilities. There were Associate Deans for Research, Education and Staff. Later there was an Associate Dean (Engagement) which covered international as well as partnerships forged with groups like the Victorian Police and Box Hill TAFE. The portfolios changed with differing needs.

The administrative structure in 2002 saw the Dean assisted by a group of Associate Deans: Professor Terri Seddon (Research), Associate Professor Peter Gronn (Development), Dr Ros Smith (Staff), Dr Debbie Corrigan and Dr Paul Richardson (Teaching) and Associate Professor Tony Taylor (Gippsland). Peter Lawford continued as Faculty Manager. The Faculty

Board was still the major governance body, with an executive under it able to deal with urgent matters that arose between board meetings. There were then five major committees: Staff, Curriculum, Research, Development and Environment and Resources. There were also specialist committees advisory to the Dean, such as Conference Travel, Outside Study Leave (OSL) and a campus management committee. Generally there was stability within these portfolios with people holding a post for 2–3 years.

In this decade Gippsland saw several people in the post of Associate Dean (Gippsland) and the rapid turnover – they had an average stay of 18 months – was seen to disadvantage the campus. There was a lack of continuity in putting their case forward.

Later (in 2007), to increase the sense of staff having a 'home' base, there were research areas designated under the leadership of a professor. The idea was to gather together people with strength in certain research areas to exchange views and give them a base. To this was added what were first called Campus Coordinators, later Associate Deans, for each campus. They chaired staff meetings and dealt with teaching and research issues at their campus as well as managing use of teaching and office space. Willis found it necessary to give leadership to each campus as she feared some staff members could become 'lost'. Despite this, Willis' aim was to create a sense of faculty and not for people to think in terms of a campus. Willis felt that staff had worked at this and could claim to be the most integrated faculty at Monash University.

Courses

There was a mushrooming of double degrees. For example, approval was given for the Gippsland campus to offer a Bachelor of Business and Commerce together with a Bachelor of Sport and Outdoor Recreation from 2001. Three more new double-degree courses were added: a Bachelor of Social Work/BEd degree, Bachelor of Law/BEd, Bachelor of Information and Management Systems/BEd.

The Bachelor of Sport and Outdoor Recreation had been developed at Gippsland by Andrew Cope. Cope's tremendous energy and enthusiasm created the course, which with its high numbers 'saved' Gippsland. The course proved a great success and quality students were attracted to it as well as good young staff. In 2005 the course was transferred to the Peninsula campus, where Monash had visions of it forming part of a larger health program. Some of the Gippsland staff saw this departure of the program as an 'asset stripper' by the greater Monash. Existing students were allowed to complete their course at Gippsland. There was further sadness when Cope was killed in a car accident in November 2006. The course proved to be a success in terms of student numbers and meant an associate professor was appointed in this area. Applications increased by 60 per cent with the move to the Peninsula campus.

There was a new course called the Bachelor of Adult Learning and Development aimed at workers in the vocational education sector including training in industry. To cater for international students, there was a Bachelor of Education Studies course tagged 'Special Education'. The Bachelor of Educational Studies became a generic degree with various tagged options.

The Bachelor of Early Childhood Studies was a degree especially designed to provide upgrading from the TAFE Diploma of Children's Services to degree level. This course was later offered in Singapore. In 1998 a city cohort was established – initially offered to students from rural areas, but within a year or two expanded to take in students from anywhere in Victoria. In addition to the government sponsorship of students entering the course, it represented a matter of social justice – that of providing university education for students who (for a variety of reasons) were not able to enrol in a university degree, but subsequently demonstrated that they were academically able to complete studies at this level.

Tags were now used to describe degrees, with the Master of Education (Policy and Management), Master of Education (Special Education) and Master of Education (TESOL) as well as courses such as Master of Educational (Policy and Administration), Master of Psychology (Education and Development), Master of Psychology (Counselling) and Master of Education (Early Childhood).

To demonstrate what was required to propose a new course or amend an existing one, we can look at the proposal for the Master in Counselling put forward in August 2005.[2] The document presented to Faculty Board comprised 76 pages. It was a course prepared and run by the faculty with Professor Dennis Moore as team leader, but in conjunction with the Asia-Pacific Management Institute in Singapore (APMI) in order to attract overseas students. It would be taught both by distance mode and face to face by Monash staff. It was planned as a high quality masters degree of one year catering for a diverse range of students who were professionals in various forms of counselling. In the 76 pages supporting the proposal were details covering the need for the course, reasons for its introduction, likely demand,

---

[2] Minutes of Faculty Board 10 August 2005.

the likely viability of the course, the course structure, admission requirements educational objectives and outcomes, administrative arrangements, course title and proposers, organisational arrangements including details of forms of delivery, expected EFTS (35 by 2007), fees, compliance requirements, resources, plus details of the course. Supplementary information included covering likely competition, market research, off-campus facilities, project management, and the role of APMI to name a few. This indicates the detail required for a new or changed course. With many changes, this meant Faculty Board papers were voluminous.

Demanded now were a host of compliance requirements – some related to occupational health and safety, an annual 'Equity and Diversity' report had to be undertaken by each faculty, and so forth.

Evaluation

While formal evaluation of courses had been undertaken in the faculty on a five-year cycle since 1993, from 2005 the university required each faculty to survey students about units as part of new quality assurance policies. This was to be a regular event. There were ten university-wide questions on a Likert scale[3] and ten questions specific to each faculty and their courses or units. All units offered by the faculty in 2005 were surveyed, with a response rate of 47 per cent (compared with an overall university rate of 40 per cent). On each of the ten university questions the education faculty ranked in the top four, and it had the highest ranking for 'the unit enabled me to achieve the learning objectives' and the question 'I found the resources provided for the unit to be helpful' (75 per cent agreeing or strongly agreeing, for the first and 71 per cent in the second). There were of course some issues: feedback needed improving, the quality of online materials needed to be improved and there was an indication that some units needed a change of structure.[4]

Approval of subjects

To introduce a new course or to modify an existing course now required elaborate documentation. Whereas previously a brief course description and approval by the relevant course committee was sufficient, now much more detail was required. These included: reasons for the course, date and regularity

---

[3] On which respondents select a response from 'strongly agree' to 'strongly disagree', 'very happy' to 'not at all happy' or similar.

[4] Lorraine Bennett's report to Faculty Board October 2005.

of offering, anticipated enrolment, location (Clayton, Peninsula, Gippsland), loading for department, staff commitment, workload requirement, prerequisites, summary of the subject, objectives, Method of teaching and assessment in relation to the stated objectives, the Faculty Handbook entry, a library impact statement, faculty endorsement, certification that all procedures had been followed and finally that what had been done conformed to university policies.[5]

The massive changes meant many subjects were dropped, and so a formal 'disestablishment of subjects' had to be undertaken and listed for Faculty Board. As staff and courses changed so did the appropriateness of many subjects.

ENTER scores

The faculty had key performance indicators which layed out the ENTER scores needed for entry to its undergraduate courses.[6] ENTER scores were replaced in 2010 by ATAR scores – Australian Tertiary Admissions Rank. In 2000 it was required to increase the intake ENTER scores by 1 per cent per annum. In 2000 no course had an ENTER score below 70, in line with a university-wide policy. For 2000 80 per cent of the offers went to student who listed Monash courses as their first preference. Balancing enrolments in the wide range of courses was difficult, with primary, secondary, specialised, undergraduate, postgraduate and high degree – not to mention also having targets for full-fee paying students both local and international. In 2004 ENTER scores were 76 for the BEd Primary at Gippsland, 89 for the BA/BEd at Clayton and 86.05 for the BA/BEd Peninsula. There was an issue with these scores and a similar pattern continued for each campus over the next decade. The faculty was criticised for its 'low' ENTER scores, particularly those of Gippsland. However, the Gippsland experience indicated that ENTER scores were not always a good guide to potentially talented teachers.

In 2008 the faculty was able to report that all students had ENTER scores over 70. Clayton had 89 per cent over, Gippsland 46 per cent over 80 and Peninsula 50 per cent over 80. In 2002, 99 per cent of students admitted to education had ATAR scores over 70.

Some, of course, entered through other selection processes. For example, the Bachelor of Early Childhood Studies program (a qualification aimed

---

[5] Faculty Board Minutes, Education Faculty, 8 March 2000.
[6] Equivalent National Tertiary Entrance Rank.

specifically at upgrading staff working in child care – an initiative supported by the then and current governments) selected students on the basis of results obtained in TAFE institutes' Diploma of Children's Services, with a minimum of distinction average required.

Research

A key measure for research was what was termed 'DETYA-recognised publications'. This included books, chapters in books, refereed articles and refereed conference papers. This measure was important as it fed directly into both education's share of university research funds and also the faculty's share of the remaining Commonwealth operating funds, which is partly determined by research performance. As the Associate Dean (Research) commented, 'it also shapes perceptions of Education's standing inside the university.'[7] This measure was closely scrutinised and in 1994 the accounting firm KPMG was engaged by the Commonwealth to check the publications listed.

Staff

Associate Professor Margaret Gill retired at the end of 1999. She continued as an Associate of the faculty for two more years, directing a major ARC project on the development of teaching standards for the English-teaching profession. This was one of three major ARC projects on teaching standards which the faculty was awarded at that time, the others for science teachers (directed by Lawrence Ingvarson) and maths teachers (directed by Alan Bishop) gave the faculty a particularly high national profile in this field. Gill had made a major impact on the faculty in her time there, both in her work in English and literacy and as a competent administrator. When Alan Bishop retired at the end of 2002 after a notable 10 years, among the farewells he was accorded a *festschrift*, or book in his honour, involving leading mathematics educators. It was called *Critical Issues in Mathematics Education: Major Contributions of Alan Bishop*, edited by Philip Clarkson and Norma Presmeg and published in 2008 by Springer Science+Business Media, LLC. It was an indication of the high regard in which Bishop was held internationally and a reminder of how fortunate Monash was to secure his services. As well as being a leading international figure in his field, he

---

[7] Minutes of Faculty Board 12 July 2000.

proved a superb member of staff, sharing many of the administrative burdens and encouraging to aspiring staff members.

In 2001, 27 per cent of staff were under 40 years old, 69 per cent had doctorates and 68 per cent of the staff was female. Late November 2001 a morning tea was held to farewell professor David Aspin, who was retiring. A noted philosopher, a dedicated Dean, Aspin was also much sought after as a speaker at conferences and seminars. He was to continue his research after leaving Monash, especially in life-long education. He was accorded the title of professor emeritus by the University Council. Glenn Rowley, who had been such a force in research and research methodology, left in 2002 to become general manager of the Victorian Curriculum and Assessment Authority.

Barry McGaw, Director of ACER, who had close links with many in the faculty over the years was confirmed again as an honorary professor. Dick Gunstone retired at the end of 2005 after a distinguished career of 32 years in the faculty, having gained an international reputation for his research and respected by students and staff alike as a helpful colleague. In 2005 Dr Zane Ma Rhea received the Vice-Chancellor's Award for Distinguished Teaching.

In 2003, two long-serving staff at Clayton left. Dr Robin Small resigned to take up a chair in New Zealand and Dr Lawrence Bartak took retirement. Small had been a key figure in the philosophy area and Bartak had been a key figure in special education, as an authority on autism and as director of the Krongold Centre.

2001

The budget in 2001 saw income and expenditure at about $12.5 million, $10.5 million of which was taken up by salaries. DETYA contributed $11,073,748 and $846,600 came from fees. For 2001 EFTS was 2,097 – made up of 158 higher (research) degrees, 783 other postgraduate degrees and 1155 undergraduate courses. For 2002 a drop in undergraduates meant a fall to 2056 EFTS. The amalgamations meant some staff were uneasy about joining the new institution and readily sought ways out. With the university keen to encourage people to 'take the package' and leave voluntarily, the faculty had to pay the bill for these retirements.

Sadly in September 2001 the Monash Education Alumni had to be disbanded as membership had slumped from 130 to 25. The trustees of the funds for the association's awards ($500 to an MEd student and a $600 to a PhD student) transferred the funds ($2,200) to the faculty.[8]

---

[8] The trustees were Robert Boyd, Leslie Greagg and Bernie Rymer.

7.3 Sue Willis and Dick Gunstone.
MUA IN-8148

Cook Island practicum

An interesting project during the 2000s was the Peninsula campus Cook Islands Teaching Practicum. This commenced in 2001 and was intended as a teaching and learning experience in a cross-cultural context, with Tony Townsend, Dick Trembath, Jill Robbins, Geraldine Burke, Lynne Surman, Len Cairns and Geoff Romeo involved in the pilot program. Initially it was a teaching practicum for students training in early childhood and primary education but in 2003 was extended to include students studying to be secondary teachers. In 2003, 37 students and 3 staff members participated in this scheme. Julie Edwards and Rod Cameron were among the main organisers and the experience included teaching practice in Cook Island schools as well as seminars and workshops, working with the Cook Islands Teachers College under Teremoana Hodges.

The Dean's views

After being Dean for five months, Sue Willis gave a report to the faculty on her impressions and plans. She found that 'Faculty members across all three campuses have said that the integration into a single department of the three Schools which originally formed the Faculty has been successful in reducing divisions between the campuses and encouraging us to work together as a Faculty.' She found some administrative processes, especially the 'academic teams', were not working well. A lack of communication was often cited as an issue. There was a need for Gippsland to change its organisational arrangements and for all staff to have the opportunity to improve induction and mentoring and provide teaching and research support. Decision-making and communication processes needed to be made more transparent and accessible.

A major requirement in Willis' view was expanding income sources beyond funding from the Commonwealth, Department of Education, Training and Youth Affairs, (DETYA). Staff costs being a high proportion of the faculty budget meant little flexibility. More income from non-DETYA sources was required. The work of the units such as the centres operating within the faculty needed to be reviewed to ensure there was a businesslike approach. Willis also saw the need to clarify academic work practice. What was academic work? How was it distributed? What was required for academic advancement? There were not only issues of teaching and teaching workloads but research quality and productivity. Also there were professional issues, sharing of administrative work in the faculty and 'citizenship' work in the community and with national and international bodies. She saw the strength of the faculty being its wide range of courses and subjects offered and the diversity and flexibility of its delivery. She saw the need to either decrease course offerings or increase student numbers. She concluded her review by setting down the tasks required to advance these goals.

Academic teaching load

A paper in November 2000 set out the Academic Load Distribution Guidelines.[9] Against a background of increasing staff workloads the document tried to set out guidelines for an equitable distribution of teaching within the faculty. There were many problems – the mismatch between staff expertise and student enrolment was one. Student demand for a course

---

[9] Minutes of Faculty Board 83/2000.

would often change unpredictably. The guidelines did not take into account academics whose responsibilities were mainly in research or in student support nor did it take into account the level of community and professional service undertaken.

All academics were expected to participate in what was called 'teaching, research and other service'. Standard contracts at the time allocated 50 per cent for teaching, 30 per cent for research and 20 per cent for other service over a 46-week year. Some offsets were allowed in special circumstances.

The formula which combined contact hours and enrolments gave points to each activity undertaken under seven headings: subject coordination, teaching, individual student feedback/marking, placements, research degrees/projects, other (consultation, PD) and major administrative responsibilities. For example a 1-hour lecture was allotted 25 points (1.5 points for a repeat lecture), a 1-hour tutorial 2 points (1 for repeat) undergraduate marking (4000 words) 1 point, postgraduate marking (6000+ words) 1.5 points. A School Review garnered 30 points and being an Associate Dean, .5 point. Course coordinator was given .5 point multiplied by EFTSU to a maximum of 50 points.

International students

By 2002 there was a dramatic change in the faculty with larger numbers of international students, all of whom were fee-paying. There were 139 EFTS of such students commencing and 93 returning international students. Half of these were in masters courses. They originated from the following countries: Singapore, 14 per cent; Japan, 12 per cent; Hong Kong, 7 per cent; Indonesia, 6 per cent; and Taiwan, 6 per cent.[10]

Widening

In 2002 a successful partnership was made with the Victoria Police. It meant 100 members of the police force undertook masters degrees, both by coursework and research, in the faculty. One of the MEd streams, 'leadership policy and change', had a cohort of 30 police as students, and 9 police were doing research degrees. There was also an evaluation by the faculty of the Police Schools Involvement Program. Another partnership was with Box Hill TAFE, with lecturers and administrative staff enrolled in coursework degrees.

---

[10] Monash University Archives MON 61 Faculty Board Minutes 25 September 2002.

Funds

A cash flow report of 30 September 2002 shows total annual income for the faculty as $12,382,348. Of this $11,073,748 came from DETYA funding, fee income was $846,600 targeted support funding was $83,000, the Faculty Development Office $270,000 and external earning levies contributed $135,000.

Expenditure showed the dominance of salary costs in the budget: $9,379,120. The practicum cost $940,000, non-salary costs were $1,819,500, the provision of long-service leave was $50,000 and $50,000 was placed in the development fund.

For a faculty that had battled to secure funding apart from DETYA, the situation was promising. The Dean reported to the Vice-Chancellor on this diversification and the achievement of funds from fee-paying students both local and international. She also pointed out the limited opportunities the faculty had for economies, as well as the disadvantaged position it was in: fewer professors than the numbers justified, a staff-student ratio of 28.5 (compared with a university wide ratio of 21.9) and the lack of administrative support for teaching and research for developing new contracts and projects. Facilities, especially at Clayton and Gippsland, were also very run down.[11]

Funding for the practicum for both nursing and education took on a new formula in 2005 and DEST provided a loading of $657 per EFTS for education. So of $11,028,528 provided for education, $993,384 was for the teaching practicum component.[12]

Courses 2003

In 2003 an overview was given of the faculty and its offerings. It stated that courses spanned initial and further education for teachers of early childhood, primary, secondary and adult learners, counselling and human development, sport and outdoor recreation and capacity building for individuals, organisations and communities. The faculty offered both undergraduate and graduate courses. Forty-two per cent of students were undergraduates in initial teacher training. That the courses were in demand was in no doubt, as Monash received two-thirds of all first preferences in the state.

Twenty-seven per cent of the students were enrolled in graduate diplomas that provided initial teacher education for students who had a bachelor

---

[11] The Dean, Professor Sue Willis to the Vice-Chancellor, Professor Peter Darvall 31 October 2002.
[12] Minutes of Faculty Board 27 April 2005.

degree in a non-education field. Within teacher education programs the faculty offered 25 curriculum specialties ranging across the humanities and social sciences, creative and performing arts, mathematics and sciences, and business and information technology. Of these initial training courses, primary, secondary and outdoor education and recreation were offered at the Gippsland campus, early childhood and primary education at Peninsula and secondary and adult education at the Clayton campus.

There were also postgraduate courses with 20 per cent of students enrolled in courses leading to postgraduate certificates and diplomas and masters degrees in coursework.

Postgraduate offerings were described as flexible and diverse recognising different starting points and pathways to learning.

There was also a large research preparation program, with over 340 students (12 per cent of all students in the faculty) enrolled in either research masters degrees or doctorates. There were doctorates in PhD and EdD, the EdD (offered since 1991) described as a degree for professionals and the PhD an opportunity to make a contribution to theory.

The faculty could boast a significant national and international profile in various fields of academic education research. There was for example a long tradition of research in science and mathematics education, and also there was research in teaching and learning and in professional practice. The Centre for Work and Learning Studies drew together research in policy studies, studies of work and organisation and leadership. The faculty was also noted for its academic studies in globalisation and international education, as well as cross-cultural and cross-national studies. This was handled through the Monash Centre for Research in International Education. Monash had combined with ACER to form the Centre for the Economics of Education and Training (CEET), where studies looked at the contribution of education and training to economic and social development and the implications for education and training given the changing nature of the Australian economy. In 2001 the centre brought revenue of $754,588 to the faculty budget.

Psychology had also been a strong area within the faculty, with contributions to knowledge through the Krongold and Elwyn Morey Centres. Language and literacy made a contribution too, both in specialised language studies and in English for speakers of other languages. There were also specialities in early childhood education, sport and outdoor recreation and studies of cultural difference and youth. It was an imposing list, well supported by research grants, books and publications.

In 2003 it was proposed that there be a faculty self-assessment, or internal review, followed by an external verification of the process culminating in a report late 2004. Guidelines were set down, a working party established and the faculty had to undertake its internal review of itself early 2004.

Numbers 2003

In 2003 the EFTS for High Degrees (HDR) was 186.8 (of which 19.2 comprised international students), other postgraduate students 922.1 (123.2 were international) and there were 837.4 in undergraduate courses (56.1 being international), giving a faculty total of 1,946.3 with 198.5 of these international students.

Operational plan

When Peter Darvall visited the faculty to address Faculty Board in September 2002, he emphasised that 'Leading the Way Monash 2020' was still the operational strategic document. He gave an overview of the Monash campuses – Malaysia (growing steadily, financially stable), South Africa (small enrolments), Berwick (a third building was planned), Gippsland (some faculties were languishing but education was doing well), Caulfield (overcrowded and a growing proportion of overseas students) and Peninsula (struggling for numbers). It gave a picture of the geographical expansion of the University.[13]

In 2003 the faculty developed the operational plan for 2004–2006.[14] It reflected the Nelson review, which focused on the need to bring extra students into teacher education. It was felt that market forces did not apply – for example, shortages of teachers do not convert into higher salaries.

One-year teacher-education program were seen as expensive as 'total cost of school placement has to be funded from only one year's fees.' The Education Department was the major employer of Monash education students and so their policies and priorities have a direct and often dramatic impact.

With university free, in the years 1974 to 1987 there were some career advantages for teachers to enrol in postgraduate education courses – and in the 1980s one in eight did. With fees and changing policies there was little advantage for teachers to undertake such professional education at their

---

[13] Monash University Archives MON 61 Faculty Board Minutes 25 September 2002.
[14] Monash University Archives MON 61 Faculty Board Minutes 2 July 2003. The Faculty of Education Operational Plan 2004–2006.

own cost. These fees were payable via HECS; they were Commonwealth-supported places.[15] Research degrees remained free for four years for PhD and two years for masters candidates. The faculty had to consider attracting different groups of students into courses, such as those wanting to train in counselling, organisational capability, leadership and work and learning studies. Links had to be forged with external organisations with requirements in these fields. Another group sought was that of international students and it seemed education could offer attractive short non-award courses. There was concern, too, that the diminished number of teachers taking postgraduate degrees would lessen the pool of potential staff for the faculty. Traditionally many staff were initially classroom teachers, adding research degrees to this professional background. 'Leading the Way' specifically refers to the 'missing generation of Education academics'. It was also asserted that academic salaries offered little incentive to teachers and similar professionals to take the steps necessary to be considered for university appointments.

The Australian Council of Deans of Education, in their report on the impact of the Higher Education Support Act (2003), stated that the overall funding for teacher education was inadequate. The removal of the funding distinction between undergraduate and postgraduate did not acknowledge the difference in costs of delivery. There was also a lack of appreciation that education faculties were unable to respond quickly to variations in demands across subject areas.

School reviews

In 2003 Anita Forsyth, who had long been associated with the economics and business studies method work, took over as director of the contract for the DEECD's School Review Services. She developed a benchmark school-review quality-assurance process. By 2013 the contract with the department had been renewed three times, and she and her team of 15 reviewers had conducted between 75–90 school reviews per year over this period, bringing important funds into the faculty.

Yet another 'plan' or set of guidelines was issued in 2002, an overview of the 'Learning and Teaching Plan 2003–2005'. Authored by Professor Alan Lindsay and Associate Professor Chris Browne it stressed the need for flexibility in modes of delivery of teaching and learning, of using technology and the 'internationalisation' of teaching and learning. The report

---

[15] From 2014, masters units will attract full fees, doubling the cost to students.

also suggested developments should be 'educationally sound, rather than electronically driven'.[16]

The Vice-Chancellor Professor David Robinson departed dramatically in 2002, over an old plagiarism issue, but Dean Willis recorded at Faculty Board the loss to Monash of an excellent leader.[17] A good opinion of Robinson was held by many others in the faculty. Deputy Peter Darvall became Vice-Chancellor until a new one could be selected. Professor Richard Larkins AO, a medical professor from the University of Melbourne, was Vice-Chancellor from 2003 until 2009 and took the lead in restoring and enhancing the university's reputation.

2003

Professor Terri Seddon in her 2003 report on the research portfolio stated that there were research officers now located on each of the three campuses of Monash. The higher degree numbers (HDR) target of 168 for 2004 had been met and there was also now a supervisor liaison officer (Jill Brown). New staff were given training in supervision and active involvement in the AARE was encouraged. An active seminar program was also part of the activity in research.

The English-language requirement for overseas students had been a score of 6 on the IELTS scale (International English Language Testing System), which required competence in reading, writing, speaking and listening in English, but this was lifted to 7 from 2004.

The reiteration of slogans intensified and in the operation plan for 2004–2006, Monash University defined itself as a global university.[18] As had been earlier stated in the 'Global Development Framework', 'Monash aspires to be among the front rank of genuine broad-based international universities'. To make the point even stronger it went on to assert that 'global development was seen as an 'essential imperative'.[19]

The 2004 review

In 2004 there was a faculty review. This comprised a seven month 'self-review' period followed by a visit by an external review panel. The review

---

[16] Minutes of Faculty Board 25 September 2002.
[17] Monash University Archives MON 61 Faculty Board Minutes 24 July 2002.
[18] Minutes of Faculty Board 30/2003.
[19] Minutes of Faculty Board 21 September 2001.

7.4 Professor Terri Seddon.
Education Faculty

resulted in glowing comments about the process itself. Among the findings were that despite some concerns, the single-model department had served the faculty well. The high degree of professionalism of the general staff was noted, as was the work of the development officers. There was a need though to develop research clusters.[20] In 2004 the faculty had a student-staff ratio of 24.7:1, above the national average for Education faculties of 23:1, and well above the figure for other faculties at Monash, 19.8:1.

Research clusters

At Clayton the groups or areas were important in fostering research collegiality, so attempts were made to retain this in the one-department structure of this large faculty. In searching for congeries of interest one idea was to have research clusters. In 2004 as Associate Dean (Research), Seddon suggested 10 areas that might be considered research clusters and a contact person for each. These were: adult learning for work, life and citizenship (Terri Seddon), Centre for the Economics of Education and Training (Gerald Burke), Centre for Childhood Studies (Marilyn Fleer), Centre for Science,

---

[20] Minutes of Faculty Board 8 December 2004.

Mathematics and Technology Education (Dick Gunstone), culture, language and diversity in education (Brenton Doecke and Jane Kenway), information and communication technologies in education (Bernard Holkner), learning in the later years (Len Cairns), Monash Centre for Research in International Education (Simon Marginson), professional learning (John Loughran) and sport, health and outdoor recreation studies (Justin O'Connor).

Grants

The year of 2004 was described as 'stunning' in terms of Australian Research Council (ARC) grants. With six Discovery Grants offered to the faculty, Monash had secured 30 per cent of all Discovery Grants given in education. There were several HMRC grants and CEET received funding from the national training authority.

The ARC Discovery grants were highly prestigious – the two sources of funds from the ARC were for Discovery Grants or Linkage Grants. The general aim was to support the highest quality research leading to the discovery of new ideas and the advancement of knowledge.

The contract with the Victorian Department of Education and Training to undertake school reviews was extended until 2007. Major research grants came to Loughran and Doecke for their teaching and Learning project, to Plunkett and Kronborg for their work on giftedness, and to the faculty as a whole for the Master of School Leadership project ($1.2 million).

Rethinking secondary teacher training

In 2004 the faculty commenced a rethinking of secondary teacher education. This was to bring about not just a review of what was being done but also some renewal. There was also the hope of bringing some alignment between secondary programs at Clayton and Gippsland. It was a period of considerable external pressures on secondary teacher education. There were new policy agendas for both state and federal governments and the schools themselves underwent major changes. After a long process of review and consultation in 2007, Dr Jane Mitchell was able to report progress.[21] What emerged was a revised structure and unit content. There were to be new core units, which were described as addressing the 'central tasks' of teacher education.[22]

---

[21] Minutes of Faculty Board 18 April 2007 and 21 March 2007.
[22] 'Central tasks' as defined by S Feiman-Nemser 'From Preparation to Practice: Designing a Continuum to Strengthen and Sustain Teaching', *Teachers College Record*, 2001, 103(6), pp. 1013–1055.

The units would also be consistent with the accreditation requirement of the Victorian Institute of Teaching established in 2001, which effectively licensed teachers. The core units involved subject matter knowledge, how this subject matter could be taught, a range of teaching practices, understanding of the diversity of the learner and their context. Issues relating to schooling, curriculum, pedagogy and assessment were also part of the core structure. In addition there were issues of values, professional identity, beliefs about teaching and the skills of educational enquiry.

There was also a major change in the method subjects or curriculum units as they were called. In 2007 there were 27 curriculum units (or method subjects) and these were to be reduced to 8–9 broad cross-disciplinary units for the first semester. In the first semester the broad units would be used to cover work in Years 7 to 10 and in the second semester the existing specialised curriculum units would cover the work in Years 11 and 12. Not all method staff liked this. There was also a rethink of fieldwork (the practicum) to try to develop a more cutting-edge approach. The practicum was separated, with the course becoming longer at 1.25 academic years, and the motives for this came under scrutiny by the staff.

As Anita Forsyth has commented:

> Many of us thought the separation of fieldwork was for financial reasons rather than for philosophical ones but it is true that it did allow a more flexible approach – for example if students 'failed' fieldwork they could still pass method and repeat just the fieldwork unit later. I guess also if the whole course was about encouraging teacher action research and reflective practice it was important perhaps that the professional experience was independent of the method units. Of course professional experience (PE) was also a growing area with the need to service so many more courses including PE requirements in all years of a 4 year education degree.[23]

Other

Music education and research in music education received a boost with the work of Dr Jane Southcott. Southcott had also developed a keyboard laboratory at Gippsland. As well as method work and supervision, Southcott brought to Clayton from Gippsland the annual revues or musicals that she produced with her music students. At Gippsland she performed in shows

---

[23] Communication with the author.

7.5 *Green Door* student revue, Gippsland, 1989. Staff participants: Tony Taylor (back row left) and Jane Southcott (front row middle).
Education Faculty

7.6 *Mob School* a Grad DipEd student revue in 1995. Can you find Libby Tudball and Jane Southcott?
Education Faculty

such as *Green Door*, a teenage rites-of-passage musical, with lyrics and music all written by the students. At Clayton there was *Mob School* in 1995, another original production, with others following annually such as *Teachalot at Camelot* in 2004 and *Papyrus Rubric* in 2007. Southcott recognised that most music teachers would be required to put on such events in their schools, usually with few resources.

Approval was given for a new award, the Jeff Northfield award for excellence in teacher research. Northfield had been a prolific researcher in that field as well as a much respected colleague at both Clayton and Peninsula campuses.[24] In December 2004, the Faculty of Education choir celebrated 30 years of singing performs its annual program of Christmas carols.

2005

As a consequence of the 2004 faculty review, the Curriculum Committee undertook a review of assessment practices and policies across all courses, and also ensured all unit guides were available online. They also took up other issues raised by the review including the practicum and the need to arrest the declining number of schools taking student teachers by building better and closer relationships with schools. For 2005 total available funds for the faculty were $19,456,613. This comprised $7,776,362 for Clayton, $2,597,758 for Gippsland and $3,100,550 for Peninsula.

Research induction

In July 2005 the position of Associate Dean (Research Induction) was created and Associate Professor Ilana Snyder was appointed, with Helen Forgasz as director of Research Degrees. There was now a Research Committee chaired by the Associate Dean [Research], Jane Kenway) and the Research Induction Committee (chaired by the Associate Dean [Research Induction]. The aim of the new post and committee was to enhance induction, supervision, completion rates, marketing research degrees and the development of new research pathways for students. The committee would also oversee allocation of supervision and would represent the faculty on the Monash Research Graduate School Committee.

---

[24] Professor Jeff Northfield died in May 2004; he had joined the faculty in 1975.

7.7 Professor Jane Kenway.
Education Faculty

2006 review

In 2007 the faculty reviewed its performance over 2006. This review was quite detailed. The headings covered evaluation, research, research training and scholarship, management, faculty KPIs. To take one example under evaluation, the stated objective was 'varied and productive pedagogies that challenge and extend all students intellectually while being respectful and inclusive of difference' – the strategies proposed to achieve this were 'continue and expand professional development programs on productive pedagogies in relation to feedback and assessment practices and flexible delivery. There were four targets specified for 2006 – one was '75 per cent of academic staff participating in at least one session to promulgate results of the 2005 Assessment Practices and Policy Project'. This item was evaluated as 'achieved around 50 per cent'.[25]

Report on teacher education

During 2006 there was a House of Representatives Report into Teacher Education. When Faculty Board discussed this report in March 2007, the Dean spoke of the 'surprising and pleasant outcome.'[26] There seemed a real awareness of the needs of teacher education; they also recommended additional funding and stressed the importance of research for strong teacher education programs. The report placed the emphasis on the exit point (the

---

[25] Minutes of Faculty Board 21 March 2007.
[26] Minutes of Faculty Board 21 March 2007.

outcomes of potential teachers) rather than the entry point. Like many reports before it, such as the Victorian Enquiry into Teacher Education (the Asche Report), it was regarded as an excellent report with helpful recommendations but in terms of any real action it was to languish. The Australian Council of Deans of Education, of which Sue Willis was president, had hopes of additional funding through this report.

Assessment policy

Much documentation was now required of the faculty. Policy statements had to be prepared on a range of issues and various forms of audits and reviews undertaken. In 2006 the faculty produced a revised assessment policy, a 22-page document.[27] Set down were the principles of assessment, the alignment with desired outcomes. The assessment tasks needed to be challenging, engaging, connected and educative. Assessment also needed to be purposeful (it could be criterion references, formative, summative, self- or peer-assessed). Details of assessment practices and processes needed to be outlined and guidance given as to the assessment load. A 6-point unit would require work of 4000 words and a 12-point unit, 8000 words. Staff responsibilities for assessment were also detailed, as was progression in courses and grievance procedures.

RQF and ERA

In 2006 notice was given that faculties were required to prepare a Research Quality Framework (RQF).[28] This was required by the Ministry of Education, Science and Training and had to be in place by 2008, with the faculty setting up three teams to do a mock audit in 2006. As part of the mock audit for RQF five research groupings were set up: education culture and identity; education, economy and society; professional learning and curriculum theory; professional practice; and educational psychology. Seventy-four staff submitted their best research outputs to be assessed as part of this project. Despite this notice and work by the faculty the RQF scheme did not eventuate, due to a change of government.

However, a year later under the new national government, a replacement scheme came in called the Excellence for Research in Australia, invariably known as ERA. The ARC is responsible for administering ERA, which

---

[27] Minutes of Faculty Board 10 October 2006.
[28] Minutes of Faculty Board 2 August 2006.

aims to identify and promote excellence across the full spectrum of research activity in Australia's higher education institutions. ERA evaluates the quality of the research undertaken in Australian universities against national and international benchmarks. The ratings are determined and moderated by committees of distinguished researchers drawn from Australia and overseas. The unit of evaluation is broadly defined as the Field of Research (FoR) within an institution based on the Australia and New Zealand Standard Research Classification (ANZSRC). The indicators used in ERA include a range of metrics such as citation profiles (common to disciplines in the natural sciences) and peer review of a sample of research outputs (more broadly common in the humanities and social sciences). The first round of this evaluation of research by universities came in 2010. Two Associate Deans (Research) were involved, first Jane Kenway and then Ilana Snyder, who headed a faculty committee to undertake the work involved. Ros Winter as Faculty Research Advisor played a key role.[29] In this first round of ERA the faculty had to submit research publications and work from 20 per cent of the academic publications for peer assessment and ranking. It was a major exercise requiring many months of work. From these peer assessments the government was to rate every faculty in each university on a five-point scale. The top mark in the scale was 5, classified as 'well above world standards', 4 was 'above world standards', 3 was 'at world standards', 2 was 'below world standards' and 1 was 'well below world standards'. The faculty was scrupulous in trying not to distort the results in its favour – the committee did not pick out the work of star academics, nor load the selection in favour of professors, but made sure it was a representative sample from all levels of the academic staff.

The results showed education faculties around Australia with an average of only 2 – that is, 'below world standards', but happily the Monash Faculty of Education was ranked 4, 'above world standards';[30] it was with two other universities at the top of the rankings. Only two universities received a ranking of 4 in every category.

Ros Winter, while officially a research fellow, had a multiplicity of roles in the faculty. Starting with the faculty in 1989 as a half-time research assistant, her skills as a librarian were often used. While she was active assisting staff

---

[29] Also involved were Trudi Brunton, Research Manager, Em Prof Gilad Leder, Prof Peter Sullivan, Assoc Prof Bruce Waldrip and Prof Marilyn Fleer.

[30] Number 13 on the ERA list is the discipline of education, and so contributions were included from other faculties as well, particularly medicine, although the faculty contributed the bulk (about 85 per cent) of the peer-assessed work.

and HDR students with their research in her role as Research & Research Degrees Advisor, she also played a key role in establishing the bibliometric tools for evaluations such as RQF and ERA.[31]

Faculty Board meetings

With the technology available, the Faculty Board shifted to the holding of electronic meetings. Whether there was a quorum or not was determined by the number of email responses. The issues were usually single ones which had arisen and needed a prompt decision.[32] From 2008 Faculty Board meetings started off acknowledging the traditional owners of the land, which for Clayton were the Kulin people and for Gippsland the Gunai/Kurnai people. At this time the faculty was used as a pilot for a new records management system known as TRIM, which was to keep all records in a systematic electronic form.

Professors and chairs

In 2007 the Vice-Chancellor Professor Richard Larkins introduced a way for staff to achieve professorial rank without holding a chair.[33] This had only been possible before when an individual was granted a personal chair – but Larkin's move enabled staff to apply for promotion to professorial office with the rank and salary of a professor. The conditions to achieve this step were rigorous and demanding – one applicant, though successful, said if they had known the ordeal involved they would not have applied. While there were frequently limits on the number of chairs a faculty could have this new mechanism enabled more staff to achieve professorial rank. This gave opportunities to talented staff where there were no vacancies for chairs to gain promotion. The first to achieve this in the faculty were Peter Gronn and Ilana Snyder.

There had been a strong push for a chair in educational psychology. Traditionally a strong area in the faculty, there was currently no chair and at one time there had been two. There were staff in psychology as well as special education, educational development, and counselling and there were also the Krongold and Elwyn Morey Centres – all fields relevant to psychology.

---

[31] She was also a key organiser of the faculty choir and often took up the cause of staff who had been in difficulty.
[32] Such meetings were held on 1 May 2006 and 27 July 2006.
[33] Professor Richard Larkins AO Vice-Chancellor 2003–2009.

There was a heavy higher degree load in these areas as well. At this time (2003) the Krongold family gave an additional grant to help 're-invigorate' the Krongold Centre.

A chair was given to Marilyn Fleer who is a significant figure in early childhood education.

7.8 Professor Marilyn Fleer.
Education Faculty

In December 2003 it was announced that Jane Kenway and John Loughran[34] had been appointed as professors and at the end of 2004 the psychology need was filled with the appointment of Professor Dennis Moore. Until then the faculty had too few professors, with 7 per cent of the staff being professorial compared with 9 per cent throughout the university.[35] Professor Marilyn Fleer's appointment to Monash as Foundation Chair of Early Childhood Education on Peninsula Campus in 2002 was to specifically build a research culture on that campus. At this time Early

---

[34] John Loughran had come up through the Fensham science education group but his work had developed into wider fields of teaching, learning and teacher education. He was styled 'professor of curriculum and pedagogy'.
[35] Minutes of Faculty Board 21 July 2003.

Childhood Education PhD students were not assigned to Peninsula staff due to lack of accredited supervisors. Over time Marilyn Fleer worked towards appointment of PhD qualified staff and developing dedicated research space for the new postgraduate community.

Today in 2014 a vibrant Faculty Research Group (Child and Community Development) exists, staff are qualified with PhD's, supervision of HDR students is growing and visiting scholar programs enrich opportunities leading to national and international early childhood research connections.

A special event in 2006 was a presentation by Professor Sue Willis, Dean of the Faculty of Education, to the University Council on the directions of the faculty. In this Willis outlined:

- the recent history of the faculty, including the need to replace retiring staff, expand research activities and diversify the range of programs offered by the faculty;

- a range of recent initiatives to further broaden the activities, research and funding base of the faculty; and that while much of the external consulting and service activities of the faculty were achieved via tender, the margins associated with such activities were slim.[36]

During discussion University Council noted advice that the faculty's operations in Singapore and Hong Kong were 'hard work' yet important – particularly in the area of postgraduate education. The Singapore link was with a group called the Asia Pacific Management Institute Partnership (a company owned by the *Washington Post* via Kaplan Industries).

The ratio of staff with PhDs was high. The faculty had possibly the best example of industry engagement in the university and had recently revised its governance structures and reduced the number of committees by approximately 50 per cent.

At Faculty Board on 6 December 2006, the Report of the Monash Experience Questionnaire 2005 was presented and discussed.[37] Results for the faculty, which aggregated 1140 responses, were very favourable. On a five-point scale, satisfaction ratings scored a mean above 3.00. The results showed an improvement over the favourable ratings of 2003. In overall terms only 6 items out of 62 were below a mean of 3.40.

---

[36] University Council Meeting 25 September 2006.
[37] The report was prepared by Sue Plowright and Nike Prince.

Staff achievements in 2006

In December 2006 it was announced that ARC Discovery Grants had been awarded to Professor Peter Sullivan, Associate Professor Barbara Clark and Professor Doug Clark from ACU ($410,000), Dr Rui Yang jointly with Professor Andrew Welch ($193,182) and Associate Professor Neville King jointly with Associate Professor Eleanora Gullone ($280,100). Associate Professor Tony Taylor was on a Commonwealth Government working party to examine the teaching of Australian history in schools. Rosalie Triolo was given the rare honour of a special award by the History Teachers' Association of Victoria for her 'outstanding contribution to the teaching and learning of history'.

2007

In 2007 the major committees (Staff Committee, Curriculum Committee, Research Committee, Development Committee and Environment and Resources Committee) were replaced by four committees: the Research

7.9 Dr Rosalie Triolo receives a special achievement award from the History Teachers' Association of Victoria, 2006.
Greg Ford, MUA IN-8170

Induction Committee, Education Committee, Research Degrees Committee and Equity and Access Committee. The Development Committee, Environment and Resources Committee and the Staff Committee were all disbanded. The Faculty Executive remained the same. The same members of the Executive Committee also comprised the membership of these four committees, with the appropriate Associate Dean taking a leading role and chairing the committee, the Education Committee by the Associate Dean (Teaching), for example. From this it is clear much power existed in this executive and particularly in the Associate Deans.

The top body was the Faculty Executive Committee, a formal advisory committee to the Dean and comprising the Associate Deans, campus co-ordinators, Faculty Manager, senior managers, one elected academic from each campus and one elected general staff member. Other committees such as Conference Travel, OSP, OHS, etc also existed but reported to one of the major committees.

A consequence of the new administrative structure, with the Associate Deans taking key roles and directing the major portfolios, was that a hierarchical structure now prevailed. With no groups or areas, this also meant a lessening of the former democratic structure of the faculty, which at Clayton had been epitomised by the Planning and Development Committee – where everyone had felt they had a say in major decisions. The three, then four campuses also enjoyed equal status in all matters. Clayton staff felt disadvantaged by this given their size and history.

Monash Peninsula has been on show in 2007, with thousands of young visitors keen to check out the offerings of the beautiful campus. Through the Schools Access Monash program, campus management initiatives and a range of Prospective Students' Office events, Peninsula has been able to offer a range of experiences and services to local secondary school students and teachers.

2008

A new Commonwealth Government came to power in 2008, elected late 2007, with Prime Minister Kevin Rudd promising the 'education revolution'. The faculty saw a possibility of redressing the inadequate funding for teacher education, but this was not to be. There was some relief with the change – the RQF scheme was cancelled, as were the proposed new minimum days for the teaching practicum. Instead there was a quality enhancement accepted for placement grants, rather than additional days of training. The minimum requirements were now for 45 days for a one-year course, 60 days for a two-year course and 80 days for three- and four-year courses. Funding for the practicum continued to be an issue with an extra amount per EFTS promised for 2008 but not given, and uncertainty prevailing as to what might be given in 2009, despite assurances from Minister Julia Gillard.[38]

Library and Media Resource Centre (LMR)

A most controversial decision was the closing of the Library and Media Resource Centre, which was known as the LMR, in 2008. It had proved a popular place for students to gather, use the resources to prepare for teaching rounds or prepare method assignments. The staff working in the LMR were highly regarded by both students and staff and feedback on the use of the LMR was very positive.[39] Formal borrowing figures did not reveal the extent of usage of the facility. The Dean, Sue Willis, felt it was inequitable that Clayton should have this resource and yet the other campuses of Monash did not. However, some staff knew that the Matheson Library at Monash was a strictly academic library, unlike the libraries at both Peninsula and Gippsland which had a wider purpose, covering the needs of trainee teachers. A sad aspect of the closure of the LMR was that enthusiastic staff Sue Egan and Angela Pye went elsewhere.

Peninsula was originally a teachers' college so the library collection there was very large and provided specifically for trainee teachers. Gippsland had a separate curriculum collection in their library, but it was severely culled in the 1990s.

A consultant recommended its closure. This was hotly debated by staff at staff meetings and strongly opposed. Terri Seddon described the centre as giving a 'sense of home' to students. The centre was closed and while in theory some of the resources were supposed to be available for students in the Matheson Library, only part of these found their way there, and the very separation of audio-visual resources, kits, books, charts, etc. destroyed the original intention of the place. So it became a place where technology prevailed, with the exception of the theses which were to be stored there. Higher degree students described the LMR website in 2000, soon after it was launched, as 'now your one-stop shop for just about anything you need to know'. In 2013 it was transformed again, and with 'state-of-the-art' open

---

[38] Minutes of Faculty Board 18 March 2009.
[39] Submission on the Library and Media Resources Centre 2005 by Rosamund Winter.

7.10 The Library and Media Resource Centre (LMR) team. Left to right: Claude Sironi, Jane Brooks, Rosamund Winter, Angela Pye, and Sue Egan.
Education Faculty

social design, the warm and encouraging space became very popular with students.

The emphasis on research induction was demonstrated in 2008 with an active program of workshops in supervision, showing an awareness that many staff were young and inexperienced in higher degree supervision. There were seminars for doctoral students too, although there were problems in involving the large number of part-time higher degree students. MEd research students also had to go through a confirmation process. All this activity was designed to 'foster a vibrant research culture'.[40]

Development Office

The faculty Development Office had to be alert to changes in government policies to be effective in tendering for projects. There were often partnerships with other faculties as well as with consultancy organisations and also government departments like AusAID. There were also tenders to lodge

---

[40] Research Induction Report by Profesror Ilana Snyder, Faculty Board 123/08.

with educational institutions. When contracts were coming to an end either renewal had to be sought or new contracts tendered for. During the period 2007–2008 non-award short courses had expanded, bringing a 65 per cent increase in revenue, as had work with courses for TAFE colleges. The global financial crisis also had an impact, especially with on-campus international students. The strong marketing emphasis that the office had to employ is reflected in their report of 'warm, to hot projects' and a chart showing a 65 per cent success rate for proposals submitted.[41] The course offered in early childhood in Singapore had attracted 60 students in 2008.

Staff achievements

Ilana Snyder was promoted to professor. Two staff members were to gain chairs elsewhere: Associate Professor Lesley Farrell to the University of Technology Sydney, where she became Associate Dean (Research and Development), and Associate Professor Trevor Gale to the University of South Australia where he became director of the National Centre for Human Equity in Higher Education. Dr Graham Parr was granted the AARE Award for Doctoral Research in Education. Dr Amy Cutter-Mackenzie was given the Australian Learning and Teaching Council Award; they cited her school-community teaching and learning practices. Dr Margaret Gearon, long-serving staff member in charge of modern languages, was awarded life membership of the Association of French Teachers in Victoria. There were many achievements by staff. Anna Hickey-Moody received the Dean's Award for Excellence in Research by an Early Career Researcher, an award that started in 2006. Brenda Beatty was awarded a lifetime fellowship in the Australian Council for Educational Leaders.[42]

Professor Terri Seddon was involved in an exciting ARC Discovery Project on the teaching profession in learning societies which involved German and Finnish as well as Australian partners.

As part of the 50th anniversary of Monash University, special awards were given to 15 people to note their outstanding research achievements. One of these was granted to Professor Peter Fensham in a special presentation ceremony at Government House in August.

A notable event was the retirement at the end of 2008 of Professor Gerald Burke, after 41 years in the faculty and 43 in the university. Burke had started at the university in 1965. A gifted teacher and researcher he was

---

[41] Faculty Development Office Report, November 2008 FB 132/08.
[42] Minutes of Faculty Board 10 December 2008.

universally liked as a contributor and friendly colleague. He had been an active member of the faculty, especially representing the social foundations field, and given great service. From 2000 he was full-time in CEET (Centre for the Economics of Education and Training), which he had helped to create. He was accorded a farewell in the faculty club, where a great crowd gathered to farewell this popular member of staff. Among other retirements were Claude Sironi after 35 years' service and Jenny Brown after 25. Sironi had been faculty photographer but had added to this task many others and become indispensable as well as universally helpful. Jenny Brown had carried many burdens in a variety of academic roles within the faculty and her superb administrative skills were often called on, usually for difficult tasks. Brown had started her links with the faculty as a DipEd student, and her husband Howard Brown also had an active role in the faculty for many years – a great team. Both had been geography method lecturers.

Overall 2008 had been a year of difficulties. Research tenders from the government had slowed down, student experience satisfaction levels had fallen and there were problems with the practicum, both in funding and in placing 2,500 students in 400 schools. International enrolments both onshore and offshore were below target. With the age structure of the faculty now changing, about half the academic staff could now be termed 'early career researchers', which presented new challenges. Annually there was a report on the faculty undertaken by a visit from what was called the 'Vice-Chancellor's Group' or VCG. This enabled the faculty to review its performance over the year and set down actions for the future as an operational plan.[43]

2009

In 2009 the Development Office reported that they had submitted 70 proposals in 12 months, with 50 per cent of these successful.

In November 2009 it was announced that Associate Professor Brenton Doecke was leaving to take a chair of education at Deakin University, and Dr Geoff Romeo a chair of education at the Australian Catholic University.

In 2001 Monash embarked on a process of enhancing the expertise of its teaching staff by requiring new staff to have formal qualifications in university teaching. The Graduate Certificate in Higher Education was the qualification offered by Monash to meet these requirements. While not taught by the faculty, the results were reported to the Faculty Board of Examiners. In 2009 it was decided to revamp this course.

---

[43] Minutes of Faculty Board 20 May 2009.

Benchmarking

With the strong moves towards accountability, compliance and accreditation in the higher education sector, the faculty undertook 'benchmarking' with the University of Queensland's education faculty. Information was exchanged, critical questions asked and comparisons made It was a suitable match, as some years later ERA (Excellence in Research for Australia) were to place the faculty at the University of Queensland and the Monash Education faculty as the top two faculties in Australia. Queensland was usually ahead, having a smaller staff (about 23) and more professors than the large multi-campus Monash faculty.

Benchmarking had been recommended by the AUQA, a body replaced in 2012 by the Tertiary Education Quality and Standards Agency (TEQSA), which with its 'Threshold Standards' required all tertiary institutions to undertake benchmarking.

2009 also saw extra funds going to the Peninsula Health and Well Being Centre provided by the Commonwealth (DEEWR).[44] The university added funds to this grant of $10 million, giving a total of $12.8 million, to enable a better facility for the sport and outdoor recreation and teacher education programs. There had been an embargo on students in education and nursing being charged the extra 25 per cent contribution, and the Federal Budget in 2009 removed this.

2010

Dr Joce Nuttall took over the education portfolio from Geoff Romeo in May 2010. Her title was now Associate Dean (Education), which had replaced the title Associate Dean (Teaching). During 2010, after the Dean's departure, Professor John Loughran became Acting Dean and the Associate Dean portfolios were: Associate Professor Helen Forgasz – Clayton, Associate Professor Barbara Clarke – Peninsula, Associate Professor Bruce Waldrip – Gippsland, Professor Ilana Snyder – Research, Dr Joce Nuttall- Education, Associate Professor Len Cairns – Development, and Associate Professor Joanne Deppeler – Research Development.

To those who were teachers in an earlier period, the annual visit of the Vice-Chancellor's Group was reminiscent of a visit from the Board of Inspectors. This group reviewed the achievements of the faculty and considered its stated plans for the future.

---

[44] Department of Education Employment and Workplace Relations.

A faculty planning retreat was held in April 2010 and former staff member Professor Lawrie Angus from the University of Ballarat was the 'critical friend'. The new mantra of the university was 'academic strengthening' – and at the April meeting of Faculty Board Professor Jayne Godfrey, the president of the Academic Board, came to speak about academic strengthening and associated key issues: review of the governance processes of the university, clarification of the organisational units of the university, and recruitment policies. It was not immediately clear what 'academic strengthening' meant or how the university was to interpret it. Joce Nuttal felt 'definitions of education achievement should be submitted for consideration at exactly the same time as definitions of research achievement.'[45]

Among new appointments in 2010 was Dr Rachel Forgasz to be a lecturer at Clayton. Among the professional staff, Marijana Gec, who had been PA to Dean Sue Willis, went with her as PA in her post as Deputy Vice-Chancellor (Social Inclusion). Darlene McGown who was PA to Sue Willis in earlier years was appointed the new PA to the Dean.

Peter Corkill, principal of the newly established John Monash Science School on the Clayton campus, spoke to the Faculty Board and outlined progress of the school. He reported that it was now in its new building, which was open plan, that they used a team teaching approach, and every student was given an individual learning plan. There were links with the university already, in the form of a maths club run by a member of the mathematics department, but other links were being sought.[46]

A number of senior early childhood staff members departed in 2010. Dr Joce Nuttall left to take up a position as associate professor at Australian Catholic University, as did Dr Suzy Edwards, while Dr Mindy Blaise assumed a leadership position in Hong Kong. Dr Jill Robbins also left, but continues to work for the faculty as an adjunct senior lecturer.

Managerialism

Previously, in a university like that of the University of Melbourne in the 1940s and 1950s, professors were appointed to what were regarded as the principal disciplines such as classics, medicine, philosophy, science, law, history, English, languages and engineering. In holding their chairs the professors professed their knowledge of their discipline, gathered staff around them and taught students in courses. From those doing bachelor

---

[45] Minutes of Faculty Board 26 May 2010.
[46] Minutes of Faculty Board 26 May 2010.

7.11 Joce Nuttall.
Education Faculty

degrees a select few might go on to higher degrees, probably a masters degree, which were of course only research degrees. While attention was given to student numbers there were often large differences between the loads of various departments. As staff were tenured there was not much flexibility to adjust. The tenured academics led by the professors ran the administration, with minimal support staff. At Melbourne it was not until 1935 that there was a salaried Vice-Chancellor. The academics also decided what courses they would teach and what subjects would be offered. Some areas were not admitted to course or subject status. These academics inherited a long standing tradition of scholarship, collegiality and academic governance which they prized.

It was not until the late 1950s that an increasing proportion of the population started going on to university. This increase in numbers together with the demands of society and the economic changed all that.

The change to a managerial structure was gradual, but saw the universities becoming in structure something like that of a public company. So the demands of the corporate structure prevailed. Money became dominant. Student numbers dictated much of the allocation. From a situation where the state paid most of the bills, the Commonwealth took over that responsibility, but later decreed that they expected universities to raise funds (or sell their services). Marketing courses became important for universities.

7.12 Lawry Angus.
Education Faculty

The Commonwealth Government would only fund a proportion of costs now, and they required universities to follow government policies in regard to courses. 'Issues' took over from the traditional disciplines in terms of favoured courses offered. There were other requirements too, that the corporate university had to meet: occupational health and safety issues, social inclusion, issues of equality and external reviews of performance.

Staff had demands on them similar to those expected of company employees. They had to show improved productivity both in research and in teaching. There were now measures to assess their performance. Promotion depended on these measures, especially of their research. Tenure was no longer freely available, more and more staff were on contract, which depending on demand for their courses and their own performance may or may not be renewed. Tenure was hard sought after. Staff too had to give attention to their physical and mental well-being and also abide by the various regulations in regard to their actions and attitudes to questions of social inclusion, equality and other rights.

Conclusion

In this decade the many staff appointments had changed the face of the faculty and given it a younger look. Important educational issues now were often interdisciplinary and new appointments reflected this.

There was now a wider client base with a range of not just teachers but now other professionals, as well as a significant number of international students. Universities now had a managerial approach to administration, there were policy documents for almost everything, there were increased government requirements for compliance on a range of issues as well as a mantra that emphasised research. Willis was a strong, well-organised Dean who was prepared to be assertive in meetings and in university settings to put the case of the faculty with some force. Informally she was a shy person and often reticent in company.

After 10 years as Dean, Sue Willis felt it was time to move on. She announced her resignation at a Faculty Day in February. Her last year had been a difficult one as she had health issues. Fortuitously she was offered the post of Pro-Vice Chancellor (Social Inclusion), an area which suited her interests. Willis had been Dean through difficult times. She had been courageous and made a significant contribution in achieving change in the faculty. As Dean she had also served as president of the Australian Council of Deans 2005–2009.

Faculty Board recorded its appreciation for her 'years of dedication and leadership as Dean', a motion which was carried with acclamation. It was noted how Sue Willis had taken the post during a period of major change and that the faculty was stronger because of her work.[47]

The university established a selection committee for a new Dean and Professors Terri Seddon, Ilana Snyder and Dr Joce Nuttall were appointed as the faculty nominees on the 11- person committee.

Staff

Tony Taylor, an associate professor at Gippsland campus, has degrees from Bristol, Birmingham and London but completed his doctorate at Cambridge: 'The Church Party and Popular Education 1893–1902'. Taylor has worked closely with a wide range of colleagues to improve the standing of history education in Australia. In 1999 he was appointed director of the Australian Government's National Inquiry into the Teaching and Learning of History

---

[47] Minutes of Faculty Board 1 February 2010.

and from 2001–2007 he was director of the Australian Government's National Centre for History Education. He has held appointments as campus coordinator at Gippsland and Associate Dean (Development). He has researched and published extensively in Australia and overseas in the field of history education, as well as in the fields of higher education policy, the politics of educational change, vocational education, rural education and history of education. From 2006 to 2010 he worked as senior consultant with successive Coalition and ALP federal governments in formulating three drafts of a national history curriculum. His research includes a 2010 Discovery Grant to conduct a comparative analysis of the political contexts for the development of history national curricula in Australia and Russia. Examples of his supervisory load include secondary school studies in history education, a linguistic post-colonial perspective on the rise of the Indian economy, curriculum innovation, and a history of Changi POWs.

Bob Greaves was appointed to the Frankston Teachers' College in 1968 after serving 18 months as a seconded lecturer in art at Melbourne Teachers' College. During the turbulent years of the Chisholm administration, Bob also taught ceramics at the Caulfield campus, sharing his time between art and design and education. However, his primary interest was in children's art and he returned to the education faculty at Frankston on a full-time basis. Greaves' interest later spread to technology studies – in his words, 'making stuff not the IT that is "Technology" today'. This interest grew from the need to develop creative thinking and the British 'craft, design and technology' model of an amalgamation of science and art. In his later years at Monash he filled an administrative role as campus coordinator for the Faculty of Education, as well as art education teacher. He always regarded himself as a 'pracademic'. Bob remained at the Frankston campus, seeing it undergo the various transformations as Chisholm and then Monash, until his retirement in 2006.

Greaves did much important voluntary work in hospitals, using woodwork and art to engage children – his work was regarded as highly therapeutic. For 15 years he also led the 'Children Working with Wood' activity at the Royal Melbourne Show, as 'Mr Woodman', bringing out 'construct sculptural forms in wood'. This work won the prestigious Royal Agricultural Society's Presidents Medal. Students who worked with Greaves found it a life-changing experience. In January 2007 he was awarded the Medal of the Order of Australia for service to the community through the provision of therapeutic play activities for children in hospital, and to education.

7.13 Bob Greaves at work, 1985.
MUA IN-6599

Staff of 2000

Michael Long joined the faculty in 2000 to work at the Centre for the Economics of Education and Training (CEET) and was, for a period, joint director of CEET. Through the centre he worked on a number of studies and evaluations in the fields of education and the labour market for many Australian Government and state and territory government departments and agencies, commercial and not-for-profit organisations and internationally for the Ministry of Education, New Zealand, the ILO, the WHO and the OECD. His work included studies of the returns to education and training, the economics of firm-based training, participation and completion in schooling, VET and higher education, the financing of education and evaluations of programs in indigenous and multimedia education. Before joining the faculty, Long was a researcher at ACER for many years and after leaving in 2010 he joined the Centre for Research on Educational Systems (CRES) at the University of Melbourne.

Staff of 2002

Janette Graetz Simmonds was appointed to the faculty in 2002, moving from a position in the Monash University Counselling Service. Her PhD was undertaken in the Faculty of Medicine, Nursing and Health Sciences at Monash. She had previously held appointments in psychology departments at Swinburne University, RMIT, Lincoln Institute of Health Sciences (now part of La Trobe University), Rutgers University (NJ, USA) and McGill University (Montreal, Canada). She began her postgraduate career as a teacher of English literature and drama in an Adelaide high school. She is a registered psychologist with dual endorsements in clinical and counselling psychology and is also a qualified group analyst. Simmonds has published more than 20 refereed journal articles to date. She has led the Masters in Psychology (Counselling) and combined MPsych/PhD in counselling psychology since 2006 and for the past three years she has served on the Australian Psychological Society Counselling Psychology College National Executive Committee.

Marilyn Fleer PhD, MA (Science and Technology Studies), MEd (Hons 1st), BEd (Computer Education), Dip Tch (Early Childhood Education) is a professor whose main research interests and expertise include cross-cultural research, family studies, early childhood science education, technology education and the building of new theoretical tools. Torn between studying psychology and education as an undergraduate, Fleer ended up choosing early childhood education, a nascent field that straddled both her areas of interest. Her current research relates to studying the early stages of concept formation – and how playtime can help promote children's imagination, and the more 'rational' thinking later on as adults. She has received many grants including three ARC grants, (totalling some $4.5 million) and has written and published extensively – 234 items in the period 1987–2013. Her book *Early Learning and Development* is regarded as a significant one in the field. Fleer is co-authoring a soon-to-released book on new theories of child development, *Family Pedagogy: Children's Learning and Development in Everyday Family Life*.

Staff of 2003

Helen Forgasz graduated from Monash with a BSc and over the years gained a DipEd, BEd, MEd Studies and PhD through the Faculty of Education. She worked as a computer programmer and high school teacher of mathematics, physics, and computing before embarking on a change of career into academia. She completed her PhD in 1995, followed by winning an ARC Postdoctoral Research Fellowship which she took up at La Trobe University. It took two more years working as a research fellow and sessional lecturer before Forgasz landed her first academic post at Deakin University where she worked for three years before her appointment (back at Monash) in the Faculty of Education. Helen was appointed Associate Dean for the Clayton campus in 2009 and in 2012 was promoted to full professor. Her main research focus has been on gender issues in mathematics education, and more generally in the science and computing areas. In 2011, she was invited to represent Australian scholars in the field of gender and science at the UN's 55th Commission on the Status of Women in New York. Helen has co-edited several monographs on gender issues in STEM, and has published extensively in scholarly and professional journals. She serves on the editorial boards of high quality journals and book series and continues to be an active member of mathematics education research associations nationally and internationally.

Cynthia Joseph completed a BSc (Ed) (Hons) and then an MEd at the Science University of Malaysia. In 2003 she completed her PhD at Monash University and was appointed to the faculty. She is currently a senior lecturer. Joseph was awarded the 2004 Mollie Holman Medal for Excellence for her doctoral thesis 'Theorisations of Identity and Difference: Ways of being Malay, Chinese and Indian schoolgirls in a Malaysian secondary school'. She draws on sociology of education, comparative education and Asian studies to research identity, cultural differences and inequality issues in education and work contexts. Her publications include *Equity, Opportunity and Education in Postcolonial Southeast Asia* (2014) and *Black and Postcolonial Feminisms: Researching Educational Inequalities* (2010), both for Routledge. Joseph has had extensive experiences within the education sectors in Malaysia, and more broadly in Southeast Asia. She also sits on the Executive Board of the Research Committee on Women in Society, International Sociological Association (ISA).

Graham Parr began as an itinerant French horn tutor in secondary schools across Melbourne, in between performing and recording with the Melbourne Symphony Orchestra. From there his interests drew him to English and literature. He subsequently taught English, literature and drama in Victoria and the USA for 10 years before joining the Department of Learning and Educational Development at the University of Melbourne as a 'links to schools' lecturer. In 2003 he moved to the Faculty of Education, Monash University, where he is currently a senior lecturer in English language and literacy education. He completed his award-winning doctorate in 2007.

Zane Ma Rhea, a graduate of Sydney University (BSoc Stud), she specialised in psychiatric social work with profoundly deaf people in both Australia and the UK. She then ran a vegetarian restaurant in the south of

Spain, returning to Australia to undertake a DipEd (Aboriginal Education) in 1990 at Flinders University. She continued on to an honours year (1991), receiving the Vice-Chancellor's Medal and winning an Australian Research in Asia award to undertake her PhD research in Thailand (1992–1996). On completion of her PhD (1997), she was awarded the Smuts Visiting Fellow in Commonwealth Studies at Cambridge University, UK, to undertake her postdoctoral studies (1997–1998). Currently, she is coordinator of Indigenous education and leadership in the Faculty of Education. She is recognised nationally and internationally for her expertise in comparative education and for improving the quality of education services to Indigenous people. She uses a rights-based framework, focusing on teacher professional development, organisational change management, and the preservation of Indigenous knowledge in mainstream schooling through meaningful school–community–university partnerships with Indigenous families. Her research program falls within the sociology of education, examining how ideas from diverse contexts are understood, produced, reproduced, legitimated and disseminated in mainstream education systems such as universities and schools.

Dr Margaret Plunkett was a secondary school teacher before becoming an academic. She completed her BEc and Grad DipEd at Monash (Clayton) in the 1970s. After moving to the Latrobe Valley in the 1980s she began an MEd at the Gippsland campus of Monash under the supervision of Dr Graham Dettrick. While completing her masters she began tutoring and lecturing in the Faculty of Education and even developed an elective unit in gifted education which she taught by DE to students across all the campuses of Monash – it became the most popular elective in the Faculty of Education. Margaret began her PhD under the supervision of Associate Professor Len Cairns in 2000 and graduated in 2006. She was promoted to senior lecturer in 2009. Margaret has won awards for teaching excellence at both the university level with a Vice-Chancellor's Teaching Excellence Award (Special Commendation) in 2010 and the Pearson/ATEA Teacher Educator of the Year Award in 2012.

Staff of 2004

Trent D Brown was originally appointed to the Gippsland campus in 2004 before moving to Peninsula in 2007 as part of the sport and outdoor recreation course re-development. He studied his undergraduate degree at the Royal Melbourne Institute of Technology (formerly Phillip Institute of Technology), graduating with a Bachelor of Applied Science in Physical Education. He taught physical education and science in Victorian secondary schools 1997–2000. In 2004, he completed a PhD degree under the supervision of Dr Bernie Holland, focusing on children's physical activity levels and teachers' knowledge of physical activity and fitness, once again at RMIT. During his decade within the faculty, Brown has taught a number of units focused primarily on secondary PE methods, curriculum and pedagogy. For a majority of his time he has also been involved in the professional association the Australian Council for Health Physical Education and Recreation (ACHPER) as board member and lately as president of the Victorian branch (2011–2015). His research is currently focused on examination physical education although he has published widely in areas of philosophy, professional learning and self-study all within the context of physical education and sport pedagogy. He became a senior lecturer in 2012.

Dennis Moore, MA, Postgrad DipPsych, PhD, came to Monash in 2004. He holds a chair in educational psychology at Monash and also heads the university's Krongold Centre for Exceptional Children and the Elwyn Morey Child Study Centre in the education faculty at the Clayton campus.

After training in his native New Zealand Professor Moore taught at the University of PNG from 1979 until 1985 – the final two years in the education research unit. From there he moved to the University of Auckland first as senior lecturer then associate professor in the Department of Education. He was also director of the university's training program for education psychology and was involved in a three-university consortium that trained resource teachers in learning and behaviour. His main fields or research currently involve the development, trialling, and evaluation of instructional processes for children with special educational needs including children with autism. He has an ongoing interest in assessment and evaluation of treatment effects and the application of functional assessment processes.

He has a substantial record of scholarship in the area together with a proven record of leadership both in significant research and teaching programs and within the university, the profession and the community. He has published extensively in his areas, especially in autism and special education.

Stephen Keast completed a BSc then a Grad DipEd (1985). He was then a secondary maths, science and computing teacher in several Wimmera schools and in 1988 was appointed as a teaching fellow to Monash University Education faculty. He began an MEd by research at Monash in 1996 which he completed in 1999 with a thesis about single-sex mathematics classrooms in a coeducational school. He worked part-time in the faculty from 1999

7.14 Professor Dennis Moore.
Education Faculty

until he obtained his first full-time ongoing academic appointment in 2001 at Deakin University. He returned to Monash as a lecturer in education in 2004 and graduated from his PhD (Monash) in 2011.

Staff of 2005

Nicky Jacobs graduated from the University of Melbourne with a Diploma in Teaching then continued her studies completing a GradDip in Special Education at Victoria College and a BEd majoring in psychology at Deakin University. After teaching briefly in Melbourne primary schools, Jacobs continued her psychology studies, completing a GradDip in Child and Adolescent Psychology at the University of Melbourne followed by a Master in Psychology (Counselling) and a PhD at the Faculty of Education at Monash University. Before joining the Faculty of Education where she is currently working as a senior lecturer, Jacobs worked as a counselling psychologist at the University of Melbourne and Swinburne University and as a psychology tutor in the School of Psychology and Psychiatry, Faculty of Medicine, Nursing and Health Sciences at Monash University.

During her time in the faculty Jacobs has been instrumental in developing the Master in Counselling program, taking it from a fledgling course to one of very high standing in Australia, Singapore and Hong Kong. Her keen interest in school bullying has prioritised her research and enabled research collaborations both within Australia and overseas.

Helen M G Watt completed a BEd (Hons) specialising in secondary mathematics in 1993 at the University of Sydney, where she won the university medal. She later completed her doctorate at the University of Sydney in the field of educational psychology and measurement, which was awarded prizes by the American Educational Research Association. She held academic appointments at Macquarie University (1997–98), the University of Sydney (1998–2003), the University of Western Sydney (2003–2004), the University of Michigan (2003–2006) before taking her position as associate professor at Monash University in 2005, and Australian research fellow 2011–2015. Her academic fields are in educational and developmental psychology, research methods (quantitative research methods, mixed methods) and teacher education. She has published widely from her two funded programs of research concerning youth motivations and career choices (www.stepsstudy.org), and teacher motivations and career trajectories (www.fitchoice.org).

Mary Lou Rasmussen is a senior lecturer in education at Monash University, Victoria, Australia. She is a leading scholar on the incorporation of Lesbian, Gay, Bisexual and Transgender (LGBT) matters within educational research, within teacher education, and within school education. Working to grow and develop scholarship in sexuality in school education in the Australian context, she has assembled and led an international interdisciplinary research team (2011–2012) that obtained the first ever Australian ARC Discovery Grant in the area of sexuality education and she was a Partner Investigator on a Canadian SSHRC grant: 'Affective Beginnings: Lesbian, Gay, Bisexual and Transgender Issues in Teacher Education'. She is the author of *Becoming Subjects* (Routledge, 2006) and co-editor, with Talburt and Rofes, of *Youth and Sexualities* (Palgrave, 2004). A monograph *Progressive Sexuality Education: The Conceits of Secularism* is also forthcoming (Routledge, 2013).

Peter Sullivan completed his DipEd (Secondary) in the faculty in 1970 and his PhD in 1988. He was appointed to the position of professor of science, mathematics and technology in 2005. He taught at universities as well as schools in Papua New Guinea, giving him experience of the influence of culture and language on learning. He was a member of the Social, Behavioural and Economic Sciences panel of the Australian Research

Council College of Experts from 2005 to 2008, and was an editor of the *Journal of Mathematics Teacher Education* for eight years. He has served as president of the Australian Association of Mathematics Teachers and was the lead developer of the Australian mathematics curriculum. Sullivan's current project is investigating the most effective methods of teaching mathematics in remote Kimberley schools.

His research and publications are extensive, including five ARC-funded projects, and the books *Teaching with Tasks for Effective Mathematics Learning* (2013), *Constructing Knowledge for Teaching Secondary Mathematics: Tasks to Enhance Prospective and Practicing Teacher Learning* (2011) and the popular teacher resource *Open-ended Maths Activities: Using Good Questions to Enhance Learning*, published in the US as *Good Questions for Math Teaching*.

Staff of 2006

Rosemary Viete has provided English academic literacy, learning and cultural support, and pastoral care to Monash students undertaking postgraduate studies, many of them international students. Her work with students on writing pays particular attention to intercultural and interdisciplinary features and attempts not to impose rigid patterns, but to help students express themselves creatively and convincingly. Her recent research focuses on affect and agency in learning, assessing, writing and teaching across cultures, with particular attention to notions of generative intertextuality. She is equally concerned with the ethics of teaching and learning languages and the need for attentiveness and respect for diversity in ways of voicing knowledge in academic communities. She is currently a senior lecturer.

Dr David Zyngier, BA, DipEd, MEd, PhD is a senior lecturer in the areas of curriculum and pedagogy, located at Peninsula. He was previously a teacher and school principal. His research on democracy in education was awarded $366,000 from the Australian Research Council for 2013–2015 and $265,000 from the Canadian Social Science Research Council.

His research focuses on teacher pedagogies that engage all students and in particular how these can improve outcomes for students from communities of disadvantage

He is the recipient of the prestigious European Union Erasmus Mundis Research fellowship. In 2010 he was an invited keynote speaker at the Inaugural Conference of Deans of Education of Latin America, in 2012 he was keynote speaker to 600 school principals in India. He has been interviewed on national and regional radio, TV and newspapers, a number of times 'setting the agenda' for journalists in relation to education. In February

2013 he was formally requested to provide oral expert evidence to the House of Representatives Committee on the Education Bill 2012 and was selected to be an online contributor about education matters for Open Forum.

Phillip Pane, BSc, MSc (Eugene Oregon), EdD (University of Georgia), came to Monash (Gippsland) in 2006, after 23 years at La Trobe University. With a background in environmental education and related curriculum, he has undertaken research in environmental education, health studies, leisure and pedagogy. As an associate professor he has headed the Bachelor of Sport and Outdoor Education program and led the Movement Environment Community and the Faculty Research Group. He has published extensively in books, monographs and journal articles as well as making many conference presentations in his fields of interest and attracting a number of research grants. He has also held many visiting appointments at overseas universities.

Chris Peers completed a Bachelor of Arts in Visual Arts at the Sydney College of Advanced Education in 1984, after which he practised as an artist and returned to study in 1996 at the then UNSW College of Fine Arts where he completed a Bachelor of Art Education with First Class Honours. Chris followed this with a doctorate in art education at UNSW, graduating in 2003. His thesis was a historical study on art-teacher training in Australia. Chris taught in primary and secondary schools in NSW until he began lecturing in art education at Monash. His research has expanded to include a range of theoretical issues raised by the history of education in Western culture, including policy studies and educational philosophy.

Staff of 2007

Joel Austin Windle was appointed to the faculty as lecturer in culture and pedagogy in 2007. He previously taught in French and Australian schools and completed his PhD jointly through the Universities of Melbourne and Bourgogne in 2008. His work at Monash focused on social inequalities in education and cultural diversity, including ARC-funded projects on literacy education for refugee-background students and school choice. In 2010 he was awarded the Vice-Chancellor's Award for Early Career Researchers. He resigned as senior lecturer in 2013 to take up a position at the Federal University of Ouro Preto in Brazil.

Dat Bao has been an academic in six countries: Vietnam, Thailand, Singapore, the USA, the UK and Australia. Prior to joining the faculty in 2007 he had worked with Ho Chi Minh Open University, Leeds Metropolitan University, Cornell University, the National University of Singapore and the Assumption University of Thailand. His expertise includes curriculum design, intercultural communication, materials development, classroom reticence, creative pedagogy and visual pedagogy in language education. He has nearly 30 publications and major books and international journals. He has given numerous presentations on four continents including being a plenary speaker at international conferences. He is also a creative writer and artist with poems, short stories and illustration art works published in Malaysia, Singapore, Hong Kong, and Mainland China. His book *Understanding Silence and Reticence in Second Language Acquisition* (with Bloomsbury, London) will come out in 2014.

Margaret Somerville is professor of education (learning and development) and research director of the Institute of Regional Studies located at Monash University's Gippsland Campus in Latrobe Valley. She has been a recognised leader in the field of place studies in Australia since the publication of the major community collaborative study, *Ingelba and The Five Black Matriarchs* (1990), described as 'the best politically informed oral history ever produced in Australia' (*The Age*, Paul Carter, 1990). She has since published four sole-authored books in the field of place studies which reach a wide popular audience, are set as readings on a range of academic courses, and have been reviewed as a body of work (e.g. Hecate, 2004, 30/1, 56–70). Since graduating with her PhD in 1996 she has published three book chapters, sixteen refereed articles, six keynote addresses, three exhibitions and led two national symposia in the field of place studies. In addition three articles about place and identity in the workplace have been published in the Swedish language. She was invited to present to the United Nations Regional Centre of Expertise in Education for Sustainable Development in the UK in April 2009.

Rachel Forgasz was in the first intake (1995) of Bachelor of Performing Arts students at Monash University. She graduated in 1997 and then went on to co-found Pocket Money Theatre, an independent theatre company dedicated to producing new work featuring strong roles for women. She completed her Grad DipEd in the Faculty of Education at Monash (1999) and taught at The MacRobertson Girls' High School where she established the school's first curricular drama department and acted as Head of Drama. Rachel returned to Monash to complete honours, then her PhD in drama and theatre studies. In 2009, she took up a position in the Faculty of Education at Monash where she lectures in the secondary teacher education program. Rachel's research interests centre on the potentiality of embodied reflection as an approach to engage pre-service teachers in their emotional experiences of learning to teach.

Angelika Anderson completed a PhD in educational psychology at the University of Auckland in 2002. Her doctoral topic was the effect of locus of control and classroom climate on motivation in the classroom. In Auckland she worked for a number of years as a research fellow, increasingly developing an interest in developmental disabilities, specifically autism spectrum disorder (ASD) and challenging behaviour. Anderson joined Monash in 2005, initially as a research fellow and since 2007 as a senior lecturer. During her time at Monash she gained the qualification of Board Certified Behaviour Analyst – doctoral designation (BCBA-D). Currently she is involved in the psychology training program teaching an introductory course in Applied Behaviour Analysis (ABA) and into other courses on developmental psychology. Her current research program primarily involves the development and piloting of novel behavioural interventions for children with ASD. She is a senior lecturer in the Institute of Human Development and Counselling at the Krongold Centre.

Michael Henderson was appointed to the faculty in 2007 as a lecturer in Information and Communication Technologies in Education. He had completed a PhD at James Cook University in 2007 and previously had taught in secondary schools for 10 years. In the faculty he worked within the teacher education and postgraduate programs and was awarded with an Australian Learning and Teaching Council Citation for Outstanding Contributions to Student Learning "for designing rich, participative online learning environments in which students are motivated and inspired to learn". He served on the Faculty Research Committee, various central university committees and continued to engage with the profession through being a member of the state council for Digital Learning and Teaching Victoria. Michael conducted research from early childhood through to higher education, covering topics such as cognitive strategies in virtual worlds through to ethical dilemmas of using social media in classrooms and in research. He has provided expert advice to government and other education providers in the field of eLearning and cybersafety and delivered many keynotes at conferences with the aim of expanding delegates understanding of the opportunities afforded by educational technology, both in online and in-class environments. Michael was the leader of the Monash Centre for Educational Multimedia (CEMM) which transformed into the Learning with New Media Research Group in which he continued as a key member.

Rebecca Cooper was appointed to the faculty as a sessional staff member in 2007 having completed a double degree, Bachelor Education / Bachelor of Science and a Master of Education (Mathematics and Science Education) through the faculty. She remained part time in a school and part time in the faculty while completing her PhD in the faculty and was appointed full-time in 2012. Rebecca was awarded her PhD in 2013. Her thesis investigated the development of pedagogical knowledge for science teacher educators through the analysis of critical experiences. During her time in the faculty, Rebecca has helped develop and taught in science education units as well as other curriculum and pedagogy units. As part of the science education faculty research group, Rebecca has established and continued to develop a reading group for teachers and researchers. She has presented at several national and international conferences and contributed to book chapters and papers. She works with pre-service and in-service science teachers and her research interests include; considering how science teachers and science teacher educators develop pedagogical knowledge throughout their career, improving the quality of science teaching to increase student engagement and working with teachers on promoting values in their science teaching in an effort to better understand the development of scientific literacy with students.

Staff of 2008

Joanne Burke completed a BSc (Hons) in 1987 and an MEd in 1998. She has taught for 25 years in Victorian and International schools in Asia, teaching years 5–12 and holding leadership positions in pastoral care, curriculum development and teacher professional learning. She has been a coordinator and examiner for the IB Diploma and vice-principal of an International School. She is currently completing her PhD on middle-school science teaching and learning. She commenced teaching in the faculty in 2008, but spent two years at Shanghai returning to the Clayton campus in 2011. She is a sessional tutor in the faculty.

Judith Joy Williams studied for her initial primary teaching qualification (DipT) at the then State College of Victoria at Frankston (1976-78), now Monash University's Peninsula campus. She worked as a primary teacher in Melbourne for approximately 25 years, during which time she completed a BA and MEd at Monash University Clayton campus. Judy enrolled in a PhD in 2004 and during her studies began sessional tutoring in the Faculty of Education at Clayton and Peninsula campuses. She gained a lecturer position at Peninsula in 2007. Her areas of teaching and research concern teacher professional learning, particularly in the context of pre-service teacher education, professional experience and school-university partnerships.

Jane Kenway's field is the sociology and politics of education. She is a professor, a professorial fellow with the Australian Research Council, and an elected fellow of the Academy of Social Sciences. She has won many prestigious grants for her research. She puts new and highly topical issues on the research agenda, often identifying trends early, and she engages the field with bodies of social and cultural theory that enable fresh and evocative interpretive perspective. Her research expertise is in socio-cultural studies of education in the context of wider social and cultural change. She has published in prestigious international journals. Her more recent jointly written books are *Masculinity Beyond the Metropolis* (Palgrave, 2006), *Haunting the Knowledge Economy* (Routledge 2006) and *Consuming Children: Education-Advertising-Entertainment*, (Open University Press, 2001).

She has published numerous book chapters and journal articles including in *British Journal of the Sociology of Education*, *Gender and Education* and *Journal of Education Policy*. She has received many grants and currently leads the international team conducting a five-year research project called 'Elite independent schools in globalising circumstances: a multi-sited global ethnography'.

Jennifer A Rennie, a graduate BEd (Hons) of Murdoch University, taught in NT Primary and secondary schools and became a lecturer in education at the Charles Darwin University. In 2005 she completed a PhD at James Cook University. She took a senior lectureship in primary literacy education beginning at the Gippsland Campus and then moved to her current position at the Peninsula campus where she teaches in both undergraduate and postgraduate primary courses. During her time at Monash she has held a number of leadership roles including Course Director Primary and Director of Student Experience. Her research interests are in reading, literacy education and Indigenous literacies.

Chris Boyle completed a BSc (Hons) in behavioural sciences (University of Glamorgan) in 1996, followed by a MSc in business information technology systems (University of Strathclyde) and a Postgraduate Certificate in Education (Secondary) (University of Glasgow) in 1998, a BA in government and politics (Open University), MSc in educational psychology (University of Strathclyde) in 2003 and finally a PhD (University of Dundee) in 2009. Boyle was a secondary school teacher and then an educational psychologist in Glasgow, Scotland from 1997 to 2009 when he emigrated to Australia. He took up a lecturing position in inclusive education at Charles Sturt University in Wagga Wagga and worked there from 2009 to 2010 before moving to Monash University. From 2010 until February 2014, Boyle was employed as a lecturer and then a senior lecturer in psychology. He taught across various programs including the PGDip in Psychology and the MPsych in Educational and Developmental Psychology. Whilst at Monash he was appointed editor of the prestigious journal *The Australian Educational and Developmental Psychologist*. He has published many articles and books in the subjects of inclusive education and psychology including *What Works in Inclusion?* (Open University Press, 2012) and *Professional Ethics in Applied Psychology* (Oxford University Press, 2014). He is currently employed as a Senior Lecturer in Educational Psychology at the University of New England.

Anastasios (Tasos) Barkatsas PhD joined the faculty in 2006 in the field of mathematics education. He became senior lecturer, program manager of the Master of Teaching Practice (Secondary) and program director of Graduate Diploma of Education (Primary) at RMIT. He held many senior positions and various educational institutes in Athens, such as senior research fellow, external advisor and evaluator of European research grants at the Pedagogical Institute. He was an external examiner for research degrees at Universities in Australia and Greece. He was a member of the Inclusive Mathematics Education Research Group at Monash 2006–2013 and a statistical advisor for HDR students. He has published widely.

Rosalie Triolo[48] was inspired to become a history method lecturer in the Faculty of Education as a consequence of mentoring as many as four Monash history student-teachers per year for 10 years at Cheltenham Secondary College. Not only did she enjoy working with and learning from the next generation of history teacher specialists, she deeply valued the rich and collegial discussions with Monash experts. She vividly recalls visits by Christine Casinader, Ann Feehan, Joan Sheen, Ann Shorten, Andy Spaull and Libby Tudball, with the latter two, along with Dick Selleck, being highly influential on the type of educator and researcher she aspired to be. Triolo is the president of the History Teachers' Association of Victoria, and has had a 33-year continuous association with it, as individual, board member and Vice-President. She has been involved in expert advisory capacities in the development of the 'Australian Curriculum: History', F–12 and in Victorian Curriculum and Assessment. She is HTAV's delegate to HTAA and the Australian Historical Association as well as an invited member of the National Archives of Australia Victorian Consultative Forum since its inception in 2003. She is active in diverse state and national

---

[48] For Rosalie Triolo's recollections of her time at Monash, see Chapter 9.

historico-cultural communities and has produced numerous history and humanities classroom, professional learning and scholarly works in paper and electronic forms. Her doctorate was published as *Our Schools and the War*; she is a senior lecturer at Clayton campus.

Dr Umesh Sharma is associate professor and coordinator of special education programs in the Faculty of Education. He has extensive training in teaching students with a range of disabilities including students with multiple disabilities. Dr Sharma is working closely with a number of professionals in the field of special education from both developed (Canada, USA, UK, Singapore and Hong Kong) and developing countries (India, China, South Africa, Fiji, the Solomon Islands, Brunei and Brazil). He is the coordinator of an international project that examines why teachers are apprehensive to work with students with diverse learning needs and what could be done to improve their efficacy. The project is being implemented in 12 countries including China, Bangladesh, Mexico, Italy and the UK. Some of his recent research projects include evaluating teaching practices using reflective teaching framework, funded by Monash; empowering parents of children with autism to manage disruptive behaviours using Positive Behaviour Support (PBS) strategies, funded by APEX Foundation; understanding and addressing misperceptions of educators for effective prevention, funded by William Angliss Foundation; and *Why Teachers are Aggressive*, funded by Monash University.

Staff of 2009

Fida Sanjakdar completed her Bachelor of Teaching and Education at RMIT University and then her MEd and PhD at the University of Melbourne. Before undertaking her doctoral studies, Sanjakdar taught at the University of Melbourne in curriculum and pedagogy while she completed her studies. In 2009 she was appointed a lecturer in the Faculty of Education at Monash University. In 2012 she was promoted to senior lecturer and now coordinates units in curriculum theory, critical pedagogy and cultural diversity. She has published widely in the areas of critical sexuality education, Muslim youth sexual identities and sociocultural theory.

Paul Richardson, an associate professor, began his career as a secondary school teacher. He taught English, history and drama in outer western suburbs and in the inner city of Sydney. He worked in teacher education at the University of Sydney before moving to the Gippsland Institute of Advanced Education in rural Victoria. He completed his PhD at Monash

University for which he was awarded the Mollie Holman Doctoral Medal. At Monash Richardson has taught both undergraduate and postgraduate courses on English curriculum and literacy education as well as research methods, particularly in the interpretation of research literature. He was an Associate Dean (Teaching) in the Faculty of Education until taking up a position as a research fellow (2004–2006) at the University of Michigan, examining the social and cultural influences on adolescent literacy development in and out of school.

Richardson's research interests focus on two areas, both of which have grown out of his professional work: the role of language and literacy in learning in academic contexts and the motivations of beginning teachers. He has a particular interest in the role that writing and other textual practices play in learning in the disciplines in higher education and is investigating the development of interest and the identification individuals have with the different disciplines.

Chapter 8

Humanising the corporate Monash

2011–2014

When Marty Sullivan was acting coordinator of DipEd he would visit students at random in this capacity. Andy Spaull recalls Marty Sullivan returning after a teaching round visit at a western suburbs school, saying 'I have just witnessed the best student I have ever seen in a classroom.' Asked who it was, Sullivan replied 'a chap called John Loughran'.[1] Loughran was not only a Monash DipEd student, but his father was a boilermaker who worked welding the hairline fractures on the cranes used in the construction of the Menzies Building.

Loughran worked in the faculty part-time, completed a masters and then a PhD and gradually became a staff member. He was well mentored by the likes of Peter Fensham, Dick White, Dick Gunstone, Jeff Northfield, Paul Gardner and Gilah Leder – the group of science educators. There was not only helpful mentoring but a team approach to much of the work and help was freely given.

Loughran, emerging from the science education tradition, developed work on teaching, learning and teacher education and especially examining alternative perspectives on aspects of teaching which are being taken for granted. So Loughran became Dean of the faculty.

In this phase, the faculty was part of a university that has gone beyond the Greater Monash or Monash Unlimited and now has a new dimension as a corporate model. Each staff member is much more on their own. Loyalty to any institution – even Monash, for some – is not as strong as in the past, as new opportunities to advance are grabbed. The Faculty of Education at Monash University having such a high reputation had a downside – it was an endorsement that people seized to jump to the next step, often meaning a curtailed time at Monash. In the past the long stays of academic staff in

---

[1] Interview with Dr Andrew Spaull by author 7 June 2012; the school was Exhibition Girls' High School. People like Margrette Fairbanks always saw Loughran as a future Dean.

the faculty have meant a continuity and the development of scholars in their fields of scholarship. People came specifically to do higher degrees in science education with Fensham, White and Gunstone, to work on women's studies with Zain'uddin, Sampson or Leder, to work on autism with Bartak, to work on the economics of education with Burke, history of education with Dick Selleck or early childhood with Marilyn Fleer.

8.1 Professor John Loughran, Dean of Education.
Education Faculty

2011

The nature of the annual visits of the Vice-Chancellor's Group to the faculty began to change in 2011. This suited the faculty as it was a faculty-review year, which involved a long process of self-review followed by a review by external people. This also coincided with AUQA (Australian Universities Quality Agency).

The extensive self-review undertaken during 2011 provides a useful overview of the faculty. The previous review had been in 2004–2005.

In 2011 there were 4,925 students enrolled in the faculty. Of these there were 862 international students. Of the total students, 42 per cent were in undergraduate programs, 48.7 per cent in postgraduate and coursework programs and 9.7 per cent were research students undertaking higher degrees. Further, 31.2 per cent of students were external, and .5 per cent were of Aboriginal or Torres Strait Islander descent. In terms of the three campuses 57 per cent were at Clayton, 23 per cent at Gippsland and 20 per cent at Peninsula. While Monash had commenced a campus at Berwick in 1994 (on the site of the old Casey airfield), education courses were not offered there until 2012. Berwick was located in a growth area of Melbourne, the southeastern corridor. It was an area with limited opportunities in education for the residents, less than 10 per cent had bachelor degrees, and it comprised small business people and young families moving into their first home. The university felt courses in education and nursing might have appeal there. Debbie Corrigan headed a team that looked into this possibility.

There was an important milestone in 2011 when the student selection and enrolments procedures were handled by professional staff. Previously these tasks had always been undertaken by academic staff with some help from the professional staff. It was hoped that this would free up academic staff for other tasks.

On-campus or internal students made up 66 per cent of the total while 34 per cent were off-campus, with 10 per cent of students described as 'multimodal'.

The growth of the Bachelor of Early Childhood Studies followed Commonwealth Government backing and there were additional plans to improve the skills of those working in early childhood. Peninsula's growth reflected too the numbers from the sport and outdoor recreation degree. There was an increase in higher degree by research students (HDR) because of increased on-shore international students (24 EFTSL in 2009 to 62 in 2010), and there was the start of off-shore enrolments.

Of the staff there were 203 people in 2011 (178.8 FTE), a 37 per cent increase on staff numbers in 2004. Of the 203, 112 were academics (teaching and research), 3 technical and 88 professional staff.

The review also reiterated the shortage of appropriate staff, especially in a period when 'academic strengthening' had become the mantra. The average age of staff in 2005 was 50, but by 2010 it had fallen to 47. Over the next five years more senior staff were to retire, and while this would provide opportunities for young appointments, the departing staff had very strong research records. The new professors appointed in 2010 had shown research

8.2 Berwick Campus.
Education Faculty

strength, but with many young and mid-career appointments there was concern and a need to provide rewards and incentives for research output.

The faculty drafted qualitative and quantitative research standards to the Taskforce on Academic Strengthening, which were commended. A table set out the various elements and targets expected. For research outputs there were items such as 'weighted publication points', number of DIISR (Department of Innovation, Industry, Science and Research) publications, high quality publications (ERA tier A) and number of non-DIISR scholarly publications. There were also categories for research inputs (such as external research income), and points for higher degree supervision.

In 2011 the Research Committee identified 12 faculty research groups with a leader nominated for each group. These were: arts education – Dr Peter De Vries; child and community development – Professor Marilyn Fleer; cultural sociology of education – Dr Mary Lou Rasmussen; inclusive mathematics education – Professor Peter Sullivan; language, literacy and education – Professor Ilana Snyder; learning with new media research – Dr Glenn Auld; movement, environment and community – Associate Professor Phil Payne; policy and practice in primary education – Professor Mike Askew; psychology of teachers and students – Associate Professor Paul Richardson; science education – Associate Professor Debbie Corrigan; social innovation and education – Professor Terri Seddon; and space, place and body – Professor Margaret Somerville. These groups were to meet regularly and aimed to construct collective policies and projects.

8.3 Debbie Corrigan.
Education Faculty

Visiting scholars

The faculty continued to attract significant numbers of international scholars to Monash. There were always seminars and sometimes lectures and the taking of courses. In 2010 the following visitors came to the faculty: Professor Shlomo Black, Dean of Kaye College Israel; Dr Monika Krajcovicova from the University of Presnov, Slovakia; Professor Hugh Glover from Nelson Mandela Metropolitan University; Associate Professor Jessica Fields from San Franciso State University; Dr Louise Allen from the University of Auckland; Professor Lynn Mario Menezes de Souza from the University of Sao Paulo, Brazil; and Tomsork, Garnet Grosjean and Deo Bishundayal from the University of British Columbia, Canada.

For 2011 there were to be even more visiting scholars. The Research Committee invited and funded two: Professor Greg Dimitriadis of the State University of New York and Professor Nikolai Veresov of the University of

Oulu, Finland. Then there were 15 collegially funded visitors and a further 12 scholars who were not funded. In 2013 Senior Fulbright Specialist Associate Professor Adam Howard from Colby College, Maine, USA came with perspectives on strategies for widening participation and redressing educational disadvantage, drawn from his extensive research into the relationship between schools, universities and social inclusion/exclusion. Among many others were Dr Horacio Walker Larraín, Dean of Education at the Universidad Diego Portales in Chile and Associate Professors Paul Carr (Lakehead University) and Gina Thésée (University of Québec at Montréal).

Staff

While there had been a significant number of new staff appointments during Sue Willis' period, there was still a problem of recruiting new staff. As the Dean observed about education faculties generally, 'Education is touted as the oldest in the tertiary sector as the baby boomer generation that was at the forefront of the wave of academic expansion now was closer to retirement'. So there was the need to regenerate but often vacancies were hard to fill. In contrast to previous times, a minimum requirement was a doctorate and preferably some publications. For the faculty it was found that most of the most senior and most active staff in terms of research were to retire in the next four to five years. There was a pleasing change in the number of women in senior positions in the faculty – double the university percentage.

Sue Willis in her move to avoid 'appointing yourself' to academic vacancies, swung away from what seemed to be a requirement of school teaching experience. With John Loughran there was more emphasis on securing people who had the academic expertise enhanced by teaching experience in schools.

Dean Loughran was awarded a Doctor of Letters (DLitt) for his work on 'Developing a Pedagogy of Teacher Education'. This was conferred in October 2011. The DLitt is the highest doctoral award for work that makes an original, substantial and distinguished contribution to knowledge. It was the first time this rare and prestigious degree had been gained by someone from Education at Monash.

In 2012 Margaret Plunkett was awarded Pearson Teacher Educator of the Year and Crystal Chatterton and Professor Terri Seddon received 25-year service awards. Jane Southcott was promoted to associate professor.

The Staff Attitude Survey (SAS), which purported to measure staff commitment to the organisation and the culture of the university, showed the faculty's response rate at 79 per cent, the best in university. Next to education was IT at 59 per cent then law with 58 per cent. The staff satisfaction surveys were positive as were efforts to reach a satisfactory work load formula for staff.

In 2011 Associate Professor Jo Deppeler took the portfolio of research degrees and Professor Ilana Snyder, research. Associate Professor Barbara Clarke stepped down as Associate Dean (Peninsula) after a distinguished period of service and was replaced by a new appointment, Associate Professor Shane Phillipson. The title Associate Dean (Teaching) was changed to Associate Dean (Education), and Associate Professor Alan Reid has made the running in raising education to a high level of performance. Another important newcomer is Mark Rickinson, Associate Dean (Engagement). Darlene McGown enthusiastically led and developed programs and opportunities, organising and enrolling staff in pilates sessions, yoga, 10,000 steps, mindfulness, Monash walks, football tipping and many other wellbeing activities. By 2014 a free medical examination and assessment was available for all staff, as well as the usuals such as 'flu vaccinations.

Deppeler pioneered the concept of two supervisors for high degree students, which the university later adopted as policy.

Maree Mayne retired after 28 years of distinguished service at the Peninsula campus.

In March 2011 came news of the death of Professor Peter Musgrave, a former Dean and professor.[2]

Courses

There were always new courses, and both major and minor amendments to existing courses. In 2011 for example a new course was developed between the Faculties of Education and Arts for a Master in Regional and Community Development. A significant course amendment was to the Bachelor of Primary Education, where units were added to strengthen the ability to communicate scientific understanding and basic science concepts. The new subjects would assist primary teachers in preparing their students better in both science and mathematics.

---

[2] Professor Peter William Musgrave (1925–2011), professor since 1970, Dean 1977–1981.

The Master of Education by research degree underwent change during 2011. The requirement of two years' full-time study plus a thesis of 40,000 words was reduced to 1.5 years study full-time (three years part-time) and between 20,000 and 25,000 words for the thesis. This was to bring the degree into line with other masters degrees at Monash and especially those at the Go8 universities.[3] The faculty review had pointed to the lower higher degree by research completion rates at Monash compared to 37 other universities in a study.[4] The larger number of words for theses required by Monash was regarded as one factor explaining this rate.

There were even more changes in courses and units during 2011 as the faculty prepared to offer courses at the Berwick campus. Two new courses were offered at Berwick, a Bachelor of Education P–10 to enable students to become teachers at all school levels, with an emphasis up to Year 10 but with opportunities for other pathways at Years 11 and 12. Units needed to be prepared and approved for this course.

Among the new units at Berwick was one entitled Indigenous People and Education (EDF4263) which while not being offered until 2014 aroused much interest. In this course there was what was being called a 'scaffolding approach' to learning, where a student with limited knowledge of a subject is encouraged to identify first what they know and second what they do not know. This approach builds on what the student has to offer as well as stimulates curiosity. Given the diversity and experiences each student would bring plus their differing opinions, this had to be recognised and identified as a starting point with mediated learning. Dr Zane Ma Rhea was the leader of the Indigenous People and Education unit.

The other new course offered at Berwick was the Master of Teaching (Secondary) – replacing the Graduate DipEd which was being phased out. The Master of Teaching was a two-year course, this now being a national requirement, and could be taken in an accelerated mode.

The year of 'reviews' came in 2011: there was a faculty review, a higher degrees (research) review, an education psychology programs review, a review for accreditation of the degrees by the Australian Psychological Society. Quality manager Crystal Chatterton had the task of overseeing the review process. Staff had the task of chairing the various review committees. In

---

[3] Faculty Board 29 June 2011.
[4] It was a national benchmarking study conducted in 2008 by Edith Cowan University. Masters with coursework and minor thesis were 30,000–40,000 words at Monash, and typically 20,000–25,000 elsewhere, and for masters by major thesis 60,000 for Monash education and 40,000 elsewhere.

addition there was much work required in preparing for the expansion of courses to the Berwick campus. To add to these burdens, 2012 was listed as a year of review for the University by AUQA.

Demand-driven funding

Under the Gillard Government there was an important change to the funding model for tertiary education by means of the *Higher Education Support Amendment Act 2011*. This 'Demand-driven funding system' meant a shift from the 'command' system approach, where the Commonwealth Government intervened to set quotas and cap enrolments in the various courses. The new approach allows demand or the market to operate. So each tertiary institution competes for students in this open-door approach, which excluded the TAFE sector. This move strengthened the market approach of universities, rewarding enrolments, recognising that Australian universities were competing in a global market. It was later accompanied by a funding cut to universities. The question is, can the workforce keep up with a demand-driven supply of graduates? Under the Abbott government, a review was instigated into this system, headed by the Hon. Dr David Kemp, former Minister for Education and Monash academic, and education researcher Andrew Norton, so there may be changes, although a demand-driven system would ideologically seem compatible with Abbot government philosophy.

2012

The reviews of 2011 spilled over to 2012 as there were reports to consider and actions to take.[5] The Dean saw the main issues to address as the exploring of the Vision/Mission statement of the faculty; reinforcing the value of the one-department structure of the faculty; the use of portfolios; aligning higher degrees by research to the research strengths of the faculty; and gaining student feedback on the issue of placements.

The faculty review had suggested the Dean have an 'Advisory Board' consisting of people external to the faculty. The group asked to undertake this role were Professor Peter Gronn, Cambridge University (former member of staff); Professor Pam Grossman from Stanford University; Professor Kwong Lee Dow, former Vice-Chancellor of the University of Melbourne;

---

5   Tribute was paid to Crystal Chatterton, the Faculty Quality Manager, who had the administrative responsibility for all these reviews.

and Francesca Beddie from NCVER, (the National Centre for Vocational Education Research).

The faculty starting teaching on the Berwick campus in 2012, with both the Master of Teaching and BEd (P–10) being offered. Deputy Dean Debbie Corrigan had overseen the Berwick development. A change brought out by AITSL[6] (the national accreditation body) that meant the one-year Graduate Diploma in Education was to be replaced by the two-year Master of Teaching.

Work on ERA (Excellence in Research for Australia) continued with Professor Ilana Snyder assisted by Trudi Brunton developing a faculty portfolio. The excellent 2010 result had been pleasing especially given the diversity of programs in the faculty compared with the more narrow focus of some of the other Go8 universities. A controversial issue was resolved when ERA ranking in journals was removed for social sciences and humanities.

ERA

The ERA results for 2012 were also favourable, the faculty gaining a 4 ranking again ('above world standards'), and sharing the honours of second place with two other universities in Australia, Sydney and Melbourne. Top with 5 (three subfields had 4, and one had 5) was the University of Queensland which was a much smaller faculty with a higher proportion of senior staff.[7]

Melbourne and Monash are roughly the same size.[8] What is different about Monash and Melbourne is the number of students and courses, especially undergraduate. Sydney had just over half Monash staffing,[9] and the University of Queensland about a quarter. The ERA numbers for staff contributing to the discipline of education: Monash 167, Melbourne 161, Sydney 93, University of Queensland 41. (These do not necessarily equate to

---

[6] The Australian Institute for Teaching and School Leadership (AITSL) came into being on 1 January 2010.

[7] The School of Education Queensland has approximately 30 full-time academic staff members and over 10 honorary or affiliated academic staff members, many of whom are national or international leaders in their fields and are recipients of a wide range of teaching awards. They have 12 administrative staff and 428 enrolled students. The academic staff comprises six professors, seven associate professors, eight senior lecturers, six lecturers and eight research officers.

[8] The University of Melbourne School of Education has 1,655 students and is a graduate school with no bachelor level students.

[9] The University of Sydney has a Faculty of Education and also a Department of Social Work included in education. It has a similar range of courses to Monash and had 723 enrolled education students (2012).

people employed in faculties.)[10] The process was complicated, and in some areas such as the ranking of journals, puzzling. Some of the more obvious weaknesses in the system had been changed for the 2012 round. A further round of rankings will be undertaken in 2015.

There remained pressure for the faculty to seek additional funding sources and to 'market' its services both locally and overseas.

With the wide range of subjects in the many courses together with changing needs and changing staff, course amendments were inevitable, both minor and major, and were a regular part of Faculty Board meetings. Close links with the Victorian Institute of Teaching also ensured helpful feedback and the appropriate amendment of courses to meet requirements.

In 2012 the Group of Eight had proposed limiting entry to their universities for school leavers to those with an ATAR score of at least 60. The University of NSW went further and stated they intended to limit entry to students with an ATAR score of 80. *The Australian* newspaper stated 'ATAR scores are a blunt and inaccurate indicator of ability to cope with academic work loads'.[11]

There were always physical infrastructure issues, especially as many of the buildings on each campus were aging.

The scale of the operations of the faculty was evident when the Dean reported at the first Faculty Board meeting in 2012 that there had been since the end of 2011, 29 new staff appointed. [12]

Associate Professor Shane Phillipson arrived as Head of the Peninsula campus replacing Associate Professor Barbara Clarke. Joining the childhood team was Associate Professor Nikolai Veresov from Russia via Finland.

International engagement faced problems in 2012, as the faculty was not price competitive in bidding for the various overseas projects. As well as the global financial crisis, the Australian dollar was high and the Monash Budget Model made the faculty more expensive. However, the search for new opportunities continued.

The Graduate Certificate in Higher Education

The Graduate Certificate in Higher Education was replaced in 2012 by the Graduate Certificate in Academic Practice (GCAP). This was designed to

---

[10] Information in this section has been supplied by Ros Winter, research officer of the education faculty.
[11] *Australian* 24 July 2013.
[12] Minutes of Faculty Board 7 March 2012.

help early and mid-career academics in their teaching, research and leadership skills.

This expanded what was offered to probationary staff, especially adding research and higher degree supervision. It was noted that most Australian universities had an equivalent certificate that they were offering, for example Melbourne had the Graduate Certificate in University Teaching and Sydney the Graduate Certificate in Educational Studies, but the revised Monash certificate was a first in its research and supervision component. A 24-point course, those taking it could select four units from seven being offered.

Operational plan

An operational plan brought before Faculty Board set out the key objectives for 2012 and beyond.[13] This provides a useful guide to the priorities of the faculty.

There were nine stated objectives:

1. Strengthen the faculty's research profile, reputation and impact.
2. Develop initiatives aimed at strengthening HDR (higher degrees by research) experiences, supervision and completion rates.
3. Recruit high quality local and international doctoral students aligned to faculty research strengths.
4. Ensure that courses and curriculum are innovative, rigorous, attractive to local and international students and professionally current.
5. Rejuvenation of pedagogies by effective use of data and unit development.
6. Enhance the impact of collaborative international engagement activities.
7. Engage in research and consultancy activities which have impact.
8. Build a strategic workforce renewal process to ensure the sustainability and strength of the faculty over the coming decade.
9. Address the faculty's current and future resource needs (physical, virtual, financial and human) particularly in light of expansion to Berwick.

---

[13] Minutes of Faculty Board 9 November 2011.

At the December 2012 Faculty Board meeting there were 60 new course units approved and just as many units or courses 'disestablished'. The emphasis on markets brought about these changes in what was offered.

There also seemed to be an almost constant review process of courses (which had to be reviewed every five years), of policies and indeed of all elements of the faculty. This involved many people, not just in the administration of the reviews but in forming the review committees. Following self-review was input from stakeholders, from students past and present and staff. The review panel included experts external to the faculty as well as students. For example in 2012, there was a report of the review of the Bachelor of Adult Learning and Development, a course which had been offered since 1999, which was unique to Monash and secured high levels of satisfaction from students. The two external senior academics on the review panel were Professor Robert Harreveld from Central Queensland University and Professor Roger Harris from the University of South Australia. There was a representative too from the Australian Higher Education Industrial Association. With all the positives from this review there was disappointment at the low student numbers. Most of the students in this course were of mature age and held full-time jobs. Links with courses that could be taken before or after (masters) were also explored.

There was also a review of the Bachelor of Sport and Outdoor Recreation course which was undertaken along similar lines. This course was often taken as a double degree with a Bachelor of Education or a Bachelor of Business. Another course reviewed was Applied Linguistics for Language Teachers, which was offered with the Faculty of Arts. Not all was rosy. The review of the Bachelor of Early Childhood course was critical, requiring a restructure of the course. The course did not attract as many school leavers as expected and the review panel was critical of some of the staff, who were not as familiar with developments in the early childhood field as they should be, a situation not helped by a high turnover of staff. A need to provide more help and to stimulate change was recognised [14]

Some of the courses reviewed were campus specific, such as the courses in regional and community development, which were at Gippsland.

The review of the Bachelor of Education (Secondary) was one which recognised that it was usually part of a double degree, with students also undertaking degrees in science, arts, music, visual arts and commerce. The review pointed out the high-achieving students entering the course.[15]

---

[14] Minutes Faculty Board 7 November 2013.
[15] As measured by high ATARs and GPAs.

With all these reviews a common element was that students had a high expectation of the faculty given its high academic reputation – this was especially so for research. This gave Monash 'the cutting edge', yet courses had to be viable; no longer could the faculty sustain courses on principle.

Gippsland and Ballarat

In 2012 there was a review of Gippsland, undertaken by Professor Kwong Lee Dow, former Vice-Chancellor of the University of Melbourne. In his report, entitled 'The Gippsland Tertiary Education Plan', he urged that more priority be given to local engagement and community involvement. The university accepted this report and endorsed moves to give Gippsland greater autonomy within what they called 'the Monash family'.[16]

Gippsland in 2013 were offering four major programs: a Bachelor of Primary Education, a Graduate Diploma in Education (one year primary and secondary), a Master of Teaching (both primary and secondary) and a Master of Regional Education and Community Development. The largest program was the Bachelor of Primary Education.

In 2013 came the news that Gippsland campus was to leave Monash University. A mutual consultation with the University of Ballarat had come up with a scheme for an expanded regionally focused university.[17] Gippsland would join with the University of Ballarat and other higher education institutions in regional Victoria to form this new university. The opportunity for all involved to have a say in the proposal was given and meetings held to enable staff to make contributions. The name chosen was Federation University Australia. It legally came into being on 1 October 2013.

The head of education at Gippsland, Simone White, expressed mixed feelings about this move. She had found the experience of being part of the one-department Faculty of Education a happy one. There had been strong support from the top with the Dean frequently at Gippsland campus. The staff were actively engaged in teaching, research and professional and community activities on a par with the other campuses of Monash, and indeed could boast some special achievements such as Margaret Plunkett receiving the Teacher Educator Award of the year from the Australian Association of Teacher Education. Gippsland had also established a Centre of Teaching Excellence funded by the Victorian Department of Education

---

[16] Global email from the Vice-Chancellor 24 February 2012.
[17] Announcement by the Vice-Chancellor Professor Ed Byrne 10 May 2013.

and Early Childhood Development. In the two years of operation there had been active participation by the staff with innovative programs emerging on pedagogy, assessment and course design. The aim was to improve student learning through improved teaching and courses. However, Monash University, despite its many campuses did not see a regional campus as part of its future. The Gippsland campus was an oddity and so while not welcoming another change, the staff saw the benefits of a new university which valued regional campuses. While the change had been approved in 2013 (effective from 1 January 2014), with many students in the pipeline, the links with Monash would only slowly be relinquished. The staff would also need to reassess their involvement in cross-campus research groups and partnerships that had been successfully developed over the years.

Some Gippsland staff lamented the departure from a prestigious Go8 university; others welcomed the chance for Gippsland to return to an institution serving its region. The latter felt that the bigger Monash had 'asset stripped' Gippsland of some of its features such as distance education and the Bachelor of Sport and Outdoor Education. Many felt that an institution in an area surrounded by a large industrial and open-cut mining area should service its need for engineers. There was also a feeling that the central control of teaching practicum placements by Monash had diminished the close contact Gippsland used to have with its neighbourhood schools. Greater Monash, having taken away much of Gippsland's autonomy, from 2004 was talking about giving some of it back but this never really eventuated.[18] Simone White herself was to surrender her post at Gippsland and move to Clayton, thus remaining with Monash University.

2013

In 2013 there was an added course, the Bachelor of Education (Special Education), which commenced with 22 students.[19] Dr Penny Round was in charge of this course. She noted that only 3 per cent of teachers in Victoria had special education training. The diverse number of students in schools had many needs and qualified teachers able to cater for these students were required. In 2014 double these numbers of students were expected to enter the course. This course was designed to produce mainstream primary and secondary teachers with a speciality in special education. In 2014 the BEd

---

[18] Minutes of Faculty Board 21 July 2004.
[19] This course was offered with assistance from the Gorman Foundation, which had been set up in the will of Dr Pierre Gorman, a former staff member.

(Early Childhood and Primary) was also to be offered. along with the Master of Teaching (Primary). Berwick had an attractive campus with excellent facilities, including the remarkable 'holodeck' room, set up like an educational room from *Star Trek* at the instigation of Debbie Corrigan, who had the oversight of developments at Berwick. It was one means of challenging the accepted norms of how you teach.

In April 2013 it was announced that the Commonwealth Government was to strip $2.3 million from university funding. There were efficiency dividends included in these cuts (a cumulative 3.5% cut) by capping self-education tax deductions – this was also expected to have a negative revenue impact on universities. These came at a time when Monash University was experiencing financial difficulties despite excellent academic and research performance.

As part of the corporate centralised process, during 2013, what were called Tier 1 current undergraduate and postgraduate coursework student enquiries were to be directed through Monash Connect, rather than handled by each faculty. These enquiries could be in person, (Monash Connect is represented on each campus), by telephone or online.[20]

Student numbers for 2013 saw a total of 5,546 students; 64.9 per cent were full-time, 35.1 per cent were part-time, 43 per cent were undergraduate students, 48 per cent postgraduate and 9 per cent were undertaking research degrees. Of the students 81.8 per cent were domestic and 18.1 per cent international. It was estimated that since 1964 there had been 95,546 students through the faculty.

Faculty Board

A further review of governance of the faculty was required in October 2013, with the decision by the University Council to make significant changes including the abolition of Faculty Boards. This came from a review of the Monash University Statutes and Regulations.[21] Council sought opinions from staff as to how this would impact on committees that report to Faculty

---

[20] Tier 1 enquiries are those enquiries where a common policy and process applies across all faculties. Monash Connect will respond to the following Course Transfers and exchange; Discontinuation, deferment and intermission; General course or Faculty information and courses; Diploma of Tertiary Studies and Monash Access Program enquiries; Special consideration Timetabling; Enrolment; Fees; Graduations; Scholarships; COE and visa related matters; Financial support in the form of loans and grants; and Letters and transcripts.

[21] Governance Review Report, November 2013, Monash University.

Board. The review looked at committee terms of reference, reporting lines, membership, frequency of meetings and appropriateness of agenda items that each committee has received/addressed over the last two years. It was not clear what legal body would replace Faculty Board. The faculty had considered an alternative to Faculty Board in the past – for example in 2008 there was talk of an Advisory Board made up of external people. Significant changes came from this review, with not only the abolition of Faculty Boards, but with the Dean, now an Executive Dean, to be assisted by a Faculty Executive which reported directly to the University Academic Board. The Executive Dean also had the power to nominate his key administrators, the Associate Deans of the various faculty portfolios, but these had to be approved by the senior management team of the University. A curious decision, as a Dean would presumably know his staff better than university administrators removed from the faculty.

December 2013 saw an historic last meeting of the Faculty Board. While the abolition would result in more efficiencies, it seemed to symbolise the dominance of the corporate model. The large and collegial gathering that was Faculty Board gave many people the opportunity to participate in faculty governance. Indeed there was an agenda item termed 'stakeholder engagement and purpose of Faculty Board' which enabled external members to provide feedback or information. The faculty often became aware of important issues and developments. Faculty Board also informed these people of the faculty's activities and similarly education representatives on other Faculty Boards had proved very useful.[22] Over the years the composition had changed but there have been representatives of the state Education Department, of secondary schools (usually a principal), of Catholic schools, of the independent schools and of the Victorian Institute of Teaching. From Monash itself there were representatives of other faculties: arts, art and design, medicine, business and economics, science, as well as a representative of the alumni office, and internally there were staff representatives of all campuses, the professors, the various Associate Deans and persons holding senior administrative positions in the faculty. At one stage representatives from education faculties of other universities were appointed and of course student representation was regarded as important.

Faculty Board may have been large and unwieldy, but it was conceptually democratic and allowed participants to have a voice. It meant that the many

---

[22] Anita Forsyth said she gained much from representing the faculty on the Faculty Board of Business and Economics.

external representatives could take back to their own institutions information as to what the faculty was doing. In earlier days Faculty Board was no mere rubber stamp. Major issues were often fought out there and some key representatives such as Dr Lawrie Shears from the Education Department and Dr Tom Coates from Wesley College made significant contributions. However, in recent years in an increasingly complex and corporate university culture, their role came to be judged as tokenistic.

Under the new arrangements the Dean of a faculty became the Executive Dean and under him was an Executive Committee – both reporting centrally. Monash was now truly corporate.

Methods

For 2013 there were 27 units in what were secondary teaching methods. The method units were: Accounting Education, Biology Education, Business Management Education, Chemistry Education, Drama Education, Economics Education, English as a Second Language Education, English Education, General Science Education, Geography Education, Health Education, History Education, Information and Communication Technology Education, Jewish Studies Education, Language Education, Legal Studies Education, Mathematics Education, Media Education, Music Education1, Music Education 2, Outdoor Education, Physical Education, Physics Education, Psychology Education, Social Education, Visual Art and Design Education 1, and Visual Art and Design Education 2.

By 2013 there was a real problem in securing placements for students who needed teaching practice as part of their course. For 2013 the faculty needed to find 6,000 places in schools. Other faculties were also making demands, and for government schools there were a number of bans related to an ongoing industrial dispute arising from enterprise bargaining.[23]

The Master of Teaching (Primary), if taken as a full-time course, was two years taking four units each year, representing 12 points each. In addition they were required to do placements in each semester for the two years: 10 days for the first semester, 15 days for the second, and for the second year 15 days in first semester and 20 days in the second.

---

[23] Anita Forsyth 15 March 2013 news item to staff about placements, Faculty of Education.

334 | *The Surprise Rival*

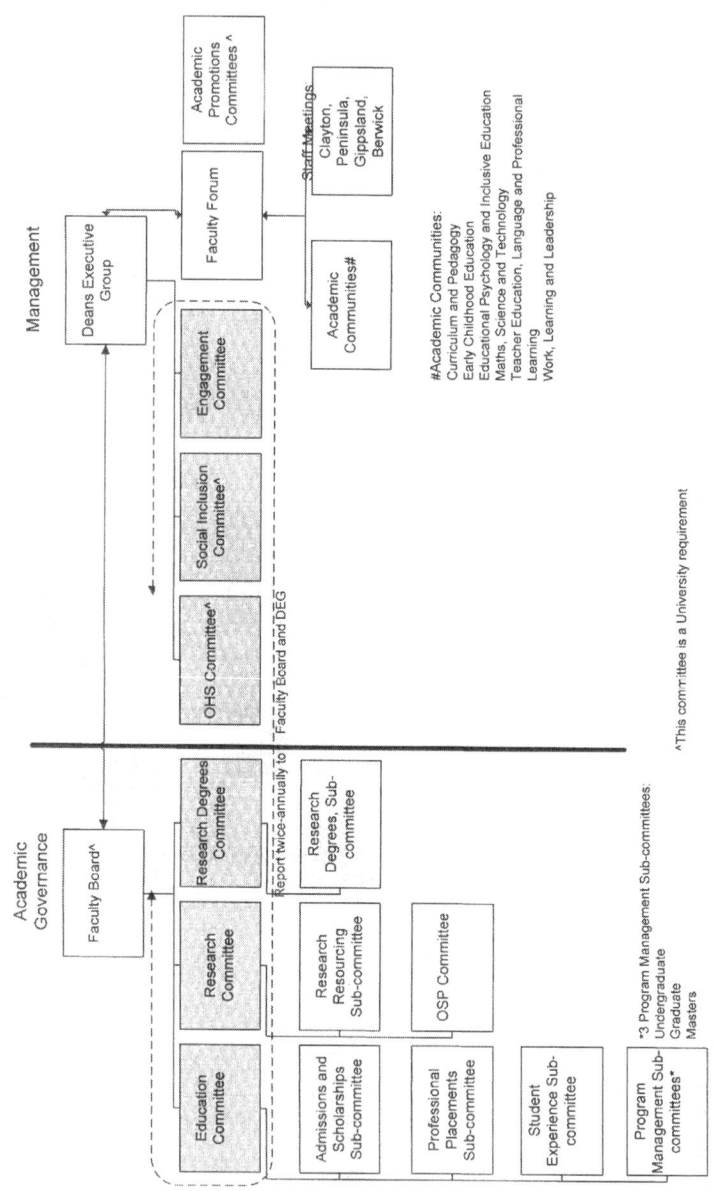

8.4 Organisational Chart.

Review

There was a review of the faculty conducted during 2013 by Crystal Chatterton, Quality Assurance Manager and Lydia Loriente, Executive Officer. This review examined how staff felt about the faculty committees and their operation and reported that the staff attitude to a committee was important in how effective the committee was. They found that interest by staff in elected positions on faculty committees was low, and for many key committee posts no nominations were received. Was this because staff did not want to waste time on committees or felt service on them did not help their career prospects? Perhaps too, diminished participation came with a changing structure which reduced democracy within the faculty. The review also looked at the cost of meetings – they concluded that 3,120 hours of staff time were spent in meetings and with an average of 12 members a committee and meetings lasting on average for two hours, the estimated cost was $302,985 per annum – the equivalent of 2.5 staff EFT. These costs did not include the costs of preparing for meetings, the use of rooms or catering. The review contrasted the need for efficiency with the history of the faculty being a democratic operation with staff able to have a real say in decision-making. Under the corporate model the democratic participation of staff in decision-making was markedly reduced. The reviewers also worked out a new committee structure for the faculty.

The Dean, John Loughran, for the June Faculty Board meeting assessed how the faculty stood. He described it as a mid-sized faculty within Monash, but with expansion to the Berwick campus and the development of a BEd (P–10) there. This meant the faculty was on four Victorian campuses of Monash yet remained a one-department faculty.

Rankings

The news came in May 2013 that according to the QS World University rankings, the education faculty was ranked sixth in the world. On 8 May 2013 the Vice-Chancellor announced that:

> You may be interested to learn that Monash University features in the world's elite (Top 200) institutions in 29 of the 30 subjects featured in this year's QS World University Rankings by Subject, was published on 8th May 2013.[24]

---

[24] On www.topuniversities.com.

For the third edition of the QS World University Rankings by Subject, they evaluated 2,858 universities and ranked 678 institutions; 68 million citations were analysed and they verified the provision of 8,391 programs.

This was good news for the faculty, making it the highest ranked faculty in Monash University. QS or Quadrelli Symonds is a London-based global higher education group which provides information and research and also published rankings of high education departments. These rankings, with a few reservations, are widely respected. They are based on four indicators: academic peer review, employer review, citations per paper and the H-index (which combines papers published and number of times they have been cited). Weightings are not evenly applied, with academic reputation weighted higher for fields like history and employer reputation weighted higher for fields like computer science.[25] In 2014 the faculty was once again ranked number six although Monash generally had slipped down the rankings.

Monash had demonstrated strong improvements in a number of subject areas, including education (up from 16th in the world in 2012 to 6th in 2013); civil and chemical engineering (from 41st and 40th respectively in 2012 to 26th and 25th in 2013); medicine (from 42nd to 29th); and linguistics (from the 51–100 band to 19th).

Monash now has two subject areas ranked in the top ten globally – pharmacy and pharmacology (dropping from 6th to 7th in 2013) and education (6th) – and are ranked in the top 50 in 22 disciplines (up from 18 in 2012).

Losses

Heather Phillips, who has worked in the faculty for 38 years announced her retirement in May 2013. At first working in the General Office and then taking administrative roles, Phillips was described as generous in sharing her knowledge (which was considerable) and possessing a strong work ethic. She is a caring person of warmth and humour who will be greatly missed.[26] Phillips retained a role on the committee for the celebration of the 50th anniversary of the faculty.

Di Chandler, who had retired in 2012 after 23 years of outstanding service as director of the Elwyn Morey Centre, died in July 2013. An expert in early

---

[25] Professor Simon Marginson, formerly of the faculty but then at Melbourne, before taking a senior post in the UK in 2013, was very critical of the ranking system, calling it 'bad social science' and describing the rankings as questionable. *The Australian*, 16 October 2013.

[26] Susan Kenton in an email to staff marking Phillips' retirement. Having refused a 'farewell', the Dean took her out to lunch.

8.5 Faculty stalwarts Anita Forsyth and Heather Phillips.
Education Faculty

childhood, Chandler was a much loved figure and her death was widely lamented by friends from the faculty.

Courses

The Bachelor of Sport and Outdoor Recreation continued to be popular. It could be taken as a three-year degree, or it could be combined to have a four-year double degree with a Bachelor of Education (Primary or Secondary) or a Bachelor of Business. The course catered for those interested in sports management, outdoor recreation, ecotourism, adventure travel, sports training and a range of recreational pursuits. The double degree enabled a student to add a business dimension or the qualifications to teach. As well as a teaching practicum component for those doing the BEd, there were professional placements and fieldwork. The course was offered at the Peninsula campus, although there were secondary education units taken at Clayton. A key new appointment in this area meant a shift of emphasis to physical education and health.

Undergraduate degrees were of three types: a four-year course to obtain a single degree in education, a four-year course to achieve a double degree or a four- or five-year degree with a major discipline followed by a Master of Teaching. The Bachelor of Education (Early Childhood) and Bachelor of Education (Primary) were single, four-year degrees offered at Peninsula and Berwick campuses (Gippsland having left Monash University). Students were also able to take a BEd that equipped them for both early childhood and primary. The four-year degree had four components: an education major, a curriculum major, education leadership units and professional experience.

There were four-year double-degree courses so students could complete a Bachelor of Education (Primary) with either a Bachelor of Arts, a Bachelor of Science, or a Bachelor of Visual Arts. There were also double degrees available for those wanting to do secondary education and these could be combined with a Bachelor of Arts, a Bachelor of Commerce, a Bachelor of Music, a Bachelor of Science, a Bachelor of Visual Arts or a Bachelor of Sport and Outdoor Recreation. In 2014 the secondary specialist teaching (or curriculum) areas were: accounting, biology, business management, chemistry, drama, economics, English, English as an Additional Language (EAL), general science, geography, health, history, information technology/computing, Languages Other than English (LOTE), legal studies, mathematics, music, outdoor education, physical education, physics, psychology, social education and visual arts. The double degree also required major and minor sequences in subjects studied.

In addition there were specialist degrees. One was the Bachelor of Education P–10, enabling the student to teach in both primary and secondary schools. An important addition was a Bachelor of Education (Special Education) a four-year course that catered for teachers able to work with children with diverse needs and in special settings. This course was offered at the Berwick campus.[27]

In addition the Master of Teaching (Primary) replaced the Grad Diploma of Education (Primary) which was meant as a pre-service teacher qualification. A Master of Organisational Leadership commenced in 2013.

CEET

While in university terms the Centre for the Economics of Education and Training (CEET) was no longer an official centre, it continued within the faculty with its research, and outside consultancies. In 2013 the Australian Council for Educational Research (ACER) published the National Report

---

[27] This initiative was made possible by a grant from the Gorman Foundation.

on Social Equity in VET 2013 which provides comprehensive information and analysis on the participation, achievement and transitions from the Australian Vocational Education and Training (VET) system for learner groups which have been identified as at risk of disadvantage. Overall, the report portrays VET as providing a diverse range of training opportunities for individuals experiencing a wide range of life circumstances.

The report includes separate chapters on: Indigenous Australians; people with a disability; people from culturally and linguistically diverse backgrounds; people living in remote areas; people from low socioeconomic status (SES) backgrounds; issues relating to gender; and those for whom VET may be seen as offering a 'second chance'. This report was regarded as an important 'first' in this field. Dr Chandra Shah was now the director of CEET and the centre worked collaboratively with other staff and external groups like ACER. Another major project is social inclusion research for the National Centre for Vocational Education Research with Sue Webb, Miriam Faine and John Pardy.

Gerald Burke retained an advisory role with the centre but has been involved in work with the Australian Workforce and Productivity Agency, and other projects like 'Gonski'. In 2013 they also held their annual conference (the 17th), which brought together researchers, policy makers and VET practitioners to discuss issues related to VET and social inclusion. Speakers included Ged Kearney, President of the Australian Council of Trade Unions, presenting on The High Road to Productivity; Philip Bullock, National VET Equity Advisory Council; Tom Karmel; Marie Persson, Australian Workforce and Productivity Agency; Kwong Lee Dow, The University of Melbourne; Brian Howe, The University of Melbourne; Gerald Burke, Australian Workforce and Productivity Agency; Peter Noonan, ACIL Allen Consulting Group; George Myconos, Brotherhood of St Laurence; Juliette Mendelovits, ACER; Phil McKenzie, ACER; and Aaron Nicholas, Deakin University.

Compliance, reports and reports

A feature of the times was the need for staff to comply with a range of requirements. These included matters such as occupational health and safety, personal well-being, social inclusion, engagement, and equal opportunity. Faculty Board required regular reports on these areas.

With social inclusion, for example the report of this faculty committee in 2010 gave details of a student leadership training camp held to prepare students for leadership roles related to peer mentoring and student ambassadorial functions. They also indicated that in 2009 17 per cent of undergraduate students in the faculty were from a low SES group – short of the target of 20.6 per cent. There was also Indigenous student engagement, including an Indigenous summer camp. The advancement of women was also an issue for the committee.[28]

The university set down rules and procedures for use of social media provided by the university and some specific prohibitions. There were also documents on the Student Academic Integrity Policy and Student Academic Integrity: Managing Plagiarism and Collusion Procedures, which provided high level information about expectations of students and the broader Monash community with regard to academic integrity and honesty.

Cameron Pettiona reported to the faculty the following documents from the May 2013 meeting of the University's Occupational Health and Safety Policy Committee:

- Hazard and Incident Report Form
- Hazard and Incident Investigation Form
- Local Area OHS Induction – General Staff, Honours or Post-Graduate Induction
- Local Area OHS Induction – Laboratory, Workshop or Studio Induction
- Health and Safety Issue Resolution Procedure

These were not all the OH and S documents, but simply the recent ones. There were human resources issues too that staff needed to watch. Helen Forgasz sent around two paragraphs of new requirements in 2013:

1. Monash University has made a recent change to the documentation required of new or re-contracted staff to ensure compliance with employment legislation and Section 245 AB of the Migration Act 1958.

   All new employees of Monash University will be asked to demonstrate proof of identity and work rights.

   If the university does not already hold the needed information, casual, sessional and fixed-term staff whose contracts will be renewed will also be asked to supply this information.

---

[28] Social Inclusion Committee report, 3 November 2010.

A copy of one of the following will be required:

AU passport; or

Expired AU passport plus drivers license; or

AU Citizenship certificate plus driver's license (or ID with photo); or

AU Birth certificate (born before 20/8/1986) showing at least one parent was born in Australia plus driver's license (or ID with photo); or

Certificate of evidence of AU citizenship plus driver's license (or ID with photo).

2. It was recently brought to our attention that some supervisors (e.g., grant holders) have asked people to commence work prior to contracts being offered and accepted. This practice carries very high risk. Not only are the people unable to claim for payment until they have been issued and accepted contracts, but they are also not covered by Workcover etc. Should a 'work-related' accident occur during the 'uncontracted' period, the supervisor/s (not the University) will be personally liable. Explanations are provided to all new casual and sessional employees during induction why they should not commence work until they have been offered and accepted a contract. Supervisors must respect this condition, recognising the consequences to the employee and to themselves in not complying.

There was also an annual report for the faculty Equity and Diversity Committee. In this report results of a staff attitude survey would be revealed, reminders about harassment issues, about work/life balance, about the work 'climate', the need to improve Indigenous awareness, discrimination against women, dealing with discrimination grievances and so forth. In terms of student equity there was socioeconomic disadvantage, rural or isolated students, students with long-term family difficulties, students with disabilities, students with medical conditions and students from non-English speaking backgrounds. Information sessions, workshops, retreats and mentoring of individuals were all employed to tackle these issues.[29]

With all these requirements and reports it is no surprise to learn that the agenda papers for the June 2011 meeting of Faculty Board went to 429 pages! All this meant more staff to handle the administration and Gerald Burke

---

[29] See Faculty Equity and Diversity Annual Report 2009.

calculated that the ratio between academic and general (or professional) staff which had been 95:5 in the 1970s became 50:50 by 2010.

Grants

In 2013, applications for ARC grants saw 5 successful ones from 14 applications made. This was a highly successful result. Dr Anne Harris received $378,442, a Discovery Early Career Researcher Award, for a study on creativity and innovative thinking in Australian secondary schools. A Discovery Project was awarded to Professor Neil Sewlyn, Dr Nicola Johnson and Dr Scott Bulfin of $325,000 for their study on why digital technologies have failed to have a consistent impact on the core processes of schools and schooling. Professor Marilyn Fleer was awarded $290,000 for looking at imaginative play and how it helps children imagine scientific explanations. Dr Stephen Keast, Professor John Loughran, Associate Professor Debra Panizzon and Dr Ian Mitchell received a Discovery Grant of $343,000 for a study on how pedagogical reasoning can be used to understand teachers' professional knowledge. Associate Professors Paul Richardson and Helen Watt received $352,000 for work looking at the coping and motivational resources used by mid-career teachers to thrive personally and professionally. All these funds were for a three-year period.

Associate Professor Joanne Deppeler with her team continued to attract major grants from groups like ARC as well as from education systems both in Australia and overseas. Deppeler with her psychological background was concerned about students facing learning challenges and did much work on improving inclusive practices. Co-author of a milestone book in this area, the book came out in a second edition in 2010.[30] Her most recent grant is for a project looking at children with disabilities in a group of Pacific nations (with Dr Umesh Sharma 2013–2015).

Helping with research and projects is the Engagement and Partnerships Office. A bulletin was issued informing staff opportunities they could tender for, or suggest a potential funding partner, help to develop an ARC Linkage proposal or the like. Andrew Jackson and Bronwyn Smith were involved in this work.

The Faculty Research Office also provided help by identifying Faculty Quality Journals and Quality Book Publishers. The office told staff that:

---

[30] Joanne Deppeler, with T J Loreman and David Harvey *Inclusive Education: Supporting Diversity in the Classroom*, London, Routledge, second edition 2010 (first edition was published in 2005).

8.6 Joanne Deppeler.
Education Faculty

8.7 Helen Forgasz.
Education Faculty

The Faculty Quality Journals list includes a total of 1,152 journals from various relevant fields that are listed in any of the 4 quartiles of ISI; and or has the Scopus SNIP factor above 0.5. This list also includes journals coded to 13 from the 2010 ERA Ranked Journal List, A*, A and B; these titles are in a smaller font, so they're easy to see quickly.

It was Ros Winter and the Research office who did the work to make these lists possible.

There was a series of reviews undertaken during 2013, one on the Master in Counselling course, from which an improvement plan was developed. The chair of the Review Panel was Associate Professor Alan Reid, who chaired a number of such review panels over the year. New to the faculty, he brought an open mind, and it proved a quick learning experience for him to get to know the faculty. These reviews well equipped him to take on the post of Associate Dean (Education).

Monash University in 2013 awarded fellowships to some distinguished alumni, including two education graduates: Stephen Newton AO, former principal of Caulfield Grammar School and Chris Wardlaw PSM, retired senior officer of the Victorian Department of Education and Early Child Development and former head coach of the Australian track and field team.

Newly created professor Helen Forgasz gave her inaugural lecture on the topic 'Negotiating Gendered Pathways'.[31] She stated that despite various targeted interventions and initiatives over the years, women remain in the minority in the nationally critical fields of Science, Technology, Engineering, and Mathematics (STEM). Given the importance of these fields for Australia's future and the need to produce sufficiently qualified people, Forgasz stressed the importance of women developing in these fields. While gender divides in school and tertiary enrolments and associated career paths remain, perceptions abound that there are no longer obstacles in the paths of women to enter and succeed in these fields. She stated though that paradoxically, there is lingering evidence that women are still considered less capable or suitable to encroach into these male enclaves.

In 2013 Dr Umesh Sharma received the Dean's Award for Innovation and External Collaboration and Dr Anne Harris was the winner of the Dean's Award for an Early Career Researcher (an award to recognise, reward and encourage excellent early career researchers).

---

[31] Delivered in June 2013.

2014

For the faculty 2014 was an important year, its 50th anniversary. Celebrations and an array of activities were planned. However, 2014 started ominously with the announcement that masters units will attract full fees, doubling the cost to students. While there was now a greater diversity of people undertaking such degrees, for teachers who took the course there was no financial reward for them from employers. It was to be a busy year with Monash University engaged in extensive negotiations with the National Tertiary Education Union (NTEU) for a new enterprise agreement.

In 2014 the faculty has 4,500 students, growing at 10 per cent annually. The DipEd was no longer being offered, students now had to do a Master of Teaching, a two-year degree, although by working an extra semester in one year, the course could be completed in one and a half years. (There would be some residual DipEd students at the Gippsland campus).

In 2014 there was a strong demand for all courses. For students entering undergraduate courses at Clayton, an ATAR score of over 80 was needed, with 130 students having scores of 85 or higher. Monash had the highest ATAR scores for education in the state. The faculty was receiving a high calibre of student for its undergraduate courses. There was also a strong demand for the Master of Teaching (which had replaced the DipEd), although Melbourne had more first-preference applicants than Monash. The new Master of Teaching has an intake of 220 students.

From 2014 there are many major policy changes which will affect the faculty.

The courses at Berwick have attracted more students than expected, with over 900 quality students. In 2014 another program was added at Berwick, the Bachelor of Education (Early Years), which provided initial training for teachers in primary schools as well as giving accreditation as an early childhood teacher. By 2014 at Berwick there were 334 students enrolled for the BEd (P–10), 179 for the Master of Teaching (Secondary), 124 for the Master of Teaching (Primary), 34 in the BEd (Special Education), 37 in the BEd (EC and Primary) and 123 doing the Diploma of Tertiary Studies (a supportive course for university study). There were six doctoral students. With Lucas Walsh, the fields of community needs and youth are receiving attention. The teaching was undertaken both by staff whose main location was the Berwick campus as well as staff from Clayton and Peninsula. The Deputy Dean, Dr Debbie Corrigan, retained a managerial role at Berwick in addition to her own research and work as Deputy Dean.

Elsewhere the students in the undergraduate courses have ATAR scores around 75, and the Master of Teaching for both primary and secondary teachers is being offered as well as the accelerated model. At Peninsula courses are well supported, with keen interest in the new emphasis on the course in sport and outdoor education with a physical education and health bias. Top-quality new staff have come in to develop this new emphasis. There has been less demand for courses in primary education as the field is oversupplied and many primary teachers are unable to find employment. Peninsula maintains its strong reputation in early childhood both for initial training and graduate courses.

Requirements and systems

In 2014 Monash University made a strategic decision to implement a new Integrated Research Administration System (IRAS) to support researchers in their core activities in the most effective and efficient way across the institution.

IRAS will manage the lifecycle of research activity from initiation and development of funding proposals for contracts and grants, to ethics, post-award, research outputs, researcher web profiles and institutional and strategic reporting. It will be used by both researchers and professional staff in research administration.

The new system will enable better tracking of research funding applications as they move between faculties and central support units, provide researchers with the facility to view project finances and milestone information during the project, enable automated harvesting of indexed research publications, and give researchers the capability to generate curriculum vitaes with their research activity data.

An important new requirement was introduced from 2014 – what the university calls 'course architecture'. Education has become involved early in this new process, with some faculties showing reluctance to participate. This is designed to stop the proliferation of courses, especially the many boutique courses being offered in the various faculties. With an aim of making it simple for students, there needs to be a critical mass before a course title can be approved. This system links up with Australian Quality Frameworks (AQF). There had to be a clear masters degree for example, with the same number of units required for all masters degrees.

The professional staff

The professional staff play a key role in the faculty, coping with the many demands for information and assisting in the compliance with the various requirements of the university and of external bodies. Leading the professional staff and playing a key role on faculty administration is the Faculty Manager.

Peter Lawford as Faculty Manager has a key role more akin to that of business manager or finance director than the former notion of Faculty Secretary. Lawford, who comes from a secondary teaching background, understands education and has a sound grasp of finance and planning. As Faculty Manager he is supported by a large administrative team, which needs to cope with the many requirements including the reviews and demands for compliance now made of faculties. Most of his managers have university degrees; some have higher degrees. While currently a large administrative or professional staff which comprises 48 per cent of the staff of the faculty, Monash policy has decreed that for the next three years the size of the professional staff has to be reduced by 5 per cent, a total of a 15 per cent reduction. The key managers in the faculty in 2014 were: Tanya Pelle (Manager, Admissions & Student Services), Seshna Maharaj (Manager,

8.8 Peter Lawford.
Kristian Lofhelm, Education Faculty

Marketing & Communications), Cameron Pettiona (Manager, Campus Services), Crystal Chatterton (Manager, Quality Assurance), Susan Kenton (Manager, Education Services), Louise Goold (Manager, Engagement), Bronwyn Smith (Manager, Strategic Initiatives), Trudi Brunton (Manager, Research Services), Mayur Katariya (Manager, Research Degrees), Samantha Curtis (Manager, Professional Experience).

The senior administrative group of the faculty for 2014 comprised the Dean, Professor John Loughran, the Deputy Dean Associate Professor Debbie Corrigan, the Faculty Manager, Peter Lawford, and the following Associate Deans with portfolios: Associate Professor Alan Reid, Education; Professor Ilana Snyder, Research Degrees; Associate Professor Mark Rickinson, Engagement; and Associate Professor Paul Richardson, Research. There were also Campus Deans: Associate Professor Lucas Walsh, Berwick; Professor Helen Forgasz, Clayton; and Associate Professor Shane Phillipson, Peninsula.

Other

In 2013 Professor Ed Byrne AO, the Vice-Chancellor, announced he was to leave in 2014 to take up the position of president and principal at King's College London. Regarded as an effective VC, Byrne had been a friend of the faculty. Taking over from him in September 2014 was Professor Margaret Gardner AO, the ninth Vice-Chancellor of Monash University and the first woman to serve in the role. Professor Gardner came from RMIT University where she was Vice-Chancellor and president. Her academic fields were in industrial relations and organisational management.

In the administrative changes made, former Dean, Sue Willis became Vice Provost (Education Programs), which added to her present work with social inclusion; adding academic leadership for course architecture; ensuring appropriate policies, procedures and systems support the educational reforms including course accreditation and review; development and implementation of the social inclusion strategy for improved access, participation and success of students from under represented communities.

There were departures from the faculty too – Professor Mike Askew, who had been such a force in primary education, and Terri Seddon to a chair at the Australian Catholic University. Seddon had an international reputation for her research and publications and was highly productive.

8.9 Professor Ilana Snyder.
Education Faculty

Social life

Socially the faculty at each campus welcomed new staff and farewelled departing staff; Faculty Days continued, rotating at each campus. Groups like the Faculty of Education Choir at Clayton continued. presenting annually a Christmas carol concert in the Religious Centre. In 2014 it celebrated 40 years. Over the years it had performed at University commencement services and also for faculty social nights including theme nights such as 'Finding the Lost Chord', featuring Victorian songs and recitations, as well as mini-musicals. People still remember Eric Friedman's rendition of 'Our Don Bradman', and solos by Judy Reyne and Floyd Ausburn.

Conclusion

In 2014 there were 135 academic staff in the faculty and 85 professional staff. An alumni newsletter was produced, aided by the capable Naren Chellappah, announcing events to celebrate the 50th anniversary: a book launch, a gala dinner in the Great Hall of the National Gallery of Victoria and an education forum carrying on from the forum theme of 2012: 'Quality in Education – What's Worth Fighting For'.

8.10 Faculty Choir in the Religious Centre Christmas Concert, 2013.
Conductor: Louise Jenkins; Piano: Annabella Fung; Trumpet: Leon de Bruin; Organ: Jeshka Earle; Other instruments: Jose Alonso, Luci Ferrier, Emily Kersing, Samantha Broadbent, Dorothy Jenkins; Sopranos: Monica Baker, Julie Harrington, Janet Hubner, Marion Miller, Kay Ritchie, Eileen Scott Stokes, Rhonda Yates; Altos: Anita Chou, Kate de Bruin, Margaret Heagney, Kate Howard, Anna Podorova, Margaret Rendell, Jackie Waylen, Rosamund Winter. Tenors: Alan Bishop, Philip Chan, Rebecca Cooper, Jane Southcott; Basses: Richard Connolly, Mircea Matthews, Renn Wortley.
Education Faculty

The university's emphasis on growth and expansion has created a treadmill atmosphere among staff. There is also the funding treadmill. Where once funding from the Commonwealth Government represented 90 per cent of university funding, today is 30 per cent. These forces create enormous pressure, yet the faculty has been fortunate in retaining quality staff.

The faculty, with its high research reputation, has had senior leaders like Ilana Snyder, Peter Sullivan, Dennis Moore, Terri Seddon, Jo Deppeler, Jane Kenworthy, Marilyn Fleer, Mike Askew and Neil Selwyn – all stand outs in their fields, as well as officially 'retired' people like Alan Bishop and Dick Gunstone, who remain important mentors. The issue facing the faculty in 2014 is how to maintain this high reputation. How to manage generational change and maintain this status. Loughran wanted able people who were good team players. These people ideally should be at the top of their fields in research, be good teachers and relate well to colleagues. Being a Faculty of Education there was the expectation that staff should be outstanding teachers! The Monash faculty is a comprehensive one, offering courses at all levels and in all fields. There are already a core of leaders for the new generation: Shane Phillipson, Lucas Walsh, Debbie Corrigan, Helen Forgasz, Alan Reid, Dawn Penny, Mark Rickinson and Simone White, adding to those senior leaders who remain. There are gaps which are being identified.

Loughran in this 50th year reflected on the great past of the faculty as well as the many changes, and how the faculty continues to be at the forefront of innovation in teaching, learning and research. He also showed the international links the faculty now had with off-shore teaching, as well as research projects and close academic links overseas.

Staff

John Loughran was contracted 0.5 as the science method lecturer in 1989. He spent 1989 and 1990 working half time in the faculty and half time at CRC Sydenham and then Xavier College before accepting a three-year full-time contract as the science method lecturer mid-way through 1990. His research and teaching interests are based on the development of teachers' knowledge and the way that this is influenced and developed through teacher preparation, beginning teaching and professional development. His research has spanned science education and the related fields of professional knowledge and reflective practice. John was the Director of Teacher Education at Monash for five years through which his interest in teacher preparation was further developed. Consequently, he has spent considerable time researching learning to teach and has been invited to work with teachers and researchers across Australia and internationally in Hong Kong, Sweden, UK, USA, Canada, Belgium, South Africa, Norway and New Zealand. John supervises a range of doctoral students across the science, reflective practice/self-study, teaching and learning fields. He continues to be involved with schools through a range of projects and through professional development and in-service roles. John has been involved in a number of research projects (faculty funded and ARC-funded) including: beginning teachers; learning about teaching in pre-service education; science teaching and learning; pedagogical content knowledge; PAVOT project and Science teacher research. John was the co-founding editor of *Studying Teacher Education* and is an executive editor of *Teachers and Teaching: Theory and Practice*. He is a also member of a number of editorial boards (*Research in Science Education; International Journal of Reflective Practice, Teacher Education Quarterly* and *Asia Pacific Forum on Science Learning and Teaching*) and is a reviewer for a number of other journals. John has had numerous research grants pertaining to science teacher education and teacher as researcher. His main research interests have been in teacher education and the knowledge base of teaching about teaching; teaching strategies that enhance greater student understanding; approaches to learning and developing a better understanding of how learning occurs; the how and why of reflective practitioners; making science teaching more interesting for students. He has authored or co-authored over 14 books and written many articles in refereed journals.

Staff of 2010

Nicola F Johnson was appointed to the faculty in February 2010 as a senior lecturer at the Gippsland campus and this is her current position. Prior to this was she was a lecturer in the Faculty of Education at the University of Wollongong (UOW) from 2007. Nicola's PhD was awarded from Deakin University in 2008 and was entitled 'Teenage Technological Experts: Bourdieu and the Performance of Expertise'. She was awarded an early career teaching award from UOW in 2009. As an early career researcher, she published two books, namely *The Mutliplicities of Internet Addiction: The Misrecognition of Leisure and Learning* (Ashgate, 2009) and *Publishing from Your PhD: Negotiating a Crowded Jungle* (Gower, 2011). Nicola is a member of the Learning with New Media Research Group (formerly CEMM) in the faculty.

Hilary Monk was appointed to the faculty (Peninsula) in 2010. A graduate of Auckland Kindergarten Teachers College in 1971 she taught in state and private kindergartens in New Zealand and Hawaii for 24 years. She completed a Bachelor of Education in 2000 at Massey University at Wellington, New Zealand and later a Master of Education (Adult Education) (Honours) in 2005 at the same university. She began lecturing at Bethlehem Tertiary Institute in New Zealand in 1996 moving to Australia to undertake her doctoral studies at Monash University which she completed in 2010. Monk was awarded the Monash Silver Jubilee Postgraduate Scholarship for the duration of her PhD candidature. Her doctoral thesis was titled 'Learning and development across the generations: A cultural-historical study of everyday family practices'. Monk is an early career researcher, a member of the Child and Community Development Faculty Research Group, and a member of the Excellence in Research in Early Years Education Collaborative Research Network funded by the Department of Industry, Innovation, Climate Change, Science, Research and Tertiary Education

(2011–2014). Her research interests are early childhood education, families, cultural-historical theory and visual methodologies.

Jennifer Bleazby was appointed to the faculty in 2010 after working as a secondary school media studies, humanities, history and philosophy teacher in both government and independent schools. While undertaking a Bachelor of Arts at La Trobe University, she completed a unit called Philosophy for Children as a part of a philosophy major and went on to complete an honours thesis about philosophy for children and feminist epistemology before enrolling in a Graduate Diploma in Education at the University of Melbourne in 2003. In 2007, she completed a PhD in the School of Philosophy at the University of New South Wales. Her PhD involved an examination of how the ideas of the philosopher John Dewey had influenced philosophy for children, as well as a defence of Dewey's philosophical and educational ideas. Her dissertation was later published by Routledge as the book *Social Reconstruction Learning: Dualism, Dewey and Philosophy in Schools* (2013). Her research involves an exploration of the implications of philosophical problems and theories (especially in the areas of epistemology, political philosophy and ethics) for educational theory and practice, as well as an investigation of the value of teaching philosophy in schools.

Staff of 2011

Shane N Phillipson is an associate professor at Monash University. He is Associate Dean (Peninsula). He was previously at the Hong Kong Institute of Education. A student of both Monash and Flinders University, after obtaining a BSc (Hons) and a Graduate Diploma in Secondary Education, he worked for many years as a mathematics and science teacher in New South Wales and South Australia. Phillipson then obtained a graduate certificate in gifted education. His PhD thesis was awarded the International Award (1999–2000) for best PhD thesis by the National Association for Gifted Children (NAGC) in the UK, and the 2001 Flinders University nomination for the Australian Association for Research in Education (AARE) Doctoral Thesis Award. Currently, Phillipson teaches educational psychology, research methods and gifted education, and his research interests include cultural conceptions of giftedness and models of achievement. He has been awarded a number of research grants, resulting in research publications in many international peer-reviewed journals, including *High Ability Studies* and *Educational Psychology*, and he is also a reviewer of research articles for these two journals. His edited books include *Learning Diversity in the Chinese*

Classroom: Contexts and Practice for Students with Special Needs (2007), and *Conceptions of Giftedness: Socio-cultural Perspectives* (with M McCann, 2007). Phillipson is a member of the American Psychological Association (APA), the Association for Psychological Science (APS), the World Council for Gifted and Talented Children and the European Council for High Ability.

Dr Sivanes Phillipson is senior lecturer at Monash and formerly an assistant professor in the Department of Education Studies at the Hong Kong Baptist University. Phillipson is also an adjunct senior lecturer with the Faculty of Education, University of Tasmania. She has diverse international experience and knowledge base in the broad field of measurements and systems approach to families and education. Phillipson's expertise includes Rasch analysis, meta-analysis and the synthesis of structural equation models of learning and achievement. She has been awarded multiple research grants and has consulted on multiple projects internationally. Her consultancies included the development of measurement tools for disability services and evaluating existing services within special care and child development services. She has published widely in books, peer-reviewed journals and book chapters. Her most recent book is *Developing Leadership in the Asia Pacific: A Focus on the Individual* (Routledge, 2014).

Mike Askew, BSc (Sheffield), MA (London), PhD (Kings College London), is the foundation Chair Professor of Primary Education at Monash University. Prior to that he was Chair Professor of Mathematics Education at Kings College London and director of BEAM Education, a publishing house specialising in materials and professional development for primary schools. He is internationally regarded as a leading expert on primary mathematics education and has directed many research projects including the influential 'Effective Teachers of Numeracy in Primary Schools', 'Raising Attainment in Numeracy' and 'Mental Calculations: Interpretations and Implementation'. He was deputy director of the five-year Leverhulme Numeracy Research Programme, examining teaching, learning and progression in number from age 5–11. The findings from such research have influenced policy in England, Australia and elsewhere. He has spoken and lectured extensively across Australia and internationally. His most recent book is *Transforming Primary Maths* (Routledge).

Sue Webb, BA (Hons, Leicester), MA (Econ) and PhD (Manchester), is a professor of education. She is known internationally for her research and leadership in the field of adult education and lifelong learning where she has published, lectured and provided external advice to a number of universities in the UK and in New Zealand. Specifically, she has researched the policy effects and practices related to access and participation of disadvantaged students in the field of lifelong learning and further and higher education in the UK. This research has been variously funded by UK government organisations and education funding agencies. Her theoretical contribution has been to develop insights into the concepts of learning identities and careers as a way of understanding risk choice and agency in decision-making and learner transitions between school, college, university and employment. Her current research includes the geographical and regional dimensions of social inclusion: the role of education and training, funded by the National Council for Vocational Education and Training (NCVER).

Adam Bertram commenced his career with Monash University in January 2011 as a lecturer in the Faculty of Education at the Gippsland Campus, soon after completing his PhD in 2010. Before becoming a lecturer, Adam taught science, mathematics and physics for eight years at the high school level at an independent college in Victoria. During this time, he began his masters thesis (with Professor Dick Gunstone as his supervisor), which explored physics teachers' understanding of their content and pedagogical knowledge. His doctoral thesis was supervised by Professor John Loughran and explored the development of science teachers' specialist knowledge of teaching through developing and articulating their pedagogical content knowledge. This led Bertram to become interested in teacher knowledge and teacher development research, particularly within the realm of science education. For his work on Pedagogical Content Knowledge (PCK), he has been invited to present and conduct workshops with teachers nationally and internationally. He continued to research and teach at Monash University until the merger with the University of Ballarat and is expected to continue on with the newly formed university.

Simone White was the Head of School and Associate Dean of Education at Monash University, Gippsland campus. Professor White's publications, research and teaching are focused on the key question of how to best prepare teachers for diverse communities. She commenced her career as a primary teacher, training at Mitchell College Bathurst where she completed DipEd and BEd. She completed her MEd from Charles Sturt University and her doctorate at the University of Sydney. She has retained a passionate interest in teacher education and published widely in the field including a role in two major books. She was the recipient of the Deakin Vice-Chancellor's Teaching Excellence Award in 2005 and a member of the College of Deakin Distinguished Educators. Professor White's current research focus is on rural and regional teacher education curriculum, early career teachers in diverse settings, teacher professional learning and university-school/community partnerships. She has a strong national competitive research grant record with several current grants from the ARC and ALTC, in addition to state government research contracts. Professor White chairs the AARE Rural Education Special Interest Group.

Dr Liang Li is a lecturer in the Faculty of Education at Monash University, Peninsula Campus and active member of Child and Community Development Research Group. Li has worked in early childhood education for more than 10 years. She began her career in Australia as a full time qualified kindergarten teacher. She has completed her studying Graduate Diploma, Master of Education (Early Childhood), Master of Education (TESOL International) and PhD specialising in early childhood education at Monash University. Li's research focuses on visual methodology, play and pedagogy, teacher education and evaluation methods, family studies and child development and learning. She has been involved in a Plan International ECCD evaluation project in rural China. She currently has a collaborative research network fellowship to research innovative visual methodologies for considering social justice, access inclusion and policy with academics from Queensland University of Technology, Charles Sturt University and at Monash University. She publishes nationally and internationally and is currently co-author with Dr Avis Ridgway and Dr Gloria Quinones of a book on pedagogy and play.

Dennis Moore, MEd, PhD, who holds a chair in educational psychology at Monash, also heads the university's Krongold Centre and the Elwyn Morey Child Study Centre. He took up the new positions on 1 November; the centre's previous director, Associate Professor David Harvey, will retire at the end of the year. After training in his native New Zealand Professor Moore taught at the University of PNG from 1979 until 1985 – the final two years in the education research unit. From there he moved to the University of Auckland as associate professor in the Department of Education. He was also director of the university's training program for education psychology and was involved in a three-university consortium that trained resource teachers in learning and behaviour. His main research was in the area of special education with interests too in inclusive education. He has a substantial record of research scholarship in the area together with a proven record of leadership both in significant research and teaching programs and within the university, profession, and the community. He has published extensively in his areas, especially in autism and special education.

Dr Nikolai Veresov, a graduate of Murmansk Pedagogical University (BA DipEd in 1982), started out teaching in Russian secondary schools. He took a position as the head of the Department of Early Childhood and Primary Education in Murmansk Teachers Training Institute in 1992. He completed his second PhD in 1998 in the University of Oulu, Finland. In 1999–2011 he took positions of senior researcher at Kajaani Department, University of Oulu. He was involved in several international educational projects as a chief investigator and the leader of the international expert teams. His publications are translated into 10 languages. He teaches at the Peninsula campus.

Toni Adele Hilland is a lecturer and researcher in physical activity and health within the Faculty of Education at Monash University. She completed her undergraduate degree at Chester University, MSc at Loughborough University, and PhD at Liverpool John Moores University (LJMU). Her PhD is entitled 'The development of the "PE Product": physically educated and physically active individuals'.

Staff of 2012

Avis Ridgway worked in education for over 40 years prior to completing her PhD at Monash University in 2010, after which she was employed as a lecturer in early childhood and primary education until retirement in 2014. Developing methodological tools for field observations that reflect broader historical, community and cultural influences on children's early learning and development led to management of professional projects for Professor Marilyn Fleer (foundation chair of early childhood) at Monash University including: DEST 'Catch the Future' 'Early Literacy and Numeracy' project (2004–2005) and Australian Research Council 'Science and Play' project (2005–2008). Ridgway's awards include Collaborative Research Network (CRN) Fellowship (2012), Service Award from Dean of Education for co-convening Monash Education Research Community (MERC) (2009), APA (Australian Postgraduate Award) scholarship (2008–2010), and earlier, an Excellence in Teaching Award (1995) from Australian College of Education. Ridgway was made an honorary member of the Reggio Emilia Australia Information Exchange in 2004. She is widely published nationally and internationally. Recent publications include *Visual Methodologies and Digital Tools for Researching with Young Children: Transforming Visuality* (Springer, 2014) and *Early Childhood Pedagogical Play: Agentic Imagination* (Allen and Unwin, 2014). She recalls the Monash beginnings in the 1960s when the Menzies Building sat alone in a paddock and tutorial groups for her BA units in German, sociology and anthropology numbered less than 10 students.

Louise E Jenkins had previously taught in the field of music education in Victorian secondary and primary schools prior to returning to study to complete her Masters of Educational Studies and her PhD at Monash University. After graduating Jenkins worked at Deakin University in the Institute for Citizenship and Globalisation as a research fellow. In this position, the focus of her research was on racism in schools, the development of cultural capital among refugee and migrant youth, and the development of inclusive learning materials for classes with culturally diverse students. Whilst at Deakin, she co-authored a book titled *Building Bridges: Creating a Culture of Diversity*, which contains modules of lessons for schools with multicultural student populations. This book was distributed to all Victorian secondary schools in 2009. Jenkins then worked at a Melbourne consultancy as Associate Director of Social Policy, before being appointed to the Monash University Faculty of Education in 2012. Her two main areas of focus at Monash are music education and sociology.

Neil Selwyn completed a BA (Hons) and PhD at Cardiff University (Wales) before going on to work in the Cardiff School of Social Sciences, the University of Bristol Graduate School of Education and the Institute of Education – University of London. His research and teaching focuses on education, technology and society and on the place of digital media in everyday life, and the sociology of technology (non-)use in educational settings.

During his time at Monash, Professor Selwyn has played a key role in the 'learning with new media' faculty research group. Neil has written extensively on a number of issues, including digital exclusion, education technology policymaking and the student experience of technology-based learning. He is the author and co-author of eight books and around 250 articles and book chapters. His work has been translated into French, Spanish, Russian, Italian and Portuguese. His publications include: *Education in a Digital World: Global Perspectives on Technology and Education* (Routledge, 2013) and *Schools and Schooling in the Digital Age: A Critical Analysis* (Routledge, 2011).

Niranjan Robert Casinader, PhD, BA (Hons), GDipEd (Melb), MEd (Monash) MACE, AMACEL, was appointed to the faculty at the Gippsland Campus in 2013 as lecturer in curriculum and pedagogy. An honours graduate in geography from the University of Melbourne, he spent over 30 years teaching and leading in Victorian secondary schools across the government, independent and Catholic sectors before entering tertiary education. As a secondary educator, he laid the foundation for a tertiary career by establishing a strong reputation in humanities teaching, specialising in development studies and the teaching of problem solving skills, as well as becoming known as an initiator of community based learning projects, the establishment of major curriculum and co-curriculum programs, and as a textbook author. He developed an ongoing involvement with Future Problem Solving Program Australia as National Director, led a non-profit group of educators in teaching thinking skills to P–12 students, and mentored the establishment of FPS programs in Malaysia, Singapore and South Africa. He was also elected onto the Board of Trustees of Future Problem Solving Program International. At Monash, his research and publications reflected the continuation of his educational concerns with the globalisation of education, particularly in respect of culture, thinking and the teaching of the humanities.

Hongming Ma is currently a lecturer in the Faculty of Education at Monash University (Gippsland). She studied engineering at Southwest Jiaotong University and used to work as a secondary vocational school teacher in China. She completed her masters and PhD study at Monash University, with both studies in the field of cross-cultural research in science education. Her main research interests are the nature of science/technology and its role in school curricula at different levels; affective learning in science and relevant teacher knowledge; and cross-cultural understanding of the aforementioned issues. She has published in the area of science education, including the book *The Images of Science Through Cultural Lenses: A Chinese Study* (Sense Publishers, 2012).

Michael Phillips, BAppSci (Phys Ed), MEd (ICTE), was a secondary school teacher with 15 years' experience teaching a variety of subject areas including physical education, outdoor education, geography, mathematics, health and ICT. As a former Head of School, Phillips became fascinated with the effective use of digital technologies and examined the influence of teachers' beliefs on their technology adoption for his Master of Education thesis. His interest in secondary school teachers' use of digital technologies as part of their teaching practice led to his PhD research examining how teachers develop technological, pedagogical and content knowledge in workplace settings. In November 2013, he was appointed to the Faculty of Education (Clayton) at Monash University. Additionally Michael's work with ICT in Education in Victoria (ICTEV) was recognised in December 2013 with an Outstanding Professional Service Award from the Council of Professional Teaching Associations of Victoria (CPTAV).

Evan Ortlieb, BS, MEd, and PhD from Louisiana State University. Ortlieb worked as an elementary school teacher before serving as a faculty member at two other institutions of higher education before Monash

University, including Texas A&M University in the United States, with responsibility for coordinating the graduate reading program and teaching in both the curriculum and instruction and reading education programs at the doctoral, masters and undergraduate levels. There, he received the Association of Literacy Educators and Researchers 2011 Jerry John's Promising Researcher Award; received the Texas A&M University System Teaching Excellence Award in 2011 and again in 2012; served as editor to the Consortium for Educational Development, Evaluation, and Research; and received the Texas A&M University Corpus Christi's Outstanding Islander Award in April 2011. Dr Ortlieb has been involved in reading education for nine years. He has served as principal investigator or co-facilitator on grants totalling more than $500,000 and has won numerous awards including the Community Partner of the Year Award in 2008 for school-based work with struggling readers in the state of Georgia (US).

Gillian Kidman, BSc, M Env Ed, Dip Teaching, PhD, came to the faculty in November 2013 from the Queensland University of Technology (QUT) where she was on academic staff for almost 20 years. Kidman is passionate about science and mathematics education. Her teaching and curriculum design is award winning at both the state and national levels. Kidman has research interests in the integration of science and mathematics, STEM, and all areas of inquiry based learning and teaching. She has published on Slowmation Animation in pre-service teacher education. She is an associate professor.

Maria Gindidis completed her DipEd at Monash in 1980 and was later appointed to the faculty as a sessional languages method tutor. She worked as a sessional in both undergraduate and postgraduate masters courses in the education faculty till 2010. During this time she was also a full-time secondary teacher, principal and project manager, innovations and excellence cluster educator to both education ministers and the DEECD. She completed her MEd Stud (1990) and PhD (2012). Her doctoral thesis investigated the marginalised voices of Arabic, Chinese and Greek community languages teachers in Victoria. She resigned from her position with the Department of Education in 2010 and accepted a full-time academic position at Monash. Her current work and research has been with bilingual education and student engagement. She was awarded a plaque by Community Languages Australia (2008) for her outstanding contribution to the training and development of community languages teachers. She is currently still at Monash and still passionate about teacher education.

Alan Reid, BSc (Lanc), PGCE (Oxon), PhD(Bath), came to Monash in 2012. Reid edits *Environmental Education Research*. Until 2012, he worked at the Centre for Research in Education and the Environment, University of Bath, and is active in a range of environmental education research activities and networks in Europe, North America and Australasia.

Reid's research interests focus on teachers' thinking and practice in environmental education, and traditions, capacities and issues in environmental education theory, research and practice. Reid is an associate professor and the Associate Dean (Education) for the faculty, the portfolio for which addresses course governance, leadership, development and evaluation, teaching and learning quality and innovation, and resources, opportunities and support for high quality education. His teaching commitments and interests principally focus on environmental and sustainability education, and research approaches and professional inquiry in education.

Renée Crawford began her work as a music educator and composer as soon as she could play a note, but sought formal qualifications that led to the completion of a BMus/BEd, BMus (Hons), MMus and PhD. As an advocate for the use of technology in education in an appropriate and contemporary way, her PhD research, completed at Monash University (2008), was based on the philosophy of authentic learning and technology in music teaching and learning practices. She has published both nationally and internationally in her field. Part of her ongoing work consists of providing consultative advice on research and evaluation matters to organisations such as the Starlight Children's Foundation. The significance and nature of the impacts and outcomes of her recent research projects has influenced governmental education, immigration and arts and culture policy. Her musical interests, which continue to influence her teaching, are in composition, film music, minimalism, the analysis of contemporary Australian music and the use of digital technology in music.

Staff of 2013

Pearl Subban was appointed to the faculty in 2013. She moved into tertiary education after teaching in a secondary school in southeast Melbourne for several years. Subban began her academic career in South Africa, completing her first course of postgraduate study at the University of South Africa in Pretoria. She migrated to Australia in 2001 and took up a leadership role at an independent school in Melbourne. Her PhD focused on the development of a scale to measure teachers' attitudes toward differentiated instruction.

Pearl has published several scholarly papers which address the view that contemporary education should accommodate student diversity. She is currently based at Monash Berwick, and teaches in both undergraduate and postgraduate units.

Staff of 2014

Amber Beth McLeod completed a BSc (Applied Biology) at RMIT and worked as a food microbiologist before completing a DipEd at La Trobe University and an MA in Linguistics at Monash University. She taught EFL in high schools in Japan and Brunei, and ESL, VCAL and adult education at TAFE in Australia for 16 years before enrolling as a PhD student at Monash Clayton. Her thesis (expected to be submitted by the end of 2014) examines issues surrounding gender and ICT. In particular it investigates the relationship between community attitudes towards ICT and the outcomes of the ARC Linkage Scheme-funded 'Digital Divas' intervention program run in Australian high schools. So far her research has led to four conference papers. While the shortage of women in ICT is a serious issue in Western countries, this is not the case in all countries and McLeod is interested in exploring community attitudes about gender and ICT in these other cultures.

Thanh Pham (Pham Thi Hong Thanh) completed a BA in Australian Studies in 2001, an MA in 2006 and then a PhD in education at the University of Queensland, Australia. Her doctoral topic was 'Designing a culturally-relevant pedagogy for Confucian Heritage Culture (CHC) college students: The case of cooperative learning in Vietnam'. In 2011 Pham was offered a postdoctoral research fellowship at the University of Queensland. Her postdoctoral research was on using activity theory as a theoretical framework to investigating educational reforms in the Asian context. Pham was also involved in teaching research methodology and educational interventions courses at the University of Queensland while doing her postdoc. She became a lecturer in education at Monash University in 2014.

Joseph Seyram Agbenyega completed a DipEd (1999) and BEd (2000) in mathematics and special education at the University of Education, Winneba in Ghana and then a BEd (Hons) in special education from Monash University in 2002. He did his EdD at Monash University in 2005. His doctoral topic was 'An investigation into the barriers and facilitators of inclusive education for students with disabilities in Ghana: A policy analysis'. Since 2008, Dr

Agbenyega has published more than 30 articles in reputable international journals in his field of expertise. He became a senior lecturer in 2011 and a course leader of masters programs in early childhood education in 2012. In 2001 he received the Sir John Monash Award for Academic Excellence, International Golden Key award, International Monash Postgraduate and Monash Research Graduate School Awards in 2002. He was awarded the Australian Leaders Fellowship in 2010. He developed the early childhood curriculum for the Orthodox Greek Church Teachers' College project in Sierra Leone, Africa in 2009. He is a member of an International Inclusive Teacher Educators Research Forum. He is currently tasked with developing training programs and train 77 directors from all the provinces in Thailand in early special education by end of 2014.

Penny Round has been working in the area of students with special needs for 25 years. She has qualifications in both special education and gifted education. Her primary research has revolved around students with special needs in regular secondary schools completing the VCE. She completed her Bachelor of Arts in 1984 at Caulfield Institute of Technology, then her Graduate Diploma in Education at Bendigo College of Advanced Education (1985). She then returned to part-time study to complete a Bachelor in Special Education at Monash University (1990), a Masters in Special Education (1992) and a Doctor of Education (2004). She then returned to a Masters in Gifted Education in 2010. She has worked in secondary schools as coordinator of inclusive education programs and the Head of English. She is currently working as a lecturer in special and gifted education at Monash University.

Anna Filipi is a graduate of the University of Melbourne (BA, MA Applied Linguistics) and Monash University (DipEd, PhD). She taught in the Victorian State secondary system. Throughout the 1980s and 1990s she held various administrative positions at the VCAA and DEECD supporting teachers in professional development in multicultural education and the development of VCE languages. During this time, she also lectured at the University of Melbourne in Italian for teachers and in the DipEd and Master of Teaching in Languages and ESL programs. In 2002, after completing her PhD in conversation analysis and language acquisition, she took up a research position at La Trobe. She was subsequently promoted to senior research fellow until 2009 when she moved with her family to Switzerland. At Monash she is currently teaching languages, TESOL and early childhood. She has developed a strong international profile in conversation analysis and its applications to mapping the acquisition of language and social interaction, and is extending this work to second language pedagogy.

Hazel Tan is a lecturer at the faculty, after completing MEd in mathematics and science education at Monash University in 2006 and a PhD in 2013. She was awarded the Faculty of Education Margaret Clarke Award in 2006 in recognition of outstanding academic results in education studies (minor thesis), and the Monash International Postgraduate Research Scholarship and the Monash Graduate Scholarship for her PhD candidature. During her candidature she worked for the faculty as research assistant and teaching associate and was the convenor of the Monash Education Research Community 2008–2009. Her doctoral topic was an investigation of factors influencing senior secondary mathematics students' interactions with advanced calculators and she has published a number of book chapters, journal articles, and peer-reviewed conference papers. She has taught senior secondary mathematics for many years, and was the Head of Mathematics Department in a Singaporean school. Hazel has also worked in the Educational Technology Division of Singapore's Ministry of Education, spearheading the pedagogical use of technologies in education.

Lucas Walsh is an associate professor and Associate Dean (Berwick) in the Faculty of Education at Monash University. He graduated with Honours from the University of Melbourne (BA, DipEd) and completed his PhD at Monash University in 2002. He was previously Director of Research and Evaluation at The Foundation for Young Australians. Lucas has worked in corporate, government and not-for-profit sectors. He has held three academic research fellowships and managed the International Baccalaureate's Online Curriculum Centre in the UK. He has been invited to advise local, state and federal governments, including the National Curriculum Board and Australian Institute for Teaching and School Leadership, presented nationally and internationally, and published one co-edited book and two co-authored books.

Marc Pruyn, PhD (UCLA), is a senior lecturer in the Faculty of Education at Monash University. His areas of expertise include curriculum, pedagogy, educational foundations and research methodologies. Pruyn worked as a bilingual primary school teacher in Los Angeles for nine years and earned his PhD from UCLA. Before moving to Melbourne in 2010, he was a faculty member for 14 years at New Mexico State University. His research interests include exploring the connections between education for social justice, multiculturalism and the social studies.

Wee Tiong (Seah), BSc, MEd, PhD. Wee Tiong is a senior lecturer of mathematics education in the faculty. He has had extensive professional experience in mathematics teaching and pastoral care across a range of school settings in Singapore and Australia. Wee Tiong's research interests include the harnessing of socio-cultural factors in the teaching of mathematics. These include values of students, teachers, parents, etc as they relate to mathematics pedagogy. He currently coordinates a multinational research team in a series of research studies relating to the harnessing of values to promote more effective teaching and learning of maths in schools. Wee Tiong has been active in the mathematics education research arena in Australia, East and Southeast Asia. Meaningful and personal engagements with colleagues have resulted in the conduct of collaborative research and consultancy activities in no less than eight countries in these regions over the last few years.

Wee Tiong's 2004 PhD thesis, entitled 'The Negotiation of Perceived Value Differences by Immigrant Teachers of Mathematics in Australia' had been supervised by Emeritus Professor Alan J Bishop and Associate Professor Barbara Clarke.

Jill Cheeseman is a lecturer of mathematics education in the faculty. Before embarking on a career as an academic, Cheeseman had extensive professional experience as a teacher of primary school and has worked as a teacher-educator in a range of settings in Australia and overseas. Cheeseman's research interests centre on how children learn mathematics and how teachers challenge children's mathematical thinking. Her PhD thesis, entitled 'Challenging Children to Think: An Investigation of the Behaviours of Highly Effective Teachers that Stimulate Children to Examine Their Mathematical Understandings' was completed in 2010. She is chief investigator for an Australia Research Council (ARC) Discovery grant entitled 'Encouraging Persistence, Maintaining Challenge: Investigating the Relationship Between Teacher Expectations, Student Persistence and the Learning of Mathematics'. The study explores what is needed to encourage students to embrace challenges and to persist even when tasks are difficult.

Cheeseman was very proud to be a member of the Early Numeracy Research Project team to which the MERGA Research Award was presented in July 2011. The award was given 'in recognition of an outstanding contribution to mathematics education research'. It is presented to long-term active Mathematics Education Research Group of Australasia members who have made a sustained and distinguished contribution to research in mathematics education in Australasia and internationally (1999–2011).

Nathan D Brubaker was appointed to the faculty in 2012. A graduate of Montclair State University (MEd, EdD) in New Jersey (USA), he previously taught in the USA at the primary, middle and tertiary levels including five years at James Madison University in Virginia. As a lecturer in curriculum and pedagogy, he taught undergraduate and postgraduate courses in multicultural education, primary level curriculum and research methods, while supervising masters and PhD students in teacher education. His research, which he conducted in Australia, New Zealand, and the USA, was concerned with preparing teachers to teach democratically, equitably and inclusively through examining teacher educators' practices involving inquiry, assessment and micropolitics.

Ibrahim Latheef completed his first teaching qualification in 1994 at Institute for Teacher Education, Maldives followed by his second training program in 1997 as primary teacher and teacher of middle school respectively. He became a headmaster and head of school in 2001 after completing a training program in school management at National Institute of Education in Sri Lanka. In 2003, he came to Australia to do Bachelor of Education (Honours) in primary. After graduating in 2006, he took up a graduate scholarship from Monash to do a postgraduate research studies program. His research area was technologies in education – specifically, interactivity around interactive whiteboards from a cultural historical activity theory perspective. He became a lecturer 2010 at the Peninsula campus. In 2013 he completed his PhD.

Louise Anne McLean, PhD, GradDip, EdPsych, BEd, began her academic career in the Faculty of Education in 2000 as a sessional lecturer and research supervisor. Prior to commencing at Monash she worked as a school counsellor and teacher of English and psychology. She completed her PhD in 2005 and took up a full time position in the Faculty of Education psychology group in the same year. She has coordinated the Postgraduate Diploma of Psychology course, for which she was awarded a Faculty of Medicine Special Commendation. In 2009 she was shortlisted for the Vice-Chancellor's Award for Excellence in Honours Supervision. Her areas of research include the identification of psychosocial risk and resilience factors related to well-being across the lifespan and the development and evaluation of interventions and preventative measures that facilitate sustained and enhanced well-being. In 2013 McLean and her research colleagues were awarded the Australasian Research Award for the best local research paper published in the *Journal of Intellectual & Developmental Disability*.

Geraldine Burke has been at the coalface of art curriculum for many years. As an artist, researcher and teacher/lecturer she has planned, developed and experienced various art curricula through early childhood, school, university and community art units and projects. This multifaceted experience provides her with a breadth of knowledge that can be drawn on to develop contextual and culturally relevant curriculum for Singaporean contexts.

Her recently submitted arts based PhD explores new approaches to visual art pedagogy across school, university, community and artistic practice.

Reviews of her teaching reflect excellent feedback on her breadth of experience, her passion for the arts and the new and inspirational possibilities that have been introduced to students. During this teaching she has drawn on the Singaporean context as an impetus for art experiences and placed it within global art and education contexts.

Andrea Reupert, a graduate of Melbourne in Arts and Education and with qualifications in counselling, completed her PhD at La Trobe University. She is a therapist, teacher and researcher. She spent over ten years as a school counsellor in the public education system, in Victoria and Queensland, working with children aged 0–18 and their families, teachers and other associated professionals. Reupert has also worked in general private practice, with various client groups and organisations including prisons, unemployment agencies and welfare departments. Reupert has authored or co-authored over 40 publications, delivered 30 conference presentations, and successfully acquitted 15 research grants totalling over $600,000 in the specialised area of parental mental illness. Along with a team of researchers, clinicians and consumers, Reupert developed a world-first model of care for families where the parent has a dual diagnosis (co-occurring drug/alcohol and mental illness). She was also involved in the first estimation of Australian children living with a parent with a mental illness. Her research interests are in parental mental health and outcomes for children; developing effective support structures and interventions for vulnerable families; whole school approaches to welfare and behaviour management.

Mark Rickinson is an associate professor and Associate Dean (Engagement) in the Faculty of Education at Monash University. Rickinson is an experienced educational researcher and evaluator who, until recently, was based in the UK as an independent consultant and research fellow at Oxford University. He has particular expertise in evidence-informed policy and practice and outdoor and environmental learning. His real interest lies in understanding and improving the use and usefulness of educational research. Mark has undertaken research, evaluation and synthesis projects relating to many aspects of education and training. His work has included projects for government departments and agencies, research funders, international organisations, national bodies, major corporates, charitable organisations, educational publishers and local authorities.

Debra Panizzon is an associate professor at Monash University with specialisations in biology and general science education. In her prior position as inaugural Deputy Director for the Flinders Centre for Science Education in the 21st Century she supported decision-making in science and mathematics education by policy makers, educational leaders, industry and other stakeholders. While in this position Panizzon coordinated a number of Science, Technology, Engineering and Mathematics (STEM) projects (research and consultancies) involving collaborations with government departments and various types of industry in South Australia. This work built upon previous experiences as Deputy Director for the National Centre of Science, Information and Communication Technology, and Mathematics Education for Rural and Regional Australia (SiMERR) located at the University of New England. In this position she was able to champion issues for rural and regional Australia while teaching in a number of science units. Critically, Debra has particular expertise around secondary teacher education. Panizzon reviews papers for two international science education journals along with key national and international conferences. Her research interests are in student learning with particular emphasis around the development of secondary and tertiary students' understandings of scientific concepts, assessment and teachers' practices, electronic assessment in science, enhancing science and mathematics teaching and learning in rural and regional areas.

Julie Harrington received a BA majoring in modern languages from McGill University, Montreal and then completed a DipEd in language education at Boston College. She taught Spanish and English at Perkins School for the Blind for three years before moving to Sydney and then to Melbourne, where she has spent a large part of her life teaching at secondary and tertiary levels, as well as in adult education. She graduated from Melbourne University with an MA in Applied Linguistics and from Monash with a PhD in education. She derives much pleasure from working with international students and has taught for Monash in South Korea, Malaysia and Singapore. Her research interests lie in the area of second and foreign language pedagogy and the supervision of HDR students. She has enjoyed singing in the education faculty Christmas Choir for over 20 years.

Emma Rowe is a PhD candidate and sessional academic in the faculty. Prior to joining the faculty, she studied a BA (Professional Writing and Literature), a Graduate Diploma in Education and Masters in Education. She attempted to write great works of fiction and worked as an editor at a publishing house before commencing a teaching career. She taught in secondary schools and vocational institutions as an English teacher and VCE coordinator. Rowe was awarded an Australian Postgraduate Award in 2011 and started her PhD in the same year. Her dissertation is currently called 'A study of collective campaigns for public education: educational geography, class and identity via school-of-choice'. It examines three different collective campaigns that are lobbying for a new public school to be built in their suburb. By collecting multiple sources of data, both qualitative and quantitative, the study questions how the public high school is operative in choice dynamics and achieves market value.

Peter J Anderson, a graduate of Deakin University and Monash, is early career research development fellow in the Faculty of Education Monash University. His current research from his PhD is on academic freedom and academic identity in Australia and the polar south. He is also teaching and researching in areas of organisational leadership and Indigenous and traditionally oriented people's education and teacher professional development. His research interests are in academic freedom, academic identities, sociology of higher education, higher education policy and development, Indigenous governance leadership and management and teacher professional development.

Chapter 9

Students and recollections

Students[1]

Missing from this narrative is the most important element for the existence of the faculty – the students and candidates. (Those pursuing doctorates are usually dignified with the title of 'candidate' rather than student). Relations between staff and students in the faculty were always close. This was especially so in the DipEd where method groups were usually small, and even the larger groups like English and history were conducted in more intimate sized groups. Given method staff would, in the period up to about 2002, always visit the students in the teaching practicum, staff usually became close to every student they visited. Teaching in a classroom is a very revealing experience for the student teacher. In the post-initial training courses, like BEd, DipEd Psych and MEd Studies, the classes were usually small: 10–15 people. With assignments and essays to be completed, requiring consultation with the lecturer in charge, staff came to know their students well. Even some of the larger classes like those in educational administration under Ray McCulloch had a social component, with wine casks and cheese, as well as individual class papers so everyone came to know each other well. In these courses students often took more than the one subject and so would meet their lecturers again. It is self-evident that with a thesis candidate relations with staff members were close. As DipEd students came to know staff reasonably well, they were encouraged to return to do postgraduate courses. In many cases a DipEd student returned to do BEd and/or MEd Studies and often then worked in method for the faculty or undertook a higher degree. There were at times formal groups for staff and students to interact socially – MUFESSA (Monash University Faculty of

---

[1] Many former staff members assisted in providing these names: Dr Brian Bullivant, Professor Diana Davis, Dr John Theobald, Professor Gerald Burke, Dr Maurice Balson, Professor Dick Gunstone and Professor Dick White.

Education Staff and Students Association), with its regular functions and even parties under the oaks, was one manifestation, and then there was the alumni group. Part-time students coming in from schools were less able to participate in social activities but came to know well the lecturers and fellow students of the class they took. Often the pattern was to adjourn the class after a 4.30pm start for a meal together at the Staff Club before resuming. Each class had its own identity – and each DipEd year too – because of the personalities and aptitudes of the people involved. The faculty was blessed by having for most years good-quality students into initial training, with a keen interest in their profession, and post initial training students who had a strong professional movitation, and brought to the course the wisdom of their own work situation.

The person assessed as Monash University's first student, Brother Michael Lynch, also graduated in education – he later became head of various schools in the Salesian Order as well as head of a university college.

9.1 Senator Dr Kay Patterson, 1987.
Geography Department, MUA IN-372

There were political figures like Bob Jolly, who became Victorian Treasurer in the Cain and Kirner governments in the 1980s; Senator Kay Patterson, Minister for Health in the Fraser government; Louise Asher, Deputy Leader of the Liberal Party and minister in the Baillieu government; Race Matthews, a Victorian cabinet minister; Paul Andrews, an MP in Western

Australia; Tony Lamb, an MHR in Victoria; Lorraine Elliott, an MLA in Victoria; Inga Peulich, MLC; the Hon. Peter Hall, Minister for Higher Education and Skills in the Naphine government; and Senator Robert Ray, Labor Federal Minister for Defence, commenced but failed to complete the DipEd. Simba Mumbengegwi of Zimbabwe did masters subjects; in 1991 he became President of the United Nations Security Council and received the surrender from Iraq at the end of the first gulf war. He is currently Minister for Foreign Affairs.

Derek Sikua did the Master of Educational Policy and Administration and later a PhD in New Zealand. He was Prime Minister of the Solomon Islands 2007 – 2010 and previously Minister for Education. Baron Waga, MEd Pol and Admin, is a famous name in the modern music industry of Nauru. He has also served Nauru as Minister of Education. He protested against the Howard government's sending of asylum seekers to Nauru. He was a popular student at Monash, providing music and entertainment at end of term parties. In June 2013 he became President of Nauru. Indonesian research students Soeparman and Sutrisno both took senior academic posts in their home country.

Ms Emeli Moala Pouvalu of Kolomotu'a, who completed an MEd (Education Policy and Administration) in 1999, was Director of the Ministry of Education, Women's Affairs and Culture. There was also Clemens Runawery, a leader of the Free Papua movement. There was Beno Boeha from Papua New Guinea who completed his PhD and caused a sensation by graduating in traditional chieftain's dress (which, as it consisted mainly of feathers, stood out among the academic gowns).

He became Deputy Vice-Chancellor at the PNG University of Technology and later director of the National Research Institute in PNG. Jamsheeda Parveen Khan from Pakistan, who came on a UNESCO fellowship, completed a doctorate and then held many consultancy posts throughout Southeast Asia.

The courses in educational administration meant there were many principals of state secondary schools and some, like Don Laird (Mt Waverley High), went on to senior posts in education. There were many other high school or secondary college principals: Jeremy Ludowyke, John Coulson, Marika Amurosiadis, Robert Jenkins, Joan Amos, Rosa Vardon, Jan Parkes, Augustus Martin, Peter Maclean, Stuart McLellan, Peter Hutton, Greg McMahon, Heather Lindsay and Elida Brereton (who also took Geography Method in the faculty very successfully).

9.2 Beno Bartholomew Tomon Boeha wearing ceremonial dress for award of Master of Educational Studies, 1981.
Richard Crompton, MUA IN-358

There were inspectors of schools and senior Department of Education administrators like Betty Mander and Chris Wardlaw, who became Deputy Secretary, head of the schools division in the Department of Education. John Mooney became a leading figure in special education, and principal of first Ashwood and then Emerson School.

There were those who took significant education posts: Tony Mackay (the private schools system and national curriculum work), Mike Rowland (VCTA and national curriculum), John Kennedy (chairman of the Teachers' Tribunal), John Miller (founder and Dean of the David Syme Business School and later holding a chair at Swinburne University) and Allen Hulls, who did a doctorate while deputy principal of RMIT. There was also Mary Bluett, who served a long term as president of the Teachers Federation and Dr Rhonda Galbally AO, an authority in health development, disability, social and health policy who has held many senior posts including Victorian Health Promotion Foundation; John Brooke OAM, a school principal, leading accountant and shire president; Ian Henderson, a notable TV newsreader; Brendon Murray, famous for his work with juvenile prisoners and principal of Parkville College; Ann Badger, the doyenne of development officers; Anne Marie Corboy, CEO of HESTA (a major superannuation fund); and Lesley Johnstone, a PhD student who became the highly respected Deputy Vice-Chancellor of Research at the Sydney Institute of Technology.

There was a host of private school principals, like Stephen Newton (Caulfield Grammar), Ann Feehan (Camberwell Girls Grammar), Christopher Black (Camberwell Grammar), Barbara Fary AM (Camberwell Girls Grammar), Di Fleming (Kilvington), Bill Toppin, Alan Ross, David Hosking, Peter Harris, Norman Fary (St Leonards), Andrew MacKenzie and Phil De Young (Carey), Rosa Storelli (MLC), Dr Helen McDonald (St Margaret's and Berwick Grammar Schools), Mal Cater (Mentone Grammar), Mark Merry (Yarra Valley Grammar School), Michael Brewin, David Hone, (Scotch College, Launceston), Pam Chessell (Shelford), Tony Conabere (Knox Grammar) and Debby Punton (St. Agnes Catholic School).

There were those who went on to senior university posts: professors such as Russell Linke, Ronald Ring, Barry Fraser, Michael Buxton, Geoff Beeson, Robert Boyd, David Wells, John Benson, Francis Archer, Verity Bottroff, Sidney Bourke, Sylvester Boudville, Des Cahill, Margaret Clayton, Brian Corbitt, Barbara Creed, Stephen Deery, Terry Evans, Peter Fitzpatrick, Edwin Galea, Martin Hayden, Wayne Hodgson, Giselle Kaplan, Douglas Lloyd, Ian Macdonald, Darrell Mahoney, Warren McGregor, Thomas McMahon, Miles Nicholls, Pauline Nugent, Maureen Ryan, Sue Rowley, Richard Snedden, Terrence Speed, Lawrence St Leger, Kay Stacey, Robert Wallis, Peter Sullivan, David Wells, Leo West, Marjorie Theobald, Olga Kanitsaki, Pamela Joyce, Robert Melchers, Carmel McNaught, Marli Wallace, Suzanne Pinchen[2] (Griffith University), Lesley Farrell (UNSW) and Professor Barbara Van Ernst AM, Deputy Vice-Chancellor of Swinburne University.

There was also Pranee Liamputtoing, who has a personal chair in the School of Public Health and Human Biosciences at LaTrobe; Dianne Siemon is a professor of maths education at RMIT, Jennifer Case now a professor in the Department of Chemical Engineering at University Cape Town, Lindsey

---

[2] For Suzanne Pinchen's recollections of her time at Monash, see Chapter 9.

Conner now associate professor at University of Canterbury (Christchurch) and Samuel Oyoo now lecturer at University of Witwatersrand (Johannesburg).

Given that the faculty offered a DipEd Tertiary for a number of years, there were notable students from other faculties including Peter Darvall, who became Dean of Engineering and later Vice-Chancellor.

9.3 Professor Pranee Liamputtoing on graduation with her daughter Zoe.
Claude Sironi, Education Faculty

How to count those who are our own? There were: John Theobald, Andy Spaull, Ailsa Zainu'ddin, Martin Sullivan, Dick White, Dick Gunstone, Gilah Leder, Diana Davis, Ilana Snyder, Helen Forgasz, Peter Gronn, Lawrie Angus, Brian Spicer, Anita Forsyth, Terri Seddon, John Loughran and even Peter Fensham who completed his DipEd with the faculty.

There were many clerical people, members of religious orders – Archbishop of Sydney Cardinal George Pell, Archbishop Philip Aspinall who became Primate of the Anglican Church of Australia, The Reverend Tim Costello and The Reverend Canon Ray Cleary, head of Anglicare and a prominent Anglican priest.

The faculty also had some judicial folk: Justice Tony Pagone (Supreme Court and then Federal Court), Judge Susan Pullen and Judge Philip Taft.

Teddy Hopkins was hero of the 1970 AFL Grand Final for coming on at half-time and kicking four match winning goals in the second half for Carlton, although he never played again. He later founded the hugely successful Champion Data, now used for statistics in major sports.

Many took to international work in education, like Professor Rupert MacLean AO with key posts for UNESCO in Asia, and then there was Albert Langer, postal officer.

9.4 Albert Langer addressing students occupying University Offices, 1969.
MUA IN-4333

Recollections

Indigenous education

Peter Anderson

Peter J. Anderson is an Early Career Research Development Fellow in the Faculty of Education Monash university. His current research is on academic freedom and academic identity in Australia and the polar south. He is also teaching and researching in areas of organisational leadership and Indigenous and traditionally oriented people's education and teacher professional development.

In 1964 Monash's Centre for Research into Aboriginal Affairs (CRAA) was established in the Department of Politics in the Faculty of Business and Politics by Dr Colin Tatz. During this period and leading up to the mid-1970s the research focus of CRAA was primarily driven by a social justice agenda and covered law, health and race relations. In 1977 the first Indigenous Director, Professor Colin Bourke was appointed. Professor Bourke shifted the CRAA into the Faculty of Education. As the faculty developed, the Centre for Aboriginal research, first headed by Dr Eggleston, was taken over by Dr Eve Fesl who ran some common projects in education with other members of staff as well as singing in the faculty choir.

9.5 Peter Anderson.
Education Faculty

During its time within the Faculty of Education the CRAA's agenda emphasised teaching and learning in the fledgling area of Aboriginal studies, which was being taught in both the Bachelor of Arts program and as a unit within the Master of Education. The overwhelming majority of students who undertook Aboriginal studies (and later Indigenous studies) were non-Indigenous or settler Australians. This remains the case today.

The Faculty of Education's long commitment to teaching and learning in Indigenous education was reinvigorated with the establishment of an education-specific faculty-wide specialist unit about Indigenous education. This unit was built into the undergraduate pre-service teacher education program. Under the leadership of Professor Henry Atkinson and Dr Zane Ma Rhea and in response to growing demand, Indigenous education units are now offered across all of the faculty's programs underpinned by a growing research culture and in partnership with peak Indigenous and government bodies. With the departure of Professor Atkinson, the Indigenous education team is now led by Peter Anderson and Bernadette Atkinson, whose research and scholarship will shape the faculty's development of Indigenous education as a vibrant cognate area into its next 50 years.

On not doing research

John Biggs

> Monash's first Education Research officer, a graduate in psychology from the University of Tasmania, PhD London, he has held academic posts in New England, Alberta, Newcastle, NSW and Hong Kong. He has published widely in psychology, being known for his SOLO Taxonomy for assessing the quality of learning outcomes, and the model of constructive alignment for designing teaching and assessment.

I was lecturer in psychology at the University of New England when my marriage broke up. The cause of the rift was in the same department as I was. Tricky. I searched for jobs. I saw a post advertised at the new Monash University: Educational Research Officer. That could mean anything but it was advertised at senior lecturer level and that was something. I applied, with a stack of private reservations that I would put on the table if I were shortlisted.

I was. In June 1966, I was interviewed by Professor Dick Selby Smith, ex-Royal Navy, recently headmaster at the exclusive Scotch College in Melbourne, now Dean of Education at Monash. He was tall, with distinguished grey hair and large, black Menzian eyebrows. Selby, as he liked to be called, was all smiles and wrinkled agreement.

I gained the impression that the post was to carry out research into anything that might be pertinent to improving teaching and learning at university. Selby told me that a brilliant young man called Don Anderson was doing the same at Melbourne University. Don's line was social psychology, sociology, something like that, so, yes indeed, a cognitive psychologist would be absolutely splendid. I had been working on a coding model of learning at New England; I suggested to Selby that maybe we could predict student performance by the ways students went about information processing, as I pretentiously called learning. Some information processing styles might be better suited to arts, some to science. How about that?

'Oh, John.' John already, eh? 'I do believe your ideas would complement Don's work beautifully!' Selby's eyes disappeared as he beamed more wrinkled agreement at me.

A senior lectureship, with what sounds like my own research laboratory. Mind you, it was called an Educational Research *Officer*. But what's in a name?

A lot, as it turned out.

The job was not what Selby had led me to expect. I was part of the administrative staff under the Academic Registrar and Chief Scout of Victoria, Jim Butchart. I was to do the bidding of the Education Committee, chaired by Vice-Chancellor Louis Matheson, on which were representatives of most faculties. From the first few meetings, it seemed that they really didn't know what they wanted from me, except to keep track of student statistics. Not my thing at all, although I did do some good work, later published, with Frank Lawson on the problems engineering students were having with chemistry.[3]

I decided I would cement my academic career by applying for an Australian Research Grants Committee (ARC) grant. I mentioned this at the next meeting of the Education Committee. Vice-Chancellor Matheson placed his elbows on the table in front of him, his hands clasped, his chin resting on his thumbs, his large dark eyebrows raised. He put it to the committee: 'Well, what do members of the Committee think?'

---

[3] Biggs, J B & Lawson, F (1970). 'Chemistry, Problem Subject for Engineering Undergraduates.' *Australian Journal of Education*, 14, pp. 14–154.

9.6 John Biggs.
Education Faculty

Professor Don Cochrane, Dean of Economic and Politics, powerbroker extraordinaire and the most to be feared, drawled: 'Why certainly, Vice-Chancellor, as long as he does his research *after* 5pm.'

Wilga Rivers, who had done some good work on the teaching of French, gave me a sympathetic I'd-love-to-help-but-what-can-I-do smile.

And so it was agreed that the Educational Research Officer was in a nine-to-five clerical job and that he was not to get any big ideas about being an academic.

Oh well, who needs research money when you've got unlimited stationery and computing facilities, ideal for sneaking in work on questionnaires, and a wonderful secretary in the form of Bon Rodell. Bon took a warm, motherly interest in her youngish boss and she was very efficient. Her first job in arriving at the office in the morning was to ring me at my home at nearby Mount Waverley to ensure that I had woken up, as it was quite possible that I mightn't have. And if I hadn't, well, it only took me 35 minutes from bed to office.

But I did have a job to do, even if I didn't find it very interesting. I repeated with Monash students the work Don Anderson at the Melbourne University Educational Research Unit and his colleague Don Fitzgerald had done on predicting first year results on the basis of various weightings of matriculation subjects. It was actuarial sort of stuff, crunched out by a program Fitzgerald had developed. (I noted that they had a 'Unit', while I only had an 'Office').

I was shocked that while correlations between matriculation performance and first year were quite high in science, around .5–.6, the corresponding figures in arts subjects were no different from zero. Yet students were being selected for the Faculty of Arts on the basis of their matric results! They might as well have been selected on the basis of their height, or the girth of their bellies.

Researchers in the United States were doing work on students' 'study habits', a term I dislike. It implies that studying is a mechanical habit, some being good habits, others bad. I used the term 'study behaviours'. I thought, with the help of my coding model, that some behaviours might be more suitable for studying arts-type subjects, while other behaviours might work better for studying science-type subjects. Might this not solve the problem of the low predictability of arts-type performance?

I collected a whole lot of self-report questionnaire items on study behaviour that seemed to reflect the ways some students typically operate: their 'cognitive styles', as the buzzword had it. 'I like studying subjects where there are clear-cut answers' is an example of an 'intolerance of ambiguity' style expressed in study behaviour. I would expect arts students to disagree and science students to agree. I put together the *Study Behaviour Questionnaire*, consisting of ten of these scales of several items each, and slipped it into a testing program for incoming students with demographic and other stuff that the Educational Research Officer might more reasonably be expected to be collecting, pursuant to his obligations. I had the idea that personality/style factors might make some ways of studying more congenial than others, and that some ways of studying suited different subject matter. Unfortunately, the scales didn't predict academic performance as well as I'd hoped.[4] Which only goes to show just how complex we human beings are.

I later realised, like 30 years later, that it was the wrong question. You don't start with student personality, but with *teaching*. Teachers can't control a student's personality but they can control how they go about teaching. Anyway, why would we want to predict which students will do well and which will do poorly? Good teachers want *all* students to do well, don't they? So the focus should be on what good teaching is all about. It seems obvious

---

[4] Biggs, J. B. (1970) 'Faculty Patterns in Study Behaviour.' *Australian Journal of Psychology*, 22, pp. 161–174, and 'Personality Correlates of Some Dimensions of Study Behaviour.' *Australian Journal of Psychology*, 22, pp. 287–297.

now, but the academic zeitgeist sometimes plays tricks with common sense. With that rethink, the original *Study Behaviour Questionnaire* morphed into the now widely used *Study Process Questionnaire*, the dimensions of which, deep and surface approaches to learning, are the outcomes, not the determinants, of teaching, with constructive alignment the way to go to maximise deep approaches and minimise surface. But I only came to work the latter out in my last year of teaching, at Hong Kong University, in 1995.

But here I'm talking early days, when I had yet to get a passport to take me back to academe proper. I thought I should write a book on that information processing model I had mentioned to Selby, and that I was currently using to help design a study behaviour questionnaire. I found to my amazed delight that Cassells Australia would be interested in publishing the book. To hurry things up, I dictated it directly to my trusty secretary, Bon, while she sat at her typewriter. *Information and Human Learning* was published in 1968, and went into North American and German editions.

Incredibly, despite my being in administration, the Educational Research Officer was entitled to study leave – presumably to carry out the research he wasn't supposed to have been doing. I applied for three months' leave to attend a month-long UNESCO-sponsored seminar in Sweden, attended by young educational psychologists from all over the world, and to visit various institutions with educational research units. I took with me my coding model and drafts of my study behaviour questionnaire. I made some fruitful connections there, which led to my giving presentations at several North American universities. One in particular, the Department of Educational Psychology at the University of Alberta, even made noises about job offers.

Meantime, Syd Dunn, who'd moved from the Australian Council for Educational Research to a chair in education at Monash, had persuaded those who needed persuading – and there weren't many – that placing the Educational Research Officer in admin wasn't working too well. Syd proposed a new Higher Education Research Unit (HERU) housed in the Faculty of Education, with Syd himself as director; me and a new appointee, John Clift, as senior fellows with academic status (*so* much better than being called an Educational Research Officer); and a full time programmer, Judy Hammond, and Bon's niece, Marilyn Fraser, as secretary to HERU. I suppose the new HERU model was a bit of a backhander to me but I couldn't have cared less as I was fairly confident that my future was not going to be at Monash.

As indeed it wasn't.

But before all that came to pass, smarting from my academic marginalisation, I sought solace by becoming a regular at the Monash Faculty Club, where, over lunch and *after* 5pm, I foregathered at the bar where the fatherly Steve Callaghan presided. Looking back, being seen as seemingly ever present at Steve's altar was probably not the most career-advancing thing for me to have been doing. I thought it even less career-advancing when I loudly voiced my opinion of my boss, the Academic Registrar, to my friends at the bar, to discover that the butt of my crude wit was standing right behind me.

But maybe that was why he had been happy to approve my study leave, and in so doing, he had done us both a great favour.

Elocution for all

Jenny Brown

> Jenny and Howard Brown have been a popular and long serving husband and wife team in the Faculty of Education, holding numerous posts. Both were initially engaged in Method work having been successful secondary school teachers, but also held important teaching and administrative posts in the Faculty.

All students who attended the faculty in the late 1960s and 1970s (to undertake DipEd) were faced with the daunting task of a speech test with Mr Keith Hudson. Keith was always immaculately suited up and very 'proper'. Morning tea was made in a teapot and consumed from a Royal Doulton cup and saucer; no hurried mug for Keith!

The trial was a one-on-one reading in a tutorial room – the student standing at the front, and Keith seated at the back with his notebook and pen poised. After completing a reading Keith would then discuss your voice: volume, pitch and articulation, not to mention mumbling, slurring and 'umming'. Keith was always very polite with his critique, but he did tell one country friend who spoke slowly with a slight drawl that he sounded as if he had been lazing in the sun for the past two hours and would be likely to send the students in his classes to sleep.

Discussion would also involve suggestions to improve the use of one's voice, especially to minimise strain – the bane of a student teacher's first teaching round. Keith would provide hints and exercises on breathing and 'throwing one's voice' to reach the back of the classroom without undue strain.

Students never 'failed' elocution, simply were sent off to practice simple breathing and other exercises, and return for a follow-up meeting with Keith. At the time many of us were rather bemused by the experience. In retrospect, often after a couple of years at the chalkface, those lessons learned in preserving and using our voices to effect (even the powerful use of silence) we were grateful for our time with Keith.

The early years of the faculty were far-sighted and very supportive. It is a pity the students of today do not have such access to a true professional 'elocutionist' and gentleman.

Memoirs of a tea-lady, 1977–1978

Howard Brown

Collegiate interaction was a strong and ongoing characteristic of the faculty, especially during the latter years of the 1970s. The staff gathered regularly in the second floor staffroom for 'morning tea' at 11.00am, provided that one did not have classes, and again at lunchtime from 1.00pm to 2.15pm when no classes were scheduled.

The new Dean, Professor Peter Musgrave, viewed this time as so special that he requested that two staff members (Howard Brown and Bev Pockney) run the tea and coffee club on behalf of the staff. Staff 'membership' fees ensured that supplies of the essentials (tea, coffee, sugar and milk) were always available. There was even an 'honesty box' for contributions towards a cuppa (20c) for visitors and casual drop-ins, especially postgraduate students who often had a class scheduled for the staffroom after hours. Judicious management of funds also allowed for cheese and dry biscuits to appear once a week during the morning gathering. There was, however, a psychological 'catch'. The provision of food was in keeping with the latest in educational psychological research. Following the early thoughts of Skinner and Pavlov, variable intermittent reinforcement was the order of the day (or in fact the week). Yes, staff knew that cheese and bikkies would be available, but on which day? This vital fact was privy only to the two 'tea-ladies'. A staff member could turn up four days of the week, and yet not even smell a cheese crumb. The comment was often heard in the corridors: 'I don't go to morning tea *one day*, and guess what – that was cheese and bikkies morning!"

Lots of serious educational conversations took place during these gatherings and 'networking' was at its zenith. As for the additional support the faculty provided: secretaries for most senior staff, and access for all staff to the 'typing pool' to have manuscripts efficiently typed and presented. One could then submit the finished material to the photocopy room where the 'photocopy ladies' Frances and her sister Hazel would quickly and efficiently run off the required number of documents to be used with classes. Strangely the photocopier (there was only one massive unit, and its orange power socket still exists on the pillar between the two current units on the second floor) seldom broke down, and waste paper was virtually non-existent. They would even make 'overheads' for lectures with diagrams carefully sized and centred.

Michael Buxton (yes that Professor Michael Buxton) was asked by the Dean to take over in 1979 when Howard Brown, who was on secondment from the Education Department, returned to the classroom.

Reminiscences from the late sixties

Gerald Burke

Professor Gerald Burke holds the record of years of service in the Faculty, serving in various capacities, teaching at all levels, undertaking considerable research and running a major Centre. A much respected figure.

I had started at university (there was only one) in 1957 on a teacher's studentship which paid my tuition fees, an allowance of £7 a week and a bond requiring three years' teaching service. The Education Department did not allow honours years for commerce students as they were likely to leave quickly but the policy changed. This enabled me after teaching at Lilydale and Reservoir High Schools for four years to get a tutoring job in the fast expanding Faculty of Economics and Politics and to commence a PhD. On advice from Professor Joe Isaac (married to Ron Taft's cousin) I took to the economics of education and my topic was the supply of teachers. The first Dean of Education Richard Selby Smith, at the instigation of John Hunt who was in charge of the social foundations area, indicated that an application for a lectureship would be welcome. Given this approach I thought I was a shoo-in and was only disabused years later by Alan Trethewey (later Dean of Education at Victoria Institute of Education, now Deakin) of my belief that it had been a very close go.

When I started in 1968 there were three professors in the faculty alongside the Dean. Syd Dunn had come two years before from ACER where he had saved it financially by developing and marketing tests, still today's major revenue. Peter Fensham had come from the chemistry department of the University of Melbourne a few months before me and Ron Taft arrived almost with me from the University of Western Australia.

Syd was a remarkable man whom you could criticise but also love. As a young man he had been a professional cyclist and he told me once at a faculty social function of the occasion he pulled out of a road race and had been strongly reprimanded by his mother for not finishing the task. He said he never forgot the lesson. Syd knew what was going on, how things worked. Syd's great strength as Peter Fensham said at the award of an honorary doctorate was 'encouraging young researchers'. In the days before email we all had regular notes in our mail boxes letting us know of an article or a researcher or other developments.

Syd became dean in 1971 after Selby (as the lecturing staff called him) had taken a position at the new college of advanced education in Tasmania. Before this appointment discussion took place on whether non-professorial staff might be represented on the Dean's selection committee. With Denis Phillips, now emeritus at Stanford and John Cleverley, emeritus at Sydney, I attended a meeting with Dr Louis Matheson, founding Vice-Chancellor. It didn't last long. He simply said yes – but added 'it was disappointing that no good Englishman had applied'.

Syd had been a part time member of the Education Research and Development Committee (ERDC), a body set up in the early 1970s especially to fund education research and support young researchers. Phil McKenzie of ACER, a prize-winning PhD, got his start in research with support from ERDC. In 1975 Syd left Monash to become ERDC's full-time head based in the Department of Education in Canberra. I worked in the planning branch of the department of education, a floor down from Syd, on secondment from Monash in 1975 and 1976. Passing his secretary one day I suggested she ask Syd if I could have a research grant to study teacher supply and demand in the south of France. A week later I asked her for Syd's response and she said he had looked puzzled for a moment and then said 'Arr, we need a more senior man for that'.

Ron Taft, now in his 90s, was an eminent social psychologist and researcher and one whom Bob Stone, a young tutor, called a 'multi-disciplinary migrantologist'. There was no doubt of Ron's range then and now – at occasional lunches Ron still asks the penetrating questions on educational reforms and has recently written a considerable article on his first visit to Israel in 1950. Nearly 40 years ago Ron told me as we were walking past the main library that he was going to his 'Forty Years On' reunion at Scotch College and I thought it remarkable that someone could be so old and still functioning.

Peter Fensham was ever-present in his time in the faculty – despite Dick White's 'Fensham's law': 'that if you stand still anywhere on the planet Peter Fensham will come by'. Always calm, encouraging, and concerned with all social and political causes, he initiated the remarkable growth in research in science education researchers and provided support across the board including to us social scientists. Peter published my first academic paper, on vouchers in school finance, in his well-remembered book *Rights and Inequality in Australian Education* in 1970. Joel Windle, Peter's grandnephew, joined the faculty as lecturer in 2006 with a range of research interests almost as extensive as Peter's. Joel had an ARC project that dealt with financing schools and I told him of my chapter but on borrowing the book from the library he found it had been cut out.

In the non-professorial ranks there were some fine scholars such as Phillips in philosophy of science. He was recruited by Stanford on a worldwide search for scholars in the top three in the world and he could also do magic tricks. But no one was more exotic than John Radvansky, also in philosophy. He was a Hungarian hereditary baron.

While John had an accent, to paraphrase the words from *My Fair Lady* his English was too good, which clearly indicates that he is foreign. His contributions at meetings were often hilarious as he found the exact words to sum up or send up the discussion. John was a staunch anti-communist. Student radical activist Albert Langer (now known as Arthur Dent) applied to do DipEd. John told me that he had pleaded with the Dean 'Dick' as he called him, to refuse the application on behalf of all of us. 'Selby' as most of us lower ranks called him allowed the enrolment. During his DipEd Albert was not widely seen but he was sent to jail for 'inciting to riot' in a demonstration the previous year. Theo MacDonald, an eccentric Canadian and the method lecturer in mathematics, arranged for Albert to meet the requirements of the teaching round by instructing other prisoners in Pentridge.

In the easier days of reporting it was not unknown for staff to attend examiners meetings with a pile of papers in their hands and to call out missing grades. John was an offender and there is a story, probably apocryphal, of his filling a long pause with 'Credit', only to be rebuked acidly by Mary Nixon with 'that is my subject John'.

On one occasion in 1970 Selby held a reception in the union building to recognise the election of Professor Wilfred Frederick, former Dean at Melbourne, as our faculty's representative on Monash council (we really had one). The Faculty Registrar (now Manager) at the time was Richard Osborn, DFC, DSO formerly World War II squadron leader and POW.

Richard had been called on to be aide de camp to the Queen during her visit to Australia to commemorate the 200 years since Captain Cook's landing. Richard arrived straight from his official duties in full uniform resplendent in gold braid. I was standing with John Radvansky and asked 'have you ever seen anything as splendid as Richard' to which he replied 'I have seen the Imperial Marshall Goering'. I asked 'did you meet him?' and he finished the exchange with 'he came on state occasions'.

John I think would not let the facts stand in the way of good repartee. His obituary includes detail on his activities during WWII, including work for an underground anti-Nazi resistance paper and with Raoul Wallenberg, the Swedish ambassador who used his diplomatic immunity to get Swedish passports for Hungarian Jews facing the Holocaust.[5]

Why a history of the Monash Faculty of Education?

Peter Fensham

Professor Peter Fensham AM, held a chair in Education from 1967 until his retirement. He was Dean from 1981–1988 and a world figure in science education, who held key posts in state, national and international organisations.

About five years ago when I was conscious that the faculty would reach 50 years in 2013 or 2014, depending on whether first staff or students was the marker, I began suggesting that a history be written. But why a history of the Monash Faculty, any more than any institution after 50 years has a chronology of persons and events that are of interest most particularly to those who participated?

To me the answer was simple. In the first 25 years I know best the Monash faculty fundamentally changed the character and role of university departments and faculties of education in Australia. This is a big claim but in this short essay I will support it in four areas of the faculty's pioneering: research, internationalism, teacher continuing development, and the politics of public education.

In 1967 I was invited by the Vice-Chancellor, Lois Matheson, and the Dean, Dick Selby Smith, to join the faculty. It must have seemed an odd appointment since I did not have a Diploma of Education and had only taught chemistry at university level. I did, however, have a research record

---

[5] John Radvansky's obituary, Obituaries Australia, http://oa.anu.edu.au/obituary/radvansky-baron-john-george-14138.

in chemistry and social anthropology, and had recently published some papers in chemical education and on the inequity of the Commonwealth Scholarship Scheme. My charge from Selby was to establish science education as a research activity as quickly as possible. The existing presence of Syd Dunn from ACER as a professor affirmed this priority for research as serious, as did the successive appointments of Ron Taft in educational psychology, Peter Musgrave in sociology of education and Dick Selleck in history of education.

Research

Early in the 1970s the Dean managed to gain a number of more highly paid doctoral scholarships for qualified teachers with a number of years of service. While this scheme held, it attracted some exceptional persons who quickly established a productive nucleus with a strong collegial research atmosphere. PhDs in education had been a rarity in the older universities with one or two at most (mainly staff) per year. In the 1970s Monash produced 44, and in the 1980s when there were 19 universities in Australia, one-third of the PhDs in education were coming from Monash! Many of these found positions in other universities, taking with them this research priority.

9.7 Peter Fensham.
Claude Sironi, Education Faculty

The Monash science education group established ASERA, the Australian Science Education Research Association (later to include NZ) in 1970, some months before members of the faculty, with others, began AARE, the Australian Association for Research in Education.

In the 1980s members of the faculty were awarded research grants for ethnographic studies, beginning a new genre of funded research in education. One of these included the first time release of senior staff as the researchers. Towards the end of the decade the faculty also gained the ARGS's (now ARC) first continuing (three-year) research grant for an educational study.

Internationalism

A very early decision to allocate a significant budgetary amount for international visitors meant the faculty had a steady flow of established researchers from many different countries that has continued to the present time. The links that were established for Monash staff through these visitors for sabbatical and then overseas study leave were invaluable. No other Australian faculty could have commanded the presence at an AERA breakfast in the 1980s of so many leading American scholars. When the Monash Faculty of Education was listed as the only Australian reference in a THES survey across many academic fields about where (other than their own university) leading academics would like to be, our pay-off for the visitor program was complete.

Teacher continuing development

When I was a member of the Universities Council (the independent body that advised the Australian Government about universities), my colleagues on it were quite perplexed when the enrolment figures for 1980 showed a majority of the students in the Monash faculty were undertaking higher degree studies. No other faculty of education, and indeed no other faculty in Australia servicing both undergraduate and higher degree studies, had such a profile. Our unique figures were certainly boosted by the strong doctoral and masters research programs, but more importantly by the development in the later 1970s of the Master of Educational Studies, a combination of coursework and a research project, that met the needs of hundreds of teachers each year for professional development and recognition. In the 1980s members of the faculty also were the pioneers of the means whereby Australian teachers, as a body of professionals, could take responsibility for developing and applying standards for teaching and learning to their members as other professional groups have done.

The politics of public education

The faculty's strong research activity has not been restricted to the halls of academe, but has been a base for the strong record it has over the years in playing an active role in the public and political spheres of education. In 1968, less than 12 months after I joined it, a number of the staff planned and gave a series of public lectures in recognition of the 20th anniversary of UN's *Universal Declaration of Human Rights*, with special reference to the right of education. Seven were given by staff and four by invited others.

The significance of these lectures was recognised by Mr F W Cheshire who published them as *Rights and Inequality in Australian Education* in 1970, just as the Australian Labor Party under Senator Sam Cohen's guidance announced it would, if elected, fund school education on a hitherto undreamt of scale on the *basis of need*. When Whitlam led the ALP to power in 1972 and established the Commonwealth Commission for Education, the Monash book became, in one of the commissioner's words 'the Bible' for this new authority. It set out, under Professor Peter Karmel as chair, to put this policy of *need* into practice. The commission also accepted the suggestion from the faculty that 'educational innovation' should be recognised as a need in Australian schooling. With much involvement from ex and current Monash staff, the highly contentious, but very successful Innovations Programme followed for almost a decade.

At numerous other times the faculty did play a significant role in the state and federal politics of education. I now only list some in which I, with others, had some involvement: the abolition of the inequitable Commonwealth Scholarship Scheme of the 1960s, the highly controversial (for the new ALP Government in Victoria) selection of students for University High School, and the winning (via the ALP Conference in 1987 when the HECS policy was introduced), of 5000 HECS-free places for teachers across Australia to undertake further degrees in education.

The history of the faculty will no doubt fill out these very special beginnings and record how they, and still further initiatives, fared in the second 25 years.

Reflections on collegiality 1996–1997

Margaret Gill

Assoc Professor Margaret Gill was in the Faculty from 1989–1999. An expert in English language and literacy she also served as Head of the School of Graduate Studies.

When I retired, I threw away filing cabinets of agendas, minutes, briefings, memos, position papers, policy papers, working party papers. But there was one set of documents I could not bear to throw away. This is the story of those documents.

My brief term as head of the School of Graduate Studies coincided with two educational upheavals: one at federal level, the other within the Faculty of Education. At federal level the then Minister for Tertiary Education, Senator Vanstone, introduced compulsory fees for students undertaking higher degrees. For the School of Graduate Studies this had potentially devastating consequences for our enrolments and budget. Second, within the faculty itself, the school faced further restructure with the possible dissolution of the three Schools of Education and their replacement with one single organisational structure. The collaborative and creative way in which staff responded to these crises remains a highlight of my years at Monash.

In the face of these changes, and as a new Head of School, it seemed a good idea to review the operation of the school by posing two questions: what would be the likely impact of the new higher education changes on the school's core endeavours, and what could be done about it? Further, did the school's current academic and administrative resources and structures maximise its present and emerging teaching and research strengths?

On 12 September 1996, I presented a position paper to all staff at a lunchtime forum. It was a sort of 'State of the Nation' address in which I pointed out the parlous situation the school could face in the near future, both in budgetary and enrolment terms. Discussion at the meeting was lively, adventurous, humorous and serious. All staff were invited to submit responses, analyses, comments, suggestions, ideas, proposals, thoughts, diagrams, flow charts – either as written papers, conversations, or via discussions at group meetings and in other committees. A second lunchtime forum was held three weeks later when a revised version of the position paper was discussed. Further drafts were reviewed by the school's Planning and Development Committee. The final document included concrete plans and a timeline for action. This consultative process took six weeks, in the course of which 19 members of staff found time to develop forensically analytical, detailed and constructive working papers. Junior as well as senior colleagues contributed to the forums. Members of the technical support and administrative staff had important things to say. One wrote:

> As I hold a somewhat unusual position in the SGS [School of Graduate Studies] and to that extent am an 'outsider' I think I may be able to offer a point of view which is relatively independent and not strongly encultured or associated with a constituency.

He went on to warn against the danger of an 'inward-looking' review process that ignored the expertise of the other schools or the sense of ourselves as part of a wider faculty.

The overwhelming message from a variety of submissions was that the organisational structure of the school had reached its use-by date. The suggestions for change were adventurous, sometimes subversive and came from all directions. One long-serving pillar of the school began his submission:

> I am attempting to offer a forward-looking response that is neither coloured by our recent, dismal history, nor by my belief that I once belonged to a 'golden age' of enterprise in this place.

A newly arrived professor drew on his expertise and professorial experience elsewhere and, though deprecatingly describing himself as the 'new boy on the block', could see that

> [i]n the coming years, we will be living in a very uncertain political and budgetary climate in which innovations and 'keeping ahead of the competition' will be the name of the game. We will need to be able to respond quickly and efficiently to new problems and opportunities. In my view, the current structure has become too large and cumbersome, designed more to protect interests than to facilitate change and innovation.

The papers tackled difficult questions head-on: what should a new organisational structure for the school look like? If the traditional 'groups' were obsolete, what should be the basis of new configurations? Disciplinary interests? Teaching/study groups? Interest groups? *Special* interest groups? Work groups? Portfolios? Or should they be fluid, overlapping entities, forming in response to market-driven initiatives? Or both? Cells? Clusters? Teams?

These questions were driven by a sharp awareness of the realities of a changed and changing educational market that included, not only schools, but TAFE, higher education, the professions, industry, families, international clients and so on. The authors were willing to look beyond the familiar faculty boundaries to possible partnerships in the wider Monash community and further. Two years earlier, when Deputy Vice-Chancellor Robert Pargetter asked me (in my role as Associate Dean [Teaching]) why the School of Graduate Studies was not planning undergraduate studies in education, I did not have an answer. Now the school was engaged in the development of two undergraduate double degrees, in partnership with other faculties and drawing on the experience of Peninsula and Gippsland colleagues for help.

Thus the review papers recorded an important moment in the history of the school, and perhaps that is one reason why I felt they should be preserved. But in reflecting on them in the context of the current bureaucratised and managerialist culture of universities I can find another reason.

At the end of his submission Lawrie Angus wrote:

> The more of us put stuff on paper (no matter how feeble it is) the more we as an institution take seriously the point that we are shapers […] and not just powerless reactors.

That sense of collegial purpose should never be entirely lost; it is central to what a university should be.

Learning the ropes...

Gilah Leder

Professor Gilah Leder is an Adjunct Professor at Monash University and Professor Emerita at La Trobe University. Her major research areea has been in Mathematics education. She is a Fellow of the Academy of the Social Sciences in Australia, a Past President and life member of the Mathematics Research Group of Australasia and a Past President of the International Group for the Psychology of Mathematics Education. She was the recipient of the 2009 Felix Klein medal.

The beginning

Turn the clock back to 1966. Six months had passed since I had stopped teaching. Despite the ruling, then still current, that a pregnant woman should resign when she was six months into her pregnancy, I had continued to work until 10 days before the birth of my first child. Whatever the joys and satisfaction of looking after a newborn baby, I missed the stimulation and challenges of teaching and the time to read and think about matters far removed from the daily house chores. Happily, we had recently moved to a location not far from Monash. Much was being written about the new university which had only recently opened its doors. Surely here was an opportunity beckoning to be grasped! Now, almost 50 years later, I reflect on my decision to return to studies with relief and an overwhelming sense of gratitude.

A student – again
At a time when small-sized tertiary classes are rare if not extinct, I look back appreciatively at my lectures and seminars in the fledgling Faculty of Education. During the first two years as a student returnee and for the subjects I chose, each class comprised just three or four students. Arriving unprepared or unwilling to contribute and participate in class discussions was simply not an option. Whatever the diversity of the physical surroundings: sparsely equipped rooms in the Menzies building, quarters in the freshly spruced new education building still hazardously surrounded by pockets of mud, or the comfortable environment of a lecturer's home (with home-baked cake and freshly brewed coffee provided during the mid-lecture break) – it was impossible to leave the class other than invigorated. How often, I can't but ask myself, do today's students, whether full or part-time, school leavers or mature age students – have this experience? (How) can such an exhilarating environment be duplicated in the now seemingly unstoppable push for the online delivery of lectures?

A full time research student
The transition from part-time coursework to full-time research student seemed seamless. Perhaps the requisite paperwork was still a novelty and something handled in a single office. The absence of a supervisor well versed in mathematics education was not considered a barrier. After all, how else could the faculty grow and diversify? Although only a pittance in buying-power terms, the boost of a scholarship to my self-esteem was immense. It seemed a vote of confidence that – whatever the obstacles – once begun the dissertation would have a successful ending. It offered opportunities to learn in other ways: to attend seminars at first glance only peripherally relevant to my area of study; to serve as the 'student rep' on requisite committees and thus become acquainted with the secrets – and treasures – of the administrative landscape; to be involved in tutorial work; to mix with a wide range of students, staff, and international visitors; and by listening to others still on the early cusp of their academic career, to become

increasingly convinced about the importance, and personal satisfaction, of not only conducting research but also disseminating its outcomes. A brief stint as a casual research assistant for Carl Wood, professor of obstetrics and gynaecology, at Monash, led to a joint publication and an early lesson that academic collaboration and mentoring could be found beyond the resources within the faculty.

New opportunities – a full time position
Move the clock forward to 1978. What stands out, as I look back on that time?

Both for the faculty and for me, newly appointed as a lecturer, this was a time of continuing growth and opportunities. At first glance, it was still very much a man's world in which, with few exceptions, senior positions were held by males. But others, too, were influential in shaping my academic journey. Foremost among them was McKenzie (Ken) Clements, an energetic and ebullient mathematics educator, a 'mover and shaker' within and beyond the Faculty. His pioneering role in establishing the Mathematics Education Research Group of Australia [MERGA], in convening at Monash University the association's first annual conference, with its still-legendary time table of three packed days of paper presentations running from 9am to 10pm, propelled mathematics education at Monash onto the national and international scene. That sense of stretching existing boundaries and conventions was consciously translated into our course content and research directions and went some way to countering the dominance of science education, and the subtle yet unbreachable barriers set by those within that group. For me those barriers became a challenge to seek alternate pathways which ultimately lead to long-term collaborations with colleagues like Shirley Sampson and Elizabeth Fennema – the former outside mathematics education, the latter outside the faculty. Shirley was a tireless champion for equal opportunity in the education of girls and careers for women. Her sterling contributions to the field were recognised but not fully appreciated within the faculty. I like to think that our common interest in equity issues enriched both our research endeavours. Certainly Shirley's sociological perspectives enhanced mine and that of her many students. Professor Fennema, located in the USA at the University of Wisconsin, was an inspirational mentor. My early research efforts were brought to her notice through the faculty's insistence that at least one examiner of a PhD thesis had to be an international scholar. Elizabeth's subsequent advice and encouragement for my research and her generosity in sharing contacts and projects proved invaluable. Her long-standing friendship remains much treasured. Without constructive support from such partners would I have had the same access to fresh fields and their attendant rich personal and professional rewards?

A final reflection
Collegiality and friendship, inner and outer circles, rewards and disappointments, the satisfaction of teaching and sharing information, watching with pride the achievements of my students, the frustrations and insights associated with research – undoubtedly I changed and matured over the 30 or so years I spent in the faculty. The faculty, too, kept evolving. Once-stark boundaries were slowly being breached, unquestioned routines replaced by bold initiatives, impediments becoming opportunities. Starting as a part-time student, I left as an experienced member of staff with a range of skills and some practice in testing existing boundaries and challenging conventions. Collectively, the myriad of experiences provided a solid base for tackling new tasks and unfamiliar ventures beyond the faculty. That journey, too, has been rewarding and ultimately brought me back where it all began: to Monash university and the faculty but in another role.

Memories

Paul Gardner

Dr Paul Gardner AM formerly a teacher in secondary schools, served in the Faculty from 1967 to 2002. He became a reader in education, and was known for his important research work in science education and in attitude measurement. During his 36 years in the faculty, he taught at all levels and chaired several faculty committees. He served as Editor of Research in Science Education from 1990 to 1994.

It was a dark and stormy night… Well, no, it wasn't, it was actually a pleasant autumn day in the Faculty of Education in 1971. Ray McCulloch, an associate professor with expertise in educational administration, was giving a staff seminar. The advertised topic wasn't related to my field of interest (or so I thought), but I attended anyway. We were just a small staff back then, and the tradition was to be collegial. (Our light teaching loads meant there was time to participate in this sort of thing. Oh, golden days.)

I was in my fifth year in the faculty, and had just begun work on my PhD, a study of the influence of teacher behaviour and pupil personality on Year 11 students' attitudes to physics. Ray spoke about Murray's needs-press model, which was based on a social psychological theory that human behaviour is influenced by an interaction between personality and the social environment.

Ray mentioned a measuring instrument, Stern's *College Characteristics Index*, used to evaluate the social environment of academic institutions. I quickly realised that the model was exactly what I needed as the theoretical framework for my study, and that I could develop an instrument similar to Stern's for the purposes of my research in high school classrooms.

Ray was just one of many people whose knowledge helped my development as a young academic. Another important episode occurred the following year, when I was analysing my data. I was employing a statistical method called analysis of covariance with unequal cell frequencies. (I am sure this will fascinate every reader.) I had written a computer program, based on a formula published in a statistics textbook by a highly esteemed American statistician, to analyse my data. I had to carry boxes of data (on Fortran punch cards, remember them?) across the campus to the Computer Centre, located close to engineering, science and mathematics and as far as geographically possible from education. (After all, why would education need easy access to the computer?) The huge machine crunched my data, spat out reams of wide continuous-fold paper, and printed out a mathematically impossible answer.

Fellow PhD student Dick White helped me out. He had actually studied statistics, whereas I was self-taught. We spent a month (on and off) wrestling with the problem. There was nothing wrong with my computer program. It was the textbook that was wrong. We developed a new statistical formula from first principles. We wrote a joint paper about it, page after page of algebraic symbols and formulas (exciting stuff!) and submitted it to an international journal. Excellent, said one reviewer: publish it. Quite right, said a second, but the textbook author has already corrected the error in the recently published second edition of his book.

These personal experiences of learning from others were not isolated events. Syd Dunn, the second professor appointed to the faculty, was an important mentor. Before his appointment to Monash, Syd had taught me about measurement in education in a postgrad BEd subject at the University of Melbourne. As deputy director of the Australian Council of Educational Research, he invited me to participate in various test development projects. His personal connections with senior education officials in the Territory of Papua New Guinea were instrumental in getting me a grant to conduct research on students' difficulties with non-technical vocabulary in learning science.

I developed expertise in attitude measurement, the major theme of my PhD, which led to a string of international publications in the 1970s and the introduction of a masters subject in the faculty which ran for years.

However, I had no particular expertise in this field when I arrived at Monash in 1967. My colleague Lindsay Mackay, appointed a year earlier, had obtained a substantial ARC grant to evaluate the new Physical Sciences Study Committee physics course (which I had taught as a high school teacher prior to coming to Monash). He invited me to collaborate with him. Would I develop a series of attitude scales to form part of the set of evaluation instruments? All my previous test construction experience was in the cognitive domain, but this looked like an interesting challenge. I assembled a small group of colleagues and we wrote, tried out, analysed and revised four scales measuring various attitude objectives of the PSSC course. Five years later, I used these scales as the major outcome measure for my PhD.

These are not earth-shattering stories (although they were all very important to me personally), but I remember them more than 40 years later because I think they epitomise something about the nature of research and academic life. 'No man is an island', said John Donne. Sir Isaac Newton acknowledged that he 'stood on the shoulders of giants'. We learn from each other, and that's as true for academics and doctoral students as it is for preschoolers. Education is a social enterprise. It takes a village to educate a child, the well-known saying goes, and it takes a socially cohesive faculty to build a world-class research institution. Monash was (and I believe still is) such a place. Science education at Monash flourished because of it (as of course did several other fields). It was this intellectual atmosphere that brought the science education staff (never given a formal name until the establishment of the Centre for Science, Mathematics and Technology Education in the 1990s) international recognition.

Such developments don't happen by themselves. Leadership is crucial. Peter Fensham, appointed in 1967 as the faculty's first professor of science education, came with extraordinary qualifications: a doctorate in chemistry and a doctorate in social psychology (and a passionate interest in social justice and the improvement of education). He led, not by making authoritarian demands, but by offering gentle suggestions and encouraging others to implement new ideas. He had an extensive network of colleagues in Australia and overseas. I know this from personal experience. He co-supervised my PhD. He recommended the Chelsea College Centre for Science Education in London as a good place to work during my first period of study leave in 1973. And almost 20 years later, it was his interest in exploring the relationship between science and technology that stimulated my own work in this area in the early 1990s.

Critical mass – the concept is borrowed from nuclear physics – helps explain how people with shared interests can coalesce to make things happen in ways that wouldn't happen otherwise. In 1970, Peter had the bright idea that it might be productive to bring together scholars from other states to form a national organisation. Two young colleagues, Lindsay Mackay and doctoral student Dick White, pitched in to help. In May of that year, Monash hosted an informal conference and the Australian (later Australasian) Science Education Research Association was born. The following year, a rather flimsy stapled paperback collection of papers presented at the second meeting in Sydney became the forerunner of a journal, eventually named *Research in Science Education*. ASERA grew, held conferences throughout Australia (and later New Zealand) and gave practical encouragement to young academics to present papers. Over a quarter of a century the journal slowly evolved into a respected publication with an editorial board supported by a long list of international referees. It is now a highly regarded, commercially produced quarterly.

My narrative is (obviously) the happy account of someone who entered the faculty as a young academic, was given numerous opportunities to grow in the job, and retired gracefully as a senior citizen 36 years later. However, I can provide definitive evidence that others (well, at least one) had similar opportunities. At one stage in the 1980s, I was briefly the acting head of my group. Another colleague and I interviewed a bright and personable young teacher who had applied for a position as a part-time lecturer in science method. He looked quite promising, we thought, and recommended his appointment. His name: John Loughran.

Teaching practice

Suzanne E Pinchen

Suzanne E Pinchen a Monash graduate (DipEd and MEd), a prominent teacher of economics and author, who worked in the Method staff at Monash and also helped run the Teachers Centre. She also worked as a training consultant. Suzanne recently returned to Victoria after living in Queensland and working at Griffith University in research and technology commercialisation. She is now with a not-for-profit organisation as an employment and training consultant. She is president-elect for 2014–2016 with the Australian College of Educators (Gippsland Region).

A Man for All Seasons was the play being performed at the Alexander Theatre, I was a Year 12 student on my first visit to the then relatively new Monash

University. I made a firm promise to myself then and there that this was the university I wanted to attend – a modern progressive university was the university where I wanted to qualify to become a secondary teacher. When I started at Monash (1968) I was on an Education Department Studentship, so was forced to face my love of teaching very early in my studies – an easy task for me. At the end of my first year at uni, at the age of 18, I had my first compulsory two weeks of teaching rounds – as a studentship holder, a compulsory round at the end of each year of uni – compulsory at the end of each year before DipEd. I was very fortunate on my first round to be accepted at Maryvale High School, where David Schapper was principal – a recognised 'experimental school'. I recall being given a class of English/poetry students, where I was placed in charge. At that time there were a number of visiting Rusden College teachers in training – in their final year. They were put in my class to observe. At least eight of them, in the classroom with me on my own. I remember so clearly a lesson on a poem about sunflowers. The lesson went so well, with the Year 9 students. At the end of the lesson the Rusden students all asked me questions. How did you manage to get the students so involved? How do you manage to organise your lesson plan? How long have you been teaching? Etc. I was honest, and they could not believe that I was only 18, at the end of my first year at uni. They had not been in a classroom before, but they were in their 'final' year of Education at Rusden.

By the time I was accepted into Monash DipEd (only accepted if you had no fails in your degree) I already had six weeks classroom experience under my belt. Of course I knew that education was in my blood. My first economics method lecture was conducted by Dr Alan Gregory. I recall his introductory comment that he was somewhat blinded by all the shiny engagement rings flashing from the female students. It made us laugh and relax somewhat as he proceeded over that year to lead us into the love of teaching economics. As I look back, I see it as a social commentary on those years. Complete a degree, get engaged and married, go overseas for the necessary backpacking trip around Europe, and return to a career in teaching.

I recall what was perhaps my first or second teaching round during Monash DipEd: Williamstown Girls High School. God it was so cold on what appeared to me as the school on that big cliff facing the sea! I knew Dr Gregory had told us that we were to be 'professionally attired', so on my first day I wore a fine wool black top over black pants, with long black boots. I think only my hands, neck and face were exposed! By recess I was called into the (male) principal's office and told that no woman could teach in his school wearing pants! Pants/slacks were not acceptable in his school, I would have to leave the premises and go home and change! I was newly married and living in Domain Road, South Yarra – a long way from Williamstown, and he expected me to go home and change? Damned impertinence of the chauvinist! I knew my top and pants were valued at over $300, yes, even in those days! But I was told I would have to leave the school if I wore pants. This male principal was threatening to cut short my required teaching practice hours!

Telling me? The student teacher who had cut her teeth on *The Female Eunuch* was obviously not happy, so the pragmatist in me triumphed – I went into the female staff toilets and removed the (offending) pants! I then appeared in his office, pants in hand, wearing a very, very mini top and long boots! The chauvinist looked askance, had the decency to look away, and allowed me to stay and continue my teaching round! Talk about misogyny! What female DipEds had to put up with, just to be able to get their teaching hours practice accepted, in 1971. How I laughed to myself about that incident years later, as an associate principal of a multi-campus college, where I regularly wore pants, in more ways than one!

In my first year of teaching I was appointed to Moorabbin High School and was allocated the Year 12 and two Year 11 economics classes, plus some junior history classes. Due to the sound economics method training I had received at Monash under Dr Gregory's watchful eye, I coped well with what some regarded as quite a challenging allotment for a first year out teacher. Within three years I was invited to the position of economics method tutor at Monash, in the days where a practicing teacher could continue to teach and be seconded to a university to provide practical teacher training. It was the first year females were given the opportunity to enter the hallowed halls of Economics teacher training! I was privileged to spend over six years in this position and highly valued the opportunity to help our teachers of the future develop their love of teaching economics.

When I first started teaching my peers used to lament the fact that they were 'bonded' to the Education Department, thus having to teach for three years, given they were on a studentship. By the time I finished tutoring DipEd students in economics method a few years later, many students were lamenting the fact they might not get jobs teaching, given that they were 'not bonded'. Yes, times in labour markets continue to change.

In the early eighties I was again privileged to be (very competitively) appointed to another position within the Education Faculty – that of manager of the externally-funded 'Work Related Curriculum Project'. It was, once again, very innovative of Monash Faculty of Education at that time. The position had as its key objectives to initiate dialogue and training between the education, business, industry, law, union and public sectors, on the role of higher education. This was at a time when universities were regarded by many as 'academic ivory towers'. Why should universities be concerned with what business expected of our graduates? The position was successful in conducting professional development seminars, implementing an Australasian conference – 'Looking Ahead' – which brought together very senior representatives from business, law, unions and higher education. The project was endorsed by the then Minister for Higher Education, Susan Ryan, as an innovative and welcome step in bringing together these crucial players in determining our future growth. As part of that same project there was also the joint collaboration with the Country Education Project TV programs I did with Peter Couchman, which were widely broadcast nationally as a teaching tool for students of economics.

I reflected on this project twenty years later when I was appointed to a position responsible for the evaluation of the Bachelor of Arts in Leisure Management at Griffith University in Queensland. I did quite a detailed survey of employers around Brisbane, to gauge what their expectations were of the BALM students. I thought at the time how similar the answers were to what had transpired during the two years I worked on the Work Related Curriculum Project and the very successful 'Looking Ahead' Conference which we held.

Any tribute to the Faculty of Education has, necessarily I suppose, the required detailed CVs and research achievements of its most highly-lauded academic staff, the details of who did the photo copying, who ran the tea club, and the details of the many committees of governance and how all of those have impacted on the Faculty over the last fifty years. To me, the most significant achievements of any university faculty is the impact on its students – yes those, to some academics, annoying little voices which will not be quieted! Yes, academics want to be high achievers in their research and 'publish or perish' environment. But let no history of the Faculty of Education be complete without highly heralding the achievements of the people who significantly impacted on the Faculty's students, and the thousands of lives which have been influenced, directly and indirectly, as a result of being eventual graduates and part of that Faculty.

In my 'recollections' of the Education Faculty, let me provide just one example of how many young lives have been influenced as a result of the 'products' of this Education Faculty. In my early years of teaching at Moorabbin High School, I well remember the very bright young student in the front row, in both Year 11 and Year 12 economics. Yes, she giggled a lot, but her results were always those of a very high achiever. I was not surprised when she entered Monash studying Ecops/Law. Four years later I was delighted to see her, in the front row, as an economics method student. She excelled of course, and I was delighted to be her referee for a position at a Melbourne private school as an economics teacher – I knew she would continue to do well. Do well, she has.

Over thirty years later I met up with her, Dr Margaret Plunkett, when I returned to Victoria from Queensland, and I became a member of the Australian College of Educators (Gippsland Region). She was president, and also a senior lecturer at the Gippsland campus (until recently) Faculty of Education, Monash University. In 2013 Dr Plunkett was awarded Australian Teacher of the Year (tertiary) – an accolade for Monash University – and was so generous to say in her media release interview that she chose education and teaching, ahead of law, due to the passion and inspiration of her Year 12 economics teacher. These honours are what we receive many years after we have forgotten how we have influenced the lives of our students.

As the now president-elect of the Australian College of Educators (Gippsland region) for the forthcoming year, I am following in Dr Margaret Plunkett's footsteps as former president, I am proud to reflect on the outcomes and achievements of the thousands of students who have been a part of Monash University's Faculty of Education, and of the even more thousands of students who have been influenced by the teachers that Faculty has produced.

A Man for All Seasons, alas I am not, but allow me to take pride in the achievements of the Faculty of Education, and all it has achieved over the last fifty years. I join all of the former students and staff in wishing it even more success in the next fifty years. Whatever those years hold, do not forget the students you touch, teach, and influence in so many ways.

Thoughts on the Faculty of Education

Professor Richard Selleck

Professor R J W Selleck Australia's leading educational historian he held a chair in the Faculty of Education from 1972–1996; he also served in many administrative roles. He was the author of many major scholarly books.

I came to Monash University, then about 14 years old, in 1972 to take up a professorial position in the education faculty after previously working at the

University of Melbourne. When I arrived at Monash the 'student troubles', which had drawn much attention to the university and in which Albert Langer had played a conspicuous part, were drawing to a close, though they had not entirely ceased. Langer had completed his DipEd the previous year: if I remember correctly he was in prison when he did his some of his teaching practice. But he had left behind a group of supporters who, for a time, continued to challenge the university's authorities.

Students in the education faculty, whatever their opinions of Langer, were an independent and lively lot, not averse to testing the university's (and the faculty's) authority. Of course, the majority of students, even the more radical ones, were aiming to complete the degrees and diplomas that gave them entry to the profession of their choice. They could then settle into the task of becoming the responsible, important and wealthy people that the university was preparing them to be.

However, that prospect was in the distant future and did not prevent students from seeking ways to persuade the university's administration to meet various demands. A mild example of this intent would sometimes come to light at the beginning of a tutorial or lecture. When the lecturer or tutor entered the classroom for a lecture or tutorial and sat on the sole chair in the front of the classroom he or she would find the class sitting peacefully (too peacefully in fact) in the rows of desks or chairs, apparently quietly waiting for the teaching to begin. Sometimes, however (and I speak with direct experience of meeting this tactic), the students would wait until the lecturer was sitting comfortably in the chair at the front of the classroom, then, in a well-choreographed move, they would stand, pick up the chairs on which they had been sitting and form a circle, making sure that the lecturer's chair was part of that circle. The lecturer, they were saying, was not an authority separate from the students. We all shall equal be!

We were not equal, of course, because the lecturer was the one who decided whether a student passed or failed. Some students seemed not to be too worried about that but fortunately most were and an awkward peace was struck.

At this time the faculty was crowded with DipEd students (rather than higher degree students), as the demand for secondary school teachers was at a level that it had never before reached in Victoria's history. Governments were well aware of the desperate need for more teachers to help reduce the intense pressure as students crowded into secondary schools in numbers that had never been previously experienced. And not only were more students entering secondary schools than ever before, but they were staying for longer, as they and their parents were planning for careers based on tertiary education. One result of these pressures was the demand for more secondary teachers and to meet that demand education faculties around the country were growing swiftly. The very establishment of Monash University was a recognition that the University of Melbourne, and the Secondary Teachers College established in its grounds, could no longer produce sufficient teachers to meet the needs of secondary education in Victoria.

Though it recognised and tried hard to meet the need for more teachers, the Monash Faculty of Education was also determined to develop a research culture. The faculty's second Dean, Syd Dunn, who was in charge when I arrived, had worked previously at the Australian Council for Educational Research: his work there had made him acutely aware of the need for the faculty to become a centre for research. The faculty's first professorial appointments clearly recognised that need and had fine research records themselves. Ron Taft was a leading psychologist; Marie Neale played a major part in the negotiations that led to the building of the Krongold Centre; Peter Fensham, a chemist, was deeply involved in science education in schools and universities; the Englishman, Peter Musgrave, was a sociologist who, somewhat to the alarm of some of his colleagues, seemed to publish a good book almost yearly. Under this leadership the faculty begun to build a reputation for producing its own high quality research and attracting many higher degree students.

The early days of the faculty were not a peaceful time for teachers. When students graduated and went to teach in a secondary or technical school they were pitched into battles about the status of the teaching profession that had long histories. They fought many of these battles while struggling with large classes and an Education Department bureaucracy which was not particularly interested in listening to what teachers had to say nor adept at handling them. Politicians also were not overly concerned to understand the conditions secondary teachers were coping with and were reluctant to negotiate with their union, the Victorian Secondary Teachers Association, which was challenging the department's authority. Such battles sapped the confidence and energy of teachers – and, in the end, despite some losses on the way, the Education Department probably won most of the battles.

The administrative structure of the faculty into which I tumbled was constructed, so far as I know, by Syd Dunn: it was built around 'groups' of staff with similar academic interests. Each group (at this time there were seven) was usually (but not always) headed by a professor. 'Group' seemed to me a deliberately vague word, but I came to understand and respect the reason for that:

it meant the faculty avoided having the formal departments that operated, sometimes divisively, in most of the university. The groups were for the most part constructed to reflect the teaching and research interests of the faculty as a whole. Their boundaries were somewhat porous and their construction was driven as much by administrative as strictly intellectual considerations, but for many years, somewhat to the bewilderment of other parts of the university as well as some members of the education faculty itself, this structure served as an efficient way of organising and administering the faculty.

One representative of each of these groups, as well as the Faculty Secretary (to use the terminology of the time), and the person in charge of the organisation of the Diploma of Education Programme, met regularly as members of the Planning and Development Committee, which was an advisory committee established by the Dean, who chaired it. As this was not a formal committee, and appeared nowhere in the university's legal and administrative structure, it had no regulatory powers, and thus mystified other members of the university. For many years, however, it worked effectively and for the most part Deans accepted its decisions, as faculty members also did. So the Planning and Development Committee was a powerful factor in the faculty's life, and continued to be so for many years.

The Monash education faculty was aware from its earliest days that it was under pressure from the Education Department, from Catholic schools and (to a lesser but still important degree) from private schools. It was called upon to produce a large number of graduates quickly, and it did so. But from its earliest days the faculty set itself to become what university faculties should always be, a centre for original research. Since its earliest days it has succeeded very markedly in that enterprise.

Memories of Monash

John Theobald

> Dr John Theobald was the first member of staff of the Faculty of Education and served from 1964 to 1990. He played a key role as Coordinator of DipEd, as well as in the planning of the Education Building, and was well known for his work in classroom testing. He was known as an outstanding administrator and teacher.

Dick Selby Smith, the principal of Scotch College, had been appointed to the chair of education at Monash University and postgraduate courses were to commence in 1964. Lectureships/senior lectureships were advertised and, thinking I stood a chance, I applied for a lectureship. Since 1960 at the STC I had been in charge of the subject Organisation of Teaching, had been first examiner in Leaving Certificate Biology, had been developing my expertise in educational measurement and was writing a manual on classroom testing for teachers-in-training. I was also an active member of the VIER and of the ACE. My application was successful and I was prevailed upon to commence at Monash in November 1963 to make arrangements with schools to provide teaching practice places for the first cohort of DipEd students, all 39 of them. So in a narrow sense, I was the 'founding' member of what was to become the Faculty of Education at Monash University. The other full-time staff members, Henry Schoenheimer and Maurice Balson, took office at the beginning of 1964 and Selby Smith joined us at Easter. Part-time methods lecturers were appointed in areas that the four of us could not cover and we were open for business. Before Selby took up his position one of our early duties was to order materials and equipment from the budget. Henry Schoenheimer had been appointed as a senior lecturer and was the chair. Among other things, we decided to buy a television set. It was only a coincidence that the English cricket team was playing matches in Australia that summer.

We were housed initially with the arts faculty on the first floor of the Menzies building, but were later to move to purpose-built accommodation on the tenth and eleventh floors in the eastern extension when that was completed. Later still we got our own building, east of the Alexander Theatre in the southeast corner of the campus. I was on the Building Committee for both sets of premises, liaising with the architect in charge, Ken Atkins. We learned much from our first attempt, particularly about sound-proofing offices from one another, the placement of toilets, the width of corridors, and keeping teaching rooms on the lower floors. We battled with a host of inflexible prescriptions, for example, on the maximum sizes of offices permitted for the various ranks of seniority, the lack of provision for a students' common room, and so on. To satisfy our requirements we had to resort to some ingenuity: for instance we provided a very wide connecting link between the first building and the northern extension that could serve as a common meeting place for students. It is difficult to predict how a faculty will develop and how a building will be used so, where there was any opportunity, we tried to plan large flexible spaces that could serve many purposes or could be modified later. I believe our worst error concerned the lift. We rightly anticipated that there may be future upward extensions and planned foundations that would bear additional floors but, because of economic constraints, we did not plan for the extension of the lift-well to serve these additional floors. The same economies resulted in a greatly reduced additional floor being added, and to have to get out of the lift and walk up a set of stairs will always be an inconvenience. At an early stage of the planning we had a largish but inconvenient area near the stairs on the ground floor and were wondering about its possible use. Selby Smith was so undemanding that he said he would be quite happy to use it as his office. We suggested that future Deans might not be so accommodating.

The early days at Monash were a great joy. I had been an early member of the staff at the Secondary Teachers' College and was now a foundation member of staff of the education 'faculty' at Monash. Everything seemed possible with our own course structures and content and, for the first couple of years, small classes. In old established universities education faculties often had little academic or social prestige but Monash's first Vice-Chancellor, Louis Matheson, was most supportive and the good relationship between many other professors and Selby Smith was an encouraging start. Louis Matheson set the tone, and cooperative relations between staff across the university were greatly enhanced by him regularly joining us for lunch in the staff common room in the Union Building. Of course this was possible while the university was small, but the friendships made lasted over the years and made my life there more fulfilling. Louis Matheson's approachability was never better displayed than during the 1970s student unrest when he set up a desk in the ground floor of the Menzies Building to be available to any disaffected students who wished to talk to him.

However, student numbers increased rapidly and, apart from the delivery of courses, the time tabling of lectures and tutorials and the placement of students in schools for their school experience became a logistic nightmare. I was given some time to administer these and other tasks of initial teacher training and shared a secretary, Christine D'Arcy-Evans, with Ray McCulloch. She was a very proper lady and insisted on a 'modesty skirt' being fitted to the front of the regulation desk so that her ankles would not show. When I took my first period of study leave in 1970–71 John Fyfield had nearly 500 students to look after. In 1974, the post of coordinator of DipEd was created and I had a full-time secretary and later an administrative assistant who was largely concerned with school placements. My first secretary was Jackie Carton, then Reba Bloomfield with Ann Shorten as an administrative assistant, and then Layla Masterton with Reba as the administrative assistant. Both Reba and Layla completed arts degrees, Reba in psychology and Layla in history, while they were working with me. As a matter of pride Layla reverted to her maiden name Godfrey and took out her degree in that name. Ann became the lecturer in history method and completed a brilliant law degree. Her son, Bill, was a talented official in the union movement and now is a Labor MP in the Federal Parliament.

As the faculty grew and new staff were appointed we wished to remain a single department, but with a number of professors to lead teaching and research. The Faculty of Education at the University of Melbourne had only one professor and was envious when the second of our several professors was appointed. Among our first professors, some of whom subsequently became the full-time Dean of the Faculty, were Dick Selby Smith, Syd Dunn, Peter Musgrave, Peter Fensham, Ron Taft, Marie Neale, Dick Selleck, Dick Tisher, Millicent Poole and David Aspin. They led areas such as psychology and special education, social foundations and educational administration, history and philosophy, teaching and curriculum, and methods of teaching.

Faculty-wide decisions about course offerings, staffing and future directions were made by a Planning and Development (P&D) Committee comprised of the Dean, the Faculty Secretary, professors and other heads of areas, a staff representative and the coordinator of DipEd. Areas and the various levels of study – DipEd, BEd, and masters – met regularly and could make submissions directly to the P&D Committee. As representative governments go, this structure seemed to me to function reasonably well in allowing wide staff consultation and participation. Students taking higher degrees by research were subject to common university-wide requirements.

Of our communal life, Alan Gregory started a faculty choir and I had great fun singing carols at an annual Christmas concert in the Religious Centre, at staff concerts and at visits to a number of old folks' homes. The staff common room was well attended for morning and afternoon teas and many robust discussions ensued. Some would want to claim that there was a certain hegemony exercised by some opinionated science staff which rather overran more collegial exchange. For a number of years the university also ran Monday lunchtime concerts in the Blackwood hall and it was here that I remember an exceptional concert by the slimmer Luciano Pavarotti in full voice, large handkerchief and all. A riveting experience.

Education with the education historians

Rosalie Triolo

Dr Rosalie Triolo previously a teacher in Victorian schools, she is a senior lecturer in the Education Faculty lectures in History Education, and is active as a researcher and presenter in state and national History Education and 'history of education' communities. She is President of the History Teachers' Association of Victoria. Well published she has led battlefield tours for history teachers as well as Australian History fellowships for pre-service teachers. Her thesis, 'Our Schools and the War', was awarded a Monash University Mollie Holman Doctoral Medal (2008) and her book of the same was commended in the Victorian History Publication Award (2012).

I was blessed professionally over a period of 11 years to be the last student of each of the faculty's last three research-dedicated education historians: Dr Martin Sullivan, Dr Andy Spaull and Emeritus Professor Dick Selleck.

I first met Andy Spaull when he visited history student-teachers placed with me at Cheltenham Secondary College. He was honest about not being a history teacher but gave a firm impression of knowing and loving history and enjoying the teaching and learning process. Several years later, I secured a sessional tutor position in the faculty and rang to ask if I could reintroduce myself and undertake a masters with him. This was in 1997 after a 16-year break from tertiary study, and I was anxious about what lay ahead. I arrived at Andy's office at the western end of the second floor to find it full of papers in and around a long row of filing cabinets, alongside expansive shelves of books complete with some books being cloth or leather covered and over a century old. I felt immediately comfortable in the presence of someone devoted to his knowledge and craft. I opted for the full research masters and embarked on a study of state school education in Victoria prior to the Great War, knowing that my doctorate to follow, also with Andy, would focus on state school education in Victoria during that war.

I needed an associate supervisor and Andy introduced me to Martin Sullivan. Martin excelled in knowledge about education during Victoria's early colonial period, a knowledge that I have not met anyone to rival. With Andy's expertise from the late 19th to mid-20th century, and Martin's, I was fully supported, although simultaneously intimidated by how much each knew. I was also somewhat intimidated by their larger-than-life characters and booming voices that could be heard not only down the corridor but a floor away.

Ultimately, I could not have asked for better supervisors to reintroduce me to tertiary study in both scholarly as well as socially appealing ways. The two were great friends and during one-on-one meetings or when we three met in the staffroom, each enjoyed a bit of fun at the other's expense, something that I also enjoyed. In return, I was able to bring to the table my knowledge of education in the 1990s, and I recall us observing that, rightly or wrongly, there are often more similarities than differences between education of the past and the present, and still much to be learned from the past. I would particularly enjoy sharing with them the occasions when an education authority would declare something to be 'entirely new' in education, yet we three knew of an historical precedent, perhaps by a different name but essentially the same. 'They don't know their education history', we would claim to ourselves. Martin retired in 1998, offering me first choice of many of the books in his office. A history of education collection began to line my own office's bookshelves.

I commenced my doctorate with Andy in 2000. Andy remains the definitive author of Australian education in the Second World War and I knew I would be working with someone who would fully understand my interest and intent. Exactly as he had done with me with my masters, he walked me over to the library and took me to the stack of history of education books, saying, 'here's where you start'. He explained each time that this was something he always did when a student embarked on research with him. I shall add here that, since the faculty's teaching collection was moved to the Matheson Library, I have walked my History Method students to the relevant shelves. I worked also with the Matheson's rare books, microfilm and microfiche collections, and primary sources held by repositories such as the Public Record Office of Victoria and Royal Historical Society of Victoria. Nothing was 'online' at the time, a fact which pleased Andy immensely (known for the story of requesting that Monash give him a Mont Blanc ink pen instead of a computer). We noted how 'history of education' was not being considered a digitisation priority at that time (and largely still is not). In any case, we each enjoyed the pleasures of neat, old-fashioned cursive script, old document formalities and formatting, and the look and feel of paper.

In 2003 Andy suffered a crippling stroke. He returned to Monash briefly but, despite responding exceptionally well to rehabilitation, decided that the time had come for retirement. Even so, he had no intention of retiring from me. He declared he would supervise me to the conclusion of my doctorate but that I should locate an additional supervisor who could manage all that Monash was suddenly and increasingly expecting to be completed by staff via email and online. In the meantime, Andy offered that I enter his office and take as many books for my own collection as I wished before what he feared would be their casting into dumpsters. My history of education collection swelled, as it did a third time when, near enough a decade after his retirement, Dick Selleck invited me to take books from his office before he gave the space to other researchers.

Dick had retired from Monash in 1996 in the year I had commenced as a 0.2 sessional. I learned in the years soon after how deeply he was respected and I regretted not having known him as someone to catch up with in 1996 or whose farewell I should have witnessed. In quite some awe, I met him at several history of education events after 1996. I read his major works and marvelled at the intellect and beauty of his writing: history of education was far from uninteresting or irrelevant under his penmanship. I was also impressed that he seemed to remember what we had discussed on any previous occasion. In 2003, seven years after his retirement, I mustered the courage to ring him to ask him to be my associate supervisor. I fumbled through an introduction which he interrupted with calm and pleasant agreement, and we met properly as a supervisor and a student several days later. My doctoral supervisors were Australia's two pre-eminent historians of education during the period of the Great War.

Aside from all advice and support pertaining to historical scholarship, what did I learn from Andy and Dick? I learned foremost that high quality research and writing takes time and that good supervisors balance patience with gentle motivations. Andy and Dick knew there was no point arguing when I said I had 'not quite finished the latest chapter', no matter how earnestly I had wished to luxuriate in its writing. They helped managed my busy world of Monash teaching with advice such as 'read or write even a little every day' so that I maintained a grip on my content and conclusions. And, they asserted that 'near enough is never good enough', giving me time and courage to re-think and re-work until we three signed off on my thesis at the point where I had said all I could want to say as well as I could say it, these being tenets I seek to uphold with my own students. The thesis received positive examiners' reports, was awarded a Monash University Mollie Holman Medal and was revised to become the book *Our Schools and the War*, commended in the 2012 Victorian Community History Awards. As a consequence of my and others' interests, I have researched the responses to the Great War of teachers, pupils and whole school communities in other states, systems and sectors, producing classroom resources for use in Australian primary and secondary schools today about 'school-life' a century ago.

There are times in life when one sets out on a path partly of one's own making but which is then blessed with opportunities to meet people more special than could have been imagined, let alone orchestrated. Such was my experience and the education I received from the faculty's education historians.

Growing internationalisation and diversity in faculty programs and practices

Libby Tudball

Libby Tudball has made an impact with her work in international education, as well as her teaching in the faculty and work in social education. She has also had senior administrative roles. Tudball's research has been on the interweaving themes of values and citizenship, internationalisation and environmental sustainability.

During the history of the faculty, global engagement and international mobility have increased rapidly, leading to internationalisation of the faculty's programs, student and academic profile and core business, including teaching and research. Internationalisation has become a buzzword in education, particularly in the past two decades, when the university opened international campuses in South Africa and Malaysia and a centre in Prato, Italy. Programs including the 'Global Passport' and study abroad opportunities, backed by scholarship incentives for students to be involved in study exchanges in overseas universities, have been additional drivers in the call to internationalise. At the same time, rapid technological innovation and the impact of high speed internet access, blogs, wikis, mobile phones, Ipads and other new technologies, have all been factors stimulating rapid changes in pedagogy and have markedly changed student learning and academic work. Email interaction with the world, online and distance learning through the use of programs such as Blackboard, then Moodle, Moocs, Google docs, and adobe conferencing, have evolved as expected means of communication embedded in our teaching and work.

In the past decade, external drivers for internationalisation have been amplified by the growth in education as an export industry, with universities globally intensifying their off shore programs in face to face or distance modes. Increasing numbers of international students have enrolled in our faculty from all over the world, but particularly from the Asian region, at all levels including undergraduate, masters and in doctoral programs, and across all Faculty campuses. The university has worked in partnership with Kaplan in Hong Kong and Singapore, in the delivery of programs including early childhood education and leadership in education. Many of these students have then continued their connection with the faculty through enrolment in higher degree research.

The flows of students have been two-way, since in the past twenty years, there has also been a range of international practicum programs developed, to provide pre-service teachers with international experiences that build their professional learning in contexts very different from Australia, and their capacity to graduate as teachers prepared to teach anywhere in the world. These practicums are consistent with the *Monash Directions 2025* policy, which emphasises that our graduates should be 'responsible and effective global citizens, who engage in an internationalised world, exhibit cross-cultural competence and demonstrate ethical values'.

The longest running of these practicum programs is in the Cook Islands, which commenced 25 years ago, and over time has led to the building of relationships with schools, teachers and Ministry officials that are of mutual benefit of all involved. Academic leaders involved include the late Julie Edwards and Judy Gray, Stephen Keast, Nerissa Albon and Judy Williams.

Through a connection with the Ministry of Education in Korea, a practicum ran for eight years in the past decade in Korean schools, where our students lived in homestays with local families. This program had a specific focus on teaching English as a second language, but students involved comment that it also provided them with rich experiences of the dynamic culture and history of Korea and the confidence and interest to teach in other parts of Asia as their careers unfold. This program was well in advance of the current emphases on readying students for the 'Asia century' and 'Asia literacy', so as a faculty we were ahead of our time in these initiatives.

In the past five years, a practicum has been built through a partnership with the Monash South Africa (MSA), Johannesburg campus. This was led for the first three years by Graham Parr, working closely with Craig Rowe, Manager of the MSA Community engagement office, who has long connections with local communities and provides sustained relationships with schools. This experience builds students' intercultural understanding and their capacity to develop an open, respectful and compassionate attitude to difference in very powerful ways. Students spend the first week in mainstream Afrikaans private Christian and government schools, which are substantially difference to Australian schools. In this period, they adjust to being in a community where the need for security and living and working behind barbed wire is a reality, since even in the post-apartheid era, socio-economic difference is marked, as large homes and gardens in secure compounds are in close proximity to informal settlements that spring up. Students teach the second part of their practicum in these shanty town schools or in new communities being constructed that provide some evidence of improvement in peoples' lives. Students comment that this experience opens their eyes to another world, and builds their resilience and skills as they adapt teaching experiences to meet diverse learner needs. When each Saturday they teach in the MSA Saturday school, providing individual and small group learning experiences for hundreds of local students, they gain tremendous satisfaction in seeing how engaged the locals are and how much they enjoy being taught by our Faculty's pre-service teachers. A feature of the program is that we work alongside MSA students and staff so the program is sustained, and we form strong bonds with local schools and teachers.

The faculty has also been involved since 2012, in collaboration with five Victorian universities, including Deakin, Latrobe, Monash and Victoria universities and RMIT, in a Malaysian teaching practicum in Kuala Lumpur and surrounding areas. This program is aimed at increasing mutual understanding between educators in the two nations about effective teacher education and mentoring of student teachers and intercultural learning. The project has generated valuable knowledge about the establishment and building of professional partnerships and networks between Australian and Malaysian schools and teacher educators, and how these partnerships can be sustained over time, so that student teachers can enhance their professional learning and intercultural capacity in Malaysia. Students particularly appreciate learning about Chinese, Malay and Indian cultures through their immersion in the schools, interaction with Malaysian student teacher buddies, and living and eating in local hostels. From the commencement of the project, strong support has been provided by the Australian Government via the Counsellor (Education) at the Australian High Commission (AHC), Malaysia, Louise McSorley, and this connection with the AHC continues. Julie Faulkner and Libby Tudball, the two faculty academics who have led this program have also provided professional learning sessions in schools and at the Institute of Teacher Education, Campus of International Languages (at IPBA) for academic staff on 'Issues on the Education Agenda' that has built and embedded ongoing relationships.

The most recent addition to the international programs has been the pilot in January 2014 of a practicum in Prato, developed in partnership with Monash Prato staff Cecilia Hewlett and Loredana D'Elia. This pilot led by faculty academics Libby Tudball and Anita Forsyth explored how an international practicum in Prato could build unique learning, through immersion in Italian culture and education contexts where our students have to work collaboratively and share in planning to teach in classrooms where often only the mentor teacher can speak English. The experiences transformed their knowledge and understanding of their own capacity to adapt to teaching in non-English speaking classrooms, to plan to teach using language immersion strategies, to challenge their student learners to take risks in speaking English and to motivate and engage them in learning about Australia and their own lives through comparative learning.

The benefits of 'people to people' connections in all of these international practicums are broad ranging. The learning for academics and pre-service teachers about how to be a globally mobile academic and a teacher who can be ready for the whole world, not just the Australian context, is powerful. We bring our knowledge back into our classes and find that we constantly tell stories about how our experiences help us to teach for diverse learners, embrace difference and show that we have the skills to be global nomad educators, in an increasingly interdependent world.

While experiences abroad provide authentic and purposeful learning for students, the faculty has also continued to build and adapt our responses to the needs of international students who come to our campuses in Melbourne to study. During the 1980s and 1990s, Rosemary Viete led the way in introducing bridging courses for international students to understand local school cultures, and to assist them in building understanding of how education differs in the Australian context. In recent years, this work has been continued through the leadership of Anna Podorova and Raqib Chowdury who assist hundreds of students to make the transition into pre-service teacher education and research studies in the faculty.

Internationalisation is also developed in our faculty in other ways. Academics come to the faculty from all over the world. They enrich our programs through sharing experiences from their home countries. We have now embedded global perspectives, intercultural learning and teaching for diversity across all undergraduate courses and through pedagogy including new media and integrated curriculum strategies. As a faculty, we continue to lead new thinking and action in teaching and learning that includes international dimensions and we are continually in the world sharing and interacting with colleagues all over Asia, the USA, the UK, Europe and the world.

Information technology

Rosamund Winter

Rosamund Winter is a Research Fellow in the Faculty of Education. In a long career in the Faculty she has undertaken many roles. She is currently the Research and Research Degrees Advisor, providing workshops and assistance to the Faculty's HDR students, particularly in relation to management of literature and qualitative research data. She also teaches in the pre-service teacher education program.

Information technology drives us crazy when it goes wrong, when the software insists on 'correcting' us, when the network is slow, when we seem chained to it and its 24/7 demands. It's also magic when it gets us to materials we want in no time at all. Although for some of us, this hasn't led to paperless or tidier offices.

When I was appointed to the faculty in 1989, it was in large part to conduct literature searches for people on the new-fangled ERIC on CD-ROM . This was an annual subscription paid for by the faculty; the university library piggy-backed on this to get a reduction on their subsequent subscription.

At that time, the university library had a relatively small collection of databases on CD-ROM, and there were computer stations for people to read them, by appointment. The library catalogue was in the process of being digitised, and the collection was print. Over the next five years, the university went online, and in 1994, PCs were put on all desks, under the DITS initiative (Desktop Information Technology Strategy; I've always loved this (ditsy) acronym – and we think up lots of unfortunate ones, like BALD, CATS, PETS, PEAS, RATS...)

When we first got networked, we had to access the library resources in the most convoluted of ways and I wrote instructions like: 'If you want to connect to SESAME2 from a departmental terminal connected to MONET: To exit from your current connection, press the Control and P keys simultaneously, then type D and press the Return/Enter key...A prompt '>' will appear. Type C LIB and press the Return/Enter key...When you have finished: Signoff by typing $$SOFF and press the Return/Enter key' or 'To exit from the CDROM network: Press F10, Press Y, Select Main Menu, and press Enter, Select DOS, and press Enter, type COLDBOOT at the prompt'– no wonder Andy Spaull wanted the university to give him a fountain pen rather than a PC.

The catalogue, other networked bibliographic resources and our word-processing, went gradually from DOS to Windows. We took up email, we discovered the Web – and very crude it was with the first browsers – like Mosaic and Netscape - on Windows 3.1, and search engines such as Web Wombat, at woeful speed. We became 'end-users', and incorporated into our vocabulary Jabberwockian words like Gopher, VAX, Cold Fusion, AARNet, ECOS1, Pegasus, VICNet, NUCOM, NUCOS, CAVAL, OPAC, RAM, Bytes, LAN, ASCII, FTP, Dongle, and were frequently alarmed by the blue screens of death with the critical error message, 'Abort, Retry, Fail?'

In the early nineties, we bought a small annual site licence for the early versions of NUD*IST (later to evolve into NVivo) long before the university did. It was pretty clunky – all the software was, and everything was stored on 5 ¼ or 3 ½ inch floppies. These days, you need a laptop to carry around an NVivo project (and many live on servers). NUD*IST provided many laughs; I remember one year just before conducting a workshop standing in the first floor corridor at Clayton chatting to David Yammouni; it was late in the year, not many people around, and a well-dressed woman came along the corridor clearly searching for something. We politely asked her if she was looking for the nudist workshop – she fled.

What happened throughout the nineties and noughties was the development of more complex software, and the level of training and support needed for this new information environment increased with it. Searching the literature is both more convenient and more complex, and assistive database software like EndNote and the ability to draw in both remote bibliographic data and the digital artefacts from online journal subscriptions, sitting in our offices or at home, is something we take absolutely for granted. When I started in 1989, most people were still using fiche and print indexes and keeping bibliographies in alphabetical box files.

We were the first faculty to have information about our researchers in a searchable database – possibly in the country, but certainly in this university. I had an annual paper publication, *Founts of Wisdom*, which was converted into a database using the same fields and text by Bernard Holkner in 1997. A snapshot of our researchers in 1998 can be found on the Web Archive[6] (thanks to Neil Selwyn for alerting me to this site).

The faculty has lived through the Information Revolution in its administrative systems, communication and authoring software, and an extensive digital library, uniting traditional and digital collections in one portal, including study guides and teaching and learning support. It gave support

---

[6] http://web.archive.org/web/19990224002439/http://penny.educ.monash.edu.au/staff/index.cfm.

to students through the Library & Media Resources Centre (LMR), which provided leadership in information and computer literacy. It conducted workshops in the use of MS Office applications, presentation software, web authoring, literature searching and management, resources development, all in the multi contexts of research, postgraduate and pre-service education courses. It was replaced in 2009 by the TLC under the leadership of Bronwyn Dethick, and over time, the learning spaces (TLS) were created at Clayton, Peninsula and Berwick, which brought a C21 interpretation, emphasising video and web conferencing, wireless connectivity to laptops and other mobile devices, in a setting which is casual, even homely, with kitchen and eating areas.

Maintaining a single faculty would not have been possible without this working environment – email made communication and collaboration easier and as we started to use voice and then video conferencing equipment and applications, real face-to-face meetings became possible in virtual space – as well as teaching. With the Academic Language and Literacy Development Team – formerly Rosemary Viete, Anne Prince and, briefly, Eleanor Peeler, and now Raqib Chowdhury and Anna Podorova – I explored with David Yammouni the running of the faculty's HDR seminar series using the new Tandberg videoconferencing suite across all campuses. With other trailblazers Phil Riley and Brenda Beatty (Master of School Leadership), we were pioneers in the use of real-time, web-streamed learning environments such as Webex, EVO and Adobe Connect. Support for this work came from Claude Sironi (LMR/AV), David Yammouni (Faculty IT/AV), Matt Rendell, and Kristian Lofhelm (TLC/AV).

We had very talented support staff over the years. In the LMR were Sue Egan and Angela Pye, both tireless and knowledgeable librarians, and Claude Sironi, A/V coordinator, and a wonderful photographer. Faculty IT support (now, unhappily, centralised) was provided by Sharon Fitzgerald, a leader in IT support, especially flexible learning, in the 1990s; David Yammouni, an AV and Mac specialist, who had a terrific understanding of the nature of teaching and research; Gordon Perkins, who loved hardware; and Suneesh Suseelan Ushakumari, who remains with us, although officially eSolutions Arts and Education staff.

We were slower to build a critical mass of ICTE academics; it has been a field that the faculty has taken less seriously than it ought to have. Anne McDougall, our first appointee in this discipline, was a significant figure in the Australian Computers in Education scene, as deputy director of the Australian Computer Society (ACS) Community Affairs Board, chair of the

ACS National Computer Education Committee, and the ACS representative on the Australian Council for Computers in Education; she was writing about laptop schools in the 1990s. Following her were Sue McNamara, with a broader interest in educational technology, Bernard Holkner, who established our website, Geoff Romeo, a fellow of the Australian Council of Computers in Education and past president of Information and Communication Technologies in Education, Victoria (ICTEV), and Michael Dyson and Glenn Russell; they represented a small group in this important field. In more recent years, we have added Michael Henderson and Michael Phillips, both State Council Members of the Victorian ICT in education teachers' association (ICTEV), Nicola Johnston, and finally, long overdue, a professor in the field, Neil Selwyn. Other staff with very strong ties with this group are Ilana Snyder, Scott Bulfin, Julie Faulkner, Wee Tiong Seah, Denise Chapman and Hazel Tan, members of the Learning with New Media Research Group.

History of Education for Girls Group 1976–1994

Ailsa Zainu'ddin

Dr Ailsa Zainu'ddin was a Senior Lecturer in the Faculty of Education, 1965–1992. Her main areas of interest and publication have been Australian and Indonesian history; the history of education; and women's history.

Between 1976 and 1994, the History of Education for Girls Group met monthly at Monash University to reflect on and discuss the history of the education of girls in Australia and beyond. Like many others during the 1970s, we were responding to increased debates and activities promoting women's liberation, with 1975 International Women's Year. For me, the flavour of those debates and the environment in which they took place is reflected in the doubts expressed by two male colleagues in the Faculty of Education when I proposed a course on the history of education for women. One colleague expressed scepticism that there would be sufficient interest to run such a course, while the other said, 'it would take all my radical women'. Dick Selleck asked me if I could start a course, and gave every support. As I remember it, Marjorie Theobald and I had already begun a concerted study of the boxes of closed school files in the State Library basement (where the Victorian government archives were then housed), with Prue Burke giving me research assistance. Marje suggested the idea of some formalised regular meetings with others working on the history of girls' schools, so that we could discuss common methodological problems peculiar to that particular area of history. The following history of HEGG is drawn from a longer account I wrote when the group disbanded in 1994, and I took the opportunity to look back on the establishment of the group and its achievements. Both of the doubting colleagues gave an occasional paper to HEGG.

Our History of Education for Girls Group (HEGG) held its inaugural meeting in Room 324 of the Education Faculty on 4 March 1976 at 2.15pm, and we kept minutes of the occasion. Six people were listed as present: Anne Calvert, Ken Clements, Betty Feith, Marje Theobald, Linda Wilkins and me. Six others had sent apologies: Prue Burke, Hazel Edwards, Lyndsay Gardiner, Judy Miller, Dick Selleck and Ann Shorten. We decided to hold our HEGG meetings on the first Thursday of the month between 1 and 2pm. Various types of activity were suggested and minuted. Let me quote two of them, with a brief comment on how far they have been attempted:

1. Work-in-progress seminars by people actively engaged in research. An initial first count listed 117 of these, but I think that may be an underestimate.

2. Methodology sessions. There were about seven which were predominantly methodological but discussion of methodology was woven into many of the work-in-progress papers.

9.8 David Aspin presents Ailsa Zainu'ddin with 25 years service award.
Education Faculty

The other proposed activities included having guest speakers providing oral history of their own schooling, and the creation of a bibliography of source materials, as well as activities regarding school archives and histories.

Having kept a list of attendees for a few meetings in 1976, I began to do so again in 1979. From the HEGG Roll Book, which had been presented to the group by John Theobald in 1980, I extracted a list of 386 names – 348 women and 38 men – who attended at least one meeting of HEGG since its formation. As I did so, I began to realise that we had quite a record to celebrate but I also recognised that occasionally I expected people to know each other from HEGG when in fact their periods of attendance did not overlap.

In November 1979 we invited Alison Mackinnon to speak to HEGG on 'deciphering women's history with an empirical eye'. To us this was a significant occasion because it involved faculty funding Alison's airfare between Melbourne and Adelaide. We had arrived! For Alison, as she told me some years later, it was a significant occasion because it involved recognition of the work she was doing.

In the course of preparing the initial version of this paper in late 1994, I was reminded of one unique meeting when Heather O'Connor spoke to us.[7] Her topic was 'Bruce cliffhanger: the experience of one woman candidate'. She had arranged to speak about her narrow defeat by Bill Sneddon, shortly after he had retained his seat in 1983. By May, when she was on the program to speak, he had resigned from Federal Parliament and she was in the midst of a second attempt to win Bruce for the ALP. It seemed an inauspicious time to have to present a paper anywhere, and so we assured her that we would quite understand if she preferred to defer it. She didn't, declaring that it was a moment of respite from that exhausting contest which would give her a glimpse of normality and help keep her sane.

It seemed important to provide a supportive audience rather than a destructive one. The academic 'cut and thrust' based on competition, drawing its metaphors from militarism or sport, was one of the ways in which the masculinity of the university environment was preserved. We needed a sanctuary in which constructive criticism could be offered supportively as against the flurry of male aggression which was a very strong element in academic debate at the time. In particular, women returning to academic life were often apprehensive and lacking in confidence, and needed some meeting place where they could participate in discussion in a sympathetic

---

[7] 19 May 1983.

atmosphere. I believe that we may also have contributed in some small way to the education of the 38 men who, at various times, participated in our activities. HEGG provided an academic peer group for those who no longer had an institutional affiliation.

From very early in our existence we became a multi-purpose group. Developments in the two decades from 1976 included the formation of more specialised groups, which came to fulfil several of these earlier functions. Several students presented research proposals and reports to us, often with some additional visitors, perhaps a supervisor. That function was later provided for higher degree students in history elsewhere in the education faculty. We provided a base for some of the postgraduate students in our faculty but that also was taken on by the current postgrad students themselves. To some extent we also became an embryonic women's studies group, providing a forum for people in disciplines other than history either to educate the historians or to try out their own excursions into history on us. In March 1980 Pat Grimshaw and other colleagues from Melbourne University initiated interdisciplinary women's studies seminars at Melbourne University which many of us also attended. (I have noted, by the way, that – with some honourable exceptions – many people connected with Melbourne University seem to believe that the distance from Melbourne out to Monash is much further than the distance in to Melbourne from Monash.)

Once a Women's Studies Centre had been established in the Monash Faculty of Arts, this became the focus of research in that area in this university. Just before retirement, Shirley Sampson and I were beginning to have the first students doing our courses while enrolled in women's studies but that option is no longer available to them. There is also a Women's Caucus of the Asian Studies Association of Australia with local branches. These were healthy signs of growth, suggesting that many of our functions were now being fulfilled on a wider scale, but it also meant that many people had to choose among a greater variety of associations. At the same time as groups were proliferating, HEGG meetings became more difficult to attend once parking problems kept former alumni off campus and gave them a sense of alienation.

As Shirley and I retired at the end of 1992 and as nobody replaced us, our courses were no longer taught and we no longer supervised students working in this area. The various functions which we initially fulfilled had been taken up by other groups on campus, and staff support within the faculty was not likely to increase, as there is now a reading group in feminist theory meeting regularly and also the seminar for and by current post-graduate students in history. Without staff membership, with no student recruits to the area and with fewer of our members engaged in active research, papers based on work in-progress would become fewer. Once attendance became an obligation, the central purpose of the original group, the sharing and enjoyment of ongoing research, would be lost. I preferred to end with a bang rather than a whimper and my analysis suggested that this was the hour to make a definite decision.

After a moment of silent meditation followed by general discussion, it was moved by Ailsa Zainu'ddin, seconded by Marjorie Theobald 'that HEGG should now disband'. The motion, the first and last to be put at a meeting of HEGG, was passed nem, con. 15 December 1994.

Postscript: in 2014 a small group of eight women, now all retired, meet monthly to support each other in continuing research projects.

Chapter 10

100,000 up – concluding thoughts

10.1 Education Building Clayton
MUA IN-7308

Education as commenced at Monash in 1964 was vastly different to the faculty of 2014. There has been an accumulative total of 95,546 students belonging to the faculty in the years up to 2013, and in 2014 another 5,960 students enrolled. This means that 2014 also celebrates the faculty having its 100,000 student! In 1964 it was a one-campus operation, providing initial teacher training for secondary teachers, most of whom had taken their first degree at Monash. In 2014 there is a vast multi-campus faculty catering for a broad range of students, both undergraduates and graduates, and for those who had a first degree from a variety of institutions. The original aim was 'Training teachers appropriately', a paraphrase of a statement by the foundation Dean Professor Richard Selby Smith in a document in which he outlined his vision of how the faculty should develop. Initial teacher training was but a first step to a vision of a research-strong faculty. Selby Smith had seen education as not a discipline in itself, but an area that applied disciplines to educational issues: psychology, philosophy, sociology, economics and so forth. He translated this into four foundation fields that underpinned the DipEd course: educational thought, social foundations, philosophy and history, and psychology. Selby Smith appointed a highly competent and diverse team, who in addition to their expertise in one of the established disciplines also had a link with schools. Selby Smith had a school-based focus and saw every member of staff capable of visiting students in their teaching practicum. Initial end-on teacher training of secondary teachers was the initial purpose of the faculty and its bread and butter for many years. Compared with the University of Melbourne, Monash gave a higher priority to method work and teaching. There were full-time method staff in many fields and the methods were staffed with outstanding practitioners. The DipEd Monash provided in the 1960s and 1970s was a rigorous course that gave young teachers a thorough and comprehensive preparation both in practical terms and in understanding the social, psychological and philosophical context of their students and teachers. Principals and administrators formed a high opinion of what Monash offered and Monash education graduates were readily employed. This was a period when employment conditions were far more favourable than today. They were happy, busy and creative times. There were disappointments, especially Selby Smith's thwarted desire to have a concurrent course. What gradually emerged were quality offerings by staff in their specialities at what was then the BEd level.

In this he saw the initial training role as only part of what the faculty should do. Essential was continuing professional development and exposure of teachers to research and development from the relevant disciplines to teaching and learning in society. This evolved into a large postgraduate program with the devalued BEd replaced by the masters degree. To cope with the demand, especially for professional development for teachers and administrators, the masters was separated into a coursework degree with a minor thesis or project and a research masters which required a major thesis, usually after appropriate courses in research methodology.

Monash has been described by Graeme Davison as the last of the old universities rather than the first of the new. As the education faculty learned, the notion of the 'God professor' prevailed, with the professors making the key decisions as to what the university offered and how it ran. Monash University commenced at a time when the State Government was the main funding source and Monash itself was a creation of that government. The State Government was content to have representation on the councils of its then two universities without substantial interference. As student numbers grew with more and more people taking the opportunity of tertiary education, Commonwealth funding and decision-making (initially through the Murray Report) changed the situation. Increasingly universities became beholden to the Commonwealth and its agencies for funding. Market forces became an issue, with much funding based on student numbers, so universities quickly adapted, offering courses in fields where there was demand and applying the same approach to course levels. The masters degree became a key feature of the education faculty in attracting students.

The image of an education faculty as a Cinderella was firmly put to rest at Monash. Matheson's insistence on equality in terms of professorial appointments was important, as was the faculty achieving the first custom-built education building in Australia. The quality and output of research quickly made it one of the top faculties in the world and has put Monash's reputation beyond doubt.

Disciplines to issues

The 50 years has seen the demise of the disciplines as they were. They have been replaced by multi- and cross-disciplinary studies or issues such as 'gender', 'global' and so forth. So a field in which the faculty excelled, educational history, has disappeared. Similarly there has been a diminution in philosophy – once one of the great pillars of any faculty of education. There was the demise too of the professors. From being a university run by 'God professors', there are now those holding 'portfolios', and without any formal groupings like areas in the faculty, there is no longer the ability to fight for one's point of view in a committee such as Planning and Development. By misadventure the processes became less democratic and more hierarchical.

One-department faculty

When Dick White, as Dean, instigated the merging of the three schools into a single-department faculty, the change in organisation brought advantages and problems. The great advantage was that though people remained separated by geography, they now had to work closely across the distances to make best use of resources human, physical, and financial. The faculty now had greater ability to respond to changes in demand. Resources could be readily shifted to new areas with new appointments, free from demands to preserve existing fields. This was a tremendous advantage, enabling it to survive in times driven by student numbers and funds. Differences in outlook declined more rapidly than they otherwise would have, to the overall improvement of the faculty. The main problem concerned internal organisation. Quasi-departments, named at various times areas, divisions or groups, had existed at Clayton from the early days. Each had consisted of scholars with similar research and education-subject interests: psychology, special education, history and philosophy, sociology, curriculum, administration, and methods of teaching, which had advantages in research and in planning appropriate course offerings in the diverse fields and in considering what was offered at each level: diploma, bachelor, masters, doctoral. Peninsula also had divisions, but they were more related to elementary school subjects: art, music, English, mathematics and science, which did not fit easily with the Clayton groups. Gippsland was less formally divided. The groups had collegiality and were the means of electing representatives on committees, ensuring a degree of democratic participation. The merging into a single-department faculty provided the opportunity to increase cross-campus collegiality, but also created the problem of determining what new arrangement could at the same time maintain the existing level of involvement in decision-making. There was general acceptance that some form of collection of staff into groups that spanned the three campuses was desirable, but it was not obvious what the groups might be. Gradually new groups formed, less formal in nature and function than their predecessors.

The current Dean, John Loughran, has continued to encourage collegiality through informal groupings of staff with similar academic interests and by helping the professors of the faculty to gather about them scholars in their fields.

Over its 50 years the faculty has been fortunate in being so well served by its deans. They have all brought different skills to the post, often at the right time. Most have been willing to listen to their staff and consult. The faculty was a pioneer at Monash of staff participation in leadership, although this tradition has been diminished by the corporate structure the university now has. There have been issues over the years, differences arise, there has been conflict – but the faculty has survived these difficulties.

Change

For most of the life of the faculty the pattern has been one of constant change, of changing requirements from both governments and the university. Staff seemed to be under constant notice to cut costs on the grounds that these are 'difficult times'. Were there ever any good times? Initially salary savings were possible, giving the faculty important leeway, and then the Whitlam years saw an extravagance of spending on education and educational research. In the last decade through hardwork and sound management there have been funds to invest in new staff and more facilities on each campus.Within the constancy of change have been elements of continuity – while computers make it more efficient, research is still conducted in much the same way as it has been for the last century and there are still aspects of the teacher-pupil interactions that do not alter either in the lecture theatre, tutorial room or classroom. It is now an uneasy alliance with change, compliance and competition, as against tradition and independence.

Society today places heavy demands on all institutions – some shaped by the law, seemingly apart from common sense, and so the faculty faces requirements for occupational health and safety, for goal-setting, for personal health, for workplace health and even desk posture. The list of what one is *not* allowed to do grows. All these requirements to conform mean more administration, more form-filling by staff and more administrators.

So how to cope with all these competing demands yet try to adhere to the ancient traditions of professing learned fields and teaching? That is the problem the faculty has to face.

Waxing and waning

One disappointing element of change in the faculty is how once strong academic fields have been eroded. One notable example is the history of Australian education, a field in which Professor Dick Selleck was once the doyen, assisted by people such as John Lawry, John Cleverly, Andy Spaull, Ailsa Zainu'ddin, Marty Sullivan and Ann Shorten. Monash had been the pre-eminent faculty in the field. Today Rosalie Triolo, is the only person in this field.

Similarly there were once a number of prestigious philosophers: John Radvansky, Denis Phillips, Ron Laura, John Watts, Robyn Small, Colin Evers, David Aspin, Andre Gallois and others with a philosophical background such as Fazal Rizvi, who brought attention to the work in international education. Today we have a single philosopher: Jennifer Bleazby.

From being a faculty noted for its work in special education with the bachelor and then the masters degree in this field, closely connected to the work of the Krongold Centre, it became one devoid of these degrees; the surrender of them was widely lamented. Important work in autism and such fields continued but preparing teachers for children with a range of special needs did not. However, this was changed in 2013 with the Bachelor of Education (Special Education) introduced, serving an important need in Victorian schools.

Educational administration is another field that has largely disappeared, although Brenda Beatty and Phil Riley had offered leadership courses from 2006 until 2013. From the early days in the faculty, educational administration courses had been popular. Originally at the BEd level, they soon became important MEd courses both as research and coursework degrees. School principals and aspiring principals came in large numbers. In the 1970s and 1980s the Education Department regarded training in educational administration as important and also developed their own college. Ray McCulloch pioneered this work, attracting able staff such as Warren Mellor, Ron King and John McArthur and later Judith Chapman and Peter Gronn. He also made good use of highly competent practitioners like Michael Norman, who gave a practical dimension. McArthur went on to a senior administrative post, Mellor to UNESCO, Chapman to a chair in Western Australia then to ACU and Peter Gronn, who had gained a chair at Monash, was appointed to a chair in Edinburgh then a chair at Cambridge, where he is currently head of department. This field has diminished, but today there is a growing demand for courses in educational leadership, and the faculty is not yet equipped to return to this area. There has been a recent return to offering courses in leadership especially for new and aspiring principals, but there is the hope of a return to a bigger program in educational leadership and administration.

An array of 'fields' and issues courses have replaced the traditional foundation studies – adult education, work studies, gender studies, vocational education, international education and so forth.

In this era of change and technological innovation, education gave the worker an edge on those without education. Is this to still apply? Friedman in looking at the American scene feels that today 'we may have come to the end of the long era in which we could look to education, as we know it, as the all-purpose solution to problems of employment and productivity'.[1]

---

[1] Benjamin M Friedman 'Brave New Capitalists' Paradise': The Jobs?' *New York Review of Books*, 7 November 2013, pp. 74–76.

Managerialism

The dominant ideology of the current corporate university has been coined managerialism. There is no shortage of critics of managerialism. Keith Windshuttle in 2013 wrote of what he calls the crisis within universities, with the 'takeover by the forces of modernity' bringing about 'one of the most disturbing breakdowns in our cultural heritage.'[2] John Biggs stated:

> We need to go in another direction entirely. The tertiary sector needs to be far more imaginative and socially beneficial than acting as corporate service provider. The managerial university, however jazzed up and streamlined it might be, is holding society in intellectual stasis, except on a narrow technological front.[3]

James Allan in the *Spectator*: 'Australian universities may have become bedevilled with overweening bureaucracy and managerialism'.[4]

The managerial dominance is in contrast to what universities used to be like. The University of Melbourne, and Monash when it started, had their faculties and departments which of course partially reflected need and demand, but also had a strong element of offering the kinds of courses and fields that it was felt universities should be about.

Today numbers or demand for courses are the major determinant, allied with demand from external clients (both international and local) with special requirements. Students numbers represents funds, as do the provision of services by universities (school reviews, evaluations of projects), as well as grants of funds for research or development projects. ARC grants are symbols of significant accomplishment. Tenure for the non-tenured, promotion, extra staff – all depends on results from these sources of funds: students, external groups and grants. Staff performance and departmental performance are both measured. Staff need to abide by a host of policy documents; their performance is measured and assessed. Staff have to comply with both regulations and policies and show that they are complying. They also need to forecast their goals and performance for the future.

Further changes came when activity such as research output became a factor in funding, and then the Commonwealth required tertiary institutions to find their own funding for an increasing proportion of their expenditure.

---

[2] Keith Windshuttle Chronicle, in *Quadrant* October 2013, p. 8.
[3] John Biggs *Changing Universities: A Memoir About Academe in Different Places and Times* Strictly Literary, Hawthorn, Vic., 2013, p. 346.
[4] James Allan 'Parting Shots' *Spectator* Australia 29 December 2012.

The managerial corporate approach has meant that only people 'doctored up' – boasting refereed publications, preferably a book and some postdoctoral research – may obtain a position at the prestigious Monash faculty. This however, can simply give them the imprimatur which enables them then to seek positions elsewhere as they climb the corporate academic ladder. Faculty staff being lured elsewhere created problems as the Dean noted in his 2011 report: 'The Faculty has experienced difficulties recruiting suitably qualified academic staff to support the University's Academic Strengthening agenda'.

Effectiveness

In 2012 the Group of Eight universities proposed limiting entry to universities for school leavers to those with an ATAR (Australian Tertiary Admission Ranks) score of at least 60. The University of NSW announced it intended to limit entry to students with an ATAR score of 80 or more. It was also realised that ATAR scores are a 'blunt and inaccurate indicator of ability to cope with the academic work load'.[5]

During 2013 there was concern that those with low ATAR scores were entering courses for teacher education. There continued to be concern about the quality of students entering the teaching profession. In 2013 the Australian Education Union reiterated its concern in this area and asked the government to recruit from the top 30 per cent of school leavers.[6]

What stood out to the observer in 2013 was the many ways one could now enter teaching.[7] Monash had as many ways as any other institution, with the primary/secondary division being only one. Some still preferred the end-on DipEd to a first degree. Increasingly popular were combined degrees. Melbourne had a Master of Teaching as a post-first degree training course. Monash in 2013 and 2014 could boast more applications than the 1000 places available. Proctor cites '500 students entering Bachelor of Education programs at Monash with ATAR scores of over 70 – placing them in the top 30 per cent of their cohort'.[8] Debbie Corrigan strongly rejected the claims of people not academically capable entering teaching – the facts showed otherwise. Today at Clayton ATAR scores are over 80 for education, with most students over 85; on other campuses they are over 70, mostly at 75.

---

[5] *The Australian* 24 July 2013.
[6] *The Australian* 6 April 2013.
[7] Julia Proctor, 'Bright Sparks Driven by Passion to Teach' *Age* 25 February 2013.
[8] Ibid.

A long-held concern was the extent to which student-teachers' skills, competencies and attitudes to teaching and learning are altered by the seasoned practitioners in the school in which they commence their teaching career. It is commonly asserted that the new teacher is told by his experienced colleagues in his first school to forget what he has been told by academics in education faculties. Field Rickards, Dean of Education at the University of Melbourne says this 'recycles teaching practices from one generation to another'.[9] This is perceived as a perpetuation that holds off change.

Politics

A feature of university life is of course the politics. Any degree of competition for students, grants and other resources engenders political battles. So unofficial groups form around a variety of issues. Henry Kissinger famously remarked that 'university politics are vicious precisely because the stakes are so small.' To the participants these stakes are not small at all. Power battles are inevitable in all forms of human organisation – how to recognise this yet also build *esprit de corps*? The Faculty of Education is no different in this respect and throughout its history there have been political battles. Sometimes these were played out at the Planning & Development meetings, at Faculty Board, sometimes at staff meetings, often over coffee and inevitably in the corridors.

In the early decades, many staff in the faculty were members of FAUSA; some indeed like Andy Spaull, Gerald Burke and Marty Sullivan were quite active. Membership from the faculty was not strong and most of those who were members were hardly militant. Issues were more nationwide ones affecting academics. Under the new union, the National Tertiary Education Union (NTEU), things became different. This was a union that included general (professional) as well as academic staff. The changing times and the move to a more corporate and centralised Monash, with more non-tenured appointments (the faculty is proud of the low ratio it has of non-tenured staff), a cycle of cutbacks and economies, and a diminished ability for staff to participate in decision-making, meant a bigger role for NTEU. More staff joined, and more issues within the faculty were taken up, as individuals had important grievances. The union and their representatives played an important role in modifying and correcting certain decisions.

The faculty has kept a strong presence on the Monash Branch Committee of the NTEU, with Rosamund Winter, Joel Windle, Anne Prince, David Zyngier, Marc Pruyn, Stephen Keast and Kay Ritchie all serving as ordinary

---

[9] Field Rickards, as reported in *The Australian* 29 August 2012.

10.2 Andy Spaull and Gerald Burke in a FAUSA picket line on Wellington Road.
Education Faculty

10.3 Rosamund Winter and Jane Southcott receiving 20 years certificates from the National Tertiary Education Union.
Education Faculty

members (i.e. non-executive). At the end of 2013, the union acknowledged the many foundation members; Jane Southcott and Rosamund Winter were among those who have been union members for 20 years.

From a committee consisting of the Dean, group heads and others meeting as P&D, came a Senior Advisory Group with the Dean and Heads of School for policy and forward planning. This has been replaced by a Senior Managers Group – and now with a Faculty Executive with an Executive Dean reporting centrally. The consultative collegial approach has gone. Former Dean Dick White, talking with some of his contemporaries about the university today, observed: 'They spoke of the growth of bureaucracy at Monash, and the concomitant shift in power and responsibility, so that deans and heads of departments no longer lead.'

Contributions – achievements

It is invidious to try to assess the achievements and contributions made by the faculty over its 50 years and list the people associated with them. Looking back though we can identify a successful initial teacher education course for secondary teachers that in its time was innovative. At Peninsula there was a tradition of excellence in the education of primary teachers that continues today. Peninsula continues to be recognised internationally for programs in early childhood teaching and research. At Gippsland innovative teacher training programs have embraced the local community to the benefit of both parties. Pioneering work in distance education has opened opportunities to more people for further education and training. Berwick campus is now offering exciting opportunities.

A continuing aim of the faculty on each campus has been the achievement of best practice in initial teacher education. Over the 50 years there have been difficult challenges. The end of free secondments and funds shortages meant institutions could no longer supervise students' teaching practice with the same degree of rigour. This took its toll on quality.

The work of the faculty has had influence at the school level on professionals both in education and wider fields and its research and teaching has made its name at both the national and international levels.

Psychology has always been recognised as a pillar discipline in education – initially with a focus on social psychology, but also including work in children's cognitive development, attitude measurement, learning theory, and new research in the field of neuropsychology. Special education has had a particularly high profile in research, teaching and in clinical work with children with special needs, including the gifted. There has also been leading work from those with an inclusive approach for children with special needs. The Krongold Centre served the community, giving help to many young people and their families. Important work was also undertaken in the fields of hearing impairment and deafness and on autism spectrum disorders. Both at Peninsula and at Clayton's Elwyn Morey Centre, research and teaching in the field of early childhood has drawn positive attention.

The faculty has had a long history of community engagement, especially with the educational community. The Parent-Teacher Centre provided programs for the community on parenting; numerous staff, particularly the method staff, served on school councils, helped with curriculum in schools, served on state education committees and boards, federal advisory committees and played key roles in the public examination system and on course committees from the earliest days of matriculation to the present VCE. Curriculum work has also been national and international. Notable too has been the faculty's work with subject associations, providing leadership in both curriculum and professional development.

For many years the faculty enjoyed close links with what used to be called the Education Department, its staff and schools. In earlier years the department was generous to the faculty with secondments of staff strengthening method programs and providing time release for teachers to undertake higher degree courses. The secondments for special education were especially important. The faculty is also proud of its links with non-government schools and with educational regions.

The field of educational measurement and testing has always been a prominent element of the faculty's work, both in courses taught, research training and in working with outside examination and measurement bodies such as ACER and the various senior secondary examination boards. Important too were alternative approaches to research methodology – anthropological approaches, ethnographic research and other qualitative methods. There have been from these groups research and publications on how students learn and how teachers teach.

The faculty's research profile has always been high, in ARC research grants to both individuals and groups, and in contract research for governments, school systems and community groups. The participation of the faculty with schools and community groups has been a special strength.

The faculty can also boast some great teachers, indeed some charismatic teachers, who have had a strong influence on students.

Social education has been another pillar of the faculty in both teaching and research, with educational sociology a major strength. Important social-science work has been undertaken at the school level as well as within the faculty. Developments have taken this work beyond sociology, addressing international issues and involving other disciplines. The development of an innovative higher education degree in adult and workplace learning was an important extension of this field.

History of education has also had a high profile, as has philosophy of education. There has been major scholarly work undertaken in both fields which has received international recognition. In history there has been significant work in regard to the history of Australian education and important scholarship too on British education. There was pioneer work on the education of women and girls. There has been a long tradition of involvement with research and teaching on higher education. Music and drama have also featured in recent years.

Science education has been a special feature of the faculty's work, evolving within a supportive research environment. There have been important projects within the faculty in relation to science education as well as key research and the setting up of research bodies in Australia. This group has established an international reputation that has attracted to the faculty significant international scholars. An important offshoot has been the PEEL project with implications for teaching and learning across the curriculum, a project that has been sustained over many years both in Australia and internationally.

Research and teaching in mathematics education and in many dimensions of mathematics have been a feature over a long period, including issues such as mathematics and gender, values and mathematics and mathematics at all levels, primary and secondary. There have been close links with the science faculty and a role in bringing to fruition the John Monash Science School. More recently has been important work in international education (not to be confused with teaching in international locations, which has also featured), and recent years have seen a number of major federally funded research projects in the field of English language and literacy. From early on the faculty has been a lead in the teaching of English and languages.

The faculty's work in the field of social justice has also been important. The publication of *On Rights and Inequalities in Australian Education* (1970), pioneered this area which was quickly taken up by the Karmel Report and the Whitlam government's education policy. This followed a 1968 seminar in the faculty focusing on the Universal Declaration of Human Rights. Other notable work included an Australian Schools Commission report and a major study of the introduction of the then new VCE. A continuing strand has been major research examining economic and social inequalities. Work in the fields of ethnicity and multiculturalism (the term being invented within the faculty) has had a strong tradition. Women's studies and Indigenous education have recently gained a higher profile. New fields have featured such as music education, both in terms of method work and research, and drama education.

From the 1970s the faculty made its mark nationally with the large number of postgraduate students undertaking both professional and research courses. The number undertaking research degrees was quite dramatic. There was also a spin-off in the number of Monash education graduates who took chairs and senior appointments both in Australia and overseas. This strength in education research has continued. In recent years for example, one of the most outstanding achievements of the vibrant student-led research community in the faculty has been the publication of a book by Monash University Publishing in which all chapters have been contributed and the volume edited by HDR students. There has been considerable support to research students and under the guidance of their supervisors many students have published in journals, books and conference proceedings. A feature has been the work of MERC (the Monash Education Research Community) – a successful association run by research students, with regular seminars both by students and invited staff and an annual four-day conference.Innovation has continued to drive the Faculty's work, both in its initial teacher training courses and at post-graduate level. The development of new courses and degrees has been a continuing feature of the Faculty's work. The Faculty developed a Doctorate of Education and pioneered a course work Masters, offering a wide range of subjects to a large number of students, catering for the needs of the time. Special Education was pioneered by the Faculty and supplied qualified teachers to schools, and to other community groups. The Bachelor of Adult Learning and Development represented a completely new field of study for the Faculty, as did the development of the undergraduate Double Degree programs. Gippsland and Peninsula have also developed special courses to meet local needs, Sport and Outdoor Recreation being one example. Variations in courses in early childhood education have been designed to meet special needs and achieve greater equity. The Faculty was a pioneer in offering summer school subjects, a trend to be continued in the new accelerated Master of Teaching degree.

A special feature of the Faculty was the creation of a continuing vacant academic post to enable prominent scholars to be invited from overseas. So the

Faculty enjoyed the company for some months each year of distinguished scholars. This greatly enriched its scholarship and also helped consolidate links with scholars worldwide. The various sections of the Faculty were able to select scholars relevant to their field. This program, which continues to this day, is different to the University-wide Visiting Professor program that the Faculty also used, however under the Visiting Lecturer scheme many more scholars could be brought to the Faculty.

Links with other faculties and departments within Monash University have waxed and waned, however there have been, at various stages, important partnerships with medicine (Special Education and Psychology), and with Arts (languages and Asian Studies) and in more recent years collaboration with Faculties jointly offering the undergraduate Double Degree programs.

In terms of courses – there have been innovations for initial teacher training courses at all levels (early Childhood, primary, secondary and even tertiary); within these courses have been experimentation to achieve more effective courses. The Faculty pioneered course work Masters offering a wide range of courses to a large number of students, catering for the needs of the time. As the Faculty grew in strength so did research by students in Masters or PhD. Special Education was pioneered by the Faculty- supplying qualified teachers in this field to schools, and to other community groups. Gippsland and Peninsula have also offered special courses to meet local needs – Sport and Outdoor Recreation being one, and variations of early childhood education to meet special needs and achieve more equity. The Faculty was a first in offering courses in summer, a trend continued with the possibility in the new Master of Teaching to undertaken an accelerated course.

Future

Change will continue and technology will have its impact. Professor Neil Selwyn has raised the issue of MOOCs – massive open online courses. Today a number of bodies, both universities as well as other institutions, offer courses at school and university level online. Some offerings are by top academics, aided by the best of teaching technology, doing courses in subjects basic to universities everywhere – introductory physics, economics, and some not-so-introductory courses. Some of these are offered for credit towards an online degree; some are provided for a fee; some are free. Students now have access to not just an enormous amount of data, but online courses taught in their specialities. Where is the dynamics of peer contact?

At an international science conference in Penang in November 2013, Gunstone drew attention to the ready availability of data:

> We are already at a point in my country (and many others) where it is correct to assume that every student carries with them at all times a device that enables them to connect with any one of a dozen encyclopaedias or other reference forms whenever we want them to. This gives the most powerful argument possible to support the point at which I began this paper – these technological developments make it even more crucial to stop the timewasting and distracting and pointless (and very disengaging) practice of focusing only on decontextualized facts as to what science is – in Schwab's terms to once and for all recognise that science is not 'a nearly unmitigated rhetoric of conclusions', and so we should not teach it and assess it as if it was.

This challenge exists for all fields, not just science.

How can educators make a contribution? At a Melbourne seminar in 1965, the eminent American economist John Kenneth Galbraith stated:

> It is the vanity of educators that they shape the educational system to their chosen image. They are not without influence, but here, as elsewhere, the determining influence is the industrial system. This has shaped the educational system of most countries in the past. It continues to do so.[10]

The material in this work suggests that Galbraith was right – the faculty has had to give way to pressures and demands from above, with the policy makers and funders reacting to the demands of what he called 'the industrial system', which might be more aptly described as the economy.

However, Galbraith did acknowledge that educators are 'not without influence', so within these confines the Faculty of Education at Monash has had more influence than most.

As Samuel Johnson in his *History of Rasselas* (1825) states:

> Ye who listen with credulity to the whispers of fancy, and pursue with eagerness the phantoms of hope; who expect that age will perform the promises of youth, and that the deficiencies of the present day will be supplied by the morrow…'[11]

---

[10] J K Galbraith 'Employment, Education and the Industrial System', 1965.
[11] Samuel Johnson *The History of Rasselas Prince of Abyssinia* (1759), Oxford Works of Samuel Johnson, 1825.

Anyone who takes an academic post in an education faculty must, despite the realities, believe in what Johnson calls 'the phantoms of hope', and also believe that they will in their teaching and research make a difference.

10.4 After a graduation ceremony, Clayton.
Claude Sironi, Education Faculty

Index

Bold type indicates a photograph.

Note: Aside from the names of the staff listed, contents of staff biographies at the end of some chapters have not been indexed, nor has the Preface or Author's introduction.

50th Anniversary of Monash   292, 349, 345, 351
AARE   292, 390
AARE prize   201
Abbott Government   324
ABC   374
Aboriginal affairs   95
Aboriginal descent   318
Aboriginal education   17, 323
Aboriginal research   377
Academic dress   17, 131, 236
Academic Registrar   379, 383
Academic strengthening   318, 319, 433
accommodation   35–7, 408
Accounting education   333
ACER   10, 17, 152, 338, 382, 389, 398, 437
achievements of faculty   436
active learning   157
Adlerian   150
administration of faculty   232, 332, 334, 239, 406
administrative staff   88, 243, 347
Admissions & Students services   347
adult learning   439
Advanced skills teacher   194
Advisory Board   324
AERA   239, 390
affiliated with Monash   212
affirmative action   160
Agbenyega, Joseph, bio   362
age of staff   318, 321
AITSL   325
Albon, Nerissa   415
Alexander Theatre   36, 130, 133
Allan, James   432
Allen, D Ian   30, 46
Allen, Louise   320
Alonso, Jose   350
ALP   391
alumni   344
Alumni Association   229
Amalgamations   203, 204, 205, 207, 210, 244
American Education Research Journal   98, 99
Amos, Joan   372
Amurosidis, Marika   372
Anderson, Angelika, bio   310
Anderson, Don   379–80
Anderson, Peter
  bio   369
  recollection   377, **377**
Anderson, Ray (biology)   100, 104, 151
Anderson, Raymond McD   208, 210, **211**, 216, 220
  bio   252
Andrews, Paul   371
Anglican   375
Angus, Lawrence   195, 237, 295, **297**, 375, 394
  bio   184
Apple, Michael   171
appointment of staff   1, 2, 13, 14, 26, 29, 31, 34, 77, 87, 89, 105, 139, 142, 143, 158, 169, 174, 243, 260, 321, 326, 408
APress   218
AQF   346
ARC grants   153, 162, 169, 192, 194, 223, 292, 342, 379, 399, 437
ARC Linkage   342
Archbishop of Sydney   375
Archer, Francis   374
Area 1, psychology   124, 141, 143
Area 2, social and comparative   143
Area 3, historical and philosophical   143
Area 4, research & evaluation   143
Area 5, Curriculum Studies   143
Area 6, Ed. Administration   143
Area 7, Special Education   124, 143
Areas   45, 77, 86, 87, 105, 174, 410
Art and Embellishment Committee   79
Art works   79
Arts Faculty, Monash   200
Asche, Austin   81
ASERA   390, 400
Ashcroft, Evelyn   30
Asher, the Hon. Louise   371
Ashwood Special School   133
Asia Pacific Education Centre   218
Asian languages   193
Asian Studies   440
Asian Studies Association   424
Askew, Mike   319, 348, 350
  bio   354
Aspin, Dean David   150, 189, 190, **191**, 195, **198**, **200**, 207, 212, 214–16, 234, 236, 410, **422**, 430
  bio   244, **245**
Aspinall, Most Reverend Phillip   375

Aspinall, Sue 146, 197
Assistant Registrar 146
Associate Dean, created 46, 239, 289, 332
Associate Dean (Education) 322, 348
Associate Dean (Engagement) 322, 348
Associate Dean (International) 239, 329
Associate Dean (Peninsula) 322
Associate Dean (Research degrees) 348
Associate Dean (Research) 225, 233, 239, 348
Associate Dean (Staff) 185, 239
Associate Dean (Teaching) 233, 239, 322, 394
Associates of the Faculty 89–90
ASTEP 225
ATAR scores 326, 345–6, 433
Atkins, Ken, architect 36, 408
Atkinson, Bernadette 378
Atkinson, Elaine 152
Atkinson, Henry 378
attitude measurement 62, 397, 398, 436
Attwood, Daphne 145
AUC 2, 3, 36, 37, 74, 124, 126, 127, 129
audit report 241
Auld, Glenn 319
AUQA 317
AusAID 291
Ausburn, Floyd 83, **96**, 349
   bio 117
Austin, Bon 100
Australian Association for Research in Education 390
Australian Association for the Teaching of English 151
Australian Association of Teacher Education 329
Australian Catholic University 348
Australian College of Education 404, 408
Australian College of Nursing 162
Australian Computer Society 420
Australian Council for Computers in Education 421
Australian Council of Deans Education 231, 298
Australian Education Council 164
Australian High Commission (Malaysia) 416
Australian Journal of Education 201
Australian Psychological Society 35
Australian Quality Frameworks 346
Australian Research Grants Committee 192, 194, 223
Australian Schools Commission 84, 438
Australian Science Education Research Association (ASERA), founded 51
Australian Science show 196
Australian Science Teachers Association 202, 225
Australian Universities Commission (AUC) 1, 3, 74
   visit 89

Australian Universities Quality Agency 317
autism 168, 437

Bachelor of
   Early Childhood 328
   Business 337
   Early Childhood Education 234
   Adult Learning and Development 328
   Early Childhood Studies 318
   Education (Early Years) 345
   Education (Primary) 337, 338
   Education (Secondary) 328
   Education (Special Education) 330, 431
   Primary Education 329
   Science Education 22
   Special Education 130, 133, 135
      becomes part-time 136, 167, 168
   Sport and Outdoor Recreation 328, 330, 337–8, 439, 440
   Teaching 214
Badger, Ann 104, 374
Baird, John 155, 156, **157**, **235**
Baker, Monica 350
Ballarat University 329
Balson, Maurice 11, **12**, 15, 34, 78, **96**, 150, 192, 408
   appointed 8
banana, faculty colour 17, 236
Bantock, G H 98
Bao, Dat, bio 308–9
Barber, Anna 151
Barkatsas, Tasos, bio 313
Barnes, Douglas 171
Bartak, Lawrence 35, 79, 84, 133, 135–6, 138, 168, 218, 220, 234
   appointed 102
   bio 115
Basten, Sir Henry 37, 38
Batten Hugh 77, 86
   appointed 31
   bio 58
   Group 70 48
   leaves 102, 104
Beatty, Brenda 292, 420, 431
BEd 16, 31, 46, 47, 73, 75, 78, 148, 163,170, 214, 328
BEd Committee 163
BEd Studies 193, 231
BEd subjects 77
BEd summer teaching 93–4
Beddie, Francesca 325
Beeson, Geoff, doctorate 85, 374
Bell, Garry 104
Bennett, David 147
   bio 181
Bennett, Rosemary, bio 257
Benson, John 374

Bertram, Adam, bio   355
Berwick   233, 318, **319**, 323, 324, 325, 330, 331, 335, 338, 345
Bessant, Bob   85
   doctorate   46
Best, Dawn   194
Best, Gil   35, 133, 134, 154, 160, 194
   appointed   102
   bio   115
Betts, Jennifer   231
bibliographies   419
Biddle, Bruce, visiting professor   43
Biggs, John   38, 432, **380**
   recollection   378–83
   resigns   44
Binary system   203, 215
Binishell   211
biology   155, 408
biology education   333
Biology method   17
Birch Cottage   24, 36
Bishop, Alan   152–3, **196**, 239, **246**, 350
   bio   246
Bishundayal, Deo   320
Black, Christopher   374
Black, Shlomo   320
Blackburn Report   144, 149, 160, 203
Blackwood Hall   410
Blackwood, Robert   7
Blane, Dudley   104, 153, 192, 231
   bio   179
Bleazby, Jennifer   430
   bio   353
Bloomfield, Reba   409
Bloomfield, the Hon. John   2, 31, 79
Bluett, Mary   373
Bodi, Leslie   52
Boeha, Beno   372, **373**
book costs   169
Bottroff, Geoff   374
Boudille, Sylvester   374
Bourke, Colin   377
Bourke, Peter   133
Bourke, Sidney   374
Boyd, Robert   374
Boyle, Chris, bio   312
Boyle, Frances   40, 52, 146, 197, 385
Bradley, Dianne   190
Brereton, Elida   151, 372
Brewin, Michael   374
Briggs, Leanne   133
Brighton Secondary College   237
Brisset, David   151
Broadbent, Samantha   350
Brooke, John   104, 151, 374
Brooks, Jane   **291**
Brown, Howard   140, 293

   bio   118
   recollection   384–5
   tea club   30
Brown, Jenny   **184**
   bio   183
   recollection   383–4
   retired   293
Brown, Justice Sally   **217**
Brown, Kay   100
Brown, Trent, bio   303
Brubaker, Nathan, bio   366
Brumby, Margaret   122, 147, 158, 180
Brunton, Trudi   325, 348
budget (Monash)   139, 148, 168–9, 233, 326
budget cuts   195, 199, 231, 233, 243, 331
building (education)   35–7, **37**
Building Committee   408
building
   costs   128
   extensions   409
   requirements   408
   stairs that led nowhere   **97**
Bulfin, Scott   342, 421
Bullivant, Brian   41, **71**, 154
   bio   69
Bullock, Philip   339
Burke, Gerald   34, **67**, 162, 169, 243, 339, 341, 434, **435**
   appointed   35
   bio   66
   recollection   385–8
   retired   292–3
Burke, Geraldine, bio   367
Burke, Joanne, bio   311
Burke, Prue   421, 422
Burrow, Sharon   237
Burwood Teachers College   161
Business Management Education   333, 338
Butchart, J D   80, 170, 379
Butler, Walter   15
Button, the Hon. John   204
Buxton, Michael   374, 385
   bio   186
Byrne, Ed   348, 329n17

Cahill, Des   374
Cairns, Len   208, 212, 213, 216, 229, **230**
   bio   250
Callaghan, Steve   383
Calvert, Anne   422
Cambridge University   152, 324
Campus, Deans   348
Campus Services   348
candidates   24, 35, 85, 89, 95, 165, 170, 221, 262, 275, 370
career paths, women   344

Carr, Paul   321
Carroll, Brian   83
    bio   113
Carton, Jackie   409
Case, Jennifer   374
Casinader, Niranjan, bio   358
Cater, Mal   374
Caulfield Institute of Technology   206
CEET   293, 338
Centre for Continuing Education   218
Centre for Health and Social Science   218
Centre for High Education   162
Centre for Human Stress Management & Research   192
Centre for International Education   218–19
Centre for Migrant Studies   89, 154
Centre for Quality Learning and Teaching   219
Centre for research   406
Centre for Research into Aboriginal Affairs   377
Centre for Research into Aboriginal Affairs   95, 377
Centre for Science, Mathematics & Technology Education   192, 218, 399
Centre for the Economics of Education and Training   293, 338–9
Centre for the Study of Higher Education   236, 239
centres   192, 218, 219
Chair in Science and Technology Education   225
Chair of areas   105
Chair of education   173, 197, 214, 220, 223, 226
    first chair   6
Chair of Educational Policy & Administration   223–5
Chair of special education   197
Chairs, naming   170
Challen, Bishop Michael   237
Chan, Helen   164
Chan, Philip   350
Chandler High School   91
Chandler, Diane   138, 336–7
change   195, 228, 350, 351, 392
Chapman, Denise   421
Chapman, Judith   **120**, 160, 161, 162, 192, 194, 195, 226, 421, 431
    bio   120
Chatterton, Crystal   321, 323, 335, 348
Cheeseman, Jill, bio   365
Chellappah, Naren   349
Chelsea College Centre for Science Education   399
Cheltenham Secondary College   411
chemistry   389
Chemistry education   333
Chessell, Pam   374
Chessman, Lee   88, 145, 147
child and community development   319
Child Development, taught   16
Child Study Centre   24, 35, 36, 126
    renamed Elwyn Morey   39
China visit   99
Chisholm Institute of Technology   207, 208
choir   *see* social life
Chou, Anita   350
Chowdury, Raqib   417, 420
Christmas party   *see* social life
Chubb, Ian   204, 213–14, 216
Churchill   211
Cinderella, faculty   4, 12, 37, 139, 428
Clark, David   104, 152
Clark, Doug   104, 152, 288
Clarke, Barbara   152, 288, 322, 326
Clarkson, Phil   152
class size   236
classroom teaching   153
Clayton   290
Clayton, Margaret   374
Cleary, Canon Ray   375
Clements, 'Ken' McKenzie   133, 152, 172, 396, 422
    bio   113
Cleverley, John   74, **85**, 386, 430
    bio   58
    appointed   31
    Group 70   48
Clift, John, HERU   39, **85**, 382
Clough Jim   47
    doctorate   85
Clunies, Ross, Ian   170
Clyne, Michael   154
Coates, Tom   80, 333
Cochrane, Don   52, 78, 148, 380
Cohen, Senator Sam   391
College of Nursing   85
collegiality   193, 244, 384, 389, 396
Comerford, Tom   104
Commercial Studies method   17, 30, 46, 100, 151
Commission on University Affairs   42
committees   232
Commonwealth Government   297, 331, 350
Commonwealth scholarship scheme   18, 391
Comparative Education   13
competencies for teaching 434
compliance   339–40, 341, 347
Compliance documentation   340
computers   87, 228
    in education   420
    in schools   144
Conabere, Tony   374
concurrent degree   17, 22, 54, 427

conference travel   237, 289
Connell, William (Bill) F   91, 148
Connolly, Richard   350
Connor, Lindsey   375
continuing posts   240
Cook Island   257, 269, 415
Cook, (Butler) Sharon   145
Cooper, Rebecca   350
    bio   310–11
Coordinator of DipEd   198, 407, 409
Cope, Andrew   bio 257, 263, 264
Corbitt, Brian   374
Corboy, Anne Marie   374
Corporate Monash   204, 244, 432
Corrigan, Deborah (Debbie)   **217**, 318, 319, **320**, 325, 331, 345, 348, 351, 433
    bio   247
Costello, the Rev. Tim   375
Couchman, Peter   403
Coulson. John   372
Coulter, Frank   47
Country Education Project   84, 403
course architecture   346
courses   328, 337
    in Special Education   125
coursework degrees   78, 170
Courtis, Wilbur   151
Cowell, Don   133
CRAA   377–8
Craven, Ron   151
Crawford, Renée   361
Crean, the Hon. Simon   **200**
Creed, Barbara   374
cricket   see social life
Cronbach, Lee   98
cross cultural issues   219
cultural sociology of education   319
culture of faculty   322, 399, 406
Cumming, Alan   190
Cunningham, Ken   170
Curriculum Development Centre   148
Curriculum Laboratory   see Library & Media Resource Centre
Curry, Norman   140, 166
Curtis, Samantha   348
cutbacks   223
Cutter-Mackenzie, Amy   292

deafness   437
Deakin, Bess, doctorate   85
Dean   189, 201, 215, 217, 226, 298, 316, 321, 348, 407
    acting   129
    executive   332
    first   8
    role of   86, 87
    new   88, 95

Dean's award   292, 344
Dean's Diary   217
DEECD   344
Deery, Stephen   374
DEET   192, 195, 219
DEETYA   236
demand for teachers   231, 406
demand-driven funding   324
demands on staff   297
demonstration (Krongold)   131–3
Dent, Arthur   387
Department of Social Security (C'wealth)   127
Departments   429
Deppeler, Joanne   322, 342, **343**, 350
    bio   122
Deputy Dean   325, 345, 348
Derham, David   55
De-schooling   99
Desktop Information Technology Strategy   418
desktop technology   228
Dethick, Bronwyn   420
Development office   291, 293
'Dick'   234
Dickinson, A R   30
DIISR   319
Dimistriadis, Grego   320
DipEd   4, 6, 13, 16, 18, 20, 3, 148, 162, 163, 170,192, 198, 221, 232, 345, 370, 388, 401, 402, 405, 427
    criticism   99, 105
    deficiencies   48
    director of   162
    experimental groups   48–50
    numbers   48, 73, 76
    quotas   51, 76, 81
    selection   74, 75
    staff   177
DipEd Coordinator   162
DipEd, tertiary   39, 73, 82
Diploma in Educational Psychology   35, 77, 148, 163
Diploma of Teaching Primary   206
direction of the faculty   89
Director of Education (Vic)   5
Director-General Education   140
disabled people   168
disciplines   297
Discovery Award   342
Discovery project   292, 342
discrimination   341
display of books, publications & theses   **241, 242**
distance education   211–12, 436
Division 1, psychology   143
Division 2, social and comparative   143
Division 3, historical and philosophical   143

Division 4, research & evaluation   143
Division 5, curriculum studies   143
Division 6, ed administration   143
Division 7, special education   143
Divisions (areas)   142
Dobson, Norman   46, 140–1
   appointed   31
   bio   63
Docking, Russell, doctorate   85
Doctor of Letters   321
Doctor of Philosophy   *see* PhD
Doctoral award   292
Doctoral candidates   221
doctoral students   165, 281, 345
Doctoral tracks   190, 191, 192
Doctorate in Education   190–1,439
doctorates   85, 95, 243, 389
Doecke, Brenton   293
donations   127
Dor, Joe   231
Double degree   214, 233, 236, 322, 328, 337–8
Douglas, Annette,   239
Dow, Gwen   100
Drake, Ian, retired   231
Drama education   333
dress of students   401–2
Duffy, Leo   46, 151
Dunbar, Noel   95
Duncan, John   201, 209
Dunn, Sydney   **19**, 39, 47, 75, 124, 126, **144**, 152, 170, 243, 382, 385–6, 398, 406, 410
   bio   17–18
   hon. degree   148
   leaves   88
   research   73
Duplicating   39, 40, 52, 197
Dyson, Michael   bio 255, 421

Earle, Jeshka   350
Early career researcher   292, 342, 344
Early Childhood Education   195, 338
Early childhood studies   318
EAS   173
Economics and Politics   171, 380, 385, 404
Economics education   333, 401
Economics method   15, 17, 30, 104,151, 401, 402
ECOPS   171, 380, 385, 404
EdD   190–1, 231, 236
Education as export   414
Education building
   Clayton   35–7
   extension   95
   naming   54–5
Education Department (Vic)   18, 21,104, 130, 135, 140. 146, 149, 166, 173, 193, 207, 385, 406, 431

Education doctorate   190–1
Education faculties, 'Cinderella'   4, 12, 37, 139, 428
Education for girls   91–2, 158, 195, 226, 396
Education for women   226, 227, 317, 344, 396, 418–25
Education forum   349
education history   97, 411–13, 421
Education Research and Development Committee   77, 88, 91
Education Research Officer   378–82
Education revolution   289-290
Education Services (Faculty)   348
Educational administration   161, 162, 195, 397, 410, 431
Educational Materials Centre   *see* Library & Media Resource Centre
Educational measurement   16, 17, 398, 437
Educational Policy & Administration (chair)   195, 223
Educational Psychology   13, 34
Educational resources   223, 290
Educational Services Centre   *see* Library & Media Resource Centre
Educational system, shaping   441
Edwards, Hazel   422
Edwards, Julie   415
Edwards, Peter   133
   bio   116
Edwards, Philip   218
EFT   335
EFTS   73, 76, 78, 86, 99, 126, 148, 168, 169, 233, 236,
EFTSL   318
Egan, Sue   223, 290, **291**, 420
Eggleston, Rosemary   377
electives   232
Elliott, Lorraine (secretary)   147
Elliott, Lorraine, MP   372
Elms, Maureen   84
elocution   383
Eltham College 84
Elwyn Morey Child Study Centre   39, 47, 131, 138, 147, 160, 168,   219, 241, 437
email interaction   414
Emerson School   133, 373
Emerson, Les   129, 130, 135
Engagement services   339, 348
Engagements and Partnerships office   342
Engineering Faculty Monash   200
English as a second language   415
English language teaching   160
English method   16, 30, 104, 151
enrolments   85, 148, 170
enrolments in pre-service courses   213
equal opportunity   92, 158, 226, 339, 344, 391, 396, 405

equal pay for women 51
equality in education 391
Equity & Diversity Committee 341
ERA 319, 325, 344
ERDC 99, 148, 386
ERIC 418
Erickson, Gaalen 171
ethnocultural pluralism 154
ethnographic research 390, 437
Eunson, Warwick 206
Evans, Hazel 40, 146, 197, 385
Evans, Terry 374
Evers, Colin 189, 201, 234 , 430
 bio 182
exceptional children 130

Faculty administration 46, 104–5
Faculty Board 16, 18, 22, 31, 45, 46, 51, 83, 86, 125, 139, 160, 208, 212, 295, 298, 328, 331
 abolished 332
 executive 80, 289, 436
 representation 80
 representatives 332
 'state of the art' reports 91
Faculty choir *see* social life
Faculty committees 86–7, 288, 335
Faculty culture 322, 341, 395
Faculty Day **220**, 349
Faculty governance 104–5, 142–3
Faculty Manager 210, 289, 347, 348
Faculty of Arts 22, 328
Faculty organisation 86
Faculty press 218
Faculty Registrar 208, 239
Faculty review 189–90, 323, 324, 335
Faculty Secretary 52, 88, 144, 146, 197, 200, 201, 208, 210, 230, 407, 410
Faine, Miriam 339
Fairbanks, Margrette 144, **145**, 163, 194
Farrell, Lesley 151, 231, 292, 374
 bio 181
Fary, Barbara 231, 374
Fary, Norman 374
Faulkner, Julie 416, 421
Federation of Australian Universities Staff Associations (FAUSA) 177, 434, **435**
Federation University Australia 329
Feehan, Ann 104, **107**, 151, 374
fees 148, 203, 231, 345
Feith, Herb 52
Feith, Betty 422
Fellows of the Faculty 89–90
female students 401–2
Feminist Readings 228
Fennema, Elizabeth 396
Fensham award 292

Fensham, Peter 29, **33**, 35, 38, 47, 55, 86, 104, **107**, 188, **144**, 152, 166, 170, 172, 173, **174**, 194, 195, 203, 219, 225, **235**, 316, 375, 385–6, 387, 399, 406, 410
 appointed 31
 ASERA 51
 bio 31–2, 201–3
 Group 70 48
 becomes Dean 142
 recollection 388–91
 retired 201–2
Ferrier, Luci 350
Fesl, Eve 95, 377
Fields, Jessica 320
Filipi, Anna, bio 363
finance 139, 199, 232, 275, 326
financial constraints 77, 172, 193,199, 233, 236, 326, 331, 409
Fitzgerald, Don 380
Fitzgerald, Sharon 165, 420
Fitzpatrick, Peter 374
fixed-term appointments 139
Flanders, Ned 79
Fleer, Marilyn 317, 319, 342, 350
 bio 301
Fleming, Di 374
Forgasz, Helen 231, **343**, 344, 348, 351, 375
 bio 302
Forgasz, Rachel, bio 309
Forster, Kathie 100
Forsyth, Anita 151, 216, **337**, 375, 417
 bio 179
Forsyth, Pam 133
Founts of Wisdom 419
Fowler, Hugh 34
Foyster, John 152
Frankston buildings 206
Frankston campus 205
Frankston State College 205
Fraser, Barry 100, 374
 doctorate 85
Fraser, the Right Hon. Malcolm 130–1, **132**, 133
Fraser, Marilyn 382
Fraser, Morag 237
Frederick, Wilfred 53, 387
French, Edgar 100
Friedman, Eric 104, 349
FTE 318
funding 199, 297, 324, 350
Fung, Annabella 350
Fyfield, John **61**, **81**, 84, **85**, **96**, 99, 147, 163, 167, 173, 409
 appointed 31
 bio 60
 chair staff meetings 46
 Group 70 48

Gagne, Robert   86, 98–9
Galbally, Rhonda   373
Galbraith, J K   441
Gale, Trevor   292
Galea, Edwin   374
Gallagher, Hec, appointed   29
Gallois, Andree   234, 430
Gardiner, Lyndsay   422
Gardner, Margaret   348
Gardner, Paul   **63**, 85, 86, 100, 104, 152, 163, 189, 192, 195, 200, 202, 235, 243, 316
   appointed   31
   bio   62
   recollection   397–400
Gearon, Margaret   229, 239, **251**, 292
   bio   251
Geelong High School   237
gender issues   103,158, 324, 438
general office   39, 40, 103
general science education   333
general staff   102, 103
Geography education   333
Geography method   17, 30, 104, 151,
Ghent, Meigs   83, 84
   appointed   47
Gilchrist, Margaret   110, 146
Gill Margaret   158, 216, **227**, 227–8, 229, 231–2, 236, 239
   bio   248
   recollection   392–4
   retired   240
Gillard Government   324
Gindidis, Mara, bio   360
Gipps, John   102, bio 123, 152
Gippsland   318, 328, 330, 394, 436, 429
   amalgamation with Monash   205, 207
   campus   **205**, 211–14
   head of   229
   leaves Monash   329
   review of courses   328
Gippsland Institute of Advanced Education   102, 205, 211
Gleeson, Fr. Chris   237
Glendonald Centre   125
Global engagement   414, 415
Glover, Hugh   320
Godfrey, Jayne   2945
Godfrey, Layla   410
gold   77
golden jubilee (50th anniversary) faculty   292, 345, 349, 351
Goldman, Ronald   80
Gonski   339
Goodall, Marilyn, bio   107
Goode, Marged, bio   253
Goold, Louise   348
Gorman, Pierre   **90**, 90–1, 148
   bio   112

governance of Faculty   see Faculty governance
governance of university   295
grades, Monash   74
Graduate certificate in Higher Education   293, 326–327
graduation   194, **442**
Gray, Judy   415
Grbich, Caroline   197
Great Debate Funding for Australian Schools   237
Greater Monash   205, 244, 316
Greaves, Bob, bio   299, **300**
Green, Marie   133
Greenway Frida   40, 53
Greenway, Phillip   34
   bio   116
Gregory, Alan   29, 94, **235**, 401
   bio   68
   leaves   198
Grimshaw, Pat   424
Gronn, Peter   147, 161, 324, 375, 431
   bio   121, **121**
Grosjean, Tomsork   320
Grossman, Pam   324
Group 2 (social foundations)   173, 174
Group 70   48–50, 74
Group of Eight (Go8)   215, 323, 325, 326, 330, 433
Groups (faculty)   174, 393, 406, 429
Guidara, Daniela   218
guidelines for research in schools   166
Gullone, Eleanora   288
Gunstone, Richard (Dick)   29, 81, 100, 104, 152, 155, 194, 195, 196, 218, **226**, 233, 234, 239, 316, 350, 375, 441
   bio   112
   Chair   225

Hall, the Hon. Peter   372
Hammond, Judy   382
Handbook, Faculty of Education   14
Hardcastle, Lesley   29, 151
   bio   182
Harreveld, Robert   328
Harrington, Julie   350
   bio   368
Harris, Anne   342, 344
Harris, Peter   374
Harris, Roger   328
Harrison, Ian   104
Harvard University   177
Hawke Government   204, 243
Hawke, R J   53–4
Hawkes, Val
   appointed   44
   bio   69
Hay, John   204

Hayden, Martin   374
Head of School Graduate Studies   231, 236
Heagney, Margaret   350
Health education   195, 333
Hearing impairment   437
HECE   240
HECS   170, 176, 236, 391
Heeps, Sandra   133
Henderson, Cath   **81**, 147, 217
Henderson, Ian   374
Henderson, Michael   421
   bio   310
Jenkins, Dorothy   350
Higher Education Research & Advisory Unit (HEARU)   82, 94
   as Higher Education Research Unit (HERU)   35, 38–9, 42, 382
   evaluates Group 70   49–50
Hewlett, Cecilia   416
Hickey-Moody, Anna   292
High Court of Australia   240
High Education green paper   176
Higher degree students   170, 200
Higher degrees   163, 164, 235, 390
Higher doctorate   190
Higher education studies   234, 240
Hillande, Toni, bio   357
Historic Schools Society of Victoria   154
History method   17, 30, 46, 87 104, 151, 411, 412
history of Australian education   97, 154–5
History of Education   16, 154, 317, 333, 404, 411–13, 438
history of education for women   154
History of Education of Girls Group (HEGG)   28, 421–5
History of Educational Thought (HET)   13
History Teachers Association of Victoria   288
Hodgson, Una   91
Hodgson, Wayne   374
Holkner, Bernard   236, **237**, 419, 421
holodeck room   331
Hone, David   374
Hong Kong   414
honorary degree   55
honorary professor   189, 268
Hopkins, Ted   376
Hopper, Max   211
Hore, Terry
   bio   66
   Group 70   48
Hosking, David   374
Howard, Adam,   321
Howard, Kate   350
Howe, the Hon. Brian   339
Hubner, Janet   350

Hudson Keith   **96**, 383
   appointed   29
   bio   68
Hulls, Alan   161, 373
Humanities & social science methods   74
Hunt, John   24, **27**, 74, 86, 143, 166, 197, **235**
   appointed   26
   bio   27–8
   Group 70   49
   retires   197
Hunt, Mel   133
Hutton, Don   23
Hutton, Peter   372

ICTEV   421
incremental creep   169
Indigenous Australians   95, 339
Indigenous education   17, 377–378, 438
Indigenous people and education   323, 339
Indigenous students   340
Indonesia   192
   history   421
industrial issues   434
Information & Communication Technology Education   333
Information revolution   419
Learning & Media Resources Centre   420
Information technology (IT)   236, 418–21
Ingvarson, Lawrence   82, 100, 149
   bio   108
initial teacher education   106, 139, 173, 417, 427
innovation   320, 351, 393, 396, 414, 436, 439
in-service education   82, 148
Institute of Teacher Education (IPBA)   416
Integrated Research Administration System   346
integration   168
interest groups   393
Interim Management Committee   204, 208
International education   414–17
International engagement   326
International students   292, 293, 318, 414
International Teaching Fellowship Scheme   51
Internationalisation   414–17
Internationalism   390
IRAS   346
Isaac, Joe   385
issues based   431
Istance, David   192

Jackson, Andrew   342
Jackson, Merrill,   35, 85, 102, 133
   appointed   31
   bio   64
Jacobs, Nicky, bio   305

James Cook University Townsville   147
Jenkins, G A   206
Jenkins, Louise   350
   bio   358
Jenkins, Robert   372
Jewell, Molly   53
Jewish Studies education   333
John Monash Science School   225, 438
Johnson, Lesley   374
   doctorate   85
Johnson, Lois   149–50
Johnson, Nicola   342, 421
   bio   352
Johnston, Gerald
   appointed   31
   bio   62
Jolly, the Hon. Robert   371
Jones, the Hon. Barry   189
Joseph, Cynthia
   bio   302
Joyce, Pamela   374

Kaiser, Jeffrey   161
   bio   111
Kanitsaki, Olga   374
Kaplan   414
Kaplan, Giselle   374
Karmel Report   124, 174, 438
Karmel, Peter   95, 391
Karmel, Tom   339
Katariya, Mayur   348
Kay, Stafford
   bio   115
Kay-Shuttleworth, James Kaye   299
Kearney, Ged   339
Keast, Stephen   342, 415, 434
   bio   304
Keating, Paul   204
Kelly, Mavis   **81**
Kelly, Viv   197, 200, 201, **202**
Kemmis, Stephen   241
Kemp, the Hon. David   324
Kennedy, John   373
Kent, Sally   **238**
Kenton, Susan   348
Kenway, Jane   262, 278, 281, **282**, 284, 286
   bio   312
Kenworthy, Jane   350
Kersing, Emily   350
Key Centres   219
Khan, Jamesheeda   372
Kidman, Gillian, bio   360
Kindergarten director   31
King, Bro Kevin   152
King, Neville   201, 288
   bio   186

King, Ron   100, 161, 431
   bio   107
   doctorate   85
King's College London   348
Kinnear, Kath   145
Kirner, the Hon. Joan   189, **235**
Kissinger, Henry   434
Klimovics, Michele   133
Knight, Russell W   52
Korea   415
Kronborg, Leonie, bio   252
Krongold Centre   168, 195, 203, 218, 219, 220, 234, 241, 406, 437
   anniversary   138
   annual report   136
   building   95, 127–8, **128**
   committee   87
   conflict   135
   opening   130–3
Krongold, Henry   127, **128**, 129, **132**, 138
Krongold, Dinah   127, **128**, **132**, 138
Kupsch, Michael   218, 233
   bio   255

Laird, Don   372
Lamb, Tony   372
Lancaster, Greg, bio   256
Landvogt, Julie   239
Langer, Albert   41, 376, 387, **376**, 405
Language across the curriculum   160
Language and literacy   319, 333, 438
languages, teachers   195, 214, 416, 417
Larrain, Horacio   321
Latheef, Ibrahim, bio   366
Laura, Ron   **81**, 102, 234, 430
   bio   118
Laverton High School   156, 157
Law Building   35
Law Faculty (Monash)   93
Lawford, Peter   210, 347, **347**, 348
Lawry, John   77, 102, 430
   appointed   31
   bio   61
   doctorate   85
   first doctorate of the faculty   47
Lawson, Frank   379
Lay, Barry   100
Layton, David   98
learning skills   156, 340, 431
learning with new media   319
Leder, Gilah   **119**, 152, 153, 195, 226, **200**, **235**, 239, 316, 317, 375
   bio   118
   recollection   394
Lee Dow, Kwong   4, 324, 329, 339
Lee, Graham   150

Lee, Vicky   229
   bio   184
Leese, John, appointed   31
Legal Studies education   151, 333
Lessons for All   218
Lewis Barbara   31, 147
Li, Liang, bio   356
Liamputtoing, Pranee   374, **375**
Library (Monash)   24, 25, 84, 169
   catalogue   418
   facilities   94
Library & Media Resource Centre (LMR)   223, 290–1
   as Curriculum Laboratory   7, 24–5, 29, 37, 47, 83–4
   as Educational Materials Centre   87
   as Educational Services Centre   89, 223
lifelong learning   236
Lindsay, Heather   372
Linguistics   328
Linke, Russell   374
   bio   72
   doctorate   85
links with faculties   22
Little, Dermot
   appointed   43
   bio   68
   Group 70   48
Lloyd, Douglas   374
Logan Mal   195, 201, 204, 215, 237
Long, Michael, bio   300
Loriente, Lydia   335
Lot's Wife   99
LOTE   338
Loughran, John   229, 231, 234, 278, 286, 294, 316, **317**, 335, 342, 348, 350, 355, 375, 400, 429
   award   239
   bio   351–2
   DLitt   321
Lovitt, Charles   152
Ludowyke, Jeremy   372
Lundgren, Ulf   98
Lynch, Brother Michael   371

Ma Rhea, Zane   268, 378
   bio   302–3
Ma, Hongming, bio   359
Macdonald, Ian   374
MacDonald, Theo   102, 152, 387
   bio   70
Macintyre, Stuart   236
MacKay, Lindsay   77, 84, 85, 86, 102, 104, 152, 203, 399, 400
   bio   59
   doctorate   47
   research grants   47

Mackay, Tony   373
MacKenzie, Alex
   appointed   100
   bio   108
   leaves   102
MacKenzie, Andrew   99, 374
Mackinnon, Alison   423
MacLean, Rupert   376
Macpherson, Mack   161
   bio   178
Macquarie University   189
Maharaj, Seshna   347
Mahoney, Darrell,   374
Main Library   84, 193
Main Library Users Committee   84
Majoribanks, Kevin   190
Malaysia   234, 414, 416
Maling, Jill   190
managerialism   210, 244, 432, 433
Mander, Betty   373
Marginson, Simon   176, 177, 219, 234, 237, 239, **240**
   bio   258
Marketing & Communications   348
Marks, Judith   145, 147
Martin Committee   55
Martin, Augustus   372
Martin, Ray   95, 171
Martin, Rosemary   133
Marton, Ference   171
Maryvale High School   401
Masarro, Vin   88, 144
Maschette, Vera   217
Master in Regional and Community Development   322
Master of Environmental Science   23
Master of Counselling   344
Master of Education (MEd)   73, 153, 165, 197, 323
   theses   95
Master of Educational Studies (MEdStud)   163, 164, 170, 197, 390
   started   78
Master of School Leadership   420
Master of Special Education   167
Master of Teaching   325, 329, 338, 345, 439
Master of Teaching (Primary)   331, 333
Master of Teaching (Secondary)   323
Masters courses   95, 219
   projects   164
Masterton, Layla   409
Mathematics and science education   219
Mathematics education   152, 153, 246, 333, 394, 396, 438
Mathematics Education Centre   153
Mathematics Education Research Group of Australia   152, 396

Mathematics method   17, 46,104, 152
Matheson, Sir Louis   4, 6, 14, 22, 24, 54–5, 124–5, 127n, 130, 139, 379, 386, 388, 409, 428
   appointed   3
   student unrest   40–2
Matriculation   10, 93, 381, 437
Matthews, Judy   133
Matthews, Mircea   350
Matthews, the Hon. Race   371
Mayberry, Hilda   145
   death   53
   secretary   15
Mayne, Maree, retired   322
McAdam, Ken   22, 34, **57**
   appointed   31
   bio   56
   leaves   102
McAlpine, Janine   145
McArthur, John   85, 161, 164, 431
   bio   109
McCarten, John   147
McCoy, Eleanor   104, **107**
McCulloch, Ray   **59**, 140, 161, 370, 397, 409, 431
   bio   58
   retired   162
McDonald, Helen   374
McDonell, Jack   171
McDonell, Win   100, 171
McDougall, Ann   147, 201, 229, 420
McGaw, Barry   189, 268
McGown, Darlene,   295, 322
McGregor, Warren   374
McKenzie, Phil   339
McLean, Louise, bio   366
McLean, Peter   372
McLellan, Stuart   372
McLeod, Amber Beth, bio   362
McMahon, Greg   372
McMahon, Thomas   374
McNamara, Sue   421
McNaught, Carmel   374
McSorley, Louise   416
measurement in Education   15, 399
MEd   *see* Master of Education
MEd Studies   *see* Master of Educational Studies
media education   333
Medical Faculty Monash   195, 200, 210
Melbourne College of Advanced Education   155
Melbourne High School   372
Melbourne Teachers' College   125, 206
Melbourne University   199, 325, 410, 424
Melchers, Robert   374

Mellor, Elizabeth   208, 231
   bio   253
Mellor, Warren   **96**, 161, 162, 208, 431
   bio   115
Mendelovits, Juliette   339
MERC   439
MERGA   152, 396
mergers   176, 204, 205, 212
Merry, Mark   374
Method lecturers   21, 100, 104, 151
Method staff   140, 151, 160, 370, 400
Method subjects   13, 15, 104
Method tutors   160, 402, 404
Methods of teaching   21, 30, 151, 153, 330, 370, 420
Meyer, Charles, retired   231
micro-teaching   26, 49, 58, 66
Mill Girl   **81**
Miller, John O   373
Miller, Judy   422
Miller, Marion   350
Minister for Education   235
Ministry of Education (Vic)   193
Ministry of Employment, Education & Training   176
Mission statement   324
Mitchell, Ian   151, 153, 155, 156, **157**, 158, **196**, 342
Mitchell, Judy   133
Modern Languages Method   15, 30, 46, 160, 161, 193
Mollie Holman Medal   302, 315, 413
Molloy, Geoffrey   201
   bio   114
Monash affiliation   204
Monash Asia Institute   234
Monash Association of Teacher Education   83
Monash budget model   326
Monash Centre for Australian Studies   234
Monash Centre for Stress Management and Research   218
Monash Connect   321
Monash Education Alumni   188, 189, 229, 268, 332, 349, 371, 424
Monash Education Research Community   439
Monash Faculty Club   383
Monash Fellowships   344
Monash High School   26, 83, 150
Monash Institute for Child and Adolescent Studies   219
Monash Research Fund   162
Monash Review Committee 105, 142
Monash South Africa   415
Monash Teachers' Centre   82, 149, 400
Monash Teachers' College   20, 26

Monash University
 founded 2
 site 3
 opened 4
Monash University College, Gippsland 208, 211, 212
Monash, Sir John 2, 181
Monheit, Dorrit 231n76
Monk, Hilary bio 352
MOOCs 440
Moody, Margaret 147
Mooney, John **129**, 130, 131–3, 373
Moorabbin High School 402
Moore, Dennis 138, 262, 264, 286, **305**, 350, 356
 bio 304
Moore, Dorothy **134**
Mordialloc High School 149
Morey, Elwyn **25**
 appointed 23
 bio 23–4
 death 39
Morgan, Margaret 146
morning tea *see* social life
Morrow, Anne 237, **238**
Movement, environment and community 319
MUFESSA 74, 370
multi-campus faculty 234, 239
multiculturalism 154
multi-professorial faculty 44–5, 95
Mumbengegwi, Simba 372
Murdoch, Dame Elisabeth 150
Murphy, Dave (building attendant) 40, 145
Murphy, David (classics) 46, 100
Murray Committee (1957) 1, 2, 428
Murray, Brendon 374
Murray-Smith, Stephen 100
Musgrave Peter **44**, 47, 76, 89, 95, 129, 135, 141–2, **144**, 145, 152, 166, 173, **198**, 384, 389, 406, 410
 acting Dean 88
 appointed 43
 bio 43
 death 322
 experimental DipEd 49
 retired 146
Music Education 100, 333
Myconos, George 339

Nash, Gerard 93
National Centre for Vocational Education Research 339
National Inquiry into Teacher Education 81
National Research Award 24
National Tertiary Education Union 345, 434

Neale, Marie D 35, 39, 87, 105, 124–7, **128**, 129, 133, 135, 136, 138, 145, 152, 173, **174**, 406, 410
 appointed 42
 bio 42–3
Nelson, Dominica, bio 117
Nettleton, Norm 34, 131, 133, 234
 bio 110
Newman, Anne 152
Newson, Val 145
Newton, Stephen 344, 374
Niall, Brenda **146**
Nichols, Aaron 339
Nicholls, Miles 374
Nixon, Mary 31, 34, 99, **238**, 387
 bio 62
non-award courses 292
non-professorial staff participation 42, 105, 142–3
non-tenured positions 240, 241, 243
Noonan, Peter 339
Norman, Michael 147, 161, 190, 431
 bio 178
Northfield, Jeff 152, 162, **178**, 183, 191, 193, 195, 218, **220**, 220–1, **229**, 234, **235**, 281, 316
 bio 117–18
Northfield, Joan 178
Norton, Andrew 324
NTEU 345, 435
NUAUS 48
NUD*IST 419
Nugent, Pauline 374
Nunn, John **27**
nursing 210
Nuttall, Joce 294, 295, **296**, 298

O'Connor, Barbara, appointed 43
O'Connor, Heather 423
Oates, Colin 104
obsolete equipment 158
Occupational health and safety 339, 340
Occupational Health and Safety Policy Committee 289, 340
OECD 192
Oldmeadow, Max 91, 171
 appointed 29
on-cost changes 140, 169, 193
one-department faculty 44, 45, 239, 324
online courses 440
Opening Education Building (Clayton) 38
Opening the Classroom Door 234
operational plan 327
organisation of Faculty 45, 86, 89, 142, 143, 334, 393, 406
Ortlieb, Evan, bio 359
Osborn, Richard B 52, 387–8
OSP 214, 289

Our Schools and the War   411, 413
outdoor education   333
overseas students   169, 318
Owen, Wyn   34, 145, 147, 163
   bio   116
      coursework degrees   163–4
Oyoo, Samuel   375

Pagone, Tony   375
Panizzon, Debra   342
   bio   368
Pardy, John   339
Paregetter, Robert   204, 394
Parents Education Centre   150, 192, 437
Parkes, Jan   372
parking   193
Parr, Graham   292, 415
   bio   302
Partridge Committee   81, 82
part-time students   371
Patterson, Senator Kay   85, **371**, 371
Patterson, Rosalind   138
'Paul'   90
Pavarotti, Luciano   410
Payne, Phil   319
Peczak, Vid   98
PEEL   155–7, 156, **159**
Peeler, Eleanor   420
peer mentoring   340
Pell, Cardinal George   375
Pelle, Tanya   347
Peninsula   192, 208, 220, 289, 318, 337, 346, 394, 429, 436
Peninsula Campus   207, 207, 212, 221, **222**, 237
Penna, Chris   **196**
Penny, Dawn   351
Pentridge gaol   387
performance indicators   72, 199, 200, 266, 432
periodical costs   169
Perkins, Gordon   103, 420
Perry, Fred   5, 77, 102
   appointed   44
   bio   69
   doctorate   85
personal computers   228
Persson, Marie   339
Pettiona, Cameron   340, 348
Pettit, Trish   **178**
Peulich, Inga   372
Pham, Thanh, bio   362
PhD   35, 78, 95, 148, 164,197, 201, 231, 389, 397
Phillips, Denis   53, 74, **85**, 234, 386–7, 430
   appointed   31
   bio   64
   leaves   97

Phillips, Heather   40, 103, 146, 336, **337**
Phillips, Judith   231
Phillips, Michael   421
   bio   359
Phillipson, Shane   320, 326, 348, 351
   bio   353
Phillipson, Sivanes, bio   354
philosophy   234, 387
philosophy of education   438
photocopier   197
photographer   102
Physical education   333
Physical Sciences Study Committee   399
physics   155, 397, 399, 400
Physics method   17, 333
Pinchen, Suzanne   374
   recollection   400–4
plagiarism   76
Planning & Development Committee   45, 46, 86, 89,124, 129, 143, 204, 209, 231, 289, 392, 407, 410, 428, 434
Plunkett, Margaret   321, 329, 404
   bio   303
Pockney, Bev   384
Podorova, Anna   350, 417, 420
politics in universities   434
Poole, Millicent   174, **175**, 189, 198, 199, 201, 223, 419
   bio   175
portfolios faculty   393
post graduate coordinator   197
Potter, Owen   80
Pouvalu, Emeli   372
practicum   20, 47, 76, 135, 162, 168, 194, 291, 333, 337, 402, 414–17, 427
Praetz, Helen   147
Prato   414, 416–17
primary education   195, 319, 322, 348
primary students in classroom   **159**
Primary teaching method   21, 30, 46
   discontinued   76
Primate of Australia   375
Prince, Anne   420, 434
Principles of Teaching   15
Print, Murray   200
professional development   192, 231, 233
Professional Development Centre   192
Professional Development Institute   218, 233, 241
professional experience (faculty)   348
Professional staff   102, 244, 342, 347
Professor of Special Education   124, 125
Professors, role   87
Project for Enhancing Effective Learning   155–7, **159**
projects   166
Pro-Vice Chancellor (London)   243

Pruyn, Marc   434
    bio   364
PSSC course   399
Psychology area   141
Psychology (education)   333, 410, 436
public education   391
Public Records Office (Victoria) PRO   412
Pullen, Judge Susan   375
Punton, Debby   374
Pye, Angela   290, **291**, 420
QS World university rankings   335–6

Quadrelli Symonds (QS)   336
qualitative research   154
quality assurance   335, 348
quality in education   349
    manager   323
    journals   344
quasi-departments   86, 105, 142, 143, 174
Queensland University   325
Queensland University of Technology   201

Radford Dr W C, on selection committee   6
Radvanksy, John   100, 387–8, 430
    appointed   31
    bio   56
Radvansky, Susan   **146**
Rainer, Valina   197
    bio   179
Ramsay Report   2
ranking of Faculty   95, 98, 173, 177, 195, 199, 325-326, 335–6
Rasmussen, Mar Lou   319
ratio academic:professional staff   342, 347
ratio staff:student   80, 139, 277
Ray, the Hon. Robert   372
razor gang   139, 148
redundancies   233, 243
regional university   329
Reid, Alan   322, 344, 348, 351
    bio   361
Relative Funding Model   199, 215
Religious Centre   79, 348, 350, 410
Rendell, Margaret   350
Report on Faculty   270
representative on university council   54, 91
reputation of Faculty   95, 98, 170, 173, 177, 195, 199, 216, 270, 273, 316, 325–6, 335–6, 350, 388, 390, 403, 404, 406, 409
research   221, 346
    clusters   277
    culture   378, 406
    grants   194, 195, 223
    groups   319
    induction   281
    office   276, 342, 348
    publications   85, 86, 98, 319

Research Committee   281, 319
research degrees 24, 85, 165, 275, 281, 318, 390, 439
    services   348
Research Degrees Committee   165, 166
research in education   66, 73, 106, 152, 168, 170, 177, 207, 267, 272, 273, 275, 319, 388, 396
    advisor   165
    excellence   195
    profile   437
    quality framework   283
    reputation   350
    strengths   195, 210
    supervision   237
research in mathematics   152
research in science education   152, 400
research students   164, 439
    scholarship   188, 395
Reupert, Andrea, bio   367
Review of Faculty   274, 276, 281, 282, 316, 323-4, 328, 332, 335
    panel   344
revues   232, 279, **280**
Reyne, Judy   349
Reynolds, Chris   164–5
Rhea, Zane Ma   268, 323, 378
    bio   302
Royal Historical Society Victoria   412
Rice, Alan   80
    bio   114
Richardson, Paul   319, 342, 348
Rickards, Field   434
Rickinson, Mark   22, 348, 351
    bio   367
Riddell, Christine, 153
Ridgway, Avis, bio   357
Rights and Inequality in Australian Education   86, 387, 391
Riley, Phil   420, 431
Ring, Ronald   374
Ripple, Dick   98
Ritchie, Kay   350, 434
Rivers, Wilga   380
Rizvi, Fazal   218, 219, 233, **224**, 234, 239, 240, 241, 262, 430
    bio   223–5
RMIT University   348
Robbins, Jill   186, 234, 269, 295
Robert Menzies School of Humanities, housed education   5, 408
Robinson, David   236, 240, 241, 258, 276
Robinson, Peter   171
Rodell, Bon   380
role of teachers   406
Romeo, Geoff   269, 293, 294, 421
Ross, Alan   374

Round, Penny   330
   bio   363
Rowe, Craig   415
Rowe, Emma, bio   369
Rowland, Mike   373
Rowley, Glen   147, 165, **167**, 268
   bio   180
Rowley, Sue   374
RQF   283
Rudd, the Hon. Kevin   289
Runawery, Clemens   372
Rusden State College   20, 161, 177, 207, 401
Russell, Glen   421
Ryan, Noel, HERU   39
Ryan, Maureen   374
Ryan, Senator Susan   403
Rye, Angela   223

salaries, staff   56n, 100, 169, 233, 236, 268, 272, 275
   savings   98, 169, 233, 430
Sampson, Shirley   84, 91–2, **92**, 147, 160, 195, 226, 227, 317, 396, 424
   bio   111
Schapper, David   401
Schneider, Bev   40, 53, 103, 146, 234
Schoenheimer, Henry   **9**, 14, 21, 104, 408
   appointed   8
   bio   10
   death   102
   scholarships   389
Schonnell, Fred   34, 170
School Days   154
School Decision Making & Management Centre   192
School Executive Officer   209
School of Computing & IT (Peninsula)   221
School of Education, Gippsland   208
School of Graduate Studies   208, 214, 228, 392, 394
School reviews   179, 233, 275, 278, 432
Schools Board   10, 64, 86, 93
Science and Technology Education (chair)   223, 225
science education   74, 152, 155, 195, 317, 319, 389, 390, 396, 399, 406, 438
   laboratory   102
   show   196
Science method   17, 15, 26, 30, 49, 50, 58, 74, 104, 143, 400
Scott, Alan   128
Scott, David   15, 40
Scott, Elaine   145
   leaves   198
Scott, Phyllis
   appointed   31
   bio   65

Scott, W A G   **132**
Seabourne, Tom   100
Seah, Wee Tiong   421
Seaton Ean   161
secondary principals   372–4
secondary teacher education   278, 333
Secondary Teachers' College (Melb)   8, 10, 11, 19, 408, 409
Secondments   21, 77, 83, 135, 136, 386, 436, 437
   end of free   140, 151, 193, 436
SECPE   208, 212, 214
secretarial assistance   87–8, 103, 145–6
Seddon, Terri   191, 228, 229, 262, 276, **277**, 321, 348, 350, 375
   bio   185
Selby Smith, Christopher   8n8
Selby Smith, Peter   6n6, 8n8
Selby Smith, Richard   **7**, 13–15,18, 20, 21, 22, 23, 26, 38, 44–5, 52, 53–4, 73, **144**, **198**, 244, 377–8, 385, 387, 388, 407, 408, 409, 410
   appointed foundation Professor   6
   bio   8
   education building   36–7
   honorary degree   55
   leaves   54
   on committee   5
   vision   426–7
selection committees   174, 262
election of staff   321
self-review   274
Sellars, Eileen   191n
Selleck, R J W (Dick)   29, **101**, 146, 152, 154–5, **156**, **178**, 208, 216, 218, 229, **230**, 234, 235, 244, **245**, 317, 389, 410, 411, 413, 422, 430
   appointed   100
   bio   100
   recollection   404–7
Selwyn, Neil   342, 350, 419, 421
   bio   358
semester system   78
Senior Advisory Group   436
Shah, Chandra   339
   bio   255
Shalley, B S   30
Shannon, Cathy   104
Sharma, Umesh   314, 342, 344
Sharples, Pat   145, 147
   leaves   198
Sharpley, Chris   147, **167**, 231
   bio   182
Shavelson, Richard   171, 190
Shaw, A G L   52
Shaw, Jean   145
Shaw, Lindsay
   faculty secretary   5, 88, 144, **146**
Shears Dr Lawrie   21, 51, 76, 80, 333

Sheen Joan   104, 151, 313
Shields, B D   166
Shorten, Ann   100, **107**, 158, 226, 409, 410, 422, 430
  bio   106
  Group 70   48
Shorten, Bill   410
Siemon, Dianne   152, 374
Sikua, Derek   372
silver jubilee (25th anniversary)   188
Singapore   414
Sir Louis Matheson Library   24, 290, 412
Sironi Claude   102, 194, 223, 420
Slattery, Monica   237, **238**, 239
  bio   183
Slowo, Nathan   133
Small, Robin   81, 189, 193, 234, 268, 430
  bio   111
Smith Bronwyn   342
Smith, Helen   147
Smith, Ros   262
Snedden, Richard   374
Snyder, Ilana   201, 262, 281, 325, 348, **349**, 350, 375, 421
  bio   249
social life   24, 29, 54, 78–9, **81**, 172, 174
  choir   78–9, 102, 172, 239, 281, 349, **350**, 377, 410
  Christmas party   172, **227**, 349
  cricket   79, **174**
  morning tea   29, 217, 383, 384
Social education   333, 410, 438
social inclusion   339
social justice   195, 438
  rights and inequalities in education   438
Social Science Citation Index   98
Social Studies method   17, 100
Socio-economic status   339, 340
Sociology (education)   438
SOEG   214
Soeparman   372
Solomon, Geulah   44
  doctorate   85
Somerville, Margaret   262, 320
South Africa   41, 274
South Pacific Centre for School & Community Development   192, 218
Southcott, Jane   279, **280**, 321, 350, **435**, 436
  bio   249
Spaull, Andrew   34, 79, 94, **96**, 154–5, **156**, 228, 316, 375, 411, 412, 413, 430, 434, **435**
  appointed   43
  bio   110
  doctorate   85
  Group 70   48
Special Education   124, 125, 133, 167, 264, 330, 345, 410, 436, 439, 440

funding   126
inquiry   127
special needs of children   125–6, 138
speech advisor   29, 383
Speed, Terrence   374
Spicer, Brian   86, 104, 234, 375
  appointed   44
  bio   68
  retired   231
Sport and Outdoor education   439, 440
St Leger, Lawrence   374
Stacey, Kay   374
staff   267–8
  age profile   268
  appointments   14, 52, 243, 260, 326
  attitudes   322, 341
  Faces of 1970   **75**
  Faces of 1990   **188**
  forum   392
  meetings   88, 143, 145
  package   233
  participation   87
  redundancies   208
  requirements   399, 341
  research   166–7
Staff & Students Association (Monash)   74, 370
Staff Club   371, 383
Stanford University   64, 97, 177, 386, 387
Starnawski, Zenon   151
State College of Victoria   206
State College of Victoria, Frankston   205, 207
statistical methods   398
status of Faculty   98, 170, 173, 177, 195, 199, 273, 325–6, 335–6, 350, 390
Steele, Phillip   221
STEM (Science, Technology, Engineering & Maths)   344
Stillwell, John   23, 153
Stokes Scott, Eileen   350
Stone, Bob   386
Storelli, Rosa   374
Strategic Management Plan   193, 327, 392
Struan Estate   206
Stuart, Connie   145, 147
Student Academic Integrity Policy   340
student numbers   193, 318, 331, 345, 426
student placements   333
students   53, Ch. 9 passim
  attitudes   397
  demands   405
  needs   341
  unrest   40–2
studentships   18, 21, 30, 76, 385, 401
study habits   381–2
Subban, Pearl   bio 361
Sub-dean   created 46, 87
subject associations   104, 151, 177, 437

subjects disestablished   231, 328
Sullivan Martin   154, **156**, 228, **234**, 237, 316, 375, 411, 412, 430, 434
   bio   106
Sullivan, Peter (professor)   **261**, 262, 284n29, 288, 319, 350
   bio   306
Sullivan, Peter (principal)   374
summer teaching   93–4, 193
Sureties, Brian   104
   appointed   31
   bio   57
Surman, Lynne   269
Sutrisno   372
Sydney University   199
Sykes, Stewart   133, **134**, 162, 195, 220
   bio   70
   left faculty   234
Szalman, Joan   192

TAFE   267
Taft, Judge Philip   375
Taft, Ron   29, **34**, 88, 99, 152 , 170, 385, 386, 406, 410
   Acting Dean   133
   appointed   32
   bio   32–3
   retires   140
Tagged degrees   264
Tan, Hazel   421
   bio   364
Tasmania   55
Tasmanian College of Advanced Education   54, 55
Tate, Frank   235
Tatz, Colin   377
Taylor Tony   262, **280**, 288
   bio   298
Taylor, Joan   46
tea club   29–30
tea lady   384
teacher education   4, 55–6, 205, 231, 234, 239, 273, 278–9, 282, 321, 415
   award   329
   funding   275
teacher supply shortages   173, 386, 405
Teachers of special education   126, 133, 138
Teaching & Leaning Space (TLC)   420
Teaching English to Speakers of Other Languages   153
teaching load   270
teaching practice   20
   placements   76, 333, 337, 401–2
   supervision   193–4
technology   103, 144, 158, 160, 195, 278, 288, 414

technophobia   228
tenured positions   240, 241, 243
Tertiary Education Commission (TEC)   95, 139, 170
TESOL   153, 154, 193, 201
The New Education   100
Times Higher Education Supplement   173, 177
Theobald, J H   **11**, 15, 24, 46, 76, 104, 162, 375, 423
   appointed   8
   bio   10
   recollection 407–10
   retired   198
Theobald, Marjorie   154–5, 162, 374, 421, 422, 425
Thésée, Gina   321
theses   166, 191, 323
Thompson, Brian   133
Thompson, Rex   83
Tiananment Square   194
Tickell, William Gerrard (Gerry)   233, 239
   bio   252–3
Tiong, Wee, bio   365
Tisher Richard (Dick)   98, **103**, 152, 162, 170, 189, 199, 410
   appointed   100–1
   bio   100–1
   leaves Monash   198
TITC   206
Toorak Teachers' College   102, 161
Toppin, Bill   374
Townsend, Tony   208, 218, 269
TPTC   206
Trembath, Richard (Dick)   208, 220, 221, 269
   bio   256
   retired   231
Trethewey, Alan   15, 77, 385
   appointed   8
   bio   12
   Group 70   48
   leaves   102
Trevaskis, Graham   206
Triolo, Rosalie   288, 313, 430
   recollection   411–14
Tsolidis, Georgina   228
TSTC   19
Tucker, Peter   102, 223
Tudball, Libby   280
   bio   254, **254**
   recollection 414–17
Turner, Ross   152
Undergraduate courses   318, 337

UNESCO   161, 171, 372, 376
Universal Declaration of Human Rights   32
Universities Council   290

Index | 461

University Council   53, 54, 80, 91, 139, 171, 221, 233, 239, 260
University High School   237
University of Ballarat   328
University of Melbourne   1, 20
University of Queensland   199
University of Western Australia   259
Ushakumari, Suneesh   420

Van Ernst, Barbara   374
Vanstone era   215, 231
Vanstone, the Hon. Amanda   231, 392
Vardon, Rosa   372
VCAA   93, 268
VCAB   101, 189, 198
Veresov, Nikolai   320, 326
   bio   356
Vernon, Clive   201, 209
Vice Provost (education)   348
Vice-Chancellor   14, 95, 171, 236, 240, 276, 348
   first   3, *see also* Matheson, Sir Louis
Vice-Chancellor's award   201
Vice-Chancellor's Group   317
Vice-Chancellors Committee (Australian)   199
Victoria College   12, 161, 207
Victoria Institute of Education   385
Victoria Police   262, 271
Victorian Certificate of Education (VCE)   203
   debate   237, **238**
Victorian College of Educational Administration   162
Victorian Commercial Teachers Association   46, 104, 151, 179
Victorian Curriculum and Assessment Authority   93, 198
Victorian Department of Education and Training (VDET)   278
Victorian Enquiry into Teacher Education   81, 283
Victorian Government archives   421, 428
Victorian Health Promotion Foundation   195
Victorian Institute of Colleges (VIC)   177
Victorian Institute of Secondary Education (VISE)   93, 102, 171
Victorian Institute of Teaching   279, 326
Victorian Post-secondary Education Committee   171
Victorian Universities Admissions Committee (VUAC)   74
Victorian Universities Schools & Examinations Board   93
video conferencing equipment   420
Victorian Institute of Education Research   408
Viete, Rosemary   201, 417, 420

Vietnam war protests   40–1
VISE   93, 102, 171
Visions for the Future   213, 214
visiting lecturers   439–40
visiting professors   43, 98, 171, 440
visiting scholars   98, 106, 171, 320, 321
Visual art & Design education   333
VIT   279, 326
Vocational Education and Training   339
voluntary retirements   268
VPSEC   171
VSTA   406
VUSEB   93

Wade, Peter   204, 241
Waga, Baron   372
Walker, David   215
Wallace, Marli   104, 151, 374
Wallenberg, Raoul   388
Wallington, Graeme   102, 147
Wallis, Robert   374
Walsh, Lucas   345, 348, 351
   bio   364
Wardlaw, Chris   344, 373
Warren, Claire   79
Waterhouse, John   53
Watt, Helen   342
Watt, John   430
   appointed   100
Waylen, Jackie   350
web   419
Webb, Sue   262
   bio   354
Webster, Hilary
   appointed   29
   leaves   47
Webster, Ruth   **167**
Wells, David   374
West, Leo   85, 374
Wheeler, James   104, 153, 154, 193, 195
   bio   65
   retired   201
White, Marj   178
White, Richard (Dick)   79, 86, 99, 100, 104, 152, 155, **178**, 189, 194, 203, 204, 207, 213, 217, 218, 219, 221, 223, 225, 226, 230, 233, 234, 233, 236, 237, **242**, 244, **245**, 259, 316, 375, 387, 398, 399, 428, 436
   appointed   44
   bio   71
   chair   141
   doctorate   47, 85
   ends as Dean   243
White, Simone,   329, 330, 351
   bio   355
Whitlam Government   77, 206, 391, 438
Wideen, Marvin   98

Wilkins, Linda   422
Wilkinson, Vern   192
Williams Report on Education and Training   82
Williams, Judy   415
Willis, Susan   259–60, **261**, 262, **269**, 276, 283, 321, 348
   bio   259
Wilson, Cliff   114, 133
Windle, Joel   387, 434
Windshuttle, Keith   432
Winter, Rosamund   158, **217**, 218, 237, 223, 344, 350
   bio   247
   NTEU   434, **435**, 436
   recollection   418–21
Wise, Jenny   133
women equal pay   51
women in education   91–2, 111, 158, 226, 227, 228, 317, 344 394–5, 396, 421–5
women in senior posts   228
women's history   423
Women's Caucus   424
Women's studies   423, 424, 438
Wood, Carl   396
Wood, Marilyn   133
word processing   158
Work Related Curriculum project   402
workloads of staff   231, 270
Worland, Bruce   100
Wortley, Renn   350

Yammouni, David   420
Yates, Peter   210, 239
Yates, Rhonda   350
Young, Jennifer   147

Zainu'ddin, Ailsa (Tommy)   152, 154, **156**, 226, 227, 317, 430
   appointed   28
   bio   28
Zigouras, Vaneete   190
Zyngier, David   307
   NTEU   434